Praise for *The HP Virtual Server Enviro*

"This book will educate professionals about the components of ... ...ual server environment and how to manage them in everyday tasks. It demonstrates how to manage resource utilization in real time and to its full capacity. Bryan and Dan are fully qualified to write this book, having been involved in creating and designing a number of the virtual server environment components."
—D'Ann Chorak
Software Engineering Project Manager

"Great overviews, technology details, and practical example details."
—George Williams
Solution Architect, Hewlett-Packard Co.

"From a customer standpoint, almost anyone can make use of the solutions and concepts portrayed in *The HP Virtual Server Environment*. Some of the solutions are free, so there are ways to take advantage at no cost. No matter what solution is used, the results are a win-win situation for the customer."
—Alan Hymes
Solution Architect, Hewlett-Packard Co.

"The material is well-written. The book will appeal to high-end enterprise system administrators and architects who are interested in implementing an 'Adaptive Enterprise' environment or in improving an existing environment."
—Rob Lucke
Chief Solutions Officer, Vista Solutions Corp.

"This book is perfect for those looking for a high level overview of VSE and those investigating the use of VSE technologies in their data center."
—Erik Bostrom
Engineering Program Manager, Hewlett-Packard Co.

"*The HP Virtual Server Environment* represents a nearly exhaustive discourse on the basic and common capabilities of the software. The casual user will come away feeling that they understand the purpose and general use of the programs and confident that they can integrate these capabilities within their server environment."
—Dave Butenof
Instant Capacity and PPU Software Architect, Hewlett-Packard Co.

The HP Virtual Server Environment

The HP Virtual Server Environment

Making the Adaptive Enterprise Vision a Reality in Your Datacenter

Dan Herington and Bryan Jacquot

invent

www.hp.com/hpbooks

PRENTICE
HALL
PTR

Prentice Hall Professional Technical Reference
Upper Saddle River, NJ • Boston• Indianapolis • San Francisco
New York • Toronto • Montreal • London • Munich • Paris • Madrid
Capetown • Sydney • Tokyo • Singapore • Mexico City

Dan — To my beautiful wife Tara, who selflessly does everything that needs to be done. I couldn't have done this without her. And to my amazing children Libby and Matt, who make me proud and keep me laughing.

Bryan — To my lovely wife Kayla, who provides unconditional and unwavering support and encouragement. To my wonderful children, Tyler, Mikayle, Ellisa, and Lucas, who provide continuous joy and delight.

Contents

Preface

What Is in This Book

This book describes each technology in HP's Virtual Server Environment (VSE) which is comprised of the industry's most complete partitioning continuum, a set of utility pricing solutions, a suite of high availability products, a complete set of management tools, and finally the industry's only goal-based workload management products. This book serves as a guide-map in deploying an efficient and flexible computing infrastructure using HP's Virtual Server Environment

Several of HP's VSE technologies are supported on HP-UX, Linux, OpenVMS and Microsoft Windows operating systems. For example, HP nPartition servers support all four operating systems running simultaneously. Additionally, the HP Serviceguard products both support HP-UX and Linux operating systems and the HP Global Workload Manager is supported on HP-UX, Linux and OpenVMS. The Pay Per Use technology supports HP-UX and Windows. This book covers the full capabilities of HP's VSE on each operating system supported by the VSE technologies and notes which operating systems are supported by each technology.

Who Should Read This Book

This book is designed to support two audiences. The first is the solution designers, architects or engineers that are considering the deployment of VSE technologies, and the second is the project managers, engineers and administrators that are tasked with the job of implementing one or more of these VSE technologies.

If you are an architect looking for information on how to design a solution using the VSE, you will be able to get a solid overview of the VSE technologies from the first two chapters of each part of the book. You can then go to the product detail chapters which follow for more information on the products that appear to be a good fit for your requirements.

If you are an administrator, you probably already know what products you need more information on, so you can go straight to the product detail chapters, which will provide guidance and examples of using the products to solve real problems.

This book is written with the expectation that the reader will already have a basic understanding of systems architecture and systems administration. An understanding of basic virtualization concepts would be helpful, but is not required.

Readers of this book will benefit from a general understanding of HP-UX, Linux, and Windows system administration. The book focuses on the VSE technologies, and thus does not attempt to address basic operating system technologies and system administration techniques.

How This Book Is Organized

This book has an introductory chapter and then three parts. Chapter 1 provides a very high level overview of the VSE which can be used to guide the reader toward the other parts of the book for more details. Parts 1 through 3 describe the various solutions available in the Virtual Server Environment in the areas of Partitioning, Utility Pricing and Management respectively. Each part of the book contains three types of chapters, including:

- An overview chapter—The first chapter of each part, chapters 2, 8, and 13, cover each of the VSE solutions with a fair amount of detail. The primary focus in these chapters is to describe the key features of each solution and what can be done with them.

- Making the Most of—Each part also contains a chapter that attempts to go beyond the many features of each solution to help you understand what you should really care about. These will provide sweet spot solutions and tips and tricks for the solutions described in that part of the book. These are chapters 3, 9, and 14.

- Product/Solution chapters—Each product or solution has a dedicated chapter. In each of these chapters, the technology is introduced along with the primary terminology. Next, the architecture of the product is described which is followed by an example scenario. The scenario is used to walk the reader through the process of implementing the solution. These scenarios provide a thorough understanding of each technology without getting bogged down in the nuances and peculiarities of each product.

At the end of the book there are three appendices. Appendix A provides a detailed list of references that can be consulted for more information on each product or solution described in the book. Of primary importance are the user guides for each product which serve as a reference for each VSE technology. Appendix B lists the software and firmware versions used in the example scenarios in the Product/Solution chapters. Finally, Appendix C provides a list of each of the VSE products' command line interfaces, along with a reference to the manual page entries and the full path to each command.

What Is Covered in This Book

This book is not intended to be a product reference. There are currently 14 products in HP's Virtual Server Environment and putting together even a brief reference for all of these technologies would not be practical in a single book. Instead, the goal of this book is to provide a thorough survey of the technologies for you to identify which solutions will best fit in your IT infrastructure and to provide enough detail so that you can assess what it would take to implement and manage the environment. There is enough information in this book for a project manager to put together a project plan and have a high level of confidence in their estimates of the work required to implement an Adaptive Enterprise strategy using the VSE. There is also enough detail in the product chapters to help managers or system administrators to know which commands and utilities are available for each of the products so that you will know where to look for more information.

Acknowledgments

The number of people who provided materials for this book are too numerous to mention. In particular, source materials for many of the figures in this book were provided by various subject matter experts, including:

- Richard Stormo and Tim Jacobson have provided a great deal of insights into how HP's IT organization are taking advantage of these VSE technologies and have provided real workload data for some of the graphs used in the book.

- Stuart Haden, Mark Shaw and Greg Huff have provided both insights and detailed architectural diagrams for HP's Superdome servers.

- Bob Sauers provided extensive information and diagrams about HP's Serviceguard suite of products.

- Steve Gonzalez provided some very useful information and diagrams describing how some of HP's customers are taking advantage of VSE technologies.

- Steve Cooke, Ute Albert, and Vicki Martel provided a wealth of VSE marketing information both in the early stages of the book proposal process to help get this book off the ground and during the review process.

There were also a large number of reviewers, as you might expect with a book covering this many topics. In particular we would like to acknowledge the folks that reviewed the entire book. This took a tremendous amount of effort, and for that we are very grateful.

- Paco Romero
- Jim Darling
- Rob Lucke

Many other folks reviewed portions of the book. Their product specific expertise is greatly appreciated. These reviewers include Erik Bostrom, Dave Butenhof, D'Ann Chorak, Edgar Circenis, Mark Coffey, Bob Cohen, Steve Cooke, Jerry Harrow, Alan Hymes, Barry Lyden, Dave Parker, Scott Rhine, Wade Satterfield, Mark Shaw, Eric Soderberg, Steve Stichler, and George Williams.

About the Authors

Dan Herington is the Chief Architect for HP's Virtual Server Environment Advanced Technology Center. The ATC is a lab-based organization that has the mission to ensure the success of customers implementing solutions based on the Virtual Server Environment technologies. For the past four years he has been an architect in the lab working on HP's industry leading Workload Manager and VSE Management products. He has also been responsible for communicating the technical vision of HP's partitioning, utility pricing, and workload management products to the field and customers. This dual responsibility has provided him with a unique opportunity to both craft the technical message being delivered to HPs field and customers, as well as ensure that future versions of the products satisfy the requirements customers have for these solutions. He has delivered hundreds of seminars on HP's Virtual Server Environment Technologies at customer visits, HP field and customer training sessions, and trade shows throughout the world. Most recently he has been a key contributor to defining the vision for the next generation Virtual Server Environment and its management tools, including a number of the new products covered by this book. This role has included working with the project teams that are responsible for delivering the individual products to ensure that they make up a well-integrated solution, and making sure it is easy for customers to realize the vision of an Adaptive Enterprise with these products.

Prior to rejoining HP in 2000, Dan held senior technical and management positions with a large systems integrator and a start-up software company. Dan started his career with HP in Cupertino, California where he held various technical positions in the OpenView Program. He was involved in the transition of this program from Cupertino to Ft. Collins, Colorado and later moved to Grenoble, France, where he helped incubate the OpenView program in Europe in the early 1990's.

Bryan Jacquot is a Software Architect in HP's Virtual Server Environment Advanced Technology Center. He has worked as both a software engineer and software architect on enterprise system administration applications for over six years. He developed the first graphical user interface for managing HP's Superdome servers, Partition Manager. Additionally, Bryan developed the first HP-UX web-based system administration interface which is used for tuning the HP-UX kernel, Kcweb. In his current position, he serves as a technical software architect for the next generation system management tools for HP's Virtual Server Environment. In addition, he works closely with customers to gather requirements and give presentations and training for HP's Virtual Server Environment. Bryan holds a Bachelor's of Science degree in Computer Science from Montana State University—Bozeman. Additionally, he is an HP Certified IT Professional, a Microsoft Certified System Administrator, and a RedHat Certified Technician.

1

The HP Virtual Server Environment at a Glance

Chapter Overview

Welcome to *The HP Virtual Server Environment—Making the Adaptive Enterprise Vision a Reality in Your Datacenter.* The HP Virtual Server Environment (VSE) is comprised of a suite of products that are designed and integrated together to allow you to get more out of your HP 9000 and Integrity servers. More means higher utilization, increased efficiency, higher availability, and improved manageability.

This chapter will provide you with a glance of what you will find in the rest of the book. The book will describe the goals of the VSE, the products and solutions included, and how they are integrated. Most important, it will provide you with some guidance on how to best take advantage of the VSE.

The Target Problem — Rampant System Over-Provisioning

The key problem the Virtual Server Environment is designed to address is rampant over-provisioning of systems for the workloads they are running. Even today most customers admit to average system utilization numbers in the 25–30% range, and that is on higher-end 64-bit HP servers. It is not uncommon for utilization in the 32-bit Windows and Linux environment to be in the single digits. Figure 1-1 shows an example of the average utilization of a large number of servers in a datacenter.

In this figure you can see that a large number of servers are seriously over-provisioned. At the same time there are a handful of servers (typically older servers) that are no longer able to handle the load that is being placed on them. The real opportunity for consolidation is to put some of the workloads running on the servers on the right-hand side with the workloads running on

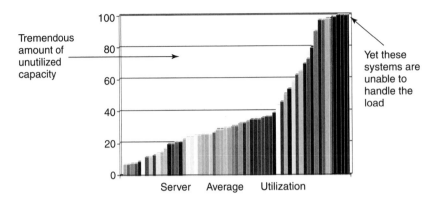

Figure 1-1 Average utilization of servers across a large datacenter

the servers on the left-hand side onto larger servers together so that the unused capacity on the left can be allocated to the applications on the right. This provides a number of compelling advantages, including:

- Higher utilization—the combined workloads could run at a higher level of utilization on the new shared server.
- Lower total cost of ownership—because you have fewer systems to purchase and manage.
- Better performance—the applications on the right will achieve better performance because they will have more resources available to them when they are busy.

The fact of the matter is that even consolidating the applications on the left-hand side will provide benefits. The biggest issue is still the systems that are over-provisioned. This brings escalating management costs for the large number of systems that are woefully underutilized. Let's explore a little about why utilization is so low in most datacenters and what can be done about it.

Why Over-Provisioning Is So Common

Over-provisioning is still the norm for a number of reasons. These include:

- The perceived need for separate servers for each workload. There were, and still are, a number of reasons why some applications might need to run on their own server. The environment can be tuned specifically to the application and you can ensure that there are no other applications that might be competing for resources.
- Business units (BUs) "own" the servers. Many companies have an IT model where the business units identify a requirement for a server, they work with IT to scope the size of the server, and then the BU pays for the cost of the server. IT then purchases the server and provisions it for the application. In this case there

is no incentive for the business unit to share those resources with workloads from other business units, even if the vast majority of the resources are going to waste—the server has already been paid for.

- Capacity planning is often little more than educated guesswork. If the application being deployed on the new server is new, there is very little information about the expected load, resource profile, or performance requirements of the workload. In these cases, most business units set the expectation that their usage will be higher than what it actually is.

- The penalty for under-provisioning is severe. One of the reasons the estimates are typically high is that the cost of underestimating is another upgrade. You will need to get another larger server and initiate yet another migration off the new server you just bought onto the larger one. Not only is this costly in that you need to get a new server, but you also need to spend an exceptional amount of time to migrate and test the application once again. This can also lead to a loss of credibility, which will result in second-guessing of future capacity-planning reports.

The bottom line is that the combination of these issues has led to the proliferation of systems that are dedicated to a single workload. The fact is, if you have a single workload running on a system, you can't possibly get utilization over 50% without risking performance problems when the application is under stress. Figure 1-2 shows a sample resource consumption profile for a typical application.

This graph shows that there are many short-term peaks and only a few large ones. And the large ones are short in duration. If you were to size a system for this workload, you would need to allow resources for the highest peak plus some amount of growth over the life of the system. The end

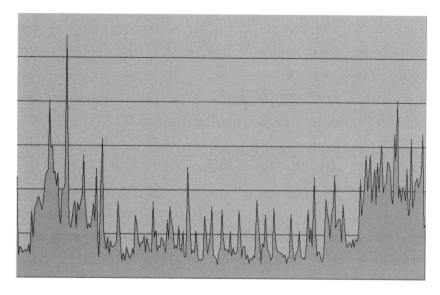

Figure 1-2 Demand Profile for an Actual Production Workload

result of this would mean that for all but an hour or so each day the system would be very lightly used and the average utilization would be less than one third of the size of the system.

Consolidation Makes Increasing Utilization Possible

Because workloads have these spikes, you need to make sure there are sufficient resources to meet the peak needs of each workload. Utilization is low because utilization peaks are usually high and short in duration. One way of increasing utilization is to provide a way for the resources to be used by other workloads when they aren't needed by this one.

Several studies show that running workloads in a consolidated environment reduces the need for CPU resources by roughly 40% with no performance degradation of any of the workloads. This is because the peaks of the different applications are usually short in duration and they do not occur at exactly the same time.

One concern with traditional consolidation (running multiple applications in a single copy of the operating system) is that there are a number of technical and political barriers to success. Technical barriers can include:

- File system namespace collisions—different applications attempting to read or write the same files
- Network port collisions—different applications attempting to attach to the same network ports
- Interprocess Communications (IPC) collisions—different applications or instances of the same applications attempting to access the same shared memory segments, message queues, named pipes, etc.
- Inconsistent kernel tunables or patch levels—each application may have specific kernel tunables or patches that are incompatible with those needed by the other applications.

Although these technical barriers can make consolidation of some combinations of applications within a single OS image impossible, they are actually pretty rare. However, political barriers are very common. These can include:

- Coordinating reboots is difficult. If the applications are owned by different user groups, it can be very difficult to coordinate among the groups sharing a server when a reboot is necessary to resolve a problem with only one of the applications.
- Multiple applications are impacted whenever a failure occurs.
- Support may be harder to get for some software products. Even if the applications will work just fine when sharing an OS, if the independent software vendor (ISV) won't support running their application with some other application, you can't put the combination into a production environment.

- User wariness. Some users just won't be comfortable about the fact that you have their application in an environment where there are one or more other applications that they don't own or understand. This wariness is usually unfounded, but it only takes one time for another application to impact their application before they ask you to put their application in an isolated environment.

What is needed is the ability to run the applications on the same system so that they can share resources AND isolate them from each other. What you need is virtualization.

Virtualization Makes Consolidation Easier

A key component of HP's Adaptive Enterprise messaging is the virtualization of the environments that applications run in. This gives the ability to reallocate unused resources in one virtual environment to workloads that need them in another. With virtualization, this can be done in a way that is transparent to the users of the application and even to the application itself.

How the Virtual Server Environment Can Help

There are actually two ways to increase utilization in this environment. The first is to consolidate multiple workloads on a server to allow resources not being used by one workload to be used by others. The other is to provide headroom in the system that is utility priced and idle until it is needed. The Virtual Server Environment (VSE) provides both of these.

Consolidation is very different today than it was even five years ago. There are now a number of partitioning alternatives that make it possible to isolate workloads from each other while allowing the resources of the system to be shared by the different workloads. However, partitioning alone is not sufficient. What we really want is dynamism. It doesn't do you any good to partition a box into four CPU partitions to run your workloads if those four partitions can't flex to allow the resources to be shared. The VSE has four different partitioning solutions that allow you to run multiple workloads on each server so that idle resources can be brought to bear on workloads that can use them. These partitioning solutions provide various levels of hardware and software isolation so the applications can't impact each other even though they are running on the same system.

There are also several Utility Pricing solutions that allow you to pay for resources as you use them. This makes it possible to provision a system with sufficient resources to meet the peak expected demands of the workloads running on the system but to have some of those resources be inactive inside the box. This makes it possible to run the system at much higher levels of utilization while still ensuring that there are sufficient resources on hand when a spike in load occurs.

Finally, the VSE has a number of management tools that provide simple configuration interfaces, automated resource allocation, and high availability. These management tools make it easier to take advantage of some of the more advanced features of the VSE.

Overview of the HP Virtual Server Environment

There are three major classifications of the solutions in the VSE. These are:

- VSE Partitioning Solutions: These are the different types of partitioning available within the Virtual Server Environment.
- VSE Utility Pricing Solutions: These are the solutions that allow customers to acquire sufficient system resources for peak loads but pay for them when only they are needed.
- VSE Management and High Availability Tools: These include workload management, configuration, capacity planning, high availability, and disaster tolerance solutions.

This book covers each of these classes of solutions. Now let's describe what tools are included in each of these areas and provide some context for the remainder of the book.

VSE Partitioning Solutions

When you think of "virtualization," partitioning is probably what you are thinking about. Partitioning allows you to run multiple workloads on a system while isolating them from each other by virtualizing the resources so the workloads can't impact each other. Another big advantage of this is that it gives you much better control over how resources are allocated to the various workloads.

Figure 1-3 shows the four partitioning solutions available with the Virtual Server Environment. These are:

- nPartitions (nPars): These are fully electrically isolated hardware-based partitions. Some of the compelling benefits here are the fact that hardware failures are isolated to the partition they occur in. You can also perform hardware maintenance activities in one partition while other partitions are running.
- Virtual Partitions (vPars): These allow users to run multiple HP-UX instances on a single system or nPar. This provides finer granularity than nPars and resources can be reallocated between partitions while they are running. The vPars product is available on both HP 9000 and Integrity platforms and is implemented by assigning hardware components to each partition.
- Integrity Virtual Machines: These are similar to vPars in that you can run multiple independent instances of the OS on a single system or nPar. Integrity Virtual

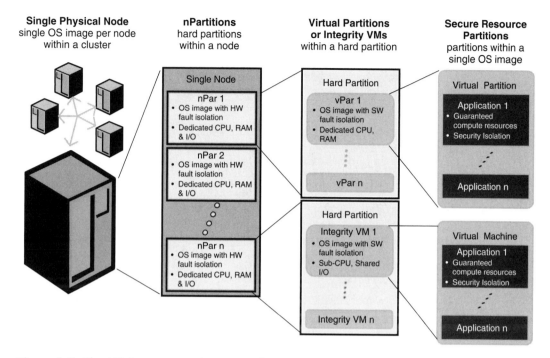

Figure 1-3 The HP Partitioning Continuum for HP 9000 and Integrity Platforms

Machines (VMs) provide fully virtualized hardware which makes it possible to have the partitions go to sub-CPU granularity, and they can also share physical I/O cards between separate OS instances. In addition, VMs can be moved from one system to another, system completely transparently to the applications running inside the VM.

- Secure Resource Partitions: These allow you to run multiple workloads in a single instance of HP-UX and isolate the workloads from each other. Isolation includes resources and communications. Each partition gets its own network interface, CPU, and memory resources even though they are running within a single copy of HP-UX.

As you can tell from Figure 1-3, you can also stack these solutions on top of one another. You can run vPars, Integrity VM, or Secure Resource Partitions inside of nPartitions. You can also run Secure Resource Partitions inside vPars or Integrity VM. Many customers have found that deploying multiple types of partitions on a single server provides a good combination of isolation and flexibility.

Part 1 of this book covers all of these partitioning solutions in full detail.

VSE Utility Pricing Solutions

HP's Utility Pricing Solutions for the HP 9000 and Integrity family of servers provide the ability to acquire hardware that is preconfigured for future requirements, but they give you flexibility about how and when you pay for those resources.

note

> These Utility Pricing Solutions provide a very compelling opportunity to save money. So much so that we make the statement that you should not be purchasing or leasing servers that don't have one or more of these solutions. We describe why in Part 2 of this book.

There are Utility Pricing solutions for both capital purchase and leased systems. The solutions for capital purchase are:

- Instant Capacity: This provides the ability to acquire a system with inactive capacity. Most of the cost of these inactive components is deferred until they are needed. This program supports both the activation of CPUs and/or whole cells with the memory attached. The instant capacity program was designed to simplify system upgrades by allowing a customer to acquire systems with ample spare capacity to support future growth without paying for all of that capacity up front.
- Temporary Instant Capacity: This provides the ability to activate instant capacity CPUs for short periods of time. This gives customers the ability to respond to short-term peaks in demand by activating additional capacity.

Customers who choose leased servers can take advantage of a Pay-per-use lease. This is what you might think of as a true utility model, where the lease payment varies each month based on the actual utilization of the server in the previous month.

These programs are described in Part 2 of this book.

VSE Management and High Availability Tools

The unprecedented level of adaptability provided by the Virtual Server Environment makes it possible to set up servers with multiple workloads that are isolated from each other while sharing resources. In addition, resources can be reallocated among workloads as required in real time and workloads can be migrated between servers. This makes it much easier to increase the utilization of servers. What's more, all of this can be done transparently to users. However, this level of virtualization and flexibility introduces new challenges in the area of management.

To address this management challenge, HP has introduced the VSE management suite of tools. This is an integrated suite of management tools that will cover the primary management functions in a datacenter, including:

- Workload provisioning: Tools will be provided that will simplify the creation of new partitions and virtual machines.

- Visualization and configuration: These are the traditional configuration and monitoring capabilities that are provided with each partitioning product. However, there will be one significant difference—starting with the first release of the HP Integrity Essentials Virtualization Manager, they are all integrated into a single common user interface so that it will be easier to identify what workloads are running in each partition on each server in the datacenter.

- Workload management: HP has been the leader in workload management since its introduction of the HP-UX Workload Manager product in April 2000. The VSE management suite will have links into this product but will have even tighter integration with the new Global Workload Manager product.

- Capacity planning: Because of the unique level of flexibility available in the VSE, it is necessary that capacity planning tools be knowledgeable about the types of flexing technologies available on the servers that are being monitored. To address this, HP has introduced the HP Integrity Essentials Capacity Advisor product as part of the VSE management suite.

- High availability and disaster tolerance: Another unique capability in the VSE is the ability to move workloads from one system to another. This can be done with Integrity VM where the "machine" itself can be rehosted, including all its resources and addresses. In addition, HP has the industry-leading Serviceguard suite of solutions for high availability and disaster tolerance. Having these products integrated into the VSE management suite makes it much easier to see what workloads are running where and to move workloads for convenience or in response to a failure.

All of these tools are being tightly integrated with each other and with the HP Systems Insight Manager so that the user experience will be one where you don't need to know what tool to use to accomplish a task.

Not all of these features will be fully supported in the first release, but these capabilities will be filled out over time.

We describe the VSE Management tools in detail in Part 3 of this book.

Integration of VSE Solutions

So far we have described a number of very useful tools for creating and managing an adaptive enterprise. What really sets these solutions apart is that they are integrated with each other. This makes it possible to stack various types of partitions on a system to run multiple workloads, provision the system with idle capacity, and automate the activation and reallocation of resources among all these things when workloads need them. This is the realization of the promise of an adaptive enterprise.

HP VSE Support for Multiple Operating Systems

HP Integrity servers support four Operating Systems — HP-UX, Linux, MS Windows and Open-VMS. It is the goal of the VSE to support all of these operating systems with most or all of these solutions. Practically speaking that is not possible due to the fact that there are underlying features required in the operating system that are not always available.

HP's flagship operating system is HP-UX. HP has spent many years building into HP-UX the security, reliability, performance and virtualization features required by their mission-critical customers. Because HP has full control of the code base for HP-UX, this is consistently where these VSE products are first provided. When there are sufficient features in the other operating systems to support the technologies, they are then ported and tested to support those as well.

Throughout this book we have made an effort to be clear as to which operating systems are supported for each of the products and solutions that make up the Virtual Server Environment. The support for operating systems other than HP-UX will evolve over time as features are added to the other operating systems that make it possible to support more of these VSE solutions.

Product and Feature Timing and Naming

In an effort to make the content of this book as timely as possible, many of the features of the products described in this book were not released as the book was being written. The most obvious result is that some of the names of the products and their features may have changed between the time the book was published and when the products were released. Where we weren't sure what the final names would be, we made an effort to use names that would be recognizable even if they were changed to something similar.

Additionally, HP is investing heavily in these technologies. You can expect that new features will be provided for these products regularly. We have tried to identify features that are deemed to be important, but weren't going to make it into the current releases. The list of new features required and how they are prioritized will evolve over time and are subject to change without notice.

Summary

The Adaptive Enterprise is HP's vision of an IT infrastructure that can easily adapt to changes required by the business. These changes could be as simple as a daily spike in load on an online transaction processing (OLTP) application or as complex as a merger or acquisition. The important thing is that today's static IT infrastructures are no longer capable of handling these changes quickly enough to satisfy the needs of the organization. We need to do better. The Virtual Server Environment is HP's answer to these requirements on HP 9000 and Integrity servers.

This book will provide you with insights into what products and solutions are available in the VSE, how they can be combined to provide unique solutions, and how to get started with these technologies. We hope you find it useful.

2

The HP Partitioning Continuum

The Partitioning Continuum at a Glance

This section provides an executive summary level of detail for the partitioning continuum. Later sections will provide a bit more detail and later chapters provide examples of how to set up each type of partition.

What Is Partitioning?

As we saw in the last chapter, the Adaptive Enterprise is all about pooling and sharing of system resources by running many workloads on the same system. However, this can sometimes be challenging because:

- One or more of the applications would consume more than its fair share of system resources

- Applications have namespace collisions. They share the same network ports, log files, configuration files, named pipes, patch levels, kernel tunables, or any one of a number of other system resources

- It can be difficult to schedule downtime on the system because multiple workloads are impacted.

Partitioning allows you to put multiple applications on a server and isolate them from each other. Each type of partition provides a different level of isolation from resource or namespace collisions, which we will cover later in this chapter.

The properties of a partition can include one or more of the following:

- Hardware-fault isolation: the ability to ensure that hardware faults and hardware maintenance in one partition won't impact other partitions on the system.
- Software-fault isolation: the ability to ensure that a software fault in one partition won't impact applications running in other partitions.
- Resource isolation: the ability to control the amount of critical system resources available to each partition.
- Security isolation: the ability to ensure that the users and processes running in one partition are not able to access or impact processes in other partitions.
- Namespace isolation: the ability to ensure that each partition has a duplicated namespace of one sort or another. It can include a copy of portions of the file system or a copy of the entire operating system.
- Application isolation: the ability to have different versions and patch levels of the same application in different partitions.
- Kernel parameter isolation: the ability to tune the kernel parameters in each partition to the application that will be running there. Many applications require a specific set of kernel parameters to ensure that the application can run at peak performance.
- Operating system isolation: the ability to run separate operating systems in each partition. This has the advantage that it typically provides most of the other types of isolation, the exception being hardware fault isolation. You can safely run a development workload in a partition on one system that is running production workloads in other partitions.
- Resource flexibility: the ability to share resources between different partitions. This is the key benefit of partitions rather than separate systems for each workload. When a workload runs out of resources on a system, it is not possible to reconfigure the system to allocate additional resources. And if the spike in load that caused the need for additional resources is rare, the utilization of the server will go down if you add resources.

HP's Partitioning Continuum

HP supports four different partitioning technologies that have progressively stronger isolation or flexibility depending on your requirements. These are depicted in Figure 2-1.

nPartitions

The first partitioning alternative is hardware-supported partitions, or nPartitions (nPars). HP introduced nPars during HP World in August 2000, when we introduced our first cell-based platform, the HP 9000 Superdome. The architecture of the system was designed to allow components of the system to be isolated from one another. The key features of nPars include:

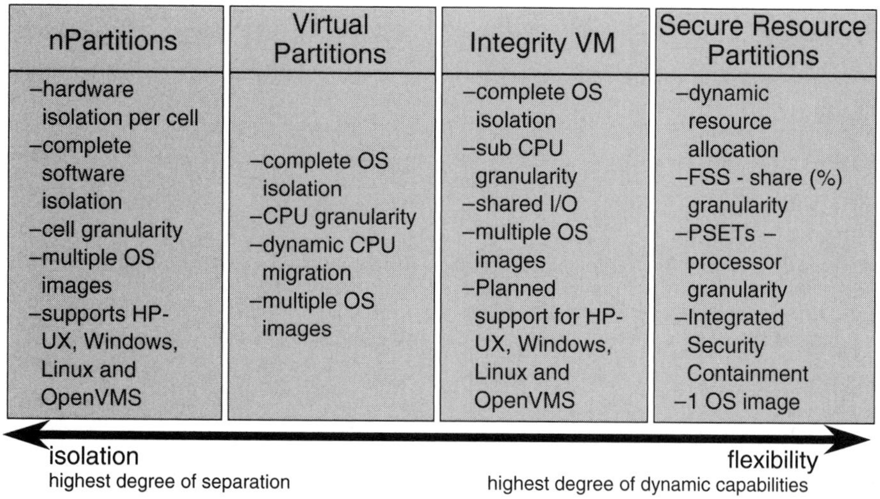

nPartitions	Virtual Partitions	Integrity VM	Secure Resource Partitions
–hardware isolation per cell –complete software isolation –cell granularity –multiple OS images –supports HP-UX, Windows, Linux and OpenVMS	–complete OS isolation –CPU granularity –dynamic CPU migration –multiple OS images	–complete OS isolation –sub CPU granularity –shared I/O –multiple OS images –Planned support for HP-UX, Windows, Linux and OpenVMS	–dynamic resource allocation –FSS - share (%) granularity –PSETs – processor granularity –Integrated Security Containment –1 OS image

isolation
highest degree of separation

flexibility
highest degree of dynamic capabilities

Figure 2-1 The HP Partitioning Continuum

- Complete hardware-fault isolation: HP's nPars is unique in the industry because it provides fully electrically isolated partitions inside a single system. This is accomplished using a custom chipset design in each cell such that firewalls are configured to ensure that electrical signals are dropped if they are destined for a cell that does not belong to the partition. This ensures that no hardware failure in one partition can affect any other partition in the system.

- Complete software-fault isolation: Clearly, if the electrical signals can't cross an nPar boundary, neither can any of the software running there. The partitions look and act like separate systems. They can run separate OS images with different versions, different patch levels, kernel tunables, etc.

- Cell granularity: One of the key benefits of nPars over separate servers for each workload is the fact that an nPar can be resized very quickly. Currently, HP-UX requires a reboot in order to move a cell from one partition to another. However, a future version of HP-UX will support addition and deletion of memory online, which will make possible a number of interesting features, including online addition and deletion of cells.

- Multiple OS images: Each partition gets its own hardware and software, including the operating system.

- Support for HP-UX, Windows, OpenVMS and Linux: The Precision Architecture–based HP 9000 Superdome only supports HP-UX. However, the Integrity Superdome, based on the Itanium processor, supports HP-UX, Windows, Linux, and OpenVMS in separate partitions on the same system. Another benefit of this flexibility is that the HP Integrity platform can be repurposed from an HP-UX platform to a Windows platform either after the HP-UX workload has been moved to another system or as an emergency spare in the case of a failed system.

- In late 2005, HP began supporting running Precision Architecture (PA) processors in one partition and Itanium processors in another. This will require up-to-date firmware but will be supported on any cell-based system with either the sx1000 or sx2000 chipsets.

Virtual Partitions

Virtual partitions is the ability to run multiple copies of the HP-UX operating system on a single core set of hardware. This can be a separate server or within an nPartition. Some of the key benefits of HP's vPars include:

- Software-fault isolation: Software faults on one partition, including kernel panics, can't impact other partitions.
- Operating system isolation: Each partition gets its own complete copy of the operating system. They can be different versions, different patch levels, different kernel tunables, etc. They also could run different versions of the applications. This is why vPars are often used to provide development and test environments.
- Single CPU granularity: vPars can be configured and run using a single CPU and can be allocated in single-CPU increments as well.
- Dynamic CPU migration: CPUs can be moved from one vPar to another while both partitions are up and running.
- Minimal overhead: HP's vPars solution was designed to allow each major hardware component—CPUs and I/O cards—for example, to be assigned to a partition in its entirety. Because these components are not shared, there is no need for a virtualization layer to manage every interface between the OS and the underlying hardware. Put differently, each OS talks directly to the hardware assigned to the vPar, ensuring that running vPars on a system has a minimal impact on performance.

Integrity VM

In 2005, HP released a new partitioning technology designed specifically for the Integrity platform called Integrity VM. This is a type of virtual partition in which the system hardware itself is fully virtualized. The result is that the operating system can operate inside the VM unmodified. This means that users will be able to run any operating system that supports the Integrity platform inside a VM, which includes HP-UX 11i V2 initially and future support for 11i V3, Windows Datacenter, Linux, or OpenVMS. Some of the key features of this technology include:

- OS isolation: Each partition runs its own full copy of the operating system. This means that the OS can be patched and tuned specifically for the applications that are running there.

- Sub-CPU or whole-CPU granularity: Since the system is virtualized, each virtual CPU inside a VM can represent a portion of a CPU or a whole CPU on the physical system.

- Differentiated CPU controls: Users have the ability to give differentiated access to the physical CPUs to specific VMs. What this means is that you will be able to define specific CPU entitlements for each VM. For example, you can assign a four-CPU VM 50% of four physical CPUs, another 25%, and a third 10%.

- I/O device sharing: Integrity VM provides fully virtualized I/O, which means multiple virtual SCSI cards can represent a single physical SCSI or fibre channel card.

- Because of the complete virtualization of the system, the OS images are unchanged. This ensures that all independent software vendor applications will run with no changes as well.

This is a nice solution for a test and/or development environment because the VMs are fully isolated and can be created and destroyed quickly and easily.

Secure Resource Partitions

HP's first consolidation solution was resource partitions, which have been shipping in HP-UX for over 10 years. They have been enhanced regularly over the years to include processor sets, memory, and I/O controls. The most recent enhancement was the addition of security containment which has been available in HP VirtualVault for many years making it possible to run applications in separate Secure Resource Partitions (SRPs) such that they can't communicate with one another. The key features of Secure Resource Partitions include:

- Sub-CPU or whole-CPU controls: CPUs can be allocated to each SRP with sub-CPU granularity using the fair share scheduler (FSS) or whole-CPU granularity using processor sets (PSETs). CPU controls are implemented by instantiating separate process schedulers for each partition in the HP-UX kernel.

- Real memory controls: HP-UX is unique in the industry in its implementation of memory resource groups (MRGs). With MRGs, HP-UX creates a separate memory-management subsystem for each partition.

- Disk I/O bandwidth controls: It is possible to define bandwidth controls for each LVM or VxVM volume group for each partition.

- Application and user assignment to partitions: Because all partitions are running in the same copy of the operating system, it is important that processes get placed into the correct partition when they start up. SRPs provides a number of utilities that allow you to start up or move application processes to the correct partition.

- Security containment: This is a new feature in HP-UX 11i V2 that has been integrated with resource partitions to create what is now called Secure Resource

Partitions. Security containment allows you to define security compartments for processes belonging to each application workload. Within a compartment, processes have full access to IPC mechanisms between processes, network interfaces and files on the file system. However, it is not possible for a process in one compartment to communicate with a process in another compartment unless a rule has been defined to allow that specific communication to occur.

Secure Resource Partitions is a set of technologies that have been implemented in the HP-UX kernel. The product that pulls all these features together is Process Resource Manager. PRM provides a single-configuration interface so users have the ability to define partitions, assign CPU, memory, disk I/O and security rules and then assign an application and/or set of users to run in that partition.

Partitioning Flexibility

A very convenient feature of the partitioning continuum is the fact that you can combine the different types of partitions in almost any combination. The only combination that is not supported is that vPars and Integrity VMs cannot run in the same nPar. Figure 2-2 shows an example of the flexibility provided.

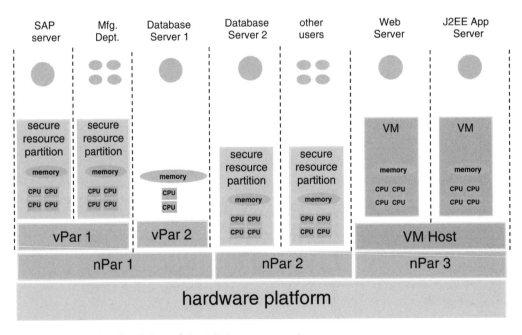

Figure 2-2 The Flexibility of the HP Partitioning Continuum

You can run Secure Resource Partitions (SRPs) in an HP-UX partition using any of the other OS-level partition options. You can run VMs in one nPar and vPars in another, with Secure Resource Partitions in one or more of those vPars. This flexibility is a tremendous advantage when trying to increase the utilization of large servers by placing multiple workloads on them.

The key advantage is that the partitioning continuum simplifies the consolidation design process because you can look at each workload individually and determine what level of isolation is required, what level of granularity is required, and what level of flexibility is required. Then you can choose an appropriate combination of partition technologies for all the workloads on the system and stack the partitions in a combination that provides all the features required for all the workloads.

Now we will look at each of the different partitioning technologies in a bit more detail. There is also a chapter covering each of these later in this part of the book. These chapters will provide examples of how to set up each type of partition.

nPartitions (Electrically Isolated Hardware Partitions)

nPartitions, or nPars, is HP's hardware partitioning solution. Because nPars is a hardware partitioning solution, it can be difficult to separate the features of the hardware from the features of nPars so we will start by discussing the hardware features that impact partitioning and then discuss partitioning itself.

Key Features

Single-System High-Availability (HA) Features

nPartitions allows you to isolate hardware failures so that they affect only a portion of the system. A number of other single-system HA features are designed to reduce the number of failures in ANY of the partitions. These include n+1, hot swappable components such as:

- Cabinet blowers
- I/O fans
- DC power supplies
- Cell backplane
- Optional redundant AC input power

These features ensure that the infrastructure is robust enough to support multiple partitions. In addition, a number of error resiliency features are designed to ensure that all the partitions can keep running. These include:

- ECC on CPU cache and front-side bus
- Parity-protected PCI-X
- Single-wire correction on fabric and I/O links
- ECC on all fabric and memory paths
- Chip-spare memory

Finally, nPars provides hardware isolation to ensure that anything not corrected will impact only a portion of the system.

Investment Protection

HP's cell-based systems were designed from the beginning to provide industry-leading investment protection. In other words, the system can go through seven years of processor and cell upgrades inside the box. One example of how this is done is shown in Figure 2-3.

This picture shows the inside of a Superdome cabinet and two generations of cells that are currently supported in this cabinet. The cell on the top is for the PA-8600, PA-8700, and PA8700+ processors. This provided three generations of processors with the same cabinet, cell, memory, I/O, etc. Moving to Itanium or PA-8800 requires a cell-board swap. However, the memory in the old cell can be moved to the new cell as part of the upgrade, so the only things changing are the processors and cell boards.

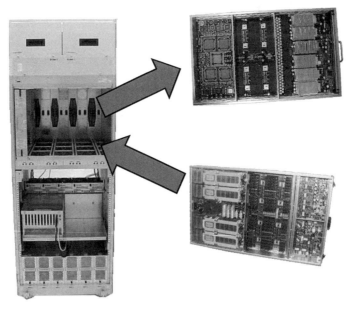

Figure 2-3 Superdome In-Box Cell Upgrade

In addition, the new cell board supports five generations of CPUs including both PA (8800 and 8900) and Itanium (Madison, Madison 9M, and Montecito). So a user could start with the PA-8800 and upgrade to Itanium later using the same cell board. There are three more years' worth of processor and memory upgrades planned for this cell board.

Finally, another upgrade is available for this same cabinet. As was mentioned earlier, there is a new chipset, the sx2000, that increases the number and bandwidth of the crossbars on the backplane. This provides yet another in-box upgrade which supports the same CPUs and I/O.

The Anatomy of a Cell-Based System

Dual-Cabinet sx1000-Based Superdome Architecture

The architecture of the Superdome based on the sx1000 chipset is depicted in Figure 2-4. A fully loaded Superdome can support two cabinets, each holding eight cells and four I/O chassis. Each cell has four CPU sockets that can hold single- or dual-core processors. The chipset also supports

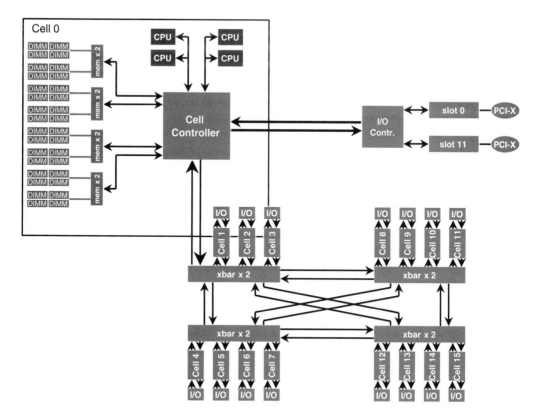

Figure 2-4 Fully Loaded Superdome Component Architecture Using the sx1000 Chipset

either PA or Itanium processors. Each cell has 32 dual inline memory module (DIMM) slots that can currently support 64GB of memory, although this will increase over time. Four cells (called a quad) are connected to each of two crossbars inside each cabinet.

A few things to note in this diagram.

- An I/O chassis can be attached to each cell. Since only four I/O chassis can fit in each cabinet, eight of the I/O chassis would need to reside inside an I/O expansion cabinet if you want the full complement of 16 I/O chassis.
- Each crossbar has dual chipsets and each cell is connected to both. In addition, all of the links are dual links, one to/from each of the crossbar chips. This provides double memory bandwidth across the backplane of the system and increases the resilience of the backplane.
- The crossbars are a fully meshed, switched fabric. So even if you lose both of the links between two of the crossbars, the switches would automatically reroute memory traffic around the failure.
- Each I/O chassis has 12 PCI-X slots, so a fully loaded system can support 192 PCI-X cards.
- Each cell has four CPU sockets. With the PA-8800, PA-8900, or Montecito processors, you can run two CPUs in each socket, allowing a fully loaded system to support 128 CPUs.

Single-Cabinet sx1000-Based Superdome Architecture

There is one significant difference between a dual-cabinet and a single-cabinet Superdome. The single-cabinet sx1000-based Superdome architecture is shown in Figure 2-5.

As you can see from this diagram, the crossover cable that connects the two cabinets in a dual-cabinet configuration can be looped back to double the number of crossbar links between the two crossbars in the single cabinet configuration. This improves the performance and flexibility of the server.

The New sx2000 Chipset

In late 2005, HP introduced a new chipset for its cell-based systems called the sx2000. Figure 2-6 shows the architecture of a dual-cabinet Superdome with the new chipset.

The key enhancements in this chipset are:

- Triple redundant crossbar mesh
- Each cell is connected to three crossbars
- Each bus has two to four times the bandwidth
- The new chipset has redundant system clocks

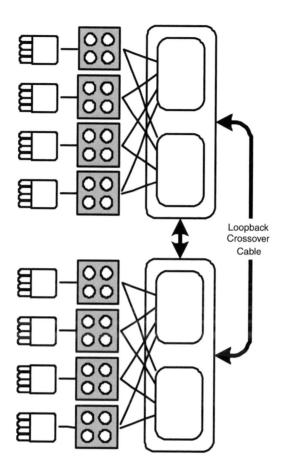

Figure 2-5 Single-Cabinet Superdome Component Architecture Based on the sx1000 Chipset

The end result of all of this is more resilience and more bandwidth. This means better performance and better availability.

Midrange System Architectures

Two other midrange systems use the same cell and crossbar architecture. The first is a four-cell system that was first introduced as the rp8400. The architecture of this system is shown in Figure 2-7. This same architecture is used in the rp8420 and rx8620 systems.

Since there are only four cells in this system, only one crossbar is required. The core architecture is effectively the same as half of that of a single-cabinet Superdome. There is approximately 60% technology reuse up and down the product line. Figure 2-8 shows a picture of the Superdome and an rp8400.

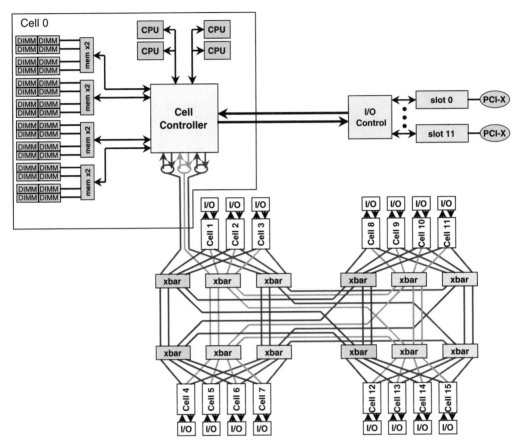

Figure 2-6 Dual-Cabinet Superdome Component Architecture Based on the sx2000 Chipset

Much of this technology is also used in the rp7410, rp7420, and rx7620, although there is no need for a crossbar in these systems. This is because there are only two cells in this system, so the cell controllers are connected together rather than having a crossbar in between. This is shown in Figure 2-9.

The key advantage to reusing system components is cost. Reuse makes it possible for HP to provide more features at a lower overall cost.

Dual-Core Processors

In 2004, HP introduced support for dual-core processors in all of its servers that use the PA-8800 or MX2 Itanium daughtercard. The MX2 is an interesting HP invention that warrants a brief description.

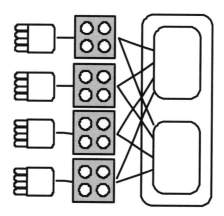

Figure 2-7 HP rp8400 Component Architecture

HP was scheduled to release the PA-8800 processor in early 2004, which would allow the Superdome to go up to 128 CPUs. At that time Intel already had a dual-core Itanium processor (Montecito) in its roadmap, but this wasn't scheduled for release until 2005. HP didn't want to wait, so the HP chipset designers came up with a clever solution. They analyzed the form factor of the Itanium processor (top of Figure 2-10) and realized that it was possible to fit two processors in the same form factor.

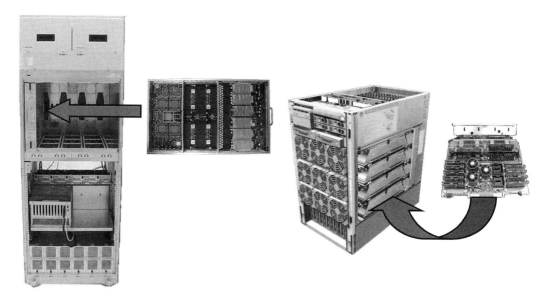

Figure 2-8 The Superdome and rp8400 Reuse Much of the Same Technology

Figure 2-9 HP rp7410 Component Architecture

They then put together a daughtercard which carried two Itanium processors, a controller chip, and a 32MB level-4 cache, and fit all this into the same form factor, power requirements, and pin-out of a single Itanium chip. They did this by laying the power pod on top of the daughtercard rather than plugging it into the side.

If you think about this, the result is that you now have two Itanium chips plus a 32MB cache in *every socket in the system.* For some workloads, the addition of the cache alone results in as much as a 30% performance improvement over a system with the same number of processors. However, in order to maintain the power and thermal envelope of a single Itanium processor the mx2 doesn't support the fastest Itanium processors.

nPar Configuration Details

Much of what we have talked about so far has been features of the hardware in HP's cell-based servers. Although this is all very interesting, what does it have to do with the Virtual Server Environment (VSE)? Well, since this section is about hardware partitioning, much of what we have

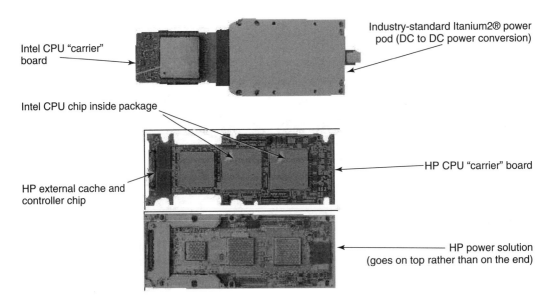

Figure 2-10 Intel Itanium Processor Compared to the HP MX2

talked about so far has been focused on helping you understand the infrastructure that you use to set up nPartitions. Now let's talk about how this all leads to an nPartition configuration.

Earlier in this section we showed you a couple of architecture diagrams of the Superdome, both the single-cabinet and double-cabinet configurations. An extensive set of documents describes how to set up partitions that have peak performance and maximum resiliency and flexibility. We are not going to attempt to replace those documents here. However, we do want to give you some guidance on where to look.

Selection of Partition Cells

One nice feature of the Superdome program is that there is a team of people to help you determine how you want the system partitioned as part of the purchasing process. That way the system is delivered already partitioned the way you want. Customer data suggests that very few customers change that configuration later. That said, many customers have become much more comfortable with dynamic systems technologies, and there should be much more of this in the future. When you get to the point that you want to reconfigure your partitions, a key resource for determining how to lay out your partitions is the *HP System Partitions Guide,* particularly for Superdomes with the sx1000 chipset. Although any combination of cells will work, there are a number of recommendations on combinations that provide the best performance and resilience. A tremendous amount of effort went into those recommendations. If you can, you should stick with them.

An additional reason to look at the recommendations in the manual is that the combinations in that document will be different for the sx2000 chipset. Because of the triple-redundant connections between all of the cells and crossbars in the sx2000, the recommendations are more open.

Memory Population

For many workloads, getting maximum memory performance is critical. Several key memory-loading concepts are helpful in making sure you get optimal performance from your system.

The first is that there are dual-memory buses in the system. To take full advantage of the architecture, you should always load your memory four to eight DIMMs at a time. This will ensure that you are using both memory buses.

The other important concept affecting memory loading is memory interleaving. This is also important to nPars, because to get optimal performance from an nPar, you need to ensure that the memory on each cell in the partition is the same. This is because the memory addressing in the partition is interleaved, which means the memory is evenly spread out in small increments over all the cells in the partition. The major advantage to this is that large memory accesses can take advantage of many memory buses at the same time, increasing overall bandwidth and performance.

HP-UX 11iV2 introduced cell-local memory. What this means is that memory allocation is done from memory locally on the cell, where the process that is allocating the memory is running. Interleaving is better when large blocks of memory are being accessed in short periods of time. Workloads that can take advantage of this include statistical analysis, data warehousing and supply chain optimization. Cell-local memory is best for workloads that do lots of small memory accesses, such as online transaction processing and web applications.

In addition, you can assign both cell-local and interleaved memory in each of your cells and each of your nPars. There are several things to remember here. The first is that you want to make sure that you still have the same amount of interleaved memory on all of the cells within each nPar. The other is that most workloads can typically benefit from a combination. Finding the right balance tends to be very workload dependent, so we recommend that you discuss your requirements with your HP Solutions Architect and then test a few combinations to determine the best balance.

More details on nPartitions and how to configure and manage them is provided in Chapter 5, "nPartition Servers."

Virtual Partitions (Peak Performance Virtualization)

HP supports two different virtual partitioning options: Virtual Partitions and Integrity Virtual Machines. These each have their own benefits and tradeoffs, so we will describe both of them here and then discuss how to choose which technology fits your needs later, in Chapter 3 — Making the Most of the HP Partitioning Continuum. Let's first look at Virtual Partitions, or vPars.

Key Features

Virtual Partitions (vPars) effectively provides you with the ability to run multiple copies of HP-UX on a single set of hardware, which can be a system or an nPar. It provides the ability to allocate CPUs and memory and I/O card slots to each of your OS images. Once that is done, the partitions boot as if they are separate systems.

Functionality

The key features of vPars include:

- Single CPU granularity: Each vPar can have as little as one CPU. Two CPUs are recommended for the same reason you want to have two of anything else — high availability — but that is not required.

- Dynamic reassignment of CPUs across virtual partitions: CPUs can be deallocated and allocated between partitions while they are up and running. This makes it possible to increase the utilization of the system by allowing unused CPUs in one partition to be moved to a partition that can use them.

- Application and OS isolation: Each vPar runs its own copy of HP-UX. This ensures that each partition is fully isolated from all others. This includes application, namespace, OS, and kernel isolation. Each partition can be updated, patched, tuned, and rebooted independently.

- Both graphical user interface (GUI) and command-line-configuration interface: The primary interface for configuring vPars is using the command-line tools. However, the VSE Manager toolset will provide a graphical view of vPars in the context of the servers and nPars they are running in. You will also be able to get configuration and resource usage information from this interface.

- Integration with Process Resource Manager (PRM), Workload Manager (WLM), and GlancePlus: All the major management tools operate appropriately with vPars. PRM can run inside vPars, allowing you to further partition your server. WLM automates the allocation of resources to resource partitions inside and across vPars. GlancePlus runs normally inside a vPar.

System and OS Support

The vPars product has been available since 2001. It supports the rp5405, rp5470, rp7400 and all of HP's cell-based servers. There are some limitations with the cards and systems supported, and these are changing regularly, so you should verify that the configuration you are considering is supported with the current vPars software.

Architecture

This section will provide some insights into the architecture of the vPars product.

Overview

vPars runs on top of a lightweight kernel called the vPar Monitor. The high-level architecture is shown in Figure 2-11.

Some interesting things to note in this figure include:

- The vPar monitor: Instead of booting the system or nPar to HP-UX, you boot what is called the vPar monitor. The monitor is configured to know what partitions should be running on this system and which hardware components belong to each partition.

- The vPars: The monitor boots the partitions to HP-UX. When the OS queries the hardware to determine what components are available, the monitor traps those firmware calls and responds with only the components that particular partition is supposed to be able to see. The OS boots normally and simply appears to be a smaller system. Each OS can be separately patched, tuned, and booted.

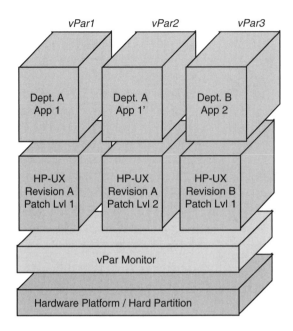

Figure 2-11 vPars Architecture Overview

- The Applications: Once the vPar is running, the only communication between the partitions is through the network via the network interface cards assigned to each partition. It appears to the applications as if they are running on a separate physical system.

Partitionable Resources

In order to decide how to divide up a system, the first step is to do an ioscan to map out the resources that are available. The ioscan will provide all the information you need to identify which resources are available for assignment to vPars.

note

> It is important that you run the ioscan and save or print the output prior to configuring and booting your first vPar. This is because once the monitor is running, the only access to the command will be from a running vPar and running ioscan from a vPar will only show you the available resources in that vPar. This means that you won't be able to identify the resources that can be assigned to other vPars. Actually, you will be able to identify the existence of I/O cards using the 'vparstatus -A' command, but there will be no information about what types of cards they are.

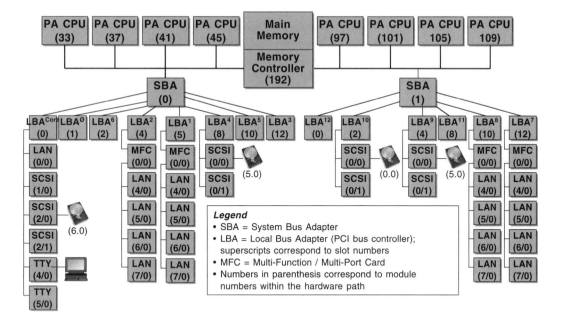

Figure 2-12 Partitionable Resources on an rp7400

Figure 2-12 shows the resources available on an rp7400 graphically.

There are a few key things to understand about this diagram before you decide how to partition this system.

Partitioning CPUs

On older versions of vPars, there was the concept of bound vs. unbound processors. The distinction is this:

* Bound processors are tagged to respond to I/O interrupts
* Unbound processors can be freely moved between vPars without requiring a reboot

An important distinction with the bound processors is that the actual I/O activity could be handled by any of the processors; only the interrupts were handled by the bound processors. On these older versions, each vPar needs to have at least one bound processor, but it may benefit from more, depending on the amount of I/O interrupt handling required by the workloads running in the vPar.

Version 4.1 of vPars resolved this issue. HP-UX version 11iV2 now supports the movement of I/O interrupts between processors, so there is no longer any need for bound processors. You still need at least one processor if you want to keep the vPar running, of course. Other than that, all the CPUs can freely move between vPars.

Partitioning Memory

Memory is allocated to vPars in 64MB ranges. It is possible to specify the blocks of memory you want to allocate to each of the vPars, but this isn't required. The memory controller (block 192 in Figure 2-12) is owned by the vPar monitor, which allocates the memory to the vPars when they boot. Changing the memory configuration of a vPar currently requires that the vPar be shut down, reconfigured, and then rebooted.

Partitioning I/O Devices

I/O devices are broken up into system bus adapters (SBAs) and local bus adapters (LBAs). The SBAs are owned by the vPar monitor. I/O devices are assigned to vPars at the LBA or SBA level. On HP systems, the LBA is equivalent to an I/O card slot. Each SBA or LBA can be assigned to a specific vPar. Whatever card is in that slot becomes owned by that vPar and will show up in an ioscan once that vPar is booted. Keep in mind that if the card is a multifunction or multiport card, then all the ports must be assigned to the same vPar.

Changing the I/O slot configuration of a vPar requires that the vPar be shut down, reconfig- ured, and then rebooted. A couple of interesting points on this:

- HP-UX and vPars supports hot swappable I/O cards. What this means is that you can physically pull a card out of a slot in one vPar and insert it into a slot in an- other vPar while both vPars are up and running if the appropriate drivers are available in both kernels. You will not want to do this often, but it might be use- ful for devices that are rarely used, such as CD drives, where you need to go to the device anyway.
- You can, and probably should, allocate one or more of your unused card slots to each of your vPars to allow for future upgrades without requiring a reboot.

Security Considerations

In order to make it possible to administer vPars from any of the partitions, the early versions of the vPar commands were accessible from any of the partitions. These include the vparmodify, vparboot, and vparreset commands. On the positive side, a root user in any of the partitions can repair the vPar configuration database. The tradeoff was that it was possible for a root user in another partition to shut down, reboot, or damage another partition configuration. Newer ver- sions of vPars will resolve this issue by allowing you to assign each vPar the designation of being a Primary or a Secondary administration domain. When these commands are run in a vPar that is a Primary administration domain, they will work as they did before. However, when running these commands in a vPar that is a Secondary administration domain, they will only allow you to operate on the vPar the command is run in. In other words, you will be able to run a vpar- modify command to alter the configuration of the local vPar, but if you attempt to modify the configuration of another vPar, the command will fail.

We do need to clear up one common misconception about this security concern, though. Each partition runs a completely independent copy of the operating system, including separate root logins. Therefore, if one of the vPars were compromised in a security attack, it would *not* be possible for them to gain access to processes running inside another vPar except through the network, as with any other separate system.

Performance Characteristics

We describe this technology as peak performance virtualization because the physical resources of the system are assigned to partitions and once they are assigned, the operating system in the partition accesses those resources directly. The tradeoff here is flexibility. For example, each I/O card slot can only be assigned to a single vPar. However, because the OS interfaces directly with the card, no translation layer is required. If I/O performance is critical for an application in your environment, you will want to ensure that the solution you are using supports this direct I/O capability.

HP Integrity Virtual Machines (Fully Virtualized Partitioning)

The newest solution in HP's partitioning continuum is called HP Integrity Virtual Machines. This is a fully virtualized environment for running applications. You can run what is called the virtual machine host on any Integrity system or nPartition. On top of the VM host, you run virtual machines, which present themselves to the operating system inside the VM as a physical server. However, all of the resources of that system are virtualized. The physical CPUs, memory, and I/O devices are managed by the VM and what the VMs see is a virtual resource that is mapped on top of the physical devices in the system. This allows the physical resources to be shared by multiple OS images.

The virtualization that is provided by Integrity VM is so complete that the operating systems running inside the VMs run without modification. This means that all the operating systems that are supported on Integrity hardware will run inside VMs. This includes HP-UX initially and future versions will support unmodified versions of Linux, Windows, and OpenVMs.

Features

The major features of Integrity VM include:

- OS isolation: Each partition runs its own full copy of the operating system. This means that the OS can be patched and tuned specifically for the applications that will be running there.

- Sub-CPU or whole-CPU granularity: Since the system is virtualized, each virtual CPU inside a VM can represent a portion of a CPU or a whole CPU on the physical system.

- Differentiated CPU controls: You can give differentiated access to the physical CPUs to specific VMs. You will be able to define specific CPU entitlements for each VM. For example, you can assign a four-CPU VM 50% of four physical CPUs, another VM can get 25%, and a third 25%.

- I/O device sharing: Integrity VM provides fully virtualized I/O, which means multiple virtual SCSI cards can represent a single physical SCSI or fibre channel card.

- Supports HP-UX initially, and will eventually support Linux, Windows, and OpenVMS: Because the system is fully virtualized, it is possible to run any of the operating systems that are supported on the Integrity platform inside a VM.

- Support for the full line of Integrity Servers: From 1 to 128 processor systems are supported for use with Integrity VM.

- Software-fault isolation: Software faults in one VM can't impact other VMs.

- Security isolation: It is not possible for a process inside a VM to access the memory or devices allocated to another VM.

High-Level Architecture

HP Integrity VM is implemented by running what is called the VM host on top of the hardware rather than running a standard operating system. Figure 2-13 shows the high-level architecture of a system running Integrity VM.

The VM host runs on top of the hardware and boots the various VMs, which each run their own copy of an operating system, which boot normally and start up whatever application workloads are intended to run in that VM.

Resource Virtualization

Each VM will have a set of virtual CPUs, a block of memory, and a set of virtual I/O interface cards. The host maps each of these resources to physical resources available on the system.

CPU Virtualization

The physical CPUs on the system are shared by the VMs, which each have one or more virtual CPUs. It is possible to have more virtual CPUs inside the VMs than there are physical CPUs in the system. In fact, this is desirable. You can get better utilization of the physical CPUs when you have several virtual CPUs for each physical CPU. However, it is not possible to have a single VM

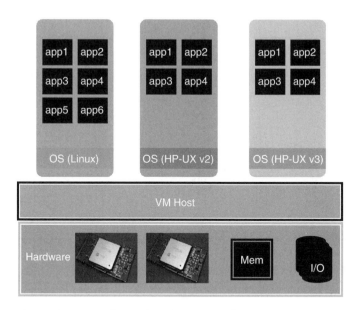

Figure 2-13 High-Level Architecture of Integrity VM

with more virtual CPUs than physical CPUs on the system. Figure 2-14 shows how the VM host manages physical CPU allocation to virtual CPUs.

As you can see from Figure 2-14, a specialized VM scheduler has been built into the VM host. This allows you to specify how much of a physical CPU each of the virtual CPUs should be able to consume. In the example in the figure, each of the virtual CPUs in the VMs on the right is guaranteed a minimum of half of a physical CPU. It may be able to get more if the resources are not being consumed by other VMs, but it can't ever get less than its entitlement if it has processes that can use it.

Another interesting thing to note here is that there are five virtual CPUs in the VMs in this figure but only four physical CPUs. This means that some of the virtual CPUs will be sharing physical CPUs and others will get dedicated physical CPUs. This results in an interesting phenomenon in a VM with multiple CPUs: the various CPUs can be running at dramatically different speeds. The scheduler in the VM host randomly shuffles the virtual CPUs across the physical CPUs to ensure that all the CPUs get equal access to the physical CPU resources. Except when you have explicitly said that you want them to be different, of course. In this case, the virtual CPUs are still shuffled, but the ticks are allocated at the ratio you have assigned. One reason this is very important is that if you are running multiple workloads inside a VM and you want to be able to encapsulate those workloads inside of Secure Resource Partitions, it is critical that the virtual CPUs all be running at approximately the same speed in order for the resource allocation to be accurate.

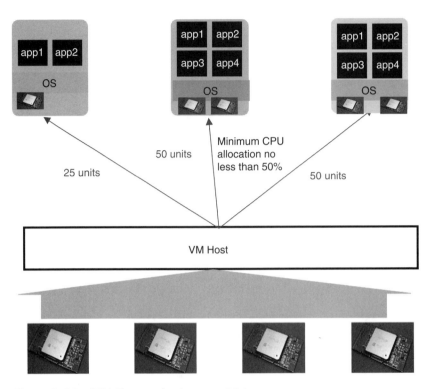

Figure 2-14 CPU-Sharing by Integrity VMs

Memory Virtualization

Integrity VM provides virtualized physical memory. Basically, what this means is that a block of physical memory is allocated to each VM and is presented to the OS running inside the VM as if it were all the physical memory that was available. This is similar in concept to how CPUs are virtualized. The OS sees four CPUs and doesn't realize that they are only virtual CPUs and may be sharing a set of physical CPUs. In the case of memory, you allocate 4GB of memory to a VM, for example. To the OS, it looks like it is running on a system with 4GB of physical memory, even though it may really be running on a system with 128GB of physical memory.

In the first release of Integrity VM, memory will not be shared by the different VMs. The reason is that allowing the VMs to share memory would, in effect, require a type of virtual memory and swapping in the VM host. This would be in addition to the swapping that is being done by the OS images running inside the various VMs. The double swapping could have a significant performance impact on the applications running in the VM. This issue isn't insurmountable, but it is not a first-release feature. The bottom line is that, with the first release of VMs you will need to ensure that there is enough physical memory in the system to satisfy the needs of all the workloads.

I/O Virtualization

Integrity VM provides I/O virtualization by allowing users to define I/O interface cards inside each VM. These interface cards are then mapped to one or more physical cards in the VM host. Although the interface cards in the VM appear to the OS as standard SCSI interface cards, they can be mapped to any SCSI or fibre channel interface card on the system. There is no performance impact when running fibre channel on the VMM and SCSI in the VM. The SCSI interfaces in the VMs just run really fast!

Figure 2-15 shows graphically how the I/O packet translation is done in the VM host. Each VM has at least one virtual SCSI interface; these are mapped to physical interface cards on the system.

In this diagram, the two VMs on the left are sharing one physical I/O interface card. The VM on the right has a dedicated physical interface mapped to its virtual interface. What this means is that you can dedicate all of the bandwidth of a physical interface card to a single VM if that is desired. The interface presented to the VM is still a virtual interface and there is still packet translation done in the VM host, but there is no competition for the bandwidth of the physical interface. This can provide significant performance benefits.

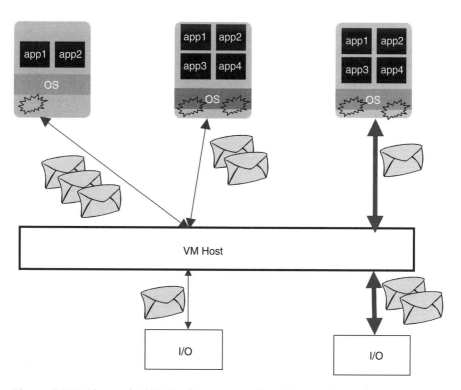

Figure 2-15 Physical I/O Cards Can Be Shared or Dedicated to Virtual I/O Interfaces in the VMs

Integrity VM also supports technologies like Auto Port Aggregation in the VM host. This allows you to configure multiple physical interfaces to act as one, providing increased bandwidth as well as higher availability because no one physical interface is a single point of failure. As an example, this is useful for providing a set of ethernet interfaces that have sufficient bandwidth to support a large number of VMs. Then you specify that at least one LAN interface in each VM shares the bandwidth available to the network. Even if one of the physical interfaces fails, the other ones will continue to function, ensuring that mission-critical applications can continue to run uninterrupted while the failing device is diagnosed and repaired.

Security Isolation

In most operating systems, there are two modes of operation. The kernel runs in "privileged mode" and processes run in "unprivileged mode." This ensures that no processes running on the system can execute privileged operations unless the kernel approves them. Only code running in ring 0 can perform privileged operations such as enabling or disabling system interrupts or managing virtual memory translations. If a process attempts to execute a privileged operation (which requires ring 0 privilege), the kernel is notified and can respond appropriately, typically by shutting down the offending process. The Itanium architecture provides four privilege levels, with ring 0 being the most privileged and ring 3 being the least privileged. Figure 2-16 shows that these privilege levels as concentric rings.

When a single operating system is running on an Itanium platform, the kernel typically runs in ring 0 and the remaining processes running on the system run in ring 3. Rings 1 and 2 are not

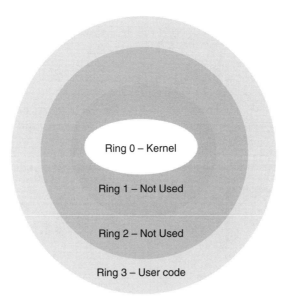

Figure 2-16 The Itanium Architecture Supports Four Privilege Rings

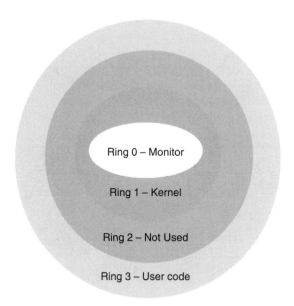

Ring 0 – Monitor

Ring 1 – Kernel

Ring 2 – Not Used

Ring 3 – User code

Figure 2-17 Integrity VM Runs the VM host at
Ring 0 and Each of the VM Kernels Run at Ring 1

used, which is the key Itanium feature that Integrity VM exploits. Figure 2-17 shows how Integrity VMs are able to run multiple kernels and ensure that none of them are able to interact with each other.

With Integrity VM, the VM host is the only thing that runs at ring 0. The VM kernels are run at ring 1, but are tricked into thinking they are running at ring 0 (sometimes called "ring compression"). Any privileged-mode operations that are executed by the kernel inside a VM are trapped and performed by the host on behalf of the VM. In this way, the host can ensure that even if the security of one of the VMs is compromised, nothing can be done on that VM to affect any of the other VMs.

Secure Resource Partitions (Partitioning Inside a Single Copy of HP-UX)

Resource partitioning is something that has been integrated with the HP-UX kernel since version 9.0 of HP-UX. Over the years, HP has gradually increased the functionality; today you can provide a remarkable level of isolation between applications running in a single copy of HP-UX. The current version provides both resource isolation, something that has been there from the beginning of resource partitions, and security isolation, the newest addition. Figure 2-18 shows how the resource isolation capabilities allows multiple applications to run in a single copy of HP-UX while ensuring that each partition gets its share of resources.

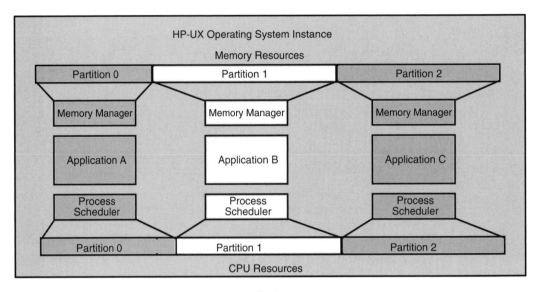

Figure 2-18 Resource Partitioning in HP-UX

Within a single copy of HP-UX, you have the ability to create multiple partitions. To each partition you can:

- Allocate a CPU entitlement using whole-CPU granularity (processor sets) or sub-CPU granularity (fair share scheduler)
- Allocate a block of memory
- Allocate disk I/O bandwidth
- Assign a set of users and/or application processes that should run in the partition
- Create a security compartment around the processes that ensures that processes in other compartments can't communicate or send signals to the processes in this Secure Resource Partition

One unique feature of HP's implementation of resource partitions is that inside the HP-UX kernel, we instantiate multiple copies of the memory management subsystem and multiple process schedulers. This ensures that if an application runs out of control and attempts to allocate excessive amounts of resources, the system will constrain that application. For example, when we allocate four CPUs and 8GB of memory to Partition 0 in Figure 2-18, if the application running in that partition attempts to allocate more than 8GB of memory, it will start to page, even if there is 32GB of memory on the system. Similarly, the processes running in that partition are scheduled on the four CPUs that are assigned to the partition. No processes from other partitions are allowed to run on those CPUs, and processes assigned to this partition are not allowed to run on the CPUs that are assigned to the other partitions. This guarantees that if a process running in any partition spins out of control, it can't impact the performance of any application running in any other partition.

A new feature of HP-UX is security containment. This is really the migration of functionality available in HP VirtualVault for many years into the standard HP-UX kernel. This is being done in a way that allows customers to choose which of the security features they want to be activated individually. The security-containment feature allows users to ensure that processes and applications running on HP-UX can be isolated from other processes and applications. Specifically, it is possible to erect a boundary around a group of processes that insulates those processes from IPC communication with the rest of the processes on the system. It is also possible to define access to file systems and network interfaces. This feature is being integrated with PRM to provide Secure Resource Partitions.

Resource Controls

The resource controls available with Secure Resource Partitions include:

* CPU controls: You can allocate a CPU to a partition with sub-CPU granularity using the fair share scheduler (FSS) or with whole-CPU granularity using processor sets.
* Real memory: Shares of the physical memory on the system can be allocated to partitions.
* Disk I/O bandwidth: Shares of the bandwidth to any volume group can be allocated to each partition.

More details about what is possible and how these features are implemented are provided below.

CPU Controls

A CPU can be allocated to Secure Resource Partitions with sub-CPU granularity or whole-CPU granularity. Both of these features are implemented inside the kernel. The sub-CPU granularity capability is implemented by the FSS.

The fair share scheduler is implemented as a second level of time-sharing on top of the standard HP-UX scheduler. The FSS allocates a CPU to each partition in large 10ms time ticks. When a particular partition gets access to a CPU, the process scheduler for that partition analyzes the process run queue for that partition and runs those processes using standard HP-UX process-scheduling algorithms.

CPU allocation via processor sets (PSETs) is quite different in that CPU resources are allocated to each of the partitions on whole CPU boundaries. What this means is that you assign a certain number of whole CPUs to each partition rather than a share of them. The scheduler in the partition will then schedule the processes that are running there only on the CPUs assigned to the partition. This is illustrated in Figure 2-19.

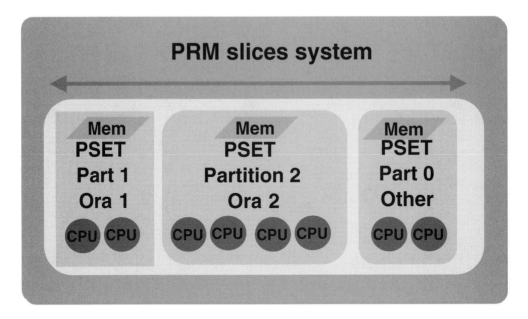

Figure 2-19 CPU Allocation via Processor Sets Assigns Whole CPUs to Each Partition

The configuration shown in Figure 2-19 shows the system split into three partitions. Two will run Oracle instances and the other partition runs the rest of the processing on the system. This means that the Oracle processes running in partition 1 will run on the two CPUs assigned to that partition. These processes will not run on any other CPUs in the system, nor will any processes from the other partitions run on these two CPUs.

Comparing FSS to PSETs is best done using an example. If you have an eight-CPU partition that you wish to assign to three workloads with 50% going to one workload and 25% going to each of the others, you have the option of setting up PSETs with the configuration illustrated in Figure 2-19 or setting up FSS groups with 50, 25, and 25 shares. The difference between the two is that the processes running in partition 1 will either get 100% of the CPU cycles on two CPUs or 25% of the cycles on all eight CPUs.

Memory Controls

In Figure 2-19, we see that each of the partitions in this configuration also has a block of memory assigned. This is optional, but it provides another level of isolation between the partitions. HP-UX 11i introduced a new memory-control technology called memory resource groups, or MRGs. This is implemented by providing a separate memory manager for each partition, all running in a single copy of the kernel. This provides a very strong level of isolation between the partitions. As an example, if PSET partition 1 above was allocated two CPUs and 4GB of memory, the memory manager for partition 1 will manage the memory allocated by the processes in that partition within the 4GB that was assigned. If those processes attempt to allocate more than 4GB, the memory manager will start to page out memory to make room, even though there may be 16GB of memory available in the partition.

The default behavior is to allow unused memory to be shared between the partitions. In other words, if the application in partition 1 is only using 2GB of its 4GB entitlement, then processes in the other partitions can "borrow" the available 2GB. However, as soon as processes in partition 1 start to allocate additional memory, the memory that was loaned out will be retrieved. There is an option on MRGs that allows you to "isolate" the memory in a partition. What that means is that the 4GB assigned to the partition will not be loaned out and the partition will not be allowed to borrow memory from any of the other partitions either.

Disk I/O Controls

HP-UX supports disk I/O bandwidth controls for both LVM and VxVM volume groups. You set this up by assigning a share of the bandwidth to each volume group to each partition. LVM and VxVM each call a routine provided by PRM that will reshuffle the I/O queues to ensure that the bandwidth to the volume group is allocated in the ratios assigned. For example, if partition 1 has 50% of the bandwidth, the queue will be shuffled to ensure that every other I/O request comes from processes in that partition.

One thing to note here is that because this is implemented by shuffling the queue, the controls are active only when a queue is building, which happens when there is contention for I/O. This is probably what you want. It normally doesn't make sense to constrain the bandwidth available to one application when that bandwidth would go to waste if you did.

Security Controls

The newest feature added to resource partitions is security containment. With the introduction of security containment in HP-UX 11i V2, we have integrated some of this functionality with resource partitions to create Secure Resource Partitions. There are three major features of the security containment product:

* Secure compartments
* Fine-grained privileges
* Role-based access control

These features have been available in secure versions of HP-UX and Linux but have now been integrated into the base HP-UX in a way that allows them to be optionally activated. Let's look at each of these in detail.

Compartments

The purpose of compartments is to allow you to provide control of the interprocess communication (IPC), device, and file accesses from a group of processes. This is illustrated in Figure 2-20.

The processes in each compartment can freely communicate with each other and can freely access files and directories assigned to the partition, but no access to processes or files in other compartments is permitted unless a rule has been defined that allows that specific access. Additionally, the network interfaces, including pseudo-interfaces, are assigned to a compartment. Communication over the network is restricted to the interfaces in the local compartment unless a rule is defined that allows access to an interface in another compartment.

Fine-Grained Privileges

Traditional HP-UX provided very basic control of special privileges, such as overriding permission to access files. Generally speaking, the root user had all privileges and other users had none. With the introduction of security containment, the privileges can now be assigned at a very granular level. There are roughly 30 separate privileges that you can assign.

The combination of these fine-grained privileges and the role-based access control we discuss in the next section allows you to assign specific privileges to specific users when running specific commands. This provides the ability to implement very detailed security policies. Keep in mind, though, that the more security you wish to impose, the more time will be spent getting the configuration set up and tested.

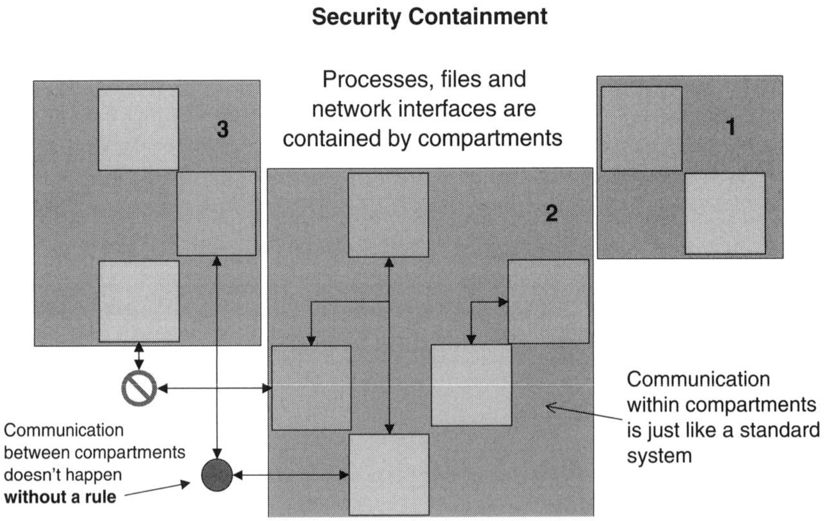

Figure 2-20 Security Compartments Isolate Groups of Processes from Each Other

Role-Based Access Controls (RBAC)

In many very secure environments, customers require the ability to cripple or remove the root user from the system. This ensures that if there is a successful break-in to the system and an intruder gains root access, he or she can do little or no damage. In order to provide this, HP has implemented role-based access control in the kernel. This is integrated with the fine-grained privileges so that it is possible to define a "user admin" role as someone who has the ability to create directories under /home and can edit the /etc/password file. You can then assign one or more of your system administrators as "user admin" and they will be able to create and modify user accounts only without having to know the root password.

This is implemented by defining a set of authorizations and a set of roles that have those authorizations against a specific set of objects. Another example would be giving a printer admin authorization to start or stop a particular print queue.

Implementing these using roles makes it much easier to maintain the controls over time. As users come and go, they can be removed from the list of users who have a particular role, but the role is still there and the other users are not impacted by that change. You can also add another object to be managed, like another print queue, and add it to the printer admin role and all the users with that role will automatically get that authorization; you will not have to add it to every user. A sample set of roles is shown in Figure 2-21.

Secure Resource Partitions

An interesting perspective of Secure Resource Partitions is that it is really a set of technologies that are embedded in the HP-UX kernel. These include FSS and PSETs for CPU control, memory resource groups for memory controls, LVM and VxVM for disk I/O bandwidth control, and security containment for process communication isolation.

	User Admin	Networ Admin	Backup Oper.	User	Admin
hpux.user.add	●				●
hpux.user.delete	●				●
hpux.user.modify	●				●
hpux.user.password.modify				●	●
hpux.network.nfs.start		●			●
hpux.network.nfs.stop		●			●
hpux.network.nfs.config		●			●
hpux.fs.backup			●		●
hpux.fs.restore			●		●

Figure 2-21 A Simple Example of Roles Being Assigned Authorizations

The product that makes it possible to define Secure Resource Partitions is Process Resource Manager (PRM). All of the other technologies allow you to control a group of processes running on an HP-UX instance. What PRM does is make it much easier for you to define the controls for any or all of them on the same set of processes. You do this by defining a group of users and/or processes, called a PRM group, and then assigning CPU, memory, disk I/O, and security entitlements for that group of processes. Figure 2-22 provides a slightly modified view of Figure 2-18, which includes the security isolation in addition to the resource controls.

This diagram illustrates the ability to control both resources and security containment with a single solution. One point to make about PRM is that it doesn't yet allow the configuration of all the features of the underlying technology. For example, PRM controls groups of processes, so it doesn't provide the ability to configure the role-based access control features of the security-containment technology. It does, however, allow you to define a compartment for the processes to run in and will also allow you to assign one or more network interfaces to each partition if you define the security features.

The default behavior of security compartments is that processes will be able to communicate with any process running in the same compartment but will not be able to communicate with any processes running in any other compartment. However, file access uses standard file system security by default. This is done to ensure that independent software vendor applications will be able to run in this environment without modifications and without requiring the user to configure in potentially complex file-system security policies. However, if you are interested in tighter file-system security and are willing to configure that, there are facilities to allow you to do that. For network access, you can assign multiple pseudo-LAN interfaces (eg. lan0, lan1, etc.) to a

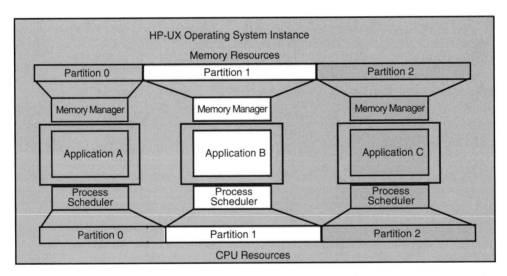

Figure 2-22 A Graphical Representation of Resource Partitions with the Addition of Security Controls

single physical network interface card. This gives you the ability to have more pseudo-interfaces and IP addresses than real interfaces. This is nice for security compartments and SRPs because you can create at least one pseudo-interface for each compartment, allowing each compartment to have its own set of IP addresses. The network interface code in the kernel has been modified to ensure that no two pseudo-interfaces can see each others' packets even if they are using the same physical interface card.

The security integration into PRM for Secure Resource Partitions uses the default compartment definitions, with the exception of network interface rules. Most modern applications require network access, so this was deemed a requirement. When using PRM to define an SRP, you have the ability to assign at least one pseudo-interface to each partition, along with the resource controls discussed earlier in this section.

User and Process Assignment

Because all the processes running in all the SRPs are running in the same copy of HP-UX, it is critical to ensure that users and processes get assigned to the correct partition as they come and go. In order to simplify this process across all the SRP technologies, PRM provides an application manager. This is a daemon that is configured to know what users and applications should be running in each of the defined SRPs.

Resource Partition integration with HP-UX

Because resource partitioning and PRM were introduced in HP-UX in 1995, this technology is thoroughly integrated with the operating system. HP-UX functions and tools such as fork(), exec(), cron, at, login, ps, and GlancePlus are all integrated and will react appropriately if Secure Resource Partitions are configured. For example:

- Login will query the PRM configuration for user records and will start the users' shell in the correct partition based on that configuration
- The ps command has two command-line options, –P and –R, which will either show the PRM partition each process displayed is in or only show the processes in a particular partition.
- GlancePlus will group the many statistics it collects for all the processes running in each partition. You can also use the GlancePlus user interface to move a process from one partition to another.

The result is that you get a product that has been enhanced many times over the years to provide a robust and complete solution.

More details on Secure Resource Partitions, including examples of how to configure them, will be provided in Chapter 11, "Secure Resource Partitions."

Summary

This chapter provided an architectural overview of each of the partitioning products available with HP's 9000 and Integrity servers. It also covered key benefits of each of these solutions. The next chapter will provide some insights into how to choose between the different solutions, and the rest of the chapters will provide examples of how to set up each type of partition.

3

Making the Most of the Partitioning Continuum

Chapter Overview

Now that you have a general understanding of the partitioning solutions available on HP's high-end servers, we try to provide some guidance on how to best take advantage of these technologies. As with any technology, some features of each of these solutions are useful to only a small number of potential customers. This chapter focuses on the key features that virtually every customer will want to take advantage of—the sweet spots, if you will.

This chapter is broken down into separate sections for each of the technologies. Additional sections cover interesting combinations of partitions and how independent software vendors support the different types of partitioning.

Choosing a Partitioning Solution

Given all the partitioning solutions that are available, it can be a daunting task to decide which of these would best meet the needs for your particular situation. The real answer is likely to be that you will want to take advantage of some combination. However, we first want to focus on each technology individually; we will discuss some interesting combinations later in this chapter.

There are a number of key benefits that you get from partitioning in general. These include:

- Application isolation: The ability to run multiple workloads on a system at the same time while ensuring that no single workload can impact the normal running of any other workload.

- Increased system utilization: This is an outgrowth of the first benefit above. If you can run multiple workloads on a system, you can increase the utilization of the server because resources that normally would have gone to waste can be used by the other workloads.

The focus of this chapter is to identify the key benefits each partitioning technology has over the other options you have with HP's servers.

Why Choose nPars?

As was mentioned in the last chapter, HP nPartitions provide for fully electrically isolated partitions on a cell-based server.

Key Benefits

A number of benefits can be gained from using nPartitions to break up a large system into several smaller ones. The few that we are going to focus on here are the ones that make this a technology that you won't want to do without. These include hardware-fault isolation, OS flexibility, and the fact that using nPars does not impact performance.

The fact that nPartitions are fully electrically isolated means that a hardware failure in one partition can't impact any other partition. In fact, it is possible to do hardware maintenance in one partition while the other partitions are running. This also makes it possible to run different partitions with different CPU speeds and even different CPU families (Precision Architecture (PA-RISC) and Itanium). The key benefit is that you can perform some upgrades on the system one partition at a time.

Another advantage of the electrical isolation is the fact that the operating system can't tell the difference between a partition and a whole system. Therefore, you can run different operating systems in each partition. The only supported OS on a PA-RISC-based HP 9000 system is HP-UX, so this is only possible on an Integrity server running Itanium processors. If you have an Integrity server, you can run HP-UX in one partition, Microsoft Windows Datacenter in another, Linux in a third, and OpenVMS in a fourth. All on one system—all at the same time.

The electrical isolation between nPars will also allow you to run PA-RISC processors in on partition and Itanium processors in another on the same system. This can simplify the upgrade process by allowing a rolling upgrade from PA to Itanium.

Another key benefit is that you can partition a server using nPars with no performance penalty. In fact, the opposite is true. Partitioning a server with nPars *increases* the performance significantly. Some performance benchmarks for a Superdome which has been partitioned into 16 four-CPU nPartitions are roughly 60% faster than the same benchmark for a fully loaded 64-CPU Superdome. There are several key reasons why this is so. The first is that there is lower multi-processing overhead with smaller partitions and the other is that there are fewer connections between the crossbars that are traversed with smaller partitions.

Key Tradeoffs

Our goal here is to ensure that you understand how to best take advantage of the Virtual Server Environment (VSE) technologies. We want to explain some of the tradeoffs of using each of them to ensure that you put together a configuration that has all the benefits you want and that you can minimize the impact of any tradeoffs. Many of the tradeoffs can be mitigated by combining VSE technologies.

The first real tradeoff of nPartitions is granularity. The smallest partition you can create is a single cell. If you are using dual-core processors, this is a two-to-eight CPU component. The granularity can also be improved by including instant capacity processors. This way you can configure a partition with up to eight physical CPUs but have as few as two of them be active. We will discuss instant capacity in Part 2 of this book.

Another tradeoff is that although you can use instant capacity processors to adjust the capacity of an nPar, its cell configuration can't be changed online. This really isn't a limitation of nPartitions but rather of the operating systems themselves. Currently HP-UX is the only supported OS that will allow activation and deactivation of CPUs while online. None of the supported operating systems allow reallocation of memory while they are running. You will need to shut down any partition to remove a cell, for example. You can, however, reconfigure both partitions while they are running and then issue a "reboot for reconfiguration" for each of them when it is convenient. A future release of HP-UX will support online addition and deletion of memory.

One other tradeoff is that because each partition is electrically isolated from the others, there is no sharing of physical resources. If you need redundant components for each workload, they will be needed in every partition. This is simply a cost of hardware-fault isolation.

You can migrate active CPU capacity between nPars, but only if you have instant capacity processors. This means that you must have sufficient physical capacity in each partition to meet the maximum CPU requirements for the partition. You would then purchase some of that capacity as instant capacity. These processors can be activated when needed by deactivating a processor in another partition or by activating temporary capacity.

A clarification about nPars: Running nPartitions is *not* the same as running separate systems. There are events that can bring all the partitions down. The most common is operator error. If an operator with administrator privileges on the Management Processor should make a serious mistake, they could bring the whole system down. Another would be a natural disaster, like a major power outage or fire. The bottom line here is that using nPartitions does not eliminate your need to implement high-availability software and hardware if you are running mission-critical workloads on the system. The complex should be configured with at least one other complex in a cluster to ensure that any failure, whether it is a single partition or multiple, would result in a minimum of downtime. This is discussed in Part 3 of this book.

nPar Sweet Spots

Now that we have provided a brief overview of the benefits and tradeoffs of nPartitions, we will provide some guidance on a few "sweet spot" solutions that allow you to get the benefits while minimizing the impact of the tradeoffs.

First of all, if you are doing consolidation of multiple workloads onto a cell-based server, you will want to set up at least two nPars. It would just not make sense to have the option of hardware-fault isolation and not take advantage of it. You might want to set up more nPars so you can provide hardware isolation between mission-critical applications. This ensures that the need to do hardware maintenance doesn't require that you take down multiple mission-critical applications at once.

Sweet Spot #1: At least two nPars

If you have a cell-based system that supports nPars and you are doing consolidation of multiple workloads, you should seriously consider setting it up with at least two. The resulting hardware-fault isolation and the flexibility with instant capacity makes this compelling.

You will want to make your nPars as big as possible. Steer clear of single-cell partitions unless you have a really good reason. Bigger partitions provide you with more flexibility in the future. If your capacity-planning estimates end up being off and one partition isn't big enough for the workload there, you can easily react to that by reconfiguring the system. But if you have many single-cell partitions you will need to rehost one of the workloads to reallocate a cell. This makes it very difficult to take advantage of the flexibility benefits of partitioning a larger server.

Sweet Spot #2: Separate nPars for each Mission-Critical Application

If you set up a separate nPar for each mission-critical application, you will ensure that a hardware failure or routine hardware maintenance will impact only one of them at a time.

Clearly, there is a tradeoff between larger partitions and more isolation. You really want to find the happy medium. Setting up a system with a few nPars and then using one of the other partition types inside the nPars to allow you to run multiple workloads provides a nice combination of isolation and flexibility. One interesting happy medium is to set up an nPar for each mission-critical production application and then use vPars or Integrity VM to set up development, production test, or batch partitions in the nPar along with the mission-critical production application. That way the lower-priority applications are isolated from the mission-critical application by a separate OS instance, yet some of the resources normally used for the lower-priority applications can be used to satisfy the production application if it ever experiences an unexpected increase in load.

Sweet Spot #3: vPars or VMs inside nPars

Subdividing nPars using vPars or VMs provides a very nice combination of hardware-fault isolation and granularity in a single solution.

Consider this scenario: You have a large Integrity server running several HP-UX partitions and because you are taking advantage of the VSE technologies you find that you have spare capacity you thought you would need. At the same time, you have a Windows server that has run out of capacity and you need a larger system to run it on. Rather than purchasing a separate Integrity server for the Windows application, you can set up another nPar on the existing system and put the application there. You might even be able to use this as a stopgap solution while waiting for the "real" server this application will be running on. You could then set up the Windows partition with the new server in a cluster and migrate it over. Because of the flexibility of the system with instant capacity processors, you can use this partition as a failover or disaster-recovery location for the primary Windows server.

Sweet Spot #4: Use Spare Capacity for Other OS Types

> If you have an Integrity server with spare capacity, you have the flexibility of creating an nPar and running any of four different operating systems on that spare capacity.

A newer feature of nPars is the ability to run PA-RISC processors in one partition and Itanium processors in another. This provides a nice solution for a rolling upgrade from PA to Itanium inside a single system. You could also add some Itanium cells to an existing system for either testing or migration.

Sweet Spot #5: Use nPars to Migrate from PA to Itanium

> Use nPars on existing HP 9000 systems to set up Itanium partitions for migration of existing partitions or other systems.

Last, when using nPartitions, you should always have some number of instant capacity processors configured into each partition. We will describe these technologies in more detail in Part 2 of this book, but suffice it to say that the flexibility it brings and the dramatic simplification of capacity planning makes this compelling. An example configuration would be a single-cabinet Superdome with dual-core processors split into four nPars. Each nPar has two cells and 16 physical processors. Since most systems are only 25% to 30% utilized, you can get half the CPUs as instant capacity processors and increase the utilization to over 50%. That way you still have the extra capacity if you need it, but you can defer the cost until later. In addition, you will get the flexibility of scaling each partition up to 16 CPUs by deallocating CPUs from the other partitions in real time. You can also get temporary capacity in case you have multiple partitions that get busy at the same time. We will talk about instant capacity and temporary capacity in the next part of the book. Figure 3-1 provides a view of this configuration which shows the dual-core processors and the configuration of inactive instant capacity processors.

This picture shows that each partition contains two cells each with eight physical CPUs. Each partition has the ability to scale up to 16 CPUs because there are eight inactive CPUs that can be activated by deactivating a CPU in another partition or by using temporary capacity.

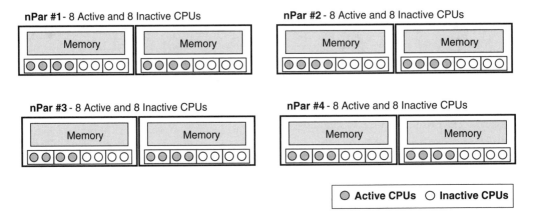

Figure 3-1 A Single-Cabinet Superdome with four nPars and Instant Capacity Processors

Sweet Spot #6: Always Configure in Instant Capacity

Instant capacity processors are very inexpensive headroom and provide the ability to flex the size of nPars dynamically.

Why Choose vPars?

When HP Virtual Partitions (vPars) was introduced in late 2001, it was the only virtual partitioning product available that supported a mission-critical Unix OS. Even today there continue to be a number of features that make vPars an excellent solution for many workloads.

Key Benefits

This section compares vPars with each of the other partitioning technologies to help you determine when you might want to use vPars in one of your solutions.

When comparing vPars to nPars, the primary benefits you get with vPars is granularity and flexibility. vPars can go down to single-CPU granularity and single card-slot granularity for I/O. With nPars, each partition must be made up of whole cells and I/O card cages. This means that you can have a vPar with a single CPU and a single card slot (if you use a LAN/SCSI combo I/O card). In addition, you can scale the partition in single CPU increments. vPars also provides the flexibility of dynamically reallocating CPUs between partitions without the instant capacity requirement. In other words, you can deallocate a CPU from one vPar and allocate the same CPU to another vPar. The tradeoff, of course, is that you won't have the hardware-fault isolation you get with nPars.

When comparing vPars with Integrity VM, the key benefits of vPars are its scalability and performance. vPars has no limit on its scalability—in other words, you could create a 64 CPU vPar and get only a slight degradation of the performance you would get with an nPar. The first release of Integrity VMs is tuned for four virtual CPUs in each VM (although you can create VMs with more). This will be increased with time, but will take some time to reach the scalability of vPars. In addition, because vPars are built by assigning physical I/O cards to each partition, the OS talks directly to the card once it is booted. There is almost no performance degradation at all.

When comparing vPars with Secure Resource Partitions, the primary benefit you get is isolation. This includes OS, namespace, and software-fault isolation. Because each vPar has its own OS image, you can tune each partition for the application that runs there. This includes kernel tunables, OS patch levels, and application versions. Also, an application or OS-level problem that each vPar isolated from software faults in other vPars and can be independently rebooted.

Key Tradeoffs

The first tradeoff is that vPars only supports HP-UX. Both nPars and Integrity VM will eventually support all four operating systems that are targeted for Integrity Servers (HP-UX, Windows, Linux, and OpenVMS) on an Integrity server.

Several other tradeoffs come as a result of the same reason vPars has better performance—the vPar monitor is emulating the firmware of the system. The two most significant tradeoffs from this are the fact that it is not possible to share I/O card slots between vPars and that vPars doesn't support sub CPU granularity. In addition, vPars is not supported on all platforms and doesn't support all I/O cards. Realistically, it does support most of the high-end systems and most of the more common I/O cards. The bottom line here is that when considering a system for vPars, you should work with your HP sales consultants, or authorized partner, and ensure you get the right configuration.

vPar Sweet Spots

You should always set up some number of nPars if you doing consolidation on a cell-based server. The key question is whether you want to further partition the nPars or system with another partitioning solution, such as vPars, VMs, or Secure Resource Partitions. If you are planning to run more than one workload in each nPar, you may want to run each workload in its own isolated environment. The key question is whether you need OS level isolation. If so, your choices are vPars or VMs. You can't run both of these at the same time on the same nPar or system. However, you can run vPars in one nPar and VMs in another on the same system. This is another nice advantage of the electrical isolation you get with nPars.

Sweet Spot #1: vPars Larger than eight CPUs

If you require finer granularity than nPars and partitions larger than eight CPUs, vPars is an excellent option.

If you need the OS-level isolation, vPars are a good choice if you need large partitions or if the workload is I/O intensive and performance is critical.

Sweet Spot #2: I/O Intensive Applications

If you require finer granularity than nPars and have I/O-intensive applications that require peak performance, vPars has very low I/O performance overhead.

Why Choose Integrity VM?

The newest addition to the partitioning continuum provides OS isolation while allowing sharing of CPU and I/O resources with multiple partitions.

Key Benefits

We will again compare VMs with each of the other partitioning alternatives to provide some context for discussing the key benefits of implementing Integrity VM.

VMs provide the same level of OS and software-fault isolation as nPars but provides it at a much higher level of granularity. You can share CPUs and I/O cards and you can even provide differentiated access to those shared resources. You have control over how much of each resource should be allocated to each partition (e.g. 50% for one VM and 30% for another). As with vPars, sharing and flexibility comes at the cost of hardware-fault isolation. This is why we recommend first partitioning the system with nPars and then using other partitioning solutions to further partition the nPars to provide finer granularity and increased flexibility. There is one other benefit when comparing VMs to nPars—you can run Integrity VM on non-cell-based platforms. Any Integrity system that supports a standard HP-UX installation can be set up to run Integrity VM.

VMs and vPars provide many of the same benefits. You have OS-level isolation, so you can create these partitions and tune the operating systems to meet the specific needs of the applications that run there. This includes kernel tunables as well as patches and shared library versions. The key differentiation for the Integrity VM product is its ability to share CPUs and I/O cards. This makes it much more suitable for very small workloads that still need the OS-level isolation.

One other interesting thing you can do with VMs that you can't do with vPars is that you can create an ISO image of a CD and mount that image as a virtual CD onto any or all of your VMs. This is very convenient for the installation of updates or patch bundles that need to be applied to multiple VMs. One other significant benefit of Integrity VM is its future support for Windows, Linux and OpenVMS. VMs also support I/O virtualization solutions like Auto-Port Aggregation on the VM host so that you can create a large I/O interface and then share it with multiple VMs. This allows the VMs to get access to losts of bandwidth as well as the redundancy you get with API without requiring any special configuration on the VMs themselves.

The last comparison for this section is with Secure Resource Partitions (SRPs). There are many similarities in how Secure Resource Partitions and Integrity VM manage the resources of the system. The implementations of these controls are different, but they have many of the same user interface paradigms. One key thing you get with VMs is OS-level isolation, including file systems, namespaces, patch levels, shared library versions, and software faults. You get none of these with Secure Resource Partitions.

Key Tradeoffs

There are a few key tradeoffs of the Integrity VM product that you should be aware of before deciding whether it is the right solution for you. These include no support for HP 9000 systems and performance of some I/O intensive workloads.

The first of these is the fact that Integrity VM requires features of the Itanium processor that are not available or very different on Precision Architecture.

Because Integrity VM is a fully virtualized system technology, all I/O traffic is handled by virtual switches in the VM monitor. This makes it possible to have multiple VMs sharing a single physical I/O card. However, this switching imposes some overhead on I/O operations. This overhead is relatively small, but it is impacted by the fact that the virtual CPU that is holding the I/O interrupt that is servicing the I/O request doesn't have all the CPU cycles on the real CPU. This makes it possible for the interrupt to come in when another VM has control of the CPU, which further delays the receipt of the I/O that was requested. When the system is lightly loaded, this impact can be fairly minor, but when the CPUs are very busy and there are I/O intensive workloads issuing many I/O requests, you can expect a higher level of overhead. Future releases of the VM product will improve this and provide alternative solutions specifically for I/O intensive workloads.

Integrity VM Sweet Spots

Most companies have a number of large applications and databases that require significant resources to satisfy their service-level requirements. Most also have a large number of applications that are used daily but have a small number of users and therefore don't require significant resources. Some of these are still mission critical and require an isolated OS instance and a mission-critical infrastructure like that available on HP's Integrity servers. These are the applications that are best suited to VMs. They have short-term spikes that may require more than one CPU, but their normal load for the majority of the day is a fraction of a CPU. These would normally be installed on a small system, possibly two to four CPUs, to meet the short-term peaks. However, the average utilization in this environment is often less than 20%. Putting these types of workloads in a VM provides the flexibility to scale the VM to meet the resource requirements when the load peaks but scale back the resources when the workload is idle. Putting a number of these workloads on an nPar or small server allows you to increase the overall utilization while still providing isolation and having sufficient resources available to react to the short term spikes.

Sweet Spot #1: Small Mission-critical Applications

If you have applications that don't need a whole CPU most of the time but do need OS isolation, Integrity VM provides both granularity and isolation.

Another sweet spot is the ability of Integrity VM to support small CPU-intensive workloads. It turns out that CPU-intensive workloads incur very little overhead inside a VM. We have seen cases where the difference in performance for some CPU-intensive benchmarks in a VM compared to a stand-alone system was less than 1%. This was using a single virtual CPU VM, so if you have small CPU-intensive workloads, a VM is a great option.

Sweet Spot #2: Small CPU Intensive Applications

Single CPU Integrity VM carry very little performance overhead for CPU-intensive applications.

The first release of Integrity VM will be tuned for 4 virtual CPUs. A real sweet spot for VMs is running a bunch of four virtual-CPU VMs on a system or nPar with four or eight physical CPUs. This way there is a very even load of virtual CPUs to physical CPUs and each VM can scale up to nearly four physical CPU speeds. If you have a handful of workloads that normally average less than one CPU of consumption but occasionally spike up from two to four CPUs at peak, running a number of these on a four- or eight-CPU system will allow the average utilization of the physical resources to exceed 50% while still allowing each VM to scale up to four CPUs to meet the peak demands when those usage spikes occur.

Sweet Spot #3: VMs with the same CPU count as the system or nPar

Running a number of four-virtual-CPU VMs on a four-physical-CPU system or partition allows sharing of CPUs and ensures an even load across the physical CPUs. This will also work if there are a number of four-virtual-CPU VMs running on an eight-CPU system or nPar — but the key is you want to have an even load on the physical CPUs.

A derivative of this sweet spot is one where you run a handful of application clusters in VMs that share the physical servers they are running on. Figure 3-2 shows an example of three application clusters with three two-CPU nodes each.

These applications will occasionally peak to the point where they need more than one CPU on each node, but the average utilization is in the 10–15% range. Now let's consider running these same clusters using VMs. This is shown in Figure 3-3.

We have configured these as four-virtual-CPU VMs and they are running on four-physical-CPU systems or nPars. Now let's consider what we have done. We have:

- Nearly doubled the maximum CPU capacity for each cluster—because each virtual CPU can be scaled to get close to a physical CPU if the other clusters are idle or near their normal average load. Each cluster can now get nearly 12 CPUs of capacity if needed.

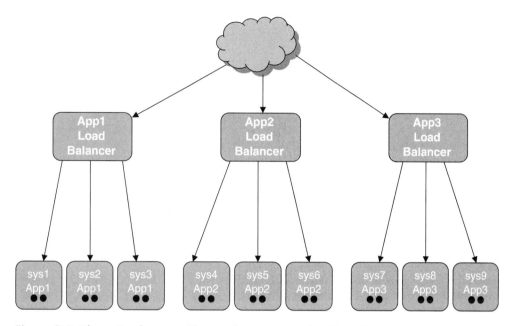

Figure 3-2 Three Application Clusters Running on Nine Two-CPU Systems

- Reduced the number of systems to manage. Although we still have nine OS images, we now have only three physical systems.
- Lowered the CPU count for software licenses from 18 to 12.
- Increased the average utilization of these systems.

To summarize, we have increased capacity, lowered the software costs, lowered the hardware costs, and lowered system maintenance costs.

Sweet Spot #4: Multiple Application Clusters in VMs

Running a number of overlapping application clusters on a set of VMs increases average utilization, increases the peak capacity of each cluster, and lowers hardware, software, and maintenance costs.

Why Choose Secure Resource Partitions?

When security compartments were added to HP-UX and integrated with Resource Partitions, the name was changed to Secure Resource Partitions (SRPs). This didn't fundamentally change the effectiveness of Resource Partitions, but it did increase the number of cases where Secure Resource Partitions would be a good fit. This is because you can now ensure that the processes running

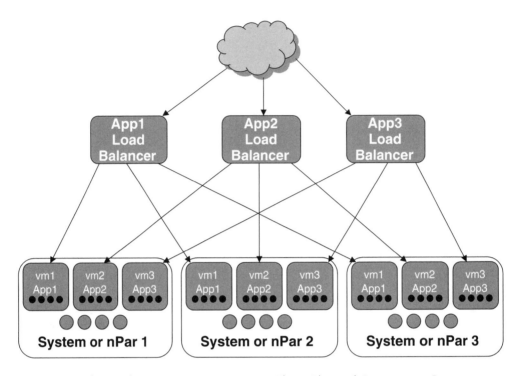

Figure 3-3 Three Clusters Running in VMs on Three Physical Systems or nPars

in each SRP cannot communicate with processes in the other partitions. In addition, each compartment gets its own IP address, and network traffic to each compartment is isolated from the other compartments by the network stack in the kernel. This, on top of the resource controls for CPU, real memory, and disk I/O bandwidth, provides a very nice level of isolation for multiple applications running in a single copy of the operating system.

Key Benefits

When comparing SRPs to nPars we could probably repeat the discussion from the section on VMs with one additional benefit, which is a reduction in the number of OS images you need to manage. Secure Resource Partitions provides much higher granularity of resource allocation. In fact, it allows you to go down below 1% CPU if you want. This might be useful if you have applications that are not always running in the compartment—either a failover package or maybe a batch job. You can also share memory and I/O. In fact, SRPs are currently the only partitioning solution in the VSE that allows online reallocation of memory entitlements. This will change with a future version of HP-UX that will begin to support online memory reallocation between partitions. The most significant advantage here is the fact that you have fewer OS images to manage. Industry analysts estimate that 40% of the total cost of ownership of a system is the ongoing maintenance and management of the system. This includes the mundane daily tasks such as backups, patches, OS upgrades, user password resets, and the like. Because you would have fewer copies of the OS and applications installed, less of your time and money would be spent managing them.

When comparing SRPs to vPars, the key things to consider are finer granularity of resource allocation, resource sharing, more-complete system support, and fewer OS images to manage. In other words, they are much the same benefits when compared to nPars. Even though vPars provide finer granularity than nPars, SRPs are still finer, and you can share CPUs and I/O cards, which lowers the costs of running small partitions. Also, the tradeoffs on the types of systems supported by vPars don't exist for SRPs. Any system that supports HP-UX will support Secure Resource Partitions.

When comparing SRPs to Integrity VM, there are only a few key benefits because the resource controls are very similar. The first is the fact that SRPs are supported on all HP-UX systems, including PA-RISC–based HP 9000 systems, whereas VMs are supported only on Integrity systems. The other was mentioned above for vPars and nPars—SRPs do not require separate OS images to be built and managed for each partition. One other benefit is that SRPs allow the sharing of memory, which none of the OS-based partitions will support until after a future release of HP-UX. You can also get slightly finer CPU-sharing granularity with SRPs. VMs allow you to have a minimum of 5% of a CPU for each VM—you can go down below 1% with SRPs, although you should be very careful when taking advantage of that. It would be pretty easy to starve a workload this way. This might be useful if you have workloads that normally are not running except under special circumstances—things such as failover or a job that only runs a small portion of the day, week, or month. In these cases it would be important to implement some type of automation (eg. Workload Manager) that would recognize that the workload has started and increase the entitlement to something more appropriate.

One other feature of Secure Resource Partitions that isn't available in the other solutions is the full flexibility to decide which resources you want to control, whether you want the security controls, and even what types of security controls you want. This, of course, can be a double-edged sword because you will want to understand what the impact of each choice will be. We provide some guidance on this later in this section.

Key Tradeoffs

The reduction of the number of OS images that need to be managed has both benefits and tradeoffs. Even though the applications are running in isolated environments, they are still sharing the same copy of the operating system. They share the same file system, the same process namespace, and the same kernel. A few examples of this are:

- There is one set of users: A user logging into one compartment has the same user ID as they would have if they logged into another compartment.
- All applications are sharing the same file system: You can isolate portions of the file system to one or more compartments, but this is not the default. A

design goal was to ensure that all applications would run normally in default compartments.

* There is one set of kernel tunables: You need to configure the kernel to support the maximum value for each tunable as required for all the compartments at the same time. Many of the more commonly updated kernel tunables are now dynamic in HP-UX 11iV2, but this is still something to be aware of.

Secure Resource Partitions Sweet Spots

The most compelling benefit of Secure Resource Partitions over the other partitioning solutions is the fact that you can reduce the number of OS images you need to manage. The tradeoff, of course, is that you have less isolation. The primary places where this isolation is an issue are:

* When the different applications need different library versions or their patch-level requirements are incompatible: If different applications need different patch levels, different kernel tunables or have some other incompatibility.
* The fact that the applications are owned by different business units: It can be difficult to get approval to reboot a partition if it will impact applications that are owned by different lines of business.

The first of these issues can be resolved by focusing on the sweet spot where you run multiple copies of the same application in a single OS image. This way they will all have the same requirements for patches and kernel tunables. It is often a well-understood process for consolidating multiple instances of the same application in a single OS instance. This is especially true if the applications are the same version of the same application. The second issue can also be resolved if you have multiple copies of the same application that are owned by the same line of business or if the different lines of business have a very good working relationship and are willing to "do the right thing" for each other.

These issues can also be mitigated by limiting the number of applications you attempt to consolidate. If you are used to doing consolidation, you have probably already worked through these issues. But if you haven't, you might want to start by limiting the number of applications you attempt to run in a single OS image. One thing to consider is that if you consolidate only two applications in each OS image, you have cut your OS count in *half*. That is a huge savings. So if each of your business units has a number of databases, or a number of application servers, you can put two to three of them on each OS image and get a tremendous savings because you cut the number of patches, backups, etc. every time you put two or more of them in the same OS image.

Sweet Spot #1: Multiple Instances of the Same Application

If you have multiple instances of the same version of the same application, put two or more of them in a single OS instance and use Secure Resource Partitions to isolate them from each other.

Another opportunity is the possibility of implementing the same overlapping cluster solution described in Figures 3-2 and 3-3 using Secure Resource Partitions. This carries the additional benefit of a reduction of the system management overhead because you would also be reducing the number of OS and application installations that need management and maintenance from nine to three.

Sweet Spot #2: Multiple Overlapping Clusters

Running multiple overlapping clusters of the same application on a set of systems or nPars provides all the benefits of this solution in VMs but also reduces the number of OS and application instances that need to be managed and maintained.

What Features of SRPs Should I Use?

You have a tremendous amount of flexibility in deciding which features of Secure Resource Partitions to activate. How do you decide which controls to use and what impact might they have on your workloads?

Choosing a CPU Allocation Mechanism

The first control to consider is for CPU. You have two choices here. You can use the fair share scheduler or processor sets. We described each of these in the last chapter, so here we will focus on the practical implications of these choices.

The key difference between FSS and PSETs is how they allocate CPUs to each of the partitions. The FSS groups allocate a portion of the CPUs cycles on all the CPUs, whereas PSETs allocates all the cycles on a subset of the CPUs. An example would help here. Let's consider running two applications on an eight-CPU system where we want one of them to get 75% and the other to get 25% of the CPU. With FSS, you would configure in 75 shares for the first and 25 shares for the second application. The first application would use all eight CPUs but would get only three out of every four CPU ticks and the second application would get the other CPU tick. With PSETs, you would configure the first application to have a PSET with six CPUs and the other with two CPUs. Each application would only see the number of CPUs in its PSET and would get every CPU cycle on those CPUs.

Given the sweet spot configuration of a small number of the same application running in an OS image, all you need to consider is whether you want to use FSS or PSETs. The only reason you would want to use PSETs is if there was some reason that the application required exclusive access to the CPUs. Because this is Unix, there are no applications that require exclusive access to CPUs. However, if you are using any third-party management tools that allocate CPU resources themselves, you might want to find out if they will work correctly when they get partial CPUs.

Another benefit of FSS is that it allows sharing of unused CPU ticks. When CPU capping is turned off, any time a partition has no processes in the CPU run queue, the next partition is allowed to use the remainder of the CPU tick. Effectively, FSS allows you to define a minimum guaranteed entitlement for each application, but if one application is idle, it allows other busy applications to use those unused shares. When everyone is busy, everyone will get their specified entitlement.

Should I Use Memory Controls?

Memory controls are implemented as separate memory-management subsystems inside a single copy of the operating system. The control mechanism is paging, so the impact on applications is transparent, with the exception of performance, of course. The key benefit you would get from turning on memory controls is when you have a low-priority workload that is consuming more than its fair share of memory and causing performance problems on a higher-priority application.

If you decide to turn on memory controls, you then need to decide if you want to isolate the memory or allow sharing. The tradeoff here is that isolating memory might result in some idle memory not being available to a different application that could use it. The other side is that without capping it is likely that more paging will occur to reallocate memory to the partition that "owns" it.

Should I Use Disk I/O Controls?

The disk I/O controls are implemented through a callout from the queuing mechanisms in the volume managers LVM and VxVM. Several things to note about this are:

- This only takes effect when there is competition for disk I/O. The queue only starts to build when there are more requests than can be met by the available bandwidth. This isn't a problem, but you should know that an application can exceed its entitlement if there is bandwidth available. There is no capping mode for I/O.
- This is only at the volume group level. Multiple compartments need to be sharing some volume groups to get the benefits of these controls.

The short answer is that turning on the disk I/O controls is useful if you occasionally have bandwidth problems with one or more volume groups and you have multiple applications that are sharing that volume group.

Should I Use Security Compartments?

The default security containment is intended to be transparent to applications. This means that processes will not be allowed to communicate to processes in other compartments, but they can communicate freely with other processes in the compartment. The default is that the file system is protected only by the standard HP-UX file system security. If you want more file system security, you will need to configure that after creating the default compartments. Other features include the fact that each SRP will have its own network interfaces.

You should consider turning security on if:

- You have multiple different applications and you need to be sure they won't be able to interfere with or communicate with each other.
- You have multiple network facing applications and you want to make sure that if the security of any of them are compromised, the damage they can cause will be contained to the compartment they are running in.
- You want each application to have its own IP address on the system and the packets on those interfaces will only be visible to the application they were destined for. Multiple interfaces can share the physical cards, but each interface and its IP addresses can be assigned only to a single SRP.

Combining Partitioning Solutions

The various partitioning solutions in the VSE are almost arbitrarily stackable. The only exception is the fact that you cannot run Integrity VM and vPars in the same nPar. Inside each partition type you can run:

- nPartitions: Virtual Partitions, Integrity VMs, or Secure Resource Partitions. In other words, you can run any one of these to subdivide each nPar. In addition, you can mix and match these in any combination in separate nPars.
- Virtual Partitions: Secure Resource Partitions. You can run SRPs inside vPars if you want to save on the management and maintenance costs of separate OS images for each application.
- Integrity VM: Secure Resource Partitions. You can run SRPs inside VMs as well.

If we take a look at all the sweet spots described in this chapter and think about how they might be combined to take advantage of all the technologies where they are most useful, we would get something along the lines of Figure 3-4.

This figure shows what is possible with the partitioning continuum. It is likely that you will choose one or two partitioning alternatives and roll those out. That said, the real benefit we are trying to show here is the flexibility; you can implement whatever combinations make sense for your solution. Let's analyze this configuration:

- We have the ability to run 32 workloads of various sizes on the two nodes.
- Each system has a total of 64 physical CPUs, but only 32 of them are active. This is sufficient to handle the normal peak load of the 32 workloads. This provides us room for growth and the ability to react to short-term peaks in load. This also makes these systems significantly less expensive than they would be if we needed

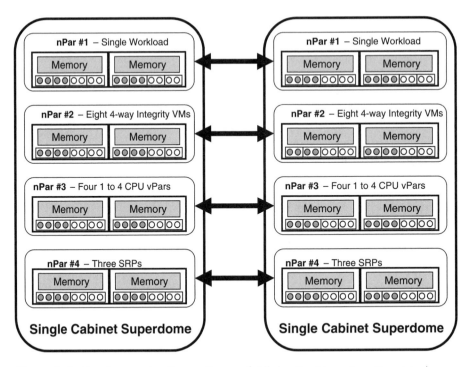

Figure 3-4 Combining the Sweet Spots of All the Partitions in a Two-Node High-Availability Cluster

to purchase all the spare capacity up front. Effectively, HP is paying for much of the cost of your headroom.

- Each system is configured with four nPars. This ensures that a hardware failure will not take down more than 25% of the system. This load can easily be absorbed by the other system on a failover because of the Instant Capacity available there.

- Each of these systems has Temporary Instant Capacity as well. This will be described in more detail in Part 2 of this book. For the purposes of this discussion, this will give us the ability to instantly activate additional capacity when needed.

- Spreading this load over two nodes allows us to provide high availability.

- Two of the workloads have their own nPars. These are relatively large workloads that normally peak out at about eight CPUs but will occasionally go over that. These nPars have 16 physical CPUs each and we will use temporary capacity for the infrequent times that they go over eight CPUs.

- We have 16 Integrity VMs that each have four virtual CPUs. These workloads can consume a small fraction of a CPU if they are idle and can go up to four full CPUs when they get busy. These nPars also have instant capacity processors, so in the infrequent case where we have more than a few of these VMs getting busy at the same time, we can instantly activate additional capacity.

- We have eight vPars, each of which can scale from one to four CPUs. These are for our smaller I/O-intensive workloads where peak performance is critical. Again, there are eight instant capacity processors available in each nPar just in case more than a few of these workloads get busy at the same time. If only a few of them are peaking at any time, the peaking vPars can be scaled up by borrowing CPUs from the other idle vPars.

- Finally we have two nPars running Secure Resource Partitions. These are all running the same version of the same application, so we get the benefits of lower maintenance costs in addition to the lower software and hardware costs because we can run six copies on the 16 active CPUs. If we put these on individual systems or partitions they would each need six CPUs. We just dropped our active CPU count for hardware and software licensing from 36 to 16. And, as before, we have instant capacity processors that can take these nPars up to a total of 32 processors if more than a few of these peaked all at once.

There you have it. These systems are using all of the partition types, have an incredible amount of flexibility and scalability, and are paired for high availability. Some of you might be concerned about how you would manage an environment like this. Have we got a deal for you! In Part 3 of this book we describe a new set of management tools designed to make the management and maintenance of a dynamic Virtual Server Environment much easier.

Independent Software Vendor Support

HP has been shipping Resource Partitioning for over 10 years and Workload Management for over five, and we frequently get the question — "How do the ISVs support this technology?" The problem can really be broken down into three key issues — whether the application can run in a partitioned environment, how it responds to automatic changes to resource entitlements, and whether there are any price breaks or penalties for using these technologies.

ISV Support of Partitions

We are primarily focused here on whether there will be any issues with an application being able to run correctly inside a partition. We will cover licensing later.

For nPars there is no issue. Each nPar is a fully electrically isolated set of hardware components. The software can't tell the difference between running in an nPar and running in a similarly sized separate system.

For vPars the same is true. Even though you don't have electrical isolation, you do assign separate hardware components to each partition. Again, the software can't tell the difference between running in a vPar and running on a separate system.

Any applications or management utilities that interact with the operating system using standard interfaces will not be affected by running in an Integrity VM. Some management applications might work differently; generally speaking, that is because they should. The design goal of the Integrity VM product is to emulate the hardware such that all management utilities should "do the right thing" when running in a VM. In other words, applications will not notice any difference and all management utilities should run without errors, or the errors you get should be expected. For example, instant capacity commands run in a VM will exit gracefully with an error that the system does not support instant capacity. This is correct because the CPUs in a VM are virtual CPUs and instant capacity operates on physical CPUs, so adding and deleting them doesn't make sense in this context. If you want to allocate additional capacity to a VM, you would activate the physical CPU in the VM host and the new CPU would then automatically be allocated to each of the VMs as appropriate.

The last partitioning solution to consider is Secure Resource Partitions. This is one where you are running multiple applications in a single copy of the operating system. The vast majority of ISV applications will run just fine with virtually any other ISV application on the same OS image. That really isn't the issue. The primary issue you need to be concerned about is whether the ISV will make life difficult for you when you call them for support. If they are going to force you to reproduce the problem on a system where their application is the only one running, it may not be worth the trouble. Of course, if you already have set up or plan to set up independent test environments, maybe this isn't such a big deal. In any event, this is one reason why we typically recommend consolidating multiple instances of the same application in an OS image. Virtually all ISVs will support running multiple copies of their own applications in a single OS instance.

ISV Support of Dynamic Resource Allocation

We are often asked whether an application will be able to take advantage of resources that are dynamically added to a partition while the application is running. How applications will handle the deallocation of resources is another common question.

The answer to the first question is yes in virtually all cases. The reason is that the OS process scheduler is responsible for allocating processes and threads on available CPUs. If additional CPUs are allocated to an OS image, the scheduler will simply spread the processes and threads out over more CPUs. This means there are fewer processes sharing each CPU and each will have access to more processing power. So the bottom line is that the application really doesn't have any choice in the matter.

The same thing can be said of the deallocation of a CPU. The process scheduler is notified that a CPU is going to be removed. It will then migrate any processes or threads that are on the run queue for that CPU to another CPU in the OS image. Once that is done, the CPU is deallocated. Once again, this is done completely transparently to the application.

The reason we said that the answer is yes in virtually all cases is that there is one case where a CPU could be added and not help. This is in the lightly loaded case—when there are not enough processes or threads in the run queue to consume all of the CPUs that are active. In this case, adding another CPU would not help because there are no threads that can be scheduled on it.

ISV Licensing When Using VSE Technologies

The last major issue with ISV support is licensing. Many ISVs price their software based on the number of CPUs running on the system the software is running on. An interesting question is this: When you have a 16-CPU system and you are running multiple different applications there, how much should the ISV license cost? The licensing issue impacts the revenue stream of ISVs, so they are being very cautious in adopting support for these technologies. That said, many ISVs are indeed starting to support more flexible licensing schemes.

Virtually all ISVs will support licensing by the number of CPUs in an nPar. In other words, if you have a 16-CPU system partitioned into two eight-CPU nPars, you will only need to pay for an eight-CPU license if you are only running the software in one of the nPars. This is also becoming true of vPars. At this point, most ISVs will recognize that if you are running their application on only one vPar on a system, you should not have to pay for CPUs that the application can't access. You should work with your ISVs to make sure they understand the maximum CPU count configured for each vPar and make sure they will only charge you for that amount.

VMs are a more complex issue. Consider the sweet spot of running, say, four VMs, each with four virtual CPUs on a system or nPar with four physical processors. If you have an application in one of the VMs, it can realistically get access to more than three physical CPUs. Therefore, you will probably always have to pay for a four CPU license if you are running a VM with four virtual CPUs. Now consider the case where you have the same application in each of the four VMs. Should you have to pay for a 16-CPU license, even though the physical system only has four? Clearly this wouldn't be fair, and most ISVs will recognize this. However, most of them don't yet have firm across-the-board policies for how VMs should be handled. Therefore, if you are considering using VMs, you should engage the ISV's sales organization and work out a fair arrangement.

Secure Resource Partitions is the last partition option. Generally speaking, ISVs don't yet provide licensing for a subset of an OS image, although some of them are starting to investigate this. A workaround to this is the sweet spot described earlier in this chapter. Running multiple copies of the same application in a single OS image allows the resources to be shared and you can still get multiple application instances with fewer overall licenses.

Summary

This chapter has provided a great deal of practical knowledge about all the different technologies in the Partitioning Continuum. As with most software products, there are some features that will be useful for a small number of customers. Here we tried to focus on the sweet spots. These are the few configurations that provide the most bang for the buck.

We also showed that combining these different partition types on a single system can provide many of the benefits of multiple partitioning technologies in a single configuration. This provides for maximum availability, flexibility, and utilization at a minimum cost.

4

nPartition Servers

Chapter Overview

On September 12, 2000, the CEO of HP, Carly Fiorina, stood in front of a live audience in New York and unveiled the first HP server to support nPartitions, the HP Superdome. Since the unveiling in New York, numerous world-record benchmarks have been set by the HP Superdome and related HP nPartition server family. After several years of development and multiple generations of hardware enhancements, HP nPartition servers continue to serve as the cornerstone of HP's Virtual Server Environment. A firm understanding of nPartitions and nPartition management enables a planner or administrator to take full advantage of HP's Virtual Server Environment.

This chapter starts with an overview of HP nPartition servers. The hardware components are discussed, along with an explanation of their role in an nPartition. Next, the fundamental data structures which allow the system to be divided into one or more nPartitions will be described. The chapter then moves into a description of the available nPartition management paradigms. This section provides a detailed view into how the nPartition management tools can be utilized to maximize the efficiency of system administration. The chapter ends with an example usage scenario that covers the viewing of an HP nPartition server's configuration, the modification of an existing nPartition, and the creation of a new nPartition.

HP nPartition Server Overview

HP nPartition servers can be configured as one large single system or divided up into multiple separate systems; the latter is the more common configuration. Each of the separate nPartitions provide both hardware and software isolation from one another. Therefore, no activity on one nPartition can affect the operation of another nPartition. As the foundation for a VSE, HP's nPartition servers provide a flexible yet robust solution for data center consolidation. nPartitions are also commonly referred to as hard partitions.

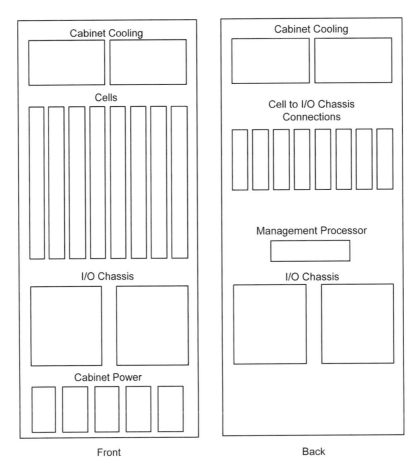

Figure 4-1 Block Diagram of HP nPartition Server Compute Cabinet

Figure 4-1 is a block diagram of an HP nPartition cabinet. The diagram shown closely resembles an HP SD32A cabinet, but the intent is not to represent any specific model. There are differences in the physical layout of the various HP nPartition cabinets, but the overall concepts presented in the figure and the accompanying text generally apply to all HP nPartition cabinets.

The following list describes the major components of HP nPartition servers, most of which are shown in Figure 4-1.

Complex: HP nPartition complexes contain a minimum of one and a maximum of four cabinets cabled together. The minimal configuration for a complex is a single compute cabinet. The maximal configuration for a complex consists of two compute cabinets and two I/O expansion cabinets.

Compute Cabinet: A cabinet containing CPU, memory, and I/O resources is called a compute cabinet.

I/O Expansion Cabinet (IOX): An I/O expansion cabinet contains I/O resources but no CPU or memory resources.

Management Processor: Every complex contains one active service processor that is referred to as either the management processor or the guardian service processor.

Cell: The physical hardware board that provides CPU and memory resources. A cell can be added, removed, or upgraded without disrupting the operation of the other partitions in the complex. Cells are the fundamental building blocks of HP nPartition servers.

I/O Chassis: I/O chassis contain peripheral component interconnect (PCI) slots suitable for installing networking and storage adapters. Both compute and I/O expansion cabinets contain I/O chassis. In order to be usable by an nPartition, every I/O chassis must be physically connected to a cell. An I/O chassis can be connected to exactly one cell. Note that a cell need not be connected to an I/O chassis to be usable by an nPartition.

Core I/O Card: Within each I/O chassis, slot 0 (zero) may contain a core I/O card. At least one core I/O card is required for every nPartition. The core I/O card provides console access and other fundamental nPartition services.

nPartition: An nPartition consists of one or more cells and at least one of the cells must be connected to an I/O chassis. In addition, at least one of the I/O chassis must contain a core I/O card. When a cell is assigned to an nPartition, the connected I/O chassis is automatically assigned to the same nPartition. nPartitions can be created, modified, and deleted without changing the physical hardware in a complex, which allows for flexible configuration over the life of the system

There are three generations of HP nPartition servers. Table 4-1 lists the generations along with the supported operating systems, processor types, model numbers, and the maximum number of cells and I/O chassis for each of the servers. The external I/O chassis listed in the table reside within an I/O expansion cabinet. Along with the maximum number of I/O chassis listed, the number of PCI slots is also shown for each configuration. The total number of PCI slots available for a given configuration is the sum of the slots in internal and external I/O chassis.

Table 4-1   HP nPartition Server Models

Generation	Supported Operating Systems	Processor	Model Numbers	Max Number of Cells	Max Number of Internal I/O Chassis (and Max PCI Slot Count)	Max Number of External I/O Chassis (and Max PCI Slot Count)
First Generation	HP-UX	PA-RISC	HP 9000 rp7410	2	2 (16)	0 (0)
			HP 9000 rp8400	4	2 (16)	2 (16)
			HP 9000 SD16000	4	4 (48)	0 (0)
			HP 9000 SD32000	8	4 (48)	4 (48)
			HP 9000 SD64000	16	8 (96)	8 (96)
Second Generation (based on sx1000 chipset)	HP-UX	PA-RISC	HP 9000 rp7420	2	2 (16)	0 (0)
			HP 9000 rp8420	4	2 (16)	2 (16)
			HP 9000 SD16A	4	4 (48)	0 (0)
			HP 9000 SD32A	8	4 (48)	4 (48)
			HP 9000 SD64A	16	8 (96)	8 (96)
	HP-UX, Microsoft Windows, Linux	Intel® Itanium® 2	HP Integrity rx7620	2	2 (16)	0 (0)
			HP Integrity rx8620	4	2 (16)	2 (16)
			HP Integrity SD16A	4	4 (48)	0 (0)
			HP Integrity SD32A	8	4 (48)	4 (48)
			HP Integrity SD64A	16	8 (96)	8 (96)

Generation	Supported Operating Systems	Processor	Model Numbers	Max Number of Cells	Max Number of Internal I/O Chassis (and Max PCI Slot Count)	Max Number of External I/O Chassis (and Max PCI Slot Count)
Third Generation (based on HP super scalable processor chipset sx2000)	HP-UX	PA-RISC	HP 9000 rp7440	2	2 (16)	0 (0)
			HP 9000 rp8440	4	2 (16)	2 (16)
			HP 9000 SD16B	4	4 (48)	0 (0)
			HP 9000 SD32B	8	4 (48)	4 (48)
			HP 9000 SD64B	16	8 (96)	8 (96)
	HP-UX, Microsoft Windows, Linux	Intel® Itanium® 2	HP Integrity rx7640	2	2 (16)	0 (0)
			HP Integrity rx8620	4	2 (16)	2 (16)
			HP Integrity SD16B	4	4 (48)	0 (0)
			HP Integrity SD32B	8	4 (48)	4 (48)
			HP Integrity SD64B	16	8 (96)	8 (96)

Data Maintained by the Management Processor

HP nPartition severs contain one active management processor (MP). The MP is responsible for a variety of tasks; the most notable are the following:

- maintaining the configuration of the entire complex
- allowing access to the console and console logs for each nPartition
- storing the chassis and event logs

- providing a command menu for performing actions on the complex
- presenting the virtual front panel (VFP) interface

The remainder of this section focuses on how the management processor maintains the configuration of the nPartitions, cells, and other configuration aspects of HP nPartition servers. The configuration data for HP nPartition servers is stored on the MP. The MP provides an interface for management applications such that administrators may configure the complex. Understanding the basics of how the data is stored on the MP provides great insights into HP nPartition server administration, configuration, and troubleshooting. Three primary data structures are stored on the MP: stable complex configuration data (SCCD), dynamic configuration data (DCD), and partition configuration data (PCD).

The SCCD structure contains several crucial pieces of data involved in the management of nPartitions. Most important, the SCCD contains the mapping of cells to nPartitions in the cell assignments array. Changes to a complex's configuration such as adding or removing cells from an nPartition are achieved by modifying the SCCD data structure. Table 4-2 lists the most notable fields in the SCCD data structure and their relevance to nPartition management.

The dynamic configuration data structure is used by the Instant Capacity, Temporary Instant Capacity, and Pay per use solutions. See the respective chapters for details on each of those VSE components.

The partition configuration data contains data for each nPartition. Each nPartition in a complex has a unique PCD data structure. Therefore, as many as sixteen separate PCD data structures could be present in a fully configured HP Superdome server containing sixteen nPartitions. Table 4-3 lists the most notable fields in each PCD data structure and their relevance to nPartition management.

Table 4-2 Key Fields in SCCD Data Structure

Field in SCCD	Importance
Cell Assignments Array	This field is an array with an element for each cell. The value contained in each array index indicates the partition ID to which the cell is assigned.
Complex Name	This field is the descriptive name of the complex.
Serial Number	The serial number is a read-only value representing the serial number of the entire complex.
Cell Type	This field determines whether the cell is to be used as a base cell (default) or floating cell. Currently only base cell types are supported.
Interleaved Memory Specifications	This field contains the memory configuration for each cell. A cell's memory can be configured as interleaved, cell local (which means no interleaving) or it may be a mix of the two.

Table 4-3 Key Fields in PCD Data Structure

Field in PCD	Importance
nPartition Name	This field contains a descriptive label for the nPartition. It is not necessarily the same as the hostname for the nPartition and is typically used to describe the workloads running in the nPartition.
Core Cell Choices	This field contains the user-specified order in which the core cell should be chosen. Should the first cell specified in this list become unusable as a core cell, firmware will proceed to the next cell in the list. If the list of core cell choices is not specified by the user, firmware will use the default algorithm to choose the core cell for the nPartition, generally based on the cell with the lowest cell ID that is capable of being a core cell.
Use on Next Boot	This field indicates whether each of the cells should be integrated into the nPartition the next time a reboot or shutdown for reconfiguration is performed on the nPartition. This field is typically used for Instant Capacity licensing purposes or for situations where a cell has experienced a hardware failure and should not be integrated into the nPartition until it can be repaired.
Admin IP Address	This field contains an IP address which can be used for administrative purposes to communicate with the operating system running in an nPartition. This field requires manual setting by administrators with the nPartition command line interfaces. If this value is set, management tools such as Partition Manager are able to communicate with each nPartition in the complex to gather operating system–specific information such as the operating system type and version.
Boot Paths	This field allows up to three boot paths to be specified. The primary, high-availability alternate, and alternate boot paths are all stored in this field. The PCD is only used for storing boot paths on HP 9000 nPartition servers. HP Integrity nPartition servers use a different storage location. As a result of this difference, when managing HP 9000 nPartition servers, boot paths are visible for all nPartitions in the complex. However, management tools on HP Integrity nPartition Servers are capable of reading the boot paths for only the nPartition where the management tools are running.

nPartition Management Paradigms

HP nPartition Servers support three management paradigms. These paradigms enable administrators to manage nPartitions in the mode which best suits their environments. The three management paradigms are as follows:

- *Local Management* has been the most commonly used paradigm for managing nPartitions because it was the only supported paradigm on the first-generation nPartition servers. Local management entails logging into an nPartition on the complex and executing the management tools directly on the nPartition. Using local management, an administrator has the ability to either make changes to the entire complex or limit management capabilities to those that affect only the local nPartition.

- *Remote Management via an nPartition* allows administrators to manage the complex from a central management station. This enables more efficient management because the administrator need not log into each nPartition to be managed and start the respective management tools. Instead, the management tools can be executed from a single location and directed toward each nPartition to be managed. In addition, only a subset of the management components needs to be running on the nPartitions.

- *Remote Management via the MP* enables administrators to fully configure an nPartition server without running any of the management software components on the nPartitions. In addition, this management paradigm affords similar benefits regarding remote management via an nPartition and the ability to manage many complexes from a central management station. Finally, this management paradigm provides a means to perform system administration even if no nPartition is active in the complex.

Local nPartition Management Paradigm

Figure 4-2 shows the paradigm of local nPartition management. This paradigm applies to all HP nPartition servers. Local nPartition management involves logging into an nPartition on the complex and performing management tasks on the local nPartition. This architecture is the simplest to use out of the box because it requires only a single system, the nPartition, to be operating in order to perform nPartition management. However, this management paradigm doesn't take full advantage of the remote management capabilities available on HP nPartition servers; this topic will be discussed in the following sections.

nPartition management applications for the original HP 9000 nPartition servers use a proprietary interface to communicate with the MP for configuration tasks. This interface enables nPartition management tools to configure the entire complex from any nPartition within the complex. nPartition management tools provide some limitations on configuration changes from one nPartition to another, such as disallowing the removal of an active nPartition from another nPartition. However, most operations are allowed from any nPartition in the complex. This provides a simplified and flexible management model, as an administrator may log into a single nPartition and perform several tasks that affect other nPartitions. The ramifications of this simplicity and flexibility should be considered when managing a shared HP nPartition server.

The second-generation HP nPartition servers, which contain the sx1000 chipset, use the Intelligent Platform Management Interface (IPMI) protocol as the interface between the MP and the management applications. IPMI is an industry-standard protocol designed to facilitate low-level system management. The IPMI interface is supported on HP-UX, Microsoft Windows, and Linux operating systems for the HP nPartition servers containing the sx1000 chipset and later chipsets. As implemented on HP nPartition servers, IPMI supports two transport mechanisms for communicating with the MP. The first is block transfer (BT) and the second is LAN. These are commonly referred to as IPMI over BT (IPMI/BT) and IPMI over LAN (IPMI/LAN). The IPMI/BT transport goes though a kernel driver on an nPartition to communicate with the MP. The IPMI/LAN transport uses the MP's LAN interface for communication.

While nPartition management has remained very similar between the generations of HP nPartition servers, several enhancements have been added. The most notable enhancement relating to Figure 4-2 and the use of the IPMI/BT interface is a feature called the nPartition configuration privilege. This feature can be enabled on the MP by using the PARPERM command from the MP's command menu as shown in Listing 4-1.

note

> The nPartition configuration privilege is supported only on HP nPartition servers based on the sx1000 chipset and later chipsets. This feature is not available on the first-generation HP 9000 nPartition servers.

Listing 4-1 Enabling the nPartition Configuration Privilege

```
                    Welcome to the

                rx8620 Management Processor

(c) Copyright 1995-2003 Hewlett-Packard Co., All Rights Reserved.

                    Version A.5.011



    MP MAIN MENU:

         CO: Consoles
        VFP: Virtual Front Panel (partition status)
         CM: Command Menu
```

```
                CL: Console Logs
                SL: Show Event Logs
                HE: Help
                 X: Exit Connection

MP> cm


                Enter HE to get a list of available commands



MP:CM> parperm

This command configures the nPartition Configuration Privilege.

WARNING: When nPartition Configuration Privilege is unrestricted,
         configuration commands issued by one partition can
         affect the configuration of another partition. When
         this privilege is restricted, configuration commands
         issued by a partition cannot affect power or partition
         assignment of hardware not already assigned to the
         partition.  Restricting nPartition configuration
         privilege does not restrict deallocation of processors
         across partition boundaries.

   nPartition Configuration Privilege is currently unrestricted.

   Do you wish to restrict partition configuration
   (preventing partitions from changing the configuration
   of the platform)?  (Y/[N]) y

   -> Partition reconfiguration is disabled
MP:CM>
```

When the nPartition configuration privilege is enabled (restricted), only configuration changes to the PCD data structure for the nPartition from which the request originated are allowed. Therefore, an administrator on one nPartition may not make changes to the SCCD or any other nPartition's PCD. In order to change the SCCD and the PCD data structures other than the PCD for the local nPartition, the administrator must use the IPMI over LAN interface; this is described in the next section.

In Figure 4-2, immediately above the IPMI or HP proprietary kernel interface component is the nPartition provider. The nPartition provider is a software component that implements the Web-Based Enterprise Management (WBEM) standard provider interface. Since an industry-standard WBEM interface for nPartition configuration is available for HP nPartition servers, third-party management tools are able to integrate with HP's nPartition servers.

Next to the nPartition provider component is the instant capacity provider. Similar to the nPartition provider, the instant capacity provider exposes an industry-standard interface for managing unlicensed components on HP nPartition servers. The nPartition management infrastructure verifies all changes to the SCCD and PCD data structures with the instant capacity provider to ensure that the complex remains in compliance with the number of unlicensed resources. All nPartition configuration changes on complexes containing unlicensed components must be made through an nPartition running HP-UX. The interface between the nPartition provider and the instant capacity provider is built to deny all configuration changes on complexes with unlicensed resources if the operating system is not HP-UX. For complexes that weren't purchased with unlicensed instant capacity components, the instant capacity provider will automatically approve all configuration changes.

Above the nPartition provider and instant capacity provider components in Figure 4-2 is the WBEM or Windows Management Instrumentation (WMI) server. When the nPartition provider is running on the HP-UX and Linux operating systems, it runs under the Pegasus open-source implementation of the WBEM server. When running on the Microsoft Windows operating system, the nPartition provider takes advantage of the (WMI) server. This allows the nPartition provider to operate as part of an existing framework on the Microsoft Windows operating system.

The next component above the WBEM or WMI Server is the nPartition commands. The nPartition commands component is the command-line interface (CLI) used for managing nPartitions. Commands such as `parcreate`, `parmodify`, and `parstatus` are represented by this component. The nPartition commands use the WBEM or WMI interface to read status information and configure HP nPartition servers. The nPartition commands are available on HP-UX, Linux, and Microsoft Windows.

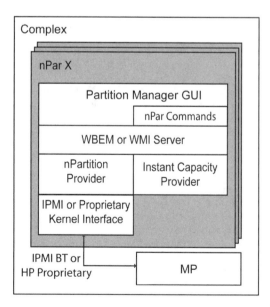

Figure 4-2 Local nPartition Management Paradigm

Finally, the uppermost box in Figure 4-2 is the Partition Manager (parmgr) graphical user interface (GUI). The Partition Manager GUI provides a web-based interface for viewing the status and making configuration changes to HP nPartition servers. Partition Manager provides graphical hardware and logical views of the entire complex to facilitate system administration. Partition Manager uses the WBEM or WMI interface to read the configuration data for the complex. It makes all changes to the complex configuration using the nPartition commands. This allows administrators to preview the commands that will be executed and even cut and paste the commands into a script or use the GUI as a learning tool. Partition Manager is available on HP-UX, Linux, and Microsoft Windows operating systems.

Remote Management via an nPartition Paradigm

Figure 4-3 shows the paradigm of remote nPartition management via an nPartition in the complex. This paradigm can be used with all architectures of HP nPartition servers.

The management paradigm depicted in Figure 4-3 involves logging into a remote system separate from the nPartition or complex to be managed. The remote system can be any HP-UX, Windows, or Linux system capable of running the nPartition commands and the parmgr GUI. This use model is extremely powerful in that an administrator may perform management of all the HP nPartition servers in the data center from a central management station. Additionally, the task of running the nPartition commands and parmgr GUI are offloaded to the remote system and the nPartitions are left to execute their production workloads.

note

> Remote management via an nPartition requires certain security measures to be taken on the remote system to establish a trust relationship between the nPartition and the remote system. See the product manual pages and documentation for specific instructions on performing these steps.

In order to perform remote management as depicted in Figure 4-3, the nPartition commands require command-line options for specifying the remote nPartition's hostname or IP address, username, and password. Given the address and authentication credentials, the nPartition commands send WBEM requests to the WBEM or WMI Server over a secure channel.

Listing 4-2 is an example execution of an nPartition command using remote management via an nPartition. In the example, the parstatus command sends remote WBEM requests to the nPartition with the hostname rex01 as the user root. Notice that the password is not specified directly on the command line; instead, the command prompts for the password. It should be noted that some of the command's output has been removed for formatting purposes.

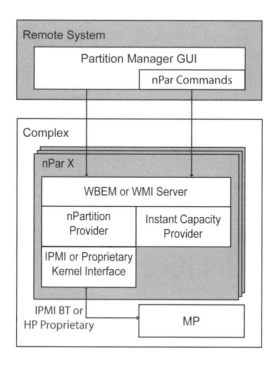

Figure 4-3 Architecture of Remote nPartition Management via an nPartition

Listing 4-2 nPartition Command Using Remote Management via an nPartition

```
# /usr/sbin/parstatus -C -h rex01 -u root:
Please enter the password for user root:


[Cell]
                            CPU      Memory
                            OK/      (GB)
Hardware     Actual         Deconf/  OK/
Location     Usage          Max      Deconf    Connected To
==========   ============   =======  ========  ====================
cab0,cell0   Active Core    4/0/8    4.0/0.0   cab0,bay0,chassis0
cab0,cell1   Active Core    4/0/8    4.0/0.0   cab0,bay0,chassis1
cab0,cell2   Active Core    4/0/8    4.0/0.0   cab8,bay0,chassis0
cab0,cell3   Active Core    4/0/8    4.0/0.0   cab8,bay0,chassis1

Notes: * = Cell has no interleaved memory.
```

The Partition Manager GUI also provides the ability to switch between the complexes being managed as shown in Figure 4-4. The top portion of the dialog labeled "A remote nPartition" provides the ability to switch between any nPartitions in the data center as long as the WBEM or WMI Server is running and the additional components shown in the figure are present on the nPartition.

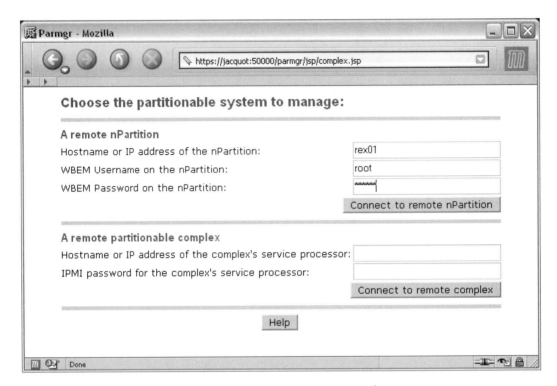

Figure 4-4 Partition Manager Remote Management Interface

Remote Management via the MP Paradigm

The final nPartition management paradigm, remote management via the MP, is presented in Figure 4-5. This paradigm is not available on the first-generation HP nPartition servers. Instead, only HP nPartition servers with the sx1000 chipset and later support this management paradigm.

The use model depicted in Figure 4-5 allows the full nPartition management stack to be run on a remote system that is separate from the complex being managed. In fact, there need not be any nPartitions running or defined in the complex for this architecture to function properly. The only requirement on the complex is for housekeeping power and network connectivity to the MP.

Performing remote management using IPMI over a local area network (LAN) as depicted in Figure 4-5 involves providing command-line options to the nPartition commands for the MP's hostname or IP address and password. The address and password are passed to the nPartition provider, which uses the credentials to send IPMI requests directly to the MP over the LAN interface.

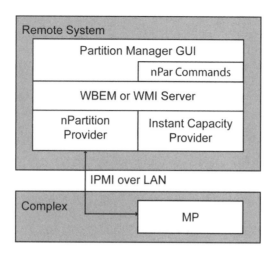

Figure 4-5 Remote nPartition Management via the MP Paradigm

note

> Remote management via IPMI over LAN is the only management paradigm that can be used to make changes to the SCCD when the nPartition configuration privilege is restricted.

Listing 4-3 shows an example execution of an nPartition command using remote management via IPMI over LAN. In the example, the parstatus command sends WBEM requests to the nPartition provider on the local system and the nPartition provider sends an IPMI message over the LAN interface directly to the MP. The hostname of the MP in this listing is rex-s. Once again, some of the command's output has been removed for formatting purposes.

Listing 4-3 nPartition Command Using Remote Management via IPMI over LAN

```
# /usr/sbin/parstatus -C -h rex-s -g
Please enter the IPMI password:
Note: The -g option may require up to 2 minutes to complete.  Please wait...


[Cell]
                          CPU     Memory
                          OK/     (GB)
Hardware    Actual        Deconf/ OK/
Location    Usage         Max     Deconf   Connected To
==========  ============  ======= ======== ===================
cab0,cell0  Active Core   4/0/8   4.0/0.0  cab0,bay0,chassis0
cab0,cell1  Active Core   4/0/8   4.0/0.0  cab0,bay0,chassis1
```

```
cab0,cell2 Active Core  4/0/8   4.0/0.0   cab8,bay0,chassis0
cab0,cell3 Active Core  4/0/8   4.0/0.0   cab8,bay0,chassis1

Notes: * = Cell has no interleaved memory.
```

The parmgr GUI provides the ability to connect directly to the MP of a complex for remote management via IPMI over a LAN. The lower portion of the dialog labeled "A remote partitionable complex" shown in Figure 4-4 provides the ability to specify the MP's hostname or IP address and the IPMI password. When parmgr is provided with the MP's hostname and IPMI password, messages will be sent from nPar provider directly to the MP via IPMI over LAN.

Example nPartition Management Scenario

The remainder of this chapter walks through an example management scenario that covers the nPartition management tasks involved with an HP nPartition server hardware upgrade. This example scenario does not cover the process of installing the physical resources; this is typically performed by an HP field engineer. Instead, the purpose of this example is to illustrate the nPartition management applications with a practical example.

The initial configuration of the complex is shown in Table 4-4. The HP nPartition server used in this scenario is an rx8620 with two cells. The two cells are contained in a single nPartition which is named rex01. There are two I/O chassis in the server and both are in use by the rex01 nPartition.

Table 4-5 shows the configuration of the complex after the hardware upgrade scenario is complete. Two new cells will be added to the server, and an I/O expansion cabinet containing two I/O chassis will also be part of the upgrade. Notice that the rex01 nPartition is extended with a portion of the newly added hardware and an additional nPartition, rex02, is created with the remaining hardware resources.

Table 4-4 Initial Complex Configuration

nPartition Name	Cells	I/O Chassis
rex01	cab0, cell0	cab0, bay0, chassis0
	cab0, cell1	cab0, bay0, chassis1

Table 4-5 Final Complex Configuration

nPartition Name	Cells	I/O Chassis
rex01	cab0, cell0	cab0, bay0, chassis0
	cab0, cell1	cab0, bay0, chassis1
	cab0, cell2	cab8, bay0, chassis0
rex02	cab0, cell3	cab8, bay0, chassis1

Viewing the Configuration of an nPartition Complex

The first step in performing the hardware upgrade is viewing the current configuration of the complex. There are three primary mechanisms for viewing the configuration of an HP nPartition server:

- the MP console's command menu
- the nPartition commands
- the Partition Manager graphical user interface.

Each of these mechanisms exposes the SCCD and PCD data in slightly different ways. The MP's interface provides high-level information about the configuration of the complex and very detailed information about the status of the hardware components. The nPartition command-line interfaces provide textual output such as that shown in Listing 4-2 and Listing 4-3. Finally, the Partition Manager GUI provides graphical views of the system configuration and status. While all three of these mechanisms can be used to view the configuration of an nPartition complex, Partition Manager will be used in this example.

The Partition Manager screen shown in Figure 4-6 is the first screen displayed in Partition Manager when the tool is started. This view shows a hardware representation of the complex, rex complex, along with the nPartition configuration and the status of the components. This screen shows the complex configuration as documented in Table 4-4. A single nPartition, rex01, contains two cells. Each of the cells is connected to an I/O chassis. The rex01 nPartition is active, as indicated by icons next to each of the hardware components. It is also evident that cell slots 2 and 3 are empty. Cells will be added to each of these empty slots as part of this example scenario.

Partition Manager color-codes the nPartitions and assigned hardware resources to assist in distinguishing resource assignment. In addition to color-coding, each hardware resource has a small icon with a number indicating nPartition assignment. In this example, rex01 is assigned nPartition id 0 (zero); therefore, the circle next to the resources assigned to the nPartition contains a

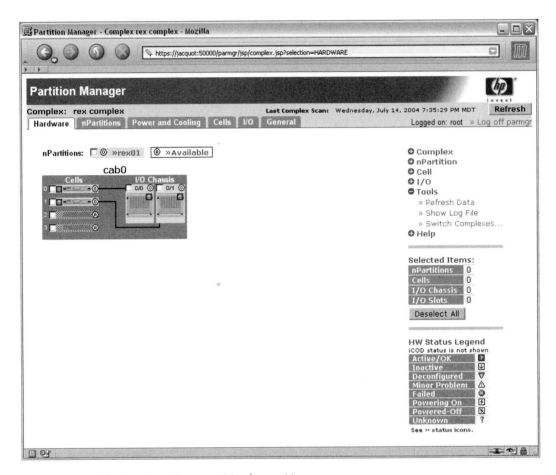

Figure 4-6 Partition Manager Hardware View

zero. Available or empty cell and I/O chassis slots contain an "A" in the circle to indicate the resource is not assigned to any nPartition and is therefore available.

Figure 4-7 shows another view of the rex complex, this time focusing on a detailed view of the cells. This view is available by selecting the "cells" tab at the top of the screen. The upper portion of the page provides several tables with summary information for the cells, CPUs, and memory in the complex. From the cells table it is clear there are two active cells and two absent cells. The two absent cell slots will be populated with new hardware in this scenario.

In addition to the summary tables, each CPU, including multi-core CPUs, is shown, as is the status of each CPU. Every DIMM is shown with its size and status. The label alongside the DIMM slot is the actual silk-screen label found on the physical cell board. Should any CPU or DIMM be deconfigured or failed, this screen provides vital information in the process of troubleshooting and physical repair because an administrator can quickly determine the problem area.

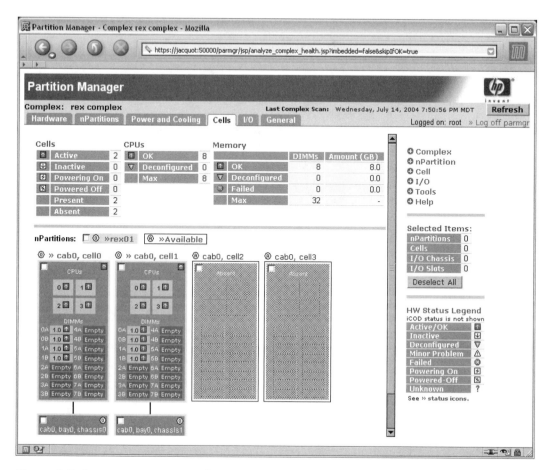

Figure 4-7 Partition Manager Cell View

Viewing the Complex after Installing Hardware

From the analysis performed, it's clear the new cells should be added into cell slots 2 and 3. Additionally, there are no empty I/O chassis slots, so an I/O expansion cabinet must be installed in order to configure additional nPartitions. The I/O expansion cabinet is required because every nPartition requires at least one cell that is connected to an I/O chassis and that chassis must contain a core I/O card.

For the purposes of this example, assume the new hardware has now been installed and power has been enabled. Figure 4-8 shows the state of the complex with the new hardware installed. Cell slots 2 and 3 now contain cells that are inactive. They are each physically connected to an I/O chassis in the I/O expansion cabinet with an ID of eight.

Why Do I/O Expansion Cabinet Numbers Start at Eight?

I/O expansion cabinets always start numbering at eight as a result of the initial platform architecture, which allowed for up to eight compute cabinets (with IDs from zero to seven) to be cabled together for extremely large systems. These configurations are not currently supported by HP, but cabinet numbering continues to reflect the initial architecture.

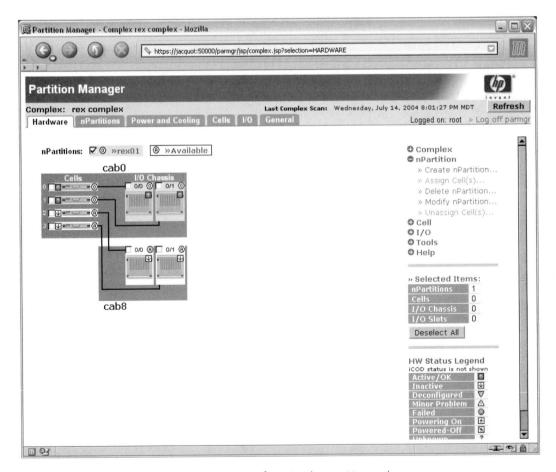

Figure 4-8 Partition Manager View after Hardware Upgrade

Extending the Existing nPartition

The first step in the process of putting the new hardware resources to use is to extend the rex01 partition. Notice in Figure 4-8 that the checkbox next to the rex01 partition is selected. From the actions menu on the left-hand side, the Modify nPartition task under the nPartition portion of the menu is selected. This task provides an interface to modify attributes for the nPartition such as the cells assigned to the nPartition and the nPartition name.

The Modify nPartition screen is shown in Figure 4-9. Notice the checkbox next to cell 2 has been selected indicating it should be added to the rex01 nPartition. Other settings for the nPartition, such as cell local memory, core cell choices, and the name of the nPartition could also be changed from this dialog by selecting the other tabs. For the purposes of this example, only the new cell will be added.

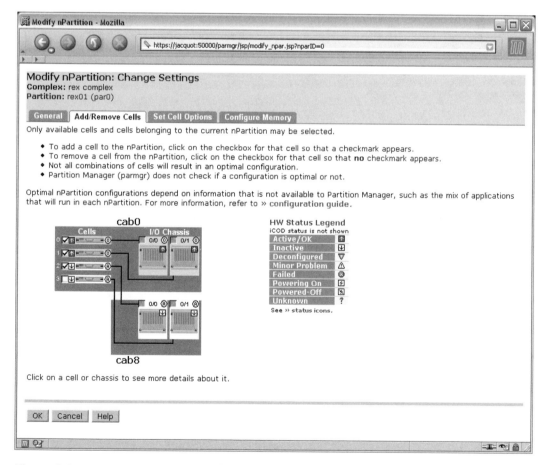

Figure 4-9 Partition Manager Modify nPartition Screen

When the OK button is pressed in the Modify nPartition dialog, the Modify nPartition Finish dialog, Figure 4-10, is displayed. This dialog provides a list of notes and warnings, a summary of the changes which will be performed to the complex, and a list of advisory high availability (HA) checks.

The Command Preview immediately below the buttons provides the *exact* command that could be executed to perform the requested changes. This is especially useful for administrators who prefer using the command-line interface but have yet to master the various command-line arguments and options.

The command parmodify is used to modify nPartitions. Of particular interest in the command are the -h and -g command-line arguments. These options are required when using the nPartition management paradigm presented in Figure 4-5 for using remote management via the MP. This is required because the nPartition configuration privilege was set to "restricted" in Listing

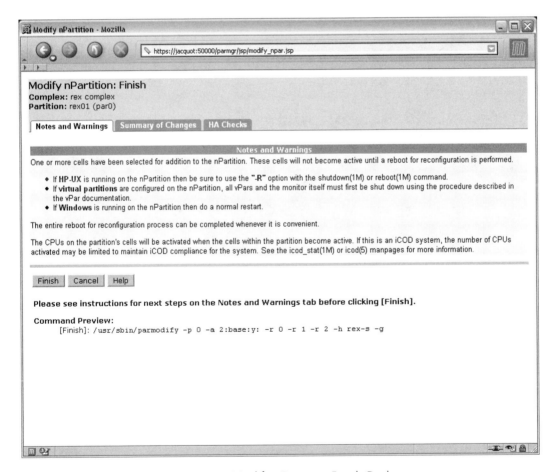

Figure 4-10 Partition Manager Modify nPartition Finish Dialog

4-1. As described earlier, this setting prevents changes to the SCCD data structure such as assigning cells to an nPartition. Pressing the OK button will result in Partition Manager executing the command shown in the Command Preview, which will assign cell 2 to the rex01 nPartition, which has the nPartition ID of 0 (zero).

Creating a new nPartition

The rex01 partition is now extended to the desired size, as shown in Table 4-5. The final configuration task associated with the hardware upgrade is to create the new nPartition, rex02. Figure 4-11 shows the rex complex with the changes made thus far. Notice that cell 2 and the attached I/O chassis 0/0 are assigned to rex01, but they are not active (as indicated by the icon next to the

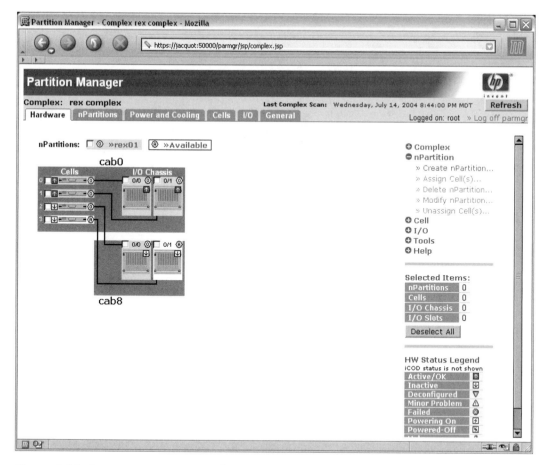

Figure 4-11 Partition Manager Hardware View before Creating Second nPartition

cell). Cell 3 and I/O chassis 8/0/1 are both available and will be used to create the new nPartition rex02.

The Create nPartition link is selected from the nPartition portion of the actions menu, which opens the Create nPartition wizard. The first step in creating an nPartition is to set the name. In this example, the name of the nPartition is rex02. The second step is to select the cells that will be assigned to the nPartition shown in the Create nPartition Select Cells screen in Figure 4-12. This screen allows simple point-and-click selection of the cells to be assigned to the nPartition. In this example, the only cell available is cell 3, so it is selected with a checkbox next to the cell.

Subsequent steps in the Create nPartition wizard are similar to the options available in the Modify nPartition dialog. Setting the core cell choice, configuring cell local memory, and other options are all available in the wizard. Before performing the requested changes to the complex,

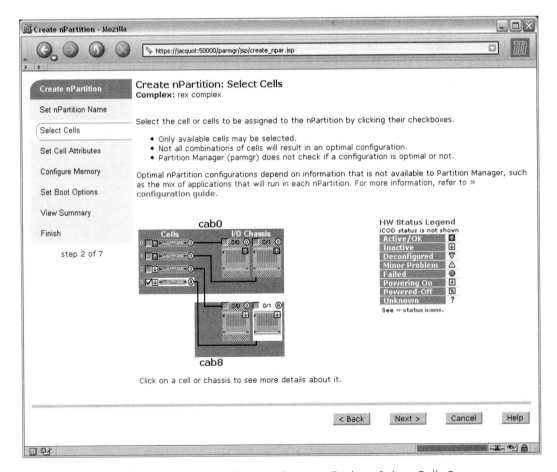

Figure 4-12 Partition Manager Create nPartition Dialog: Select Cells Page

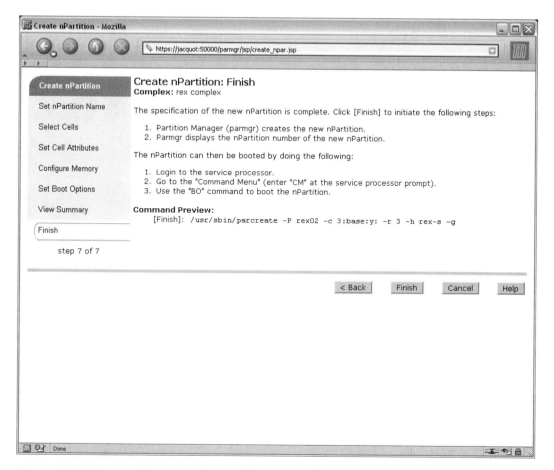

Figure 4-13 Partition Manager Create nPartition Dialog: Finish Page

consult the summary pages Partition Manager provides, which give detailed information regarding the nPartition that will be created. The final step in the process of creating an nPartition is the Finish page, show in Figure 4-13. As with the Modify nPartition task, the Command Preview is presented. Once again, remote management via IPMI over LAN is being utilized, as is evident by the -h and -g command-line options.

The changes to the rex complex are now complete. The rex01 nPartition has been extended to include the newly added cell 2 and I/O chassis 8/0/0. The rex02 nPartition has been created using the remaining new hardware resources, cell 3 and I/O chassis 8/0/1. Figure 4-14 shows the final configuration of the complex. Notice, however, that the newly added resources are inactive, as shown by the icon next to each hardware component. Rebooting the rex01 nPartition and booting the rex02 nPartition are the final steps in this example scenario.

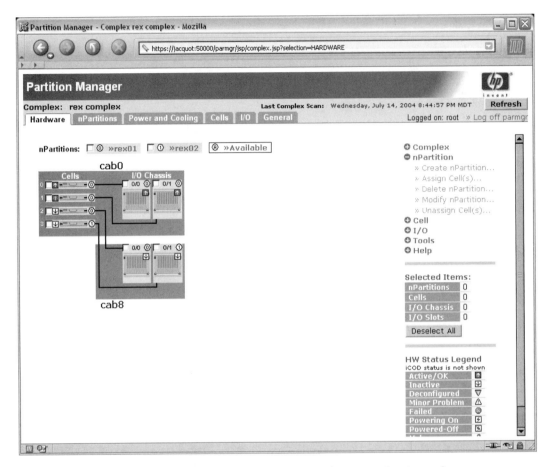

Figure 4-14 Partition Manager Hardware View after Complex Reconfiguration

Rebooting and Booting nPartitions

The complex configuration tasks related to the hardware upgrade are complete. However, the new resources are not usable for workloads. The rex01 nPartition must be rebooted and the rex02 nPartition must be booted in order for the new hardware to be usable. Before jumping into the process of rebooting and booting nPartitions, a discussion of the states of cells is warranted to clarify the process of configuration an HP nPartition server.

As shown in Figure 4-15, there are four cell states. When cells are not physically installed, the nPartition management tools refer to the cells as absent. After initially installing a cell, it will be in the Powered-Off state. Enabling power to the cell causes the cell to go through a series of power-on self-tests. These tests ensure that the CPUs, memory, I/O, and other hardware entities are functioning appropriately. After the power-on self-test sequence, a cell stops at the "Inactive" state; this is also known as the Boot Is Blocked (BIB) or Boot Inhibit Bit (BIB) state. Cells

2 and 3 are Inactive, or at BIB, in Figure 4-14. The final cell state is the "Active" state. This is the state that will most commonly be observed on production systems, as only active cells are able to run operating systems and workloads. Cells 0 and 1 are Active in Figure 4-14.

While it is possible to make changes to a complex when cells are in the Active state, it is generally not the recommended approach. Every cell contains a copy of the SCCD data structure that mirrors the copy contained in the MP. When changes are made to the SCCD affecting an active cell, the change cannot be pushed out to any cells until the affected cell becomes inactive. Therefore, a Pending SCCD data structure results. This Pending SCCD will persist until the affected cell becomes inactive, which could be an indefinite amount of time. In addition, no other changes can be made to the SCCD data structure until the change is pushed out. In some cases it is necessary to make changes to the SCCD that affect an active cell, and in those cases, it is recommended that the nPartition be rebooted as soon as possible to minimize the amount of time the Pending SCCD data structure persists. The addition of cell 2 to the rex01 nPartition did not create a Pending SCCD because the only affected cell, cell 2, was inactive when the change was made. Therefore, the copy of the SCCD for cell 2 was pushed out immediately. Similarly, when the rex02 nPartition was created, only cell 3 was affected, and it was inactive when the nPartition was created.

The state of an nPartition is related to the cell states shown in Figure 4-15; when one or more assigned cells are in the active state, then the nPartition is said to be active. Otherwise, the nPartition is inactive.

The rex01 nPartition must be rebooted for reconfiguration in order for cell 2 to communicate with the other cells in the nPartition and become active. The HP-UX operating system

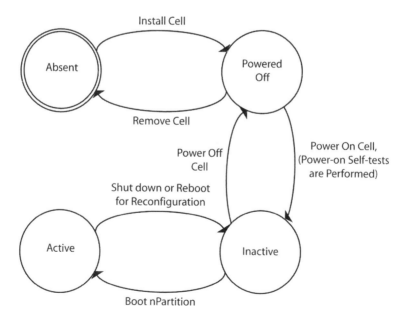

Figure 4-15 HP nPartition Server Cell State Diagram

requires special command-line options when rebooting the operating system in order for complex configuration changes to take effect. The -R option is required for both the shutdown and reboot commands on HP-UX. This requirement is shown in the Notes and Warnings section of Figure 4-10. If rex01 were running Microsoft Windows or Linux, a normal reboot would result in activation of cell 2 and the original two cells. The difference in behavior on HP-UX allows an administrator to alter the SCCD but have finer control over exactly when the changes to the SCCD take effect. A normal HP-UX shutdown or reboot command with the -R option omitted reboots the operating system without activating the newly added hardware in the nPartition.

Finally, rex02 must be booted by using the MP's command menu. The boot, bo, command boots the nPartition, releasing the cell from BIB and allowing it to become active. The cell proceeds to either the BCH firmware interface on a cell that contains PA-RISC processors or to the Extensible Firmware Interface (EFI) on a cell that contains Intel Itanium Processor Family (IPF) processors. From the firmware interface, an operating system can be installed and then workloads can be started.

Figure 4-16 shows the final hardware view of the complex after the upgrading the hardware, reconfiguring the complex, rebooting rex01, and booting rex02.

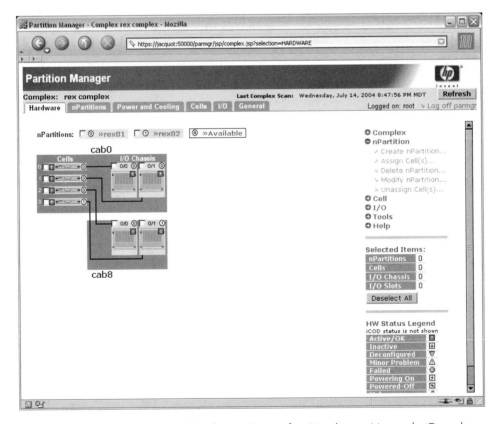

Figure 4-16 Partition Manager Hardware View after Hardware Upgrade Complete

Summary

As the foundation for HP's Virtual Server Environment, HP nPartition servers are a crucial building block in a data center. This chapter has covered the basic hardware in HP nPartition servers including complexes, cabinets, cells, and I/O chassis. The nPartition Management paradigms were discussed to provide an in-depth understanding of the powerful management options available for HP nPartition servers. Finally, an example scenario was covered to illustrate the process of modifying nPartitions and creating new nPartitions.

5

HP Virtual Partitions

Chapter Overview

It's 7:00 PM. By now most end users are sitting down in their recliners at home, reading the paper. Not Toshi. Toshi has been asked to consolidate workloads in the data center onto fewer servers. Toshi logs into a few of his primary servers and begins to gather data. He is using HP OpenView to gather the empirical utilization data for each server, but Toshi fully understands the usage patterns of the workloads in his data center. In fact, he probably knows them better than OpenView does. He knows that 90% of the web server use is during normal business hours. Additionally, there are several build machines that are only used during the night for automated software builds. Toshi understands that further investigation will only serve to confirm what he already knows. In addition, he knows HP Virtual Partitions will meet his needs. He can consolidate the web server and automated build server to a single nPartition. In fact, the size of the nPartition only needs to be the size of one of the current servers, not the sum of the two. Toshi also knows that he can dedicate a fixed amount of resources to each workload. He can then use the dynamic migration capabilities of HP Virtual Partitions to ensure that each workload has adequate resources during their peak utilization times.

The character Toshi and this story are typical of many system administrators and their weekly routines. A common issue in today's data centers is how to do more with less resources. HP Virtual Partitions play a crucial role in the process of consolidating servers and providing a dynamic Virtual Server Environment.

This chapter begins with an overview of HP Virtual Partitions and then discusses the planning process. Thorough planning for virtual partition configurations is a key step for success in the deployment of Virtual Partitions. The remainder of the chapter goes through an example deployment scenario for Virtual Partitions. The example begins with the planning phase and continues through the process of setting up a scheduled task to automatically migrate CPUs on a daily basis to meet the demands for each workload.

Throughout this chapter, the term "*server*" will be used to describe either a single nPartition or a stand-alone server. Virtual Partitions operate almost identically regardless of whether the underlying hardware is an nPartition or stand-alone server. The generic term will be used to describe both hardware platforms. The Virtual Partitions product documentation covers the platform differences in detail; refer to the Installing and Managing HP-UX Virtual Partitions (vPars) user's guide for platform specifics.

Virtual Partitions Overview

HP Virtual Partitions (vPars) allows the hardware of a single server to be divided into separate entities, each of which is capable of running a distinct operating system. This allows the workloads on multiple servers, none of which are fully utilizing their allocated hardware, to be combined to a single server and yet retain their operating system isolation. Figure 5-1 is a diagram showing three traditional servers running separate operating systems and workloads. Certainly the three workloads could be combined on one server without vPars; however, it is common for workloads to require some level of isolation. Operating system isolation is commonly used to provide the workload separation.

Figure 5-2 provides a view of a server running vPars. One of the key differences in this diagram is the *Virtual Partition Monitor* layer. This layer serves as an intermediary between the operating systems and the firmware. The vPar monitor reads the configuration of the Virtual Partitions from disk, loads the configuration into memory, and allocates resources to the Virtual Partitions based on the configuration. Using the vPar configuration information, the firmware calls of each of the operating systems are intercepted and filtered by the vPar monitor. For example, an operating system's firmware calls requesting data for the CPUs and I/O devices in the hardware platform will be filtered to return only the information for the assigned hardware resources. Consequently, applications built to run in non-vPar environments typically operate without modification because the interfaces between the HP-UX operating system and the workloads have remained unchanged.

Virtual Partitions allow consolidation to a single server in order to increase system utilization. In addition, vPars allow dynamic CPU migration. The granularity and flexibility of vPars allow

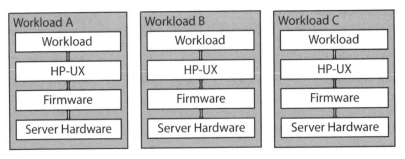

Figure 5-1 Workloads in a Non-Virtual Partition Environment

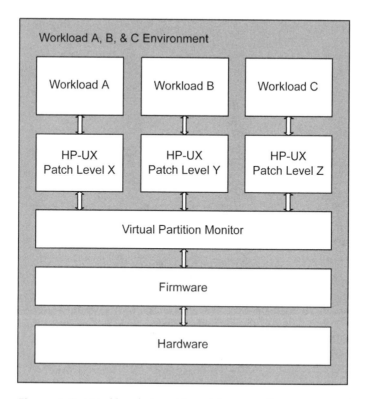

Figure 5-2 Workloads in a Virtual Partition Environment

each workload to continue operating in a highly customizable environment. Each vPar is running a separate operating system, which means it can be patched and tuned precisely to the needs of the workload. Additionally, the operating system isolation results in protected workloads. An errant workload consuming all of the file descriptors, for example, will not affect any of the other vPars in the server. In addition, kernel panics and other software faults will not affect the availability of any vPar other than the one where the fault occurred.

Each vPar must consist of at least the following resources:

- one bound CPU
- sufficient memory to boot HP-UX and run a workload
- I/O connectivity to bootable media
- network connectivity (not required, but common)

Given these minimum system requirements, a large SD64000 Superdome with 64 processors is capable of running a maximum of 64 distinct virtual partitions. However, these virtual partitions cannot reside within a single nPartition. There can be at most eight vPars within each nPartition. To achieve the full 64 virtual partitions, the Superdome would first need to be divided into eight nPartitions, and each of the nPartitions can then be divided into eight virtual partitions. The final requirement for a Virtual Partition configuration is all the Virtual Partition kernels together must fit within the(lower 2GB of address space and each kernel must reside in contiguous address space.

Virtual Partition Terminology

The following list of terms is(used throughout the remainder of this chapter and in the vPar product documentation.

General

Virtual Partition Database is where the configuration of every vPar in the server is represented. The default location for the vPar database is /stand/vpdb. If this file does not exist when the command to create the first vPar is executed, the file will be created. When the vPar monitor is loaded, it reads the vPar database into memory. Upon booting each of the vPars, a copy of the vPar monitor's in-memory database is written to the file system for every vPar in the server. This results in all of the vPars having a current copy of the vPar configuration. The vPar infrastructure also supports alternate databases, which allows for differing configurations based on the database loaded by the monitor.

Virtual Partition Monitor is the layer shown in Figure 5-2 that intercepts the operating system's firmware calls and filters the responses appropriately.

CPUs

Bound CPU is a CPU that services I/O interrupts. Starting with HP-UX 11i v2, interrupts can be dynamically migrated. However, previous releases of HP-UX did not support interrupt migration, therefore a bound CPU can be added or removed from a vPar only while the vPar is down. Since bound CPUs service interrupts, it is recommended vPars with I/O-intensive workloads have more bound CPUs than unbound CPUs. There are two subtypes of bound CPUs, monitor bound and user bound.

Monitor-Bound CPU is a CPU bound by the monitor as a result of meeting the minimum number of CPUs assigned to a vPar. Monitor-bound CPUs are chosen by the monitor at boot time and cannot be dynamically migrated from one Virtual Partition to another.

User-Bound CPU is a CPU bound because the user has explicitly specified the path of the CPU to be assigned to a vPar.

Unbound CPU is a CPU that does not service interrupts. Unbound CPUs can be dynamically migrated from one vPar to another while the vPars are in the up state.

Unbound CPUs are ideal for CPU-intensive workloads, especially in environments where migrating CPUs enable higher server utilization.

Minimum CPUs is the minimum number of CPUs to be assigned to the vPar. This value represents the number of CPUs that will be bound by the monitor if no CPUs are explicitly assigned.

Maximum CPUs is the maximum number of CPUs that can be assigned to the vPar. The sum of bound and unbound CPUs cannot exceed this value.

Memory

Memory Size is the amount of memory in MB assigned to the vPar. The memory size must be in multiples of 64MB. Memory sizes that are not multiples of 64 MB will be rounded *up* to the nearest 64MB boundary.

Memory Range is a specific base address and size that dictates exactly which range of memory should be assigned to the vPar. Memory ranges should only be used with systems and applications that support non-uniform memory access (NUMA) architectures.

I/O

Local Bus Adapter (LBA) is the hardware layer that can be assigned to a single vPar. The assignment of an LBA to a vPar assigns the I/O slot, the contained PCI card, and all devices attached to the PCI card.

Explicit I/O Path is the path of the LBA being explicitly assigned to a vPar. All devices below the specified LBA are owned by a single vPar.

Implicit I/O Path is the path of an LBA that is implicitly assigned to a vPar as a result of a device below the LBA being assigned to a vPar. This situation typically occurs when a boot device is assigned to a vPar but the LBA containing the boot device is not explicitly assigned to the vPar.

Boot Attributes are added to an I/O path to specify the primary and alternate boot paths for a vPar's operating system. Configuration of boot paths is a mechanism commonly used to assign implicit I/O paths. This situation is illustrated in the example scenario below.

Virtual Partition Example Scenario

The remainder of this chapter focuses on an example scenario. The purpose of this scenario is to demonstrate the power and flexibility provided by Virtual Partitions. The scenario begins with an overview that outlines the steps that are generally required when deploying vPars. It then describes the environment in which Virtual Partitions will be deployed. Proper planning of the virtual partition configuration greatly eases the implementation; therefore, a few tips and suggestions are provided to facilitate the planning process. Next, the sequence of creating and booting the initial virtual partition is described. After the first virtual partition is running, the second vPar is created and booted from an Ignite-UX server. With two vPars running HP-UX, a shell script is written to illustrate the dynamic capabilities of vPars. Finally, the shell script is added as a scheduled task using the cron tool, which results in the dynamic reconfiguration of the system based on the timing of workload utilization peaks.

It should be noted that portions of command output shown throughout this example have been modified for formatting purposes and to provide additional clarity.

Example Scenario Overview

This example scenario consists of the following steps. These steps are covered in detail throughout the example scenario. There are many possible ways to deploy vPars, and the intent of this example is to illustrate just one of them.

1. *Determine the Virtual Partition Environment*

   This step encompasses choosing where vPars will be installed, determining how many vPars will be deployed, and deciding the initial configuration of the vPars. In this example, two vPars will be deployed on an nPartition with four CPUs.

2. *Plan for Virtual Partitions*

   This step involves capturing the hardware configuration of the system where vPars will be deployed. Most important aspect of this phase is capturing the output of ioscan for I/O configuration purposes.

3. *Install Virtual Partition Software*

   This step consists of installing the Virtual Partitions software on the instance of HP-UX where the first vPar will be created. In this example, HP-UX is already running on the nPartition where the first vPars will be booted so the installation of the Virtual Partitions software is performed in the same way traditional HP-UX software bundles are installed.

4. *Create the First vPar*

   After installing the vPar software, the first vPar can be created. The vPar command-line interface is used to create Virtual Partitions.

5. *Boot the Virtual Partition Monitor*

After creating the first vPar, it must be booted. In order to boot a vPar, the virtual partition monitor must be loaded. The vPar monitor is loaded by shutting down the operating system running in the server and then booting the vPar monitor from the firmware interface in much the same way the HP-UX kernel is loaded.

6. *Load the First Virtual Partition*

Having loaded the virtual partition monitor, a text-based interface is available for performing various vPar tasks, such as loading vPars. Loading a vPar starts the HP-UX boot process as it would traditionally be performed from the firmware interface.

7. *Create the Second Virtual Partition*

The next step is to create the second vPar. This step involves using the vPar command-line interface from within the first vPar to create the second vPar.

8. *Boot the Second Virtual Partition*

Booting the second vPar is a bit simpler than booting the first one because the vPar monitor is already running. As a result, a command can be issued from the first vPar to boot the second vPar. In fact, as is shown in this example, the second vPar can be directed to boot directly from an Ignite-UX server.

9. *Configure vPars to Automatically Boot*

After creating and booting both vPars, there are steps that must be performed in order for all of the vPars to be booted automatically.

10. *Automate the CPU migration*

The final step in this scenario involves an elementary example of how CPUs can be automatically migrated from on vPar to another.

The Virtual Partition Environment

The environment for this scenario is an HP nPartition server. An nPartition with one cell, four CPUs, and 2GB of memory will host two vPars. See Table 5-1 for the details of the nPartition.

Table 5-1 Configuration of nPartition

nPartition Name	nPartition ID	Num CPUs	Amount Mem	I/O Slots
zoo6	6	4	2 GB	12

Table 5-2 Configuration of Virtual Partitions

vPar Name	Num Bound CPUs	Max CPUs	Amount Mem	I/O Slots
zoo24	1	3	1 GB	2
zoo25	1	3	1 GB	3

Within the zoo6 nPartition, two vPars will be created. Each of the vPars will be assigned one bound CPU. Each vPar will also be assigned 1GB of memory, a networking interface, and interfaces for two boot devices. This configuration leaves two unbound CPUs for the purpose of migrating between the vPars as the workloads demand.

Figure 5-3 shows the hardware diagram of the zoo6 nPartition. HP nPartition servers have exactly one I/O PCI slot per LBA. When an LBA is assigned to a vPar, the associated PCI slot, card, and all devices under the LBA are assigned to the vPar.

The I/O device hardware paths in HP-UX within HP nPartition servers have the following format:

```
<cell id>/<SBA>/<LBA>/<PCI card specific>
```

The hardware paths for this nPartition start with 6 because the zoo6 nPartition contains a single cell with an ID of 6. There is a single system bus adapter (SBA), SBA 0, which yields a zero (0) in the second field of the hardware paths. Finally, there are 12 LBAs below each SBA. The LBAs are numbered starting at zero, but they are not numbered sequentially because of the double-bandwidth (2X) PCI slots. Therefore, ioscan output should be relied upon to find the hardware paths associated with each LBA for input to the Virtual Partitions commands.

The core I/O card in slot 6/0/0 contains the console device for the nPartition and a LAN card. This is the LAN interface that will be used as the primary LAN card for the zoo24 vPar. The SCSI card in slot 6/0/6 will also be assigned to zoo24. The zoo25 vPar will be assigned the slots 6/0/8, 6/0/9, and 6/0/10, with the result that the vPar will own a LAN card and two SCSI cards. In this scenario, there are extra LBAs and I/O cards that not being used and are not assigned to

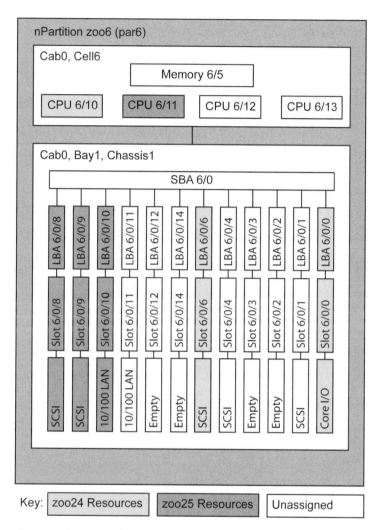

Figure 5-3 Superdome nPartition I/O Hardware Diagram

any virtual partition. These LBAs and I/O cards can be utilized in the future by assigning the LBA to the vPar requiring the capabilities.

Planning for Virtual Partitions

Proper planning for vPars greatly simplifies the implementation process. Before performing any vPar tasks, the state of the server should be captured for future reference. At a minimum, output of the parstatus and ioscan commands should be saved or printed.

The output of `parstatus`, shown in Listing 5-1, provides the details of the nPartition where the vPars will be created. The nPartition's boot paths, CPU count, and memory information have been highlighted.

Listing 5-1   Status of nPartition

```
# parstatus -V -p 6
[Partition]
Partition Number       : 6
Partition Name         : zoo6
Status                 : active
IP address             : 0.0.0.0
Primary Boot Path       : 6/0/6/0/0.2.0
Alternate Boot Path     : 0/0/0/0/0.0.0
HA Alternate Boot Path : 0/0/0/0/0.0.0
PDC Revision           : 35.3
IODCH Version          : 5C70
CPU Speed              : 552 MHz
Core Cell              : cab0,cell6


[Cell]
                        CPU     Memory
                        OK/     (GB)
Hardware    Actual      Deconf/ OK/
Location    Usage       Max     Deconf    Connected To
========== ============ ======= ========= ====================
cab0,cell6 active  core  4/0/4     2.0/ 0.0 cab0,bay1,chassis1

[Chassis]
                                  Core Connected  Par
Hardware Location   Usage         IO   To         Num
================== ============ ==== ========== ===
cab0,bay1,chassis1  active        yes  cab0,cell6 6
```

Capturing the I/O configuration of the server with `ioscan` is crucial because booting the vPar monitor results in limited I/O visibility. Only the I/O information for the resources that have been assigned to the local vPar is visible through tools such as `ioscan` after the vPar monitor is booted. Creating or modifying vPars can be difficult without a snapshot of the server's configuration before booting the vPar monitor.

I/O visibility is limited because the vPar monitor applies a filter to restrict the hardware components visible to each vPar to only those which have been assigned. Even though the I/O data being sought is for resources that are not assigned to any vPar, the only detailed I/O information available is for resources assigned to the local Virtual Partition. The `vparstatus` command has an option to show the available resources, but this option does not provide any I/O details beyond the LBA level. Therefore, `ioscan` output such as the one shown in Listing 5-2 should be captured for future reference. The most relevant items are highlighted, as they will be referenced in upcoming vPar commands.

tip

Always capture the output of ioscan before booting the virtual partition monitor. After the vPar monitor is booted, only resources assigned to the local vPar are visible.

Listing 5-2 Ioscan of nPartition before Virtual Partition Creation

```
# ioscan -k
H/W Path          Class       Description
=========================================================
                  root
6                 cell
6/0               ioa         System Bus Adapter (804)
6/0/0             ba          Local PCI Bus Adapter (782)
6/0/0/0/0         tty         PCI Serial (103c1048)
6/0/0/1/0         lan         HP PCI 10/100Base-TX Core
6/0/1             ba          Local PCI Bus Adapter (782)
6/0/1/0/0         ext_bus     SCSI C87x Ultra Wide Differential
6/0/1/0/0.7       target
6/0/1/0/0.7.0     ctl         Initiator
6/0/2             ba          Local PCI Bus Adapter (782)
6/0/3             ba          Local PCI Bus Adapter (782)
6/0/4             ba          Local PCI Bus Adapter (782)
6/0/4/0/0         ext_bus     SCSI C87x Ultra Wide Differential
6/0/4/0/0.7       target
6/0/4/0/0.7.0     ctl         Initiator
6/0/4/0/1         ext_bus     SCSI C87x Ultra Wide Differential
6/0/4/0/1.7       target
6/0/4/0/1.7.0     ctl         Initiator
6/0/6             ba          Local PCI Bus Adapter (782)
6/0/6/0/0         ext_bus     SCSI C896 Ultra2 Wide LVD
6/0/6/0/0.2       target
6/0/6/0/0.2.0     disk        HP 18.2GST318404LC
6/0/6/0/0.4       target
6/0/6/0/0.4.0     disk        HP 18.2GST318404LC
6/0/6/0/0.6       target
6/0/6/0/0.6.0     disk        HP 18.2GST318404LC
6/0/6/0/0.7       target
6/0/6/0/0.7.0     ctl         Initiator
6/0/6/0/1         ext_bus     SCSI C896 Ultra2 Wide LVD
6/0/6/0/1.7       target
6/0/6/0/1.7.0     ctl         Initiator
6/0/8             ba          Local PCI Bus Adapter (782)
6/0/8/0/0         ext_bus     SCSI C895 Ultra2 Wide LVD
6/0/8/0/0.7       target
6/0/8/0/0.7.0     ctl         Initiator
6/0/8/0/0.8       target
6/0/8/0/0.8.0     disk        HP 18.2GST318406LC
6/0/9             ba          Local PCI Bus Adapter (782)
6/0/9/0/0         ext_bus     SCSI C895 Ultra2 Wide LVD
6/0/9/0/0.7       target
```

```
H/W Path          Class     Description
===========================================================
6/0/9/0/0.7.0     ctl       Initiator
6/0/9/0/0.8       target
6/0/9/0/0.8.0     disk      HP 18.2GST318406LC
6/0/10            ba        Local PCI Bus Adapter (782)
6/0/10/0/0        lan       HP A5230A/B5509BA PCI 10/100Base-TX
6/0/11            ba        Local PCI Bus Adapter (782)
6/0/11/0/0        lan       HP A5230A/B5509BA PCI 10/100Base-TX
6/0/12            ba        Local PCI Bus Adapter (782)
6/0/14            ba        Local PCI Bus Adapter (782)
6/5               memory    Memory
6/10              processor Processor
6/11              processor Processor
6/12              processor Processor
6/13              processor Processor
```

Installation of Virtual Partitions

Installing Virtual Partitions is straightforward. The two most common methods used for installing the vPar software are (a) using an Ignite-UX server to install HP-UX and vPars together, and (b) installing and booting HP-UX and then installing the vPar software as a separate step afterward. It is generally recommended that you set up an Ignite-UX server and install HP-UX and the vPar software in a single step because it expedites the process of deploying vPars. See the Ignite-UX & vPars Cookbook referenced in Appendix A for details on setting up an Ignite-UX server for vPar deployment.

For this example, the process of installing vPars will not be covered in detail. It is assumed the vPars software has been installed on the zoo6 nPartition. Running the swlist command shows the vPars software is in fact installed on the zoo6 nPartition.

```
# swlist ¦ grep Virtual
  T1335AC                   A.03.01.03    HP-UX Virtual Partitions
```

Even though the vPars product is installed, it has not been configured for use. The vPar monitor is not running and no vPars have been created. This is evident by running the vparstatus command.

```
# vparstatus
vparstatus: Error: Virtual partition monitor not running.
```

Create the First Virtual Partition

Creating the first vPar is similar to the creation of subsequent vPars with one important difference. Because the vPar Monitor is not yet running, the resources assigned to the vPar are not validated by the vPar commands. It is possible to create the first vPar in such a way that it will not be bootable. For example, too much memory could be assigned to the vPar, or I/O devices that don't exist in the nPartition could be assigned. As a result, it is important to ensure that the paths and resources assigned to the first vPar are manually validated against the resources available in the system as captured during the planning process. The command shown in Listing 5-3 creates the first vPar.

note

The LBA with the hardware console must be assigned to the first vPar created.

Listing 5-3 Create Virtual Partition Command

```
# /usr/sbin/vparcreate -p zoo24 \
> -a cpu::1 \
> -a cpu:::1:3 \
> -a mem::1024 \
> -a io:6/0/0 \
> -a io:6/0/6/0/0.2.0:boot \
> -a io:6/0/6/0/0.4.0:altboot
```

The following list describes each argument and its purpose in the command:

-p zoo24: The vPar is named zoo24.

-a cpu::1: The number of CPUs that are assigned to the vPar.

-a cpu:::1:3: The minimum number of CPUs that will be bound to this vPar is one and maximum number of CPUs is three.

-a mem::1024: The vPar contains 1GB of memory.

-a io:6/0/0: All of the I/O devices below the LBA with hardware address 6/0/0 are assigned to the zoo24 vPar. Adding the 6/0/0 LBA assigns the core I/O card to the zoo24 vPar. This assigns the physical console and core LAN device to the vPar. Remember, I/O resources assigned at the LBA level assigns everything below the 6/0/0 LBA to zoo24.

-a io:6/0/6/0/0.2.0:boot: This option specifies the primary boot device.

-a io:6/0/6/0/0.4.0:altboot: This option specifies the alternate boot device.

The final two options are of particular importance because beyond specifying the primary and alternate boot devices, the options also implicitly assign the LBA 6/0/6 to the vPar. Just as assigning 6/0/0 adds everything under that path, the implicit assignment of 6/0/6 results in no other vPar having access to devices under the 6/0/6 LBA. The addition of the option -a io:6/0/6 would have explicitly assigned the LBA to the vPar, but it would not have changed the behavior of the vPars; the only effect would have been the output shown by vparstatus. LBAs implicitly assigned to vPars are not shown by vparstatus; only explicitly assigned LBAs are shown.

The command shown in Listing 5-3 creates the first vPar using the default vPar database file located at /stand/vpdb. If the default vPar database doesn't exist it will be automatically created. In this example, zoo24 was the first vPar to be created and the file didn't exist, so the vparcreate command created the file and defined the zoo24 partition.

The zoo24 vPar has now been created, but it is not yet active. Listing 5-4 shows the output of the vparstatus command after creating the first vPar. The initial warning makes it clear the vPar monitor is still not running. The zoo24 vPar exists in the database and has a minimum of one CPU and a maximum of three. Additionally, the LBA 6/0/0 is assigned to the vPar and the two boot devices are also specified. Notice the 6/0/6 LBA is not explicitly mentioned in the vparstatus output, but in fact it is assigned to the vPar.

Listing 5-4 Detailed Virtual Partition Status

```
# vparstatus -v -p zoo24
vparstatus: Warning: Virtual partition monitor
not running, Requested resources shown.
[Virtual Partition Details]
Name:          zoo24
State:         N/A
Attributes:    Dynamic,Autoboot
Kernel Path:   /stand/vmunix
Boot Opts:

[CPU Details]
Min/Max:   1/3
Bound by User [Path]:
Bound by Monitor [Path]:   <no path>
Unbound [Path]:

[IO Details]
   6.0.0
   6.0.6.0.0.2.0.0.0.0.0   BOOT
   6.0.6.0.0.4.0.0.0.0.0,  ALTBOOT

[Memory Details]
Specified [Base   /Range]:
          (bytes) (MB)
Total Memory (MB):   1024
```

Virtual Partition States

Before diving into the process of booting the vPar monitor and the first vPar, a discussion of the vPar states is in order. The states of a vPar are shown in Figure 5-4. These states are helpful in interpreting the output of the vparstatus command and managing vPars. Listing 5-4 shows the zoo24 vPar is in the *N/A* state. In this case, the vPar monitor has not been booted, so the vPar can't be in any other state. The following list describes all of the vPar states and an explanation of when a vPar can be in each state.

N/A is the initial state for vPars when the vPar monitor is not running or an alternate database has been passed to the vparstatus command. In both of these cases, the

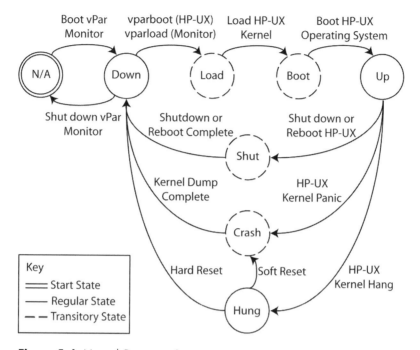

Figure 5-4 Virtual Partition States

vPar is not running and cannot be started without first booting the vPar monitor with the given vPar database.

Down is the vPar state that occurs when the vPar monitor is running but the vPar has not been booted with the `vparboot` command from the HP-UX command line or the `vparload` command from the vPar monitor.

Load is the first state a vPar will transition to upon being booted with the `vparboot` or `vparload` command. While in this state, the vPar's kernel is being loaded into memory. After loading the kernel into memory, the vPar automatically transitions to the boot state without user intervention. Therefore, this state is labeled as a transitory state.

Boot is the state a vPar goes through while booting the HP-UX operating system. As with the load state, the boot state is transitory and the vPar will transition to the up state without user interaction.

Up is the state a vPar will occupy a majority of the time. This state is where workloads are running and traditional HP-UX administration tasks, such as configuring users and installing software, can be performed.

Shut is the state a vPar goes through when it has been shut down with the HP-UX `shutdown` or `reboot` commands. This state is also transitory; the vPar will automatically transition to the down state after the shutdown process is complete.

Crash is a state administrators hope to never see. A vPar enters this state when the HP-UX kernel panics. While in this transitory state, a kernel dump is performed. When the kernel dump is complete, the vPar returns to the down state.

Hung is another undesirable vPar state. In this state the vPar is not responding and most likely needs to be reset using the `vparreset` command. Depending on the type of reset performed, the vPar will transition either to the crash state (as a result of a soft reset) or the down state (as a result of a hard reset).

Booting the First Virtual Partition

In order to boot a vPar to the up state, the next step is booting the vPar monitor. This is accomplished by booting the vPar monitor by interacting with the firmware interfaces to specify the path of the vPar monitor. Listing 5-5 shows an example of interacting with the Initial System Loader (ISL) to boot the vPar monitor at /stand/vpmon instead of the default HP-UX kernel.

Listing 5-5 Virtual Partition Monitor Boot Process

```
---- Main Menu -------------------------------------------------

    Command                         Description
    -------                         -----------
    BOot [PRI¦HAA¦ALT¦<path>]       Boot from specified path
    PAth [PRI¦HAA¦ALT] [<path>]     Display or modify a path
    SEArch [ALL¦<cell>¦<path>]      Search for boot devices
    ScRoll [ON¦OFF]                 Display or change scroll capability

    COnfiguration menu              Displays or sets boot
    INformation menu                Displays hardware info
    SERvice menu                    Displays service commands

    DIsplay                         Redisplay the current menu
    HElp [<menu>¦<command>]         Display help for menu
    REBOOT                          Restart Partition
    RECONFIGRESET                   Reset to allow Reconfig
----
Main Menu: Enter command or menu > bo

    Primary Boot Path:  6/0/6/0/0.2


 Do you wish to stop at the ISL prompt? (y/n) >> y

Initializing boot Device.


Boot IO Dependent Code (IODC) Revision 0


Boot Path Initialized.
```

```
HARD Booted.

ISL Revision A.00.43  Apr 12, 2000

ISL> hpux /stand/vpmon

Boot
: disk(6/0/6/0/0.2.0.0.0.0.0;0)/stand/vpmon
679936 + 190216 + 17306888 start 0x23000

Welcome to VPMON (type '?' for a list of commands)

MON>
```

When the vPar monitor is loaded without arguments as shown in Listing 5-5, it will not automatically boot any of the vPars. Instead the monitor stops at the vPar monitor prompt, MON>.
From this prompt, several vPar specific commands are available. The most commonly used commands are vparload and reboot.

The vparload command can be used in several ways. To boot all of the vPars that have their
auto attribute set (the default setting) simply specify the vparload -auto command. All vPars
can be booted, regardless of their auto attribute by using the vparload -all option. Finally, specific vPars can be booted using the vparload -p <partition> option. This is the option used
in Listing 5-6 to boot the zoo24 vPar. The output from the HP-UX boot process has been suppressed from the listing.

Listing 5-6 Loading First Virtual Partition

```
MON> vparload
Usage: vparload -auto ¦ -all
       vparload -p <partition> [-o <boot opts>] [-b <kern path>]
               [-B <boot device>]
MON> vparload -p zoo24
[MON] Booting zoo24...
[MON] Console client set to zoo24
[MON] Console server set to zoo24

[zoo24]

[MON] zoo24 loaded

<normal HP-UX boot follows>
```

With the HP-UX boot process completes, the first vPar has been successfully booted and
in the up state. The output of the vparstatus command executed from the HP-UX within
the first vPar is shown in Listing 5-7. The vPar zoo24 is assigned one bound CPU, the minimum
number of CPUs is one, and the maximum number of CPUs is three. The vPar has 1024MB of
memory.

Listing 5-7 Virtual Partition Status

```
# vparstatus -v -p zoo24
[Virtual Partition Details]
Name:         zoo24
State:        Up
Attributes:   Dynamic,Autoboot
Kernel Path:  /stand/vmunix
Boot Opts:

[CPU Details]
Min/Max:   1/3
Bound by User [Path]:
Bound by Monitor [Path]:  6.10
Unbound [Path]:

[IO Details]
   6.0.0
   6.0.6.0.0.2.0.0.0.0.0  BOOT
   6.0.6.0.0.4.0.0.0.0.0, ALTBOOT

[Memory Details]
Specified [Base  /Range]:
        (bytes) (MB)
Total Memory (MB):  1024
```

Before creating the second vPar, closely examine Listing 5-8. Notice that the `ioscan` output shows only the I/O devices under LBAs 6/0/0 and 6/0/6. There are 12 LBAs in the zoo6 nPartition, so the remaining 10 LBAs are hidden from view by the vPar monitor. This illustrates the importance of capturing the `ioscan` output during the planning phase so it can be referred to during the creation of subsequent vPars.

Listing 5-8 Ioscan after Booting Virtual Partition

```
# ioscan -k
H/W Path        Class      Description
=========================================================
                root
6               cell
6/0             ioa        System Bus Adapter (804)
6/0/0           ba         Local PCI Bus Adapter (782)
6/0/0/0/0       tty        PCI Serial (103c1048)
6/0/0/1/0       lan        HP PCI 10/100Base-TX Core
6/0/6           ba         Local PCI Bus Adapter (782)
6/0/6/0/0       ext_bus    SCSI C896 Ultra2 Wide LVD
6/0/6/0/0.2     target
6/0/6/0/0.2.0   disk       HP 18.2GST318404LC
6/0/6/0/0.4     target
6/0/6/0/0.4.0   disk       HP 18.2GST318404LC
```

```
H/W Path        Class      Description
=======================================================
6/0/6/0/0.6     target
6/0/6/0/0.6.0   disk       HP 18.2GST318404LC
6/0/6/0/0.7     target
6/0/6/0/0.7.0   ctl        Initiator
6/0/6/0/1       ext_bus    SCSI C896 Ultra2 Wide LVD
6/0/6/0/1.7     target
6/0/6/0/1.7.0   ctl        Initiator
6/5             memory     Memory
6/10            processor  Processor
6/11            processor  Processor
6/12            processor  Processor
6/13            processor  Processor
64              tty        Virtual Console Client
65              tty        Virtual Console Server
```

Creating the Second Virtual Partition

After booting the first virtual partition, the second will be created. Most of the options for creating the vPar are similar to those specified when creating the first vPar. Of particular interest, though, is the fact that the boot and alternate boot devices are no longer under the same LBA. This provides an additional level of availability, as the failure of the PCI device under LBA 6/0/8 will not make the vPar unbootable. Instead, the PCI device under the LBA 6/0/9 can be used as an alternate boot device. This configuration assigns 6/0/8, 6/0/9, and 6/0/10 to the zoo25 vPar. The first two LBAs are implicitly assigned and the last one is explicitly assigned.

Listing 5-9 Create Second Virtual Partition Command

```
# vparcreate -p zoo25 \
> -a cpu::1 \
> -a cpu:::1:3 \
> -a mem::1024 \
> -a io:6/0/8/0/0.8.0:boot \
> -a io:6/0/9/0/0.8.0:altboot \
> -a io:6/0/10
```

At this point, both vPars have been created. The vparstatus output shown in Listing 5-10 shows both vPars exist but the zoo25 vPar has not been booted; it is in the down state. If the boot disk specified in the vparcreate command for zoo25 already contains the HP-UX operating system and the vPar software, then the vPar may be booted from its primary boot disk using the vparboot command. In this case, the boot disk does not contain an operating system so it must be installed using Ignite-UX.

Listing 5-10 Status of Virtual Partitions

```
# vparstatus
[Virtual Partition]
Boot
Virtual Partition Name          State Attributes Kernel Path
Opts
============================== ===== ========== =============
zoo24                            Up    Dyn,Auto   /stand/vmunix
zoo25                            Down  Dyn,Auto   /stand/vmunix

[Virtual Partition Resource Summary]
                                        CPU    Num
                                CPU    Bound/  IO
Virtual Partition Name          Min/Max Unbound devs  Total MB
============================== ======= ======== ====  ========
zoo24                            1/ 3     1    0     4   1024
zoo25                            1/ 3     1    0     5   1024
```

Booting the Second Virtual Partition

The zoo25 vPar can now be booted from an Ignite-UX server with the hostname of seminole. In this example, there is only one remaining vPar to be installed with Ignite-UX. In situations where multiple vPars have been created and require an operating system to be installed, the process of installing operating systems can be streamlined by using the approach shown in Listing 5-11. Each vPar that requires installation of an operating system can be booted in parallel from an Ignite-UX server.

tip

> Multiple operating systems may be installed in parallel after booting the first vPar. The vparboot command with the -I option can be used for each vPar requiring an operating system to be installed. This results in provisioning the operating systems for each vPar in parallel.

The output shown in Listing 5-11 illustrates the process of booting the newly created zoo25 vPar from an Ignite-UX server. Notice the <ctrl-a> in the listing after the vPar is loaded. The <ctrl-a> command was manually issued at the console to toggle between the vPar consoles. In this case, the vparboot command was issued from the zoo24 operating system on the physical console assigned to zoo24.

The consoles for all the vPars in a server are accessible from the physical console. From the physical console, each of the individual vPar consoles can be accessed using the <ctrl-a> keys. This command cycles through the consoles for all of the vPars in the server.

The output shown at the end of the listing is that of the standard Ignite-UX interface. The operating system for zoo25 is configured and installed just as any operating system would be in a non-vPar environment, assuming the Ignite-UX depot contains the vPar software.

warning

Booting vPars from an Ignite-UX server provides a streamlined installation process. However, the Ignite-UX depots must be properly configured with the vPar software and its dependencies in order for the operating system to boot in a vPar environment.

Listing 5-11 Booting of Second Virtual Partition

```
# vparboot -p zoo25 -I seminole,WINSTALL
vparboot: Booting zoo25.  Please wait...
#
[MON] zoo25 loaded
<ctrl-a>
[zoo25]
.
.
.


                     Welcome to Ignite-UX!

  Use the <tab> key to navigate between fields, and the arrow
  Keys within fields.  Use the <return/enter> key to select
  an item.  Use the <return> or <space-bar> to pop-up a choices
  list.  If the menus are not clear, select the "Help" item
  for more information.

  Hardware Summary:        System Model: 9000/800/SD64000
  +--------------------+----------------+------------------+
  ¦ Disks: 2  ( 33.9GB) ¦ Floppies: 0   ¦ LAN cards:   1   ¦
  ¦ CD/DVDs:        0  ¦ Tapes:    0   ¦ Memory:    942Mb ¦
  ¦ Graphics Ports: 0  ¦ IO Buses: 2   ¦ CPUs:        3   ¦
  +--------------------+----------------+------------------+

              [      Install HP-UX       ]

              [    Run a Recovery Shell  ]

              [     Advanced Options     ]


      [  Reboot  ]                       [  Help  ]
```

Listing 5-12 shows the status of the vPars after the installation of the HP-UX operating system is complete and the vPar has been booted. Notice both zoo24 and zoo25 are in the up state.

Listing 5-12 Status of Final Virtual Partition Configuration

```
# vparstatus
[Virtual Partition]
Boot
Virtual Partition Name          State Attributes Kernel Path
Opts
=============================== ===== ========== ==============
zoo24                           Up    Dyn,Auto   /stand/vmunix
zoo25                           Up    Dyn,Auto   /stand/vmunix

[Virtual Partition Resource Summary]
                                              CPU    Num
                                 CPU       Bound/   IO
Virtual Partition Name          Min/Max   Unbound  devs  Total MB
=============================== ========= ======== ==== ========
zoo24                             1/  3     1    0     4  1024
zoo25                             1/  3     1    0     5  1024
#
```

Configuring an nPartition and Virtual Partitions for Auto-Booting

The two vPars are now configured and running properly. However, the boot sequence for the vPar monitor and the two vPars requires manual interaction. This may not be obvious because the vparstatus output shown in Listing 5-12 indicates that both of the vPars have the auto attribute set. However, additional configuration steps are necessary for two reasons. First, each vPar's auto attribute is used by the vPar monitor, not the firmware of the server where vPars are running. Therefore, firmware must be set to automatically boot independent of the vPars' attributes. Secondly, the vPar monitor must be invoked in such a manner as to automatically boot all vPars whose auto attribute set. If you don't configure these settings, the vPars will require manual interaction during booting.

The vPar architecture allows the monitor to be booted from the boot disk of any of the vPars. No one vPar is the "master" vPar. Even if the disk that is used as the primary boot device for the monitor experiences a hardware failure, the worst-case scenario is the loss of a single vPar. The vPar monitor can be booted from another vPar's boot disk and the configuration will be the same as if it was booted from the original.

The following steps are required for an nPartition and the contained vPars to be booted automatically.

1. Configure the auto attribute for each vPar that should be automatically booted. This can be done through vparcreate, vparmodify, or setboot. By default, vPars will be set to automatically boot. In most cases, this step involves ensuring that the default value hasn't been changed.

2. Set primary and alternate boot paths in stable storage. Use either `parmodify` or the firmware interfaces directly to set the boot paths.

3. Modify the `AUTO` file for each boot device to boot the vPar monitor. The vPar monitor must be directed to boot all of the vPars. The `mkboot` command is used to modify the `AUTO` file from the vPar that owns the boot device.

4. Configure firmware to automatically boot from the specified boot paths. This step must be performed from the firmware interface.

note

In a vPar environment, the `setboot` command does not affect the boot paths used by firmware to boot the vPar monitor. Instead, the `setboot` command only affects the boot paths for the local vPar.

Listing 5-13 shows the nPartition status for zoo6. Notice that the primary, alternate, and HA alternate boot paths are set to the same boot devices configured for the zoo24 and zoo25 vPars. The `parmodify` command can be used to set the boot paths when they have not already been set using the nPartition commands or the firmware interfaces for the nPartition.

Listing 5-13   nPartition Status with Boot Paths

```
# parstatus -V -p 6
[Partition]
Partition Number      : 6
Partition Name        : zoo6
Status                : active
IP address            : 0.0.0.0
Primary Boot Path     : 6/0/6/0/0.2.0
Alternate Boot Path   : 6/0/8/0/0.8.0
HA Alternate Boot Path : 6/0/9/0/0.8.0
PDC Revision          : 35.3
IODCH Version         : 5C70
CPU Speed             : 552 MHz
Core Cell             : cab0,cell6

[Cell]
                        CPU     Memory
                        OK/     (GB)
Hardware    Actual      Deconf/ OK/
Location    Usage       Max     Deconf    Connected To
==========  ==========  ======= =========  ===================
cab0,cell6 active core  4/0/4    2.0/ 0.0 cab0,bay1,chassis1
```

```
[Chassis]
                                     Core Connected  Par
Hardware Location    Usage          IO   To          Num
==================== ============== ==== ========== ===
cab0,bay1,chassis1   active         yes  cab0,cell6 6
```

After setting the boot paths used by firmware, each of the boot disks must be configured to load the vPar monitor. Notice that in Listing 5-14, the primary boot device for zoo24 is shown in the ioscan output. The raw disk device is used as an argument to the mkboot command. The mkboot command shown at the end of the listing modifies the AUTO file on the specified disk. The AUTO file is used when booting and in this case boot the vPar monitor. Also note that the -a argument is passed to the vPar monitor. This argument causes the vPar monitor to boot all of the vPars whose auto attribute is set. The mkboot command must be executed on the vPar that owns the respective boot devices. In this example, only the nPartition's primary boot device for the zoo6 nPartition is owned by the vPar zoo24.

Listing 5-14 Set Primary Boot Disk to Auto Boot vPar Monitor (from zoo24)

```
# ioscan -funC disk
Class    I  H/W Path        Driver S/W State   H/W Type
============================================================
disk     0  6/0/6/0/0.2.0   sdisk CLAIMED       DEVICE
                            /dev/dsk/c3t2d0     /dev/rdsk/c3t2d0
disk     1  6/0/6/0/0.4.0   sdisk CLAIMED       DEVICE
                            /dev/dsk/c3t4d0     /dev/rdsk/c3t4d0
disk     2  6/0/6/0/0.6.0   sdisk CLAIMED       DEVICE
                            /dev/dsk/c3t6d0     /dev/rdsk/c3t6d0
# mkboot -a "hpux /stand/vpmon -a" /dev/rdsk/c3t2d0
```

To achieve the highest level of availability, the nPartition's alternate and HA alternate devices must also have their AUTO file set to automatically boot the vPar monitor. Since the zoo25 vPar owns both of the zoo6 nPartition's alternate and HA alternate boot devices, the mkboot command is executed for both of those devices from the same vPar. The mkboot commands are identical except for the path of the target device, and the firmware boots the monitor in the same fashion regardless of the physical boot device.

Listing 5-15 Set Alternate Boot Disks to Auto Boot vPar Monitor (from zoo25)

```
# ioscan -funC disk
Class    I  H/W Path        Driver S/W State   H/W Type
============================================================
disk     3  6/0/8/0/0.8.0   sdisk CLAIMED       DEVICE
                            /dev/dsk/c5t8d0     /dev/rdsk/c5t8d0
disk     4  6/0/9/0/0.8.0   sdisk CLAIMED       DEVICE
                            /dev/dsk/c6t8d0     /dev/rdsk/c6t8d0
# mkboot -a "hpux /stand/vpmon -a" /dev/rdsk/c5t8d0
# mkboot -a "hpux /stand/vpmon -a" /dev/rdsk/c6t8d0
```

The nPartition's primary, alternate, and HA alternate boot devices have been properly configured to boot the vPar monitor and all of the vPars. The final step is configuring firmware to automatically boot from these boot paths. Listing 5-16 shows the boot console handler (BCH) firmware commands for setting the boot order and actions. This sequence of commands tells the firmware to attempt to boot from the nPartition's primary, HA alternate, and alternate boot paths, in that order. The value at the end of each of the commands specifies the action to take if booting from a given path is unsuccessful. The value 2 specifies that the firmware should continue on to the next path when booting fails. The value 1 specifies that firmware should return to BCH upon failure to boot. In this case, firmware is configured to attempt booting from all three booth paths and return to BCH only if all three are unsuccessful.

Listing 5-16 Set Firmware Path Flags to Automatically Boot

```
Configuration Menu: Enter command > pf PRI 2

    Primary Boot Path Action
        Boot Actions:  Boot from this path.
                       If unsuccessful, go to next path.

Configuration Menu: Enter command > pf HAA 2

HA Alternate Boot Path Action
        Boot Actions:  Boot from this path.
                       If unsuccessful, go to next path.

Configuration Menu: Enter command > pf ALT 1

   Alternate Boot Path Action
        Boot Actions:  Boot from this path.
                       If unsuccessful, go to BCH.

Configuration Menu: Enter command >
```

All of the steps necessary for automatically booting the nPartition and the contained vPars have been completed. The nPartition zoo6 will automatically boot the vPar monitor and pass the vPar monitor the appropriate flag to indicate that it should automatically boot all vPars. Listing 5-17 shows the fully automatic boot process.

Listing 5-17 Example Automatic Booting of Virtual Partition Monitor and Virtual Partitions

```
Firmware Version  35.3

Duplex Console IO Dependent Code (IODC) revision 1
    ----------------------------------------------------------------------
      (c) Copyright 1995-2002, Hewlett-Packard Company, All rights reserved
    ----------------------------------------------------------------------
```

```
          Cab/    Cell     ------- Processor --------   Cache Size
   Cell   Slot    State     #    Speed      State       Inst    Data
   ----   ----   --------  ---   --------  ----------   ------  ------
     6    0/6    Active     0    552 MHz   Active       512 KB  1 MB
                            1    552 MHz   Idle         512 KB  1 MB
                            2    552 MHz   Idle         512 KB  1 MB
                            3    552 MHz   Idle         512 KB  1 MB


      Primary Boot Path:  6/0/6/0/0.2
         Boot Actions:  Boot from this path.
                        If unsuccessful, go to next path.

HA Alternate Boot Path:  6/0/9/0/0.8
         Boot Actions:  Boot from this path.
                        If unsuccessful, go to next path.

   Alternate Boot Path:  6/0/8/0/0.8
         Boot Actions:  Boot from this path.
                        If unsuccessful, go to BCH.

         Console Path:  6/0/0/0/0.0


Attempting to boot using the primary path.
-----------------------------------------------------------


  To discontinue, press any key within 10 seconds.

  10 seconds expired.
  Proceeding...


Initializing boot Device.


Boot IO Dependent Code (IODC) Revision 0


Boot Path Initialized.


HARD Booted.

ISL Revision A.00.43  Apr 12, 2000

SL booting  hpux /stand/vpmon -a

Boot
: disk(6/0/6/0/0.2.0.0.0.0.0;0)/stand/vpmon
679936 + 190216 + 17306888 start 0x23000
[MON] Booting zoo25...
[MON] Booting zoo24...
[MON] Console client set to zoo25
```

```
[MON] zoo25 loaded
[MON] Console server set to zoo24

[zoo25]

[MON] zoo24 loaded
```

Using a Script to Migrate CPUs

Having booted the vPars and with them up and running, the example could stop here. Each of the vPars is running as an independent operating system with full operating system isolation. However, there are two unused CPUs in the nPartition. Furthermore, the nature of the workloads in zoo24 and zoo25 allows the CPUs to be migrated between the two vPars, which would mean better performance for each of the workloads during their peak utilization times.

The CPUs could be migrated manually on demand, but a preferred method would be an automated process for moving CPUs when they are needed. The script shown in Listing 5-18 automates the process of migrating a specified number of CPUs from one vPar to another. The script starts by parsing the command-line arguments and ensuring that all required arguments are given. The final steps remove the specified number of CPUs from the source vPar and add the CPUs to the destination vPar.

While this script illustrates the flexibility of vPars and the power provided by having the ability to dynamically move CPUs based on workload demand, it isn't suited for production use. Most important, it does no error-checking to ensure that the commands will succeed. Instead, it just tries to perform the operation and if it doesn't work, it returns the error. In addition, before this script is initially executed, the two unassigned CPUs must be assigned to one of the vPars.

Listing 5-18 Script for Migrating CPUs

```
#!/usr/bin/sh
# *************************************************************
# Migrate CPUs
# -------------------------------------------------------------
#
# Usage:
#  migrate_cpus -s <source vpar> -d <dest vpar> -c <count>
#
# Description:
#
# This script will move <count> CPUs from <source vpar> to
# <dest vpar>.
#
# This script is for illustration purposes only.
#
# *************************************************************
```

```
#
# Initialize variables
#
SOURCE=""
DEST=""
COUNT=""
USAGE="migrate_cpus -s <source vpar> -d <dest vpar> -c <count>"

#
# Parse the command line arguments, see getopt(1) for usage details.
#
set -- $(getopt c:d:s: $*)

if [ $? -ne 0 ]; then
  print -u2 "$USAGE"
  exit 1
fi

while [ $# -gt 0 ]; do
  case "$1" in
  '-c')
    COUNT=$2
    shift 2
    ;;
  '-d')
    DEST=$2
    shift 2
    ;;
  '-s')
    SOURCE=$2
    shift 2
    ;;
  --)
    break      # this is the end of parameters
    ;;
  esac
done

#
# Ensure all of the required parameters were specified
#

if [ -z "$SOURCE" -o -z "$DEST" -o -z "$COUNT" ]; then
  print -u2 "ERROR: Missing required argument(s)"
  print -u2 "$USAGE"
  exit 1
fi

vparmodify -p $SOURCE -d cpu::$COUNT || exit $?

sleep 10

vparmodify -p $DEST -a cpu::$COUNT

exit $?
```

The `sleep` command between the two `vparmodify` commands is required because the removal of CPUs from a vPar is asynchronous. The `vparmodify` command that removes the CPUs will return immediately. However, the CPUs will be delayed for an indeterminate amount of time before they are actually removed from the vPar and become available for assignment to another vPar. This is a result of pending threads and processes being serviced by the CPUs. A 10-second sleep is sufficient for most cases, but in fact a busy system could delay the removal of CPUs even longer. This script could be enhanced to poll the `vparstatus` command to check for the availability of the removed CPU.

Using Cron to Automatically Migrate CPUs

The `migrate_cpus` script doesn't provide much value alone. For manual CPU migration, simply invoking the two vparmodify commands in succession isn't difficult. The value of a script such as `migrate_cpus` is realized when it is integrated with a task scheduler such as cron. In this case, two cron entries results in a simple but dynamic computing environment. The `migrate_cpus` command could be added as a set of cron entries such as:

```
# crontab -l
00 22 * * * /usr/local/bin/migrate_cpus -s zoo24 -d zoo25 -c 2
00 06 * * * /usr/local/bin/migrate_cpus -s zoo25 -d zoo24 -c 2
```

The combination of the `migrate_cpus` script and the cron entries illustrates the power and flexibility provided by vPars. However, there are several technical issues with this solution. The `migrate_cpus` script has no concept of what the initial and final states should be. As a result, it is unable to ensure that the configuration is correct at the end of the script. For example, assume that the 10-second delay is not adequate for the removed CPUs to become available. In this situation, assigning the CPUs to the destination vPar would fail. Assuming no user intervention, the next time the script was executed, the first vparmodify command that removes the CPUs from the source vPar would fail. This effectively would result in no CPUs being migrated until an administrator manually intervened and corrected the situation. The HP Virtual Server Environment has a robust solution for this problem. Both *Chapter 15, "Workload Manager,"* and *Chapter 19, "Global Workload Manager,"* describe how to provide tight integration with vPars to enable much more powerful and flexible vPar workload management than shown with the `migrate_cpus` script and cron jobs.

Shutting Down Virtual Partitions

Virtual partitions are shut down and rebooted independent of one another using the traditional HP-UX `reboot` and `shutdown` commands. The only recommended modification to the shutdown process is to run the `vparstatus` command immediately before shutting down the operating system. This forces the vPar monitor's in-memory copy of the database to be synchronized with the file on the vPar's file system. This ensures that the copy of the database on the vPar's file system reflects the most recent configuration changes that may have been made. In a dynamic environment where CPUs are being migrated from one vPar to another on a regular basis, this is especially important.

When vPars are running within nPartitions, there is a special situation that should be understood. If a change is made to an active nPartition containing vPars that results in a pending SCCD such as removing a cell from an nPartition, then all of the vPars must be shut down before the change can take effect. When a pending SCCD is present and a vPar is rebooted, the vPar will not be restarted until all of the vPars are shutdown and the nPartition becomes inactive. This is true regardless of the auto attribute for the vPar. Therefore, it is recommended that changes to an nPartition containing vPars that require the nPar to be shut down for reconfiguration be performed when all of the vPars are in the down state and the cells are inactive.

Summary

Virtual Partitions provide flexibility while retaining isolation in a dynamic Virtual Server Environment. While this chapter did not cover all of the vPar commands, the fundamental vPar terminology was discussed in detail. The example usage scenario discussed the process of creating two vPars in a single nPartition. Each vPar was assigned individual CPU, memory, and I/O resources. This configuration left two unbound CPUs that were migrated between the two vPars. The vPars were then configured to automatically boot from firmware up to the HP-UX operating systems. Finally, a script was presented that enabled a simple interface to be used with cron. This made possible the automated migration of CPUs between the two vPars based on the time of day.

After reading this chapter, it should be clear the problems that Toshi faced at the opening of the chapter can be solved by vPars. vPars make it possible to create dynamic computing environments while retaining operating system isolation. It should also be apparent that vPars play a significant role in HP's Virtual Server Environment.

6

Integrity Virtual Machines

Chapter Overview

The Compatible Time Share System (CTSS) was one of the first time-sharing operating systems invented. The largely forgotten but influential operating system was developed at MIT and first operated in a time-sharing environment in 1961. Its notable accomplishments include being one of the first operating systems to have interuser electronic mail and computerized text editing capabilities. But CTSS's most significant contribution to the computing industry was its demonstration that time-sharing was viable.[1] Time-sharing is an operating system feature that allows multiple users or tasks to be running concurrently on a single hardware platform. Without time-sharing, even the most powerful computers available were limited to a single user or task. The CTSS's time-sharing implementation paved the way for the time-sharing capabilities that are standard in virtually every operating system. Today's servers commonly have thousands of users connected simultaneously, and to a large degree the foundation for that capability was set many decades in the past with the CTSS.

Integrity Virtual Machines in HP's Virtual Server Environment take the time-sharing capabilities first demonstrated by the CTSS to a whole new level. Instead of simply allowing multiple users or tasks to run simultaneously on a single computer, Integrity Virtual Machines (Integrity VM) allows multiple operating systems to be running on a single computer. Integrity Virtual Machines allows a single server with four CPUs, for example, to host multiple operating system instances at the same time. In fact, the number of operating systems isn't even limited to the number of physical CPUs.

Employing Integrity Virtual Machines in an enterprise data center enables higher utilization of hardware resources and provides a flexible and dynamic foundation for workloads. Since multiple operating systems are able to run simultaneously on a single server platform, the operating

---

[1]Fernando J. Corbató, Marjorie Merwin Daggett, Robert C. Daley, "An Experimental Time-Sharing System," available at http://larch-www.lcs.mit.edu:8001/~corbato/sjcc62.

systems with demanding workloads can be allocated the necessary resources to handle the peaks in resource requirements. Those operating systems with workloads demanding little resources receive a fraction of what they would be allocated in a nonvirtualized environment.

As an illustration, consider a software development environment. In typical development environments, each engineer has a dedicated hardware system. When the engineers are not using their system, the resources are left idle and unused. The same development environments can be deployed by using a single server that has a fraction of the hardware resources compared to the total of all the developers' individual systems. Then a virtual machine can be created for each of the developers, giving each of them a fully customizable and isolated operating environment. In such a system, which requires fewer hardware resources, the developers often experience higher performance because the underlying hardware hosting the Integrity Virtual Machines can be more powerful than the individual systems. When resource-intensive tasks such as source-code compilations occur, the resources that are not being used by other developers are allocated to the compilation processes, thereby increasing the overall performance and system utilization.

Another major benefit of Integrity Virtual Machines is the utilization of virtual hardware resources. While this statement may not seem profound, it has dramatic ramifications. When hardware resources are virtualized, an operating system running within Integrity Virtual Machines can be moved from one hardware platform to another without the traditional configuration and compatibility problems one encounters when the hardware resources are not virtualized.

This chapter begins with a discussion of the terminology of Integrity Virtual Machines, then it provides overview of the technology and a VM configuration overview. Next it describes the VM management paradigms. It concludes with an example scenario that illustrates the configuration and management capabilities of Integrity Virtual Machines.

It should be noted this chapter was written using a pre-release version of Integrity VMs and the Integrity VM management GUI. The screens and commands shown in this chapter will vary slightly from the final product.

Integrity Virtual Machines Terminology

Virtual Machine (VM) is a virtualized environment created by the virtual machine monitor that emulates a server and is capable of running an operating system. In fact, unmodified operating systems and executables are capable of running within a virtual machine. Multiple virtual machines are capable of running within a single VM host, and each virtual machine retains a high level of software isolation. Since virtual machines rely on software to provide operating system isolation and resource sharing, they are often referred to as soft partitions.

VM Guest is an operating system running within a virtual machine. The terms "virtual machine" and "VM guest" are often used interchangeably because a VM guest often refers to the guest operating system and the virtual machine as a whole. Every VM guest is allocated a portion of the physical system's CPU, memory, and I/O resources. Multiple VM guests can share CPU and I/O resources; however, the VM guests are unaware the resources are shared. The sharing is handled in the VM host by the VM application.

VM Host is an operating system that acts as the controller for the VM guests. The VM host owns the hardware and performs all of the hardware-dependant operations on behalf of the virtual machine monitor. The VM host is the operating system where management of the physical system is performed and where the VM guests are configured and managed.

Virtual CPU is a CPU allocated to a VM guest. A virtual CPU can be backed by the equivalent of an entire physical CPU or a portion of a CPU in the VM host. In any case, the VM guest is unaware of the mapping between virtual CPUs and physical CPUs. From the VM guest's perspective, it has visibility and complete ownership of the number of CPUs assigned to the VM guest. The VM host is responsible for ensuring that each VM guest receives its minimum CPU entitlement.

Virtual CPU Entitlement is the minimum allocation of CPU resources a VM guest is entitled to. If a VM guest is not consuming all of its entitlement, other VM guests are permitted to utilize the unused resources. When a VM guest requires more resources, it is allowed to borrow from other VM guests provided the resources are not being used. Virtual CPU entitlements are discussed further in the following section.

Virtual Network Switch (vSwitch) is a software component that runs on the VM host. Virtual network switches allow multiple VM guests to connect to one another for a high-speed internal network within the VM host. In addition, virtual network switches allow multiple VMs to connect to the physical network and share network interface cards. Other nodes on the physical network are unaware a virtual network switch is being used when communicating with a VM because every virtual interface has a unique hardware address that is used on the physical network. A virtual network switch is also referred to as a vswitch.

VM Application (vm_app) runs on the VM host and allocates resources on behalf of the VM guest. There is one instance of the vm_app running on the VM host for every running VM guest. The vm_app appears as a process on the VM host and contains one kernel thread for every virtual processor allocated to the VM guest. The vm_app's memory usage is the same as the amount of memory assigned to the VM guest. Finally, the vm_app has open devices for all of the virtual devices assigned to the VM guest.

VM Driver (VMDVR) is a dynamically loadable kernel pseudo-driver that is loaded on the VM host. The purpose of the VMDVR is to perform tasks such as creating, starting, and stopping VM guests at the request of system administrators.

VM Monitor (VMM) is responsible for providing virtualized Itanium processor family (IPF) processors and a virtualized IPF platform.

Integrity Virtual Machines Overview

Integrity Virtual Machines provides soft partitioning that includes sub-CPU granularity, shared I/O devices, security isolation, and dynamic resource allocation. Figure 6-1 shows the high-level architecture of Integrity Virtual Machines. The image depicts three VM guests running on a single VM host. Each of the VM guests has the ability to run workloads in an isolated instance of an operating system, such as HP-UX. In addition, as shown in Figure 6-1, each of the VM guests has virtualized CPU, memory, and I/O hardware resources.

The topmost layer in the VM host portion of the diagram is the virtual machine monitor (VMM). The VMM provides the virtualized platform and virtualized IPF processors to the VM guests. In essence, the VMM emulates a hardware platform that has the configured CPU, memory, and I/O resources that have been assigned to each particular VM guest. The VMM layer presents a hardware platform to the VM guest that makes the virtualized platform indistinguishable from a real hardware platform; so much so that any operating system capable of running on a physical HP Integrity hardware platform is also capable of running within an Integrity VMs environment without modification.

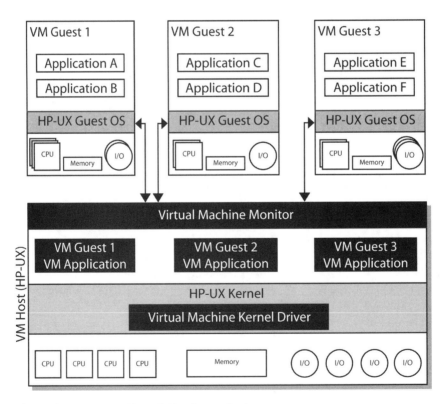

Figure 6-1 Integrity Virtual Machines Architecture

Below the VMM in the VM host lie the VM applications (vm_apps). Each of the vm_apps is a process running on the VM host. There is one vm_app process for every booted VM guest. The purpose of the vm_app is to request resources to be allocated to the associated VM guest. The memory size of the vm_app process in the VM host will be the same as the amount of memory that has been assigned to the VM guest. In addition, there is one kernel thread within the vm_app for every virtual processor allocated to the VM guest.

The final component in the VM host portion of the diagram is the VM driver (VMDVR). The VMDVR is a dynamically loadable kernel driver that is responsible for starting, stopping, creating, and removing VM guests.

VM Configuration Overview

Configuration of Integrity Virtual Machines consists primarily of defining CPU resource allocation, memory allocation, storage devices, and network connectivity. In addition, each VM guest requires configuration for its name, boot attributes, and other miscellaneous settings, but these topics are straightforward and don't require a detailed explanation.

CPU Resource Allocation

CPUs are specified in two components in Integrity Virtual Machines. The first is the number of virtual CPUs configured in a VM guest and the second is the percentage of a physical CPU that should be allocated to each virtual CPU.

The number of virtual CPUs configured in a VM guest dictates how many CPUs the VM guest operating system is able to use for running workloads. For example, if a VM guest is configured with four virtual CPUs, running the top command on the VM guest would show four CPUs. This means a multiprocess or multithreaded application has the ability to execute four processes or threads simultaneously on the VM guest. However, each of the virtual CPUs does not necessarily translate to a dedicated physical CPU for the VM guest.

The second component of the CPU configuration is the entitlement (the percentage of physical CPU guaranteed to each virtual CPU). This value can be specified such that each virtual CPU corresponds to a percentage of a physical CPU. For example, a virtual CPU can be defined such that is backed by 50% of a physical CPU. Or virtual CPUs can be specified according to a desired clock speed. For example, a virtual CPU can be defined such that it is backed by the equivalent of a CPU running at 1GHz, regardless of the physical CPU frequency. (Of course the frequency of the virtual CPU cannot exceed that of the physical CPU.)

Even though virtual CPU entitlements can be quite specific in their relationship to the physical CPUs, Integrity Virtual Machines allows CPU resources to be shared. Busy VM guests may use unused resources, even if that guest receives more than its entitlement. The entitlements are enforced only when all of the VM guests are busy simultaneously, at which point the entitlements represent the guaranteed amount of processor resources available to each VM guest. Said another way, CPU resources that are entitled to a VM guest but are not currently being used will be made available to other VM guests that require the resources. Thus, for a VM guest with four virtual CPUs that are each entitled to 50% of a physical processor, the entitlement is not a minimum, nor is it a maximum; it is a guarantee of resources when they are needed by the VM.

It should be understood that many Integrity Virtual Machines configurations simply assign a certain number of virtual CPUs to each VM guest, such as two or four virtual CPUs, and specify the default percentage of physical CPU to back the virtual CPUs. This configuration is easy to configure and maintain, and each VM guest receives an entitlement sufficient to run an operating system. This type of configuration also provides the ability for all VM guests to equally share unassigned CPU resources as needed. The example scenario uses this approach when allocating CPU resources.

Memory Allocation

Each virtual machine must be assigned a portion of the VM host's physical memory. The memory assigned to each virtual machine can be changed by shutting down the VM guest and modifying the amount of assigned memory. When each VM guest is booted, a check is performed to ensure that adequate memory is available on the VM host to boot the VM guest; if there is not enough available memory, the VM guest will not be permitted to boot. When each VM guest operating system is booted, the amount of memory assigned to the VM is locked. Therefore, if a VM guest is assigned 1GB of memory on a VM host with 4GB of memory, booting the VM guest will cause the entire 1GB of memory to become unavailable to the VM host and other VM guests, regardless of the amount of memory the owning VM guest is using. Therefore, the amount of memory assigned to each VM guest should be carefully considered. Allocating too much memory could result in underutilized memory resources, and allocating too little memory could result in excessive memory-swapping and poor performance in the VM guest.

Networking Configuration

Network configuration for a virtual machine using Integrity Virtual Machines can be set up in a manner very similar to a stand-alone system, nPartition, or virtual partition. In this type of environment, each VM guest is assigned one or more dedicated network adapters that are not shared. However, one of the primary benefits of Integrity Virtual Machines is the ability to share hardware to achieve higher utilization. Therefore, most configurations of Integrity Virtual Machines involve a virtual network switch that runs on the VM host. The vswitch is configured with zero or more physical network adapters as backing devices. When zero physical network adapters are backing the vswitch, it is referred to as a local switch, which means that no network traffic leaves the VM host. Instead, local vswitches serve as a high-speed internal LAN connection between VM guests. Alternatively, virtual network switches can be configured with a single network adapter that provides sharing by multiple VM guests. Finally, using the HP Auto Port Aggregation (APA) product, multiple network adapters can be grouped together to serve as a backing device for a vswitch.

Virtual network switches can be configured as either dedicated or shared. As these terms indicate, a shared vswitch can be used multiple VM guests, whereas a dedicated vswitch is limited to a single VM guest.

Storage Configuration

The configuration of storage devices for VM guests involves creating a mapping between the desired virtual devices for the VM guest to the physical backing devices in the VM host. Virtual storage devices for Integrity Virtual Machines can be a disk or a DVD. The physical backing devices for the virtual devices can be a raw disk device, a block disk device, a logical volume, a DVD, or a file. The most common mapping between virtual storage devices and physical backing devices uses a virtual disk device to map to a physical raw disk. This provides the VM guest with direct access to the disk device while introducing the least amount of overhead. After configuring this mapping, the VM guest is able to create a volume group, logical volumes, and file systems on the virtual device just as would be done on a stand-alone system.

Virtual Machine High Availability

The process of making a system highly available can be greatly simplified using Integrity Virtual Machines. The simplicity comes from the ability to configure the VM host once as a highly available system and the consequent ability of each VM guest to partake of the high-availability features without individually configuring each VM guest for high availability. Networking and storage connectivity are two of the primary features that can be configured on the VM host to simplify the high-availability configuration in each VM guest.

Networking High Availability

The networking configuration of VM guests can be one of the most powerful benefits of using Integrity Virtual Machines. The networking configuration of VM guests can be built upon the HP Auto Port Aggregation (APA) product. APA allows multiple physical network interfaces, or links, to be logically grouped together for a single, high-performing, fault-tolerant network interface. Consider a VM host system with four physical network adapters. If four VM guests were to be created on this VM host, one configuration approach would be to assign each VM guest direct access to one of the four physical network adapters. However, if the network adapter assigned to any one of the VM guests were to fail, the associated VM guest would experience complete loss of network connectivity.

An alternate configuration approach is to configure all of the network adapters together using APA on the VM host; in this scenario, all four VM guests can be configured to use the APA device. The end result is that each VM guest has hardware-fault isolation without degradation in performance or the added cost of redundant hardware devices. In fact, unless all of the VM guests are busy at the same exact time, each VM guest can experience higher performance because each VM has access to all four physical network devices. Further, should a network interface card or network cable experience a hardware failure, the VM guests can continue operating, but in a slightly degraded state.

Finally, the most significant reason for employing APA on the VM host is because the configuration of APA is performed only on the VM host and all of the VM guests are afforded the benefits of the configuration. Configuration of the VM guest operating system is greatly simplified because there is no need to perform special network configuration; APA configuration does not need to be performed on each guest. This feature alone greatly simplifies the administration of each VM guest operating system instance while providing a high-performance and fault-tolerant network infrastructure.

Storage High Availability

Another Integrity Virtual Machines configuration component that provides high availability while simplifying administration for VM guests is storage configuration. As with networking configuration, high-availability features that have been available in HP-UX for several years can be exploited to simplify the configuration of VM guests. Each VM host can be configured with multiple fiber adapters for connectivity to a storage array, as is typical for systems with high-availability requirements. Because the redundant paths can be put in place on the VM host, all of the VM guests are able to benefit from the redundant links without configuring them in the VM guest. From the perspective of the VM guest, storage configuration is greatly simplified. There is no need to configure multiple physical paths to the storage device. Instead, all of the VM guests are able to benefit from the VM host's fault-tolerant and high bandwidth storage connections.

For example, consider four stand-alone servers with fiber-channel connectivity to a storage array. This configuration would traditionally require at least one, usually two, fiber-channel host bus adapters. Using Integrity Virtual Machines, the same four stand-alone servers can be consolidated to a single VM host with the same four fiber-channel host bus adapters. Instead of each system having a single fiber-channel connection to the storage array, as many as four channels would be available at times of high bandwidth requirements. This results in better performance without additional hardware requirements. Additionally, failure of a fiber-channel host bus adapter, fiber-channel cable, or fiber-channel switch will not result in a loss to storage connectivity. Instead, all of the VM guests will retain connectivity, albeit in a degraded state.

Having discussed the most significant VM configuration components and the high availability configuration features, a discussion of the VM management paradigms that are used to configure these components follows.

VM Management Paradigms

Integrity Virtual Machines supports two management paradigms. The first is shown in Figure 6-2, which depicts local management from the VM host. Using this management paradigm, the VM host serves as the management platform and runs the applications necessary for VM management. The HP System Management Homepage is used to launch the virtual machine management GUI. This application relies on the virtual machine WBEM provider to read data from

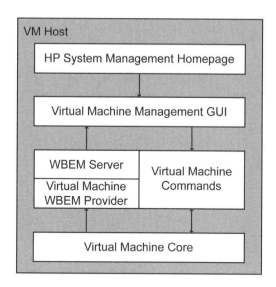

Figure 6-2 Local Integrity Virtual Machines
Management Paradigm

the virtual machine core interfaces. When the virtual machine management GUI makes a change to the VM guest configuration, the virtual machine commands are used. One difference in the management paradigms between nPartitions and VMs is that the virtual machine commands do not rely on the virtual machine WBEM provider, whereas the nPartition commands utilize the nPartition WBEM provider for all tasks. The ramification of this difference is the VM commands are only capable of performing administrative tasks on the local VM host. The VM commands can be executed remotely by relying on standard remote command execution tools such as remote shell or secure shell.

The second VM management paradigm is shown in Figure 6-3. This diagram illustrates VM management from an HP Systems Insight Manager central management station (CMS). There are three primary differences between the mode shown in Figure 6-2 and that shown in Figure 6-3:

1. The VM management GUI accesses WBEM providers remotely to collect data for the VM host and the VM guests. Since this paradigm relies on network connectivity between the CMS and the WBEM providers, the WBEM connection between the VM management GUI and the WBEM server is encrypted and transported over the network using HTTPS.

2. The VM management GUI executes VM commands remotely on the VM host using secure shell to make VM configuration changes.

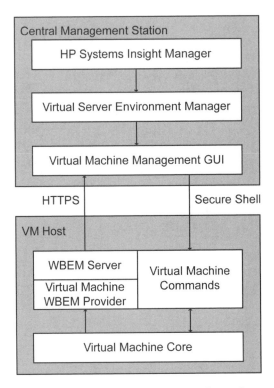

Figure 6-3 Remote Integrity Virtual Machines Management Paradigm

3. The VM host is not required to run the HP System Management Homepage. This offloads the responsibility of running the user interface to the CMS that is intended to host management applications.

An important similarity should be noted when examining the two VM management paradigms. VM guests are largely uninvolved in both paradigms. The management paradigms for VM management intentionally omit the VM guests from having involvement. This results in simplified management because all VM management tasks are performed from the VM host. Furthermore, this model allows individual VM guest administrators to focus on management of the operating system, as they typically would with a stand-alone system, and rely on the VM administrator to perform the VM-specific administration tasks.

While the VM guests are largely uninvolved in the VM management paradigms, HP recommends several WBEM providers to run on each VM guest and on the VM host—the VM WBEM provider, the IO tree WBEM provider, and resource utilization WBEM provider. When the VM WBEM provider runs within the VM guest, its purpose is to identify that it is a VM guest and to provide the universally unique identifier (UUID) of its VM host. This allows tools such as HP Systems Insight Manager to associate VM guests discovered on the network with the appropriate VM host. The IO tree WBEM provider allows I/O data to be gathered from each VM guest. The resource utilization WBEM provider is used to collect resource usage for the VM guest for the purposes of displaying utilization metrics, allocating resources, and capacity planning.

Finally, it's important to understand that this management paradigm discussion does not involve the typical administration tasks for operating systems running within the VM guests such as tuning the kernel, adding users, and configuring applications. This discussion applies only the administration of VM guests. It should also be understood that the two management paradigms are not mutually exclusive. Both the local and remote management paradigms can be utilized in the same environment depending on system administration policies and preferences.

Integrity Virtual Machines Example Scenario

This Integrity Virtual Machines example scenario discusses the creation and monitoring of several VM guests within a single VM host. Table 6-1 shows the physical configuration of the VM host server. The VM host is an nPartition in an Integrity rx8620 server with four cells. The VM host is running in an nPartition that has one cell, four CPUs, and 16 Gb of memory.

Table 6-2 shows the configuration of the VM guests that will be created during this scenario. Of particular interest in the table are the storage devices. Notice that each VM guest is allocated one disk device. Furthermore, the device files for virtual devices in the VM guests are identical. This greatly simplifies the administration of the individual VMs because the I/O devices are identical for every VM guest. As a simple example, this type of configuration allows (though does not require) files such as /etc/fstab to be identical for each VM guest.

Finally, the virtual networking devices shown in Table 6-3 further emphasize the simplicity and consistency available through the use of VMs. The virtual networking device is identical in each of the VMs and they are all connected to the same virtual network switch, named intranet.

Table 6-1 VM Host Configuration

VM Host	Physical Memory	Physical Processor
rex01	16 Gb	4 @ 2 GHz

Table 6-2 VM Guest Configurations

VM Guest Name	Processor Entitlement	Memory Allocation	Storage Devices (Virtual: Physical)	Networking Devices (Virtual: vswitch)
rex05	2 @ default entitlement	2 GB	Disk - /dev/rdsk/c0t0d0: /dev/rdsk/c1t6d0	/dev/lan0: intranet
rex06	4 @ default entitlement	4 GB	Disk - /dev/rdsk/c0t0d0: /dev/rdsk/c1t5d0	/dev/lan0: intranet
rex07	2 @ default entitlement	2 GB	Disk - /dev/rdsk/c0t0d0: /dev/rdsk/c1t4d0	/dev/lan0: intranet
rex08	2 @ default entitlement	2 GB	Disk - /dev/rdsk/c0t0d0: /dev/rdsk/c1t3d0	/dev/lan0: intranet

Integrity Virtual Machines Scenario Overview

The Integrity Virtual Machines example scenario discusses the following steps that are commonly performed during the initial deployment of Integrity Virtual Machines.

1. *Prepare the VM Host*

    The first step for deploying Integrity Virtual Machines is to prepare the host system both from a hardware and software perspective. As previously described, many hardware and software configuration tasks can be performed one time on the host system and all VM guests will reap the high availability and performance benefits.

2. *Creating a VM Guest*

    The next step is configuring a VM guest. Either the Integrity Virtual Machines commands or the virtual machine management GUI can be used to perform these steps.

3. *Booting the VM Guest*

    After creating the VM guest, an operating system must be installed. This step is performed in much the same way as a nonvirtualized HP Integrity server.

4. *Viewing the VM Guest*

    The next step illustrated in this scenario is viewing the VM guest. The virtual machine management GUI or the virtual machine commands can be used to view the configuration of a VM guest.

5. *Viewing all VM Guests' Configuration*

    One of the most compelling features of the virtual machine management GUI is the ability to visualize the VM guest general, network, and storage configuration attributes. This step shows examples of the graphical views of the VM guests.

Preparing the VM Host

Installing the VM software is the first task when using Integrity Virtual Machines. It consists of the VM monitor, the VM application, the VM kernel driver, the VM WBEM Provider, the VM command-line interfaces, and the VM management GUI, all of which can be installed from a single depot. After installing the VM software and tuning the HP-UX kernel as required, the physical disks and networking must be set up to support all of the VM guests that will be configured. As previously described, proper configuration of the VM host's networking and storage can greatly simplify the configuration of the VM guests. After installing the VM host software and configuring the hardware, the VM guests can be created.

Creating a VM Guest

The next step is creating the first VM guest. The screen shown in Figure 6-4 is the initial VM host configuration. Since this is the first VM guest to be created on the VM host rex01, the initial screen of the VM management application displays information about the VM host and its capacity. From the initial screen, creating a new VM guest is one of the possible actions.

Figure 6-5 shows the initial screen of the Create VM Guest wizard. The first step consists of specifying the name of the VM guest. In this case, the rex05 VM is the first VM to be created so its name is specified in the appropriate field. When specifying the name of the VM, it's important to keep in mind all of the VM commands rely on the VM guest name as the identifier when performing management tasks. Second, a description can be used to provide a brief explanation of the VM guest's role or function. The description is used only for display purposes to help identify the VM guest. Finally, the hostname or IP address of the VM guest should be specified on this screen. This field does not set the IP address for the VM guest. Instead, this field allows management applications that are communicating with the VM host to contact the VM guests to gather additional information, including resource utilization and I/O configuration information.

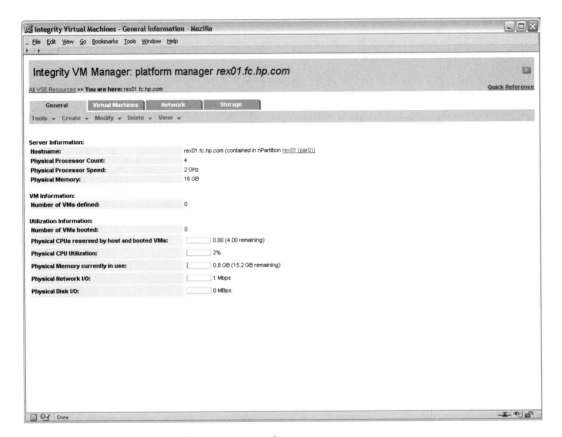

Figure 6-4 Initial Virtual Machine Configuration

Figure 6-6 shows the next screen in the wizard, which is the processor specification screen. This page sets the number of processors and their entitlements for the VM guest. In this screen's simplest form, only the number of virtual CPUs assigned to the VM guest must be specified. If the entitlement is not explicitly configured, the VM guest will receive a minimum entitlement necessary to run an operating system and will be allowed to share resources with other VMs.

The CPU specification screen also provides an advanced mode for specifying the exact CPU entitlements. The CPU entitlement can be specified as a percentage of a physical CPU or it can be specified according to the desired clock speed of the virtual CPU. The advanced CPU configuration portion of the screen is not shown.

After specifying the processors, the next step in the wizard, which is not shown, is to allocate memory to the VM guest. In this scenario, 2GB of memory is being allocated to the rex05 VM.

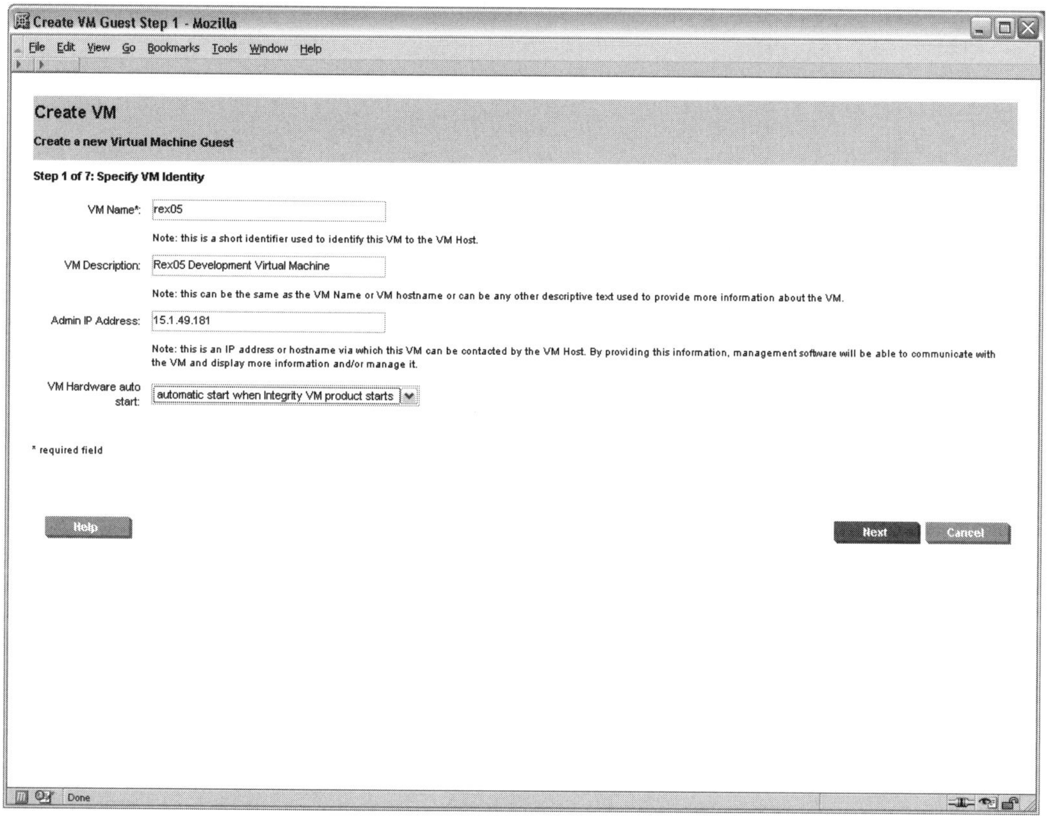

Figure 6-5 Identify Virtual Machine

To assist with the allocation of memory, the screen provides the amount of memory allocated to the VM host, the amount available that can be allocated to VM guests, and the amount that has already been allocated to other VM guests. Integrity Virtual Machines support VM guests with as little as 256 MB of memory, but the recommendations of the VM guest operating system should be consulted. For HP-UX as the VM guest operating system, HP recommends a minimum of 1GB of memory.

Specifying the networking devices for the VM guest is the next step. While you are creating a VM guest, you may need to create a new virtual switch (vswitch). A vswitch is a virtual network that runs within the VM host. All of the VM guests connected to a given vswitch can communicate with one another using the vswitch and realize significant performance benefits because the network traffic never leaves the physical VM host. In addition, using vswitches allows multiple VM guests to share the same physical network interface card or APA device. When VM

Figure 6-6 Specify Virtual Machine Processor Entitlements

guests are communicating with systems outside the VM host, the network packets look as if they have been sent from physically separate systems as the hardware addresses are unique for every VM guest.

When creating a virtual network switch (vswitch), the following attributes are required:

* The name of the vswitch (such as backup, mgmt, or corp)
* The vswitch type, either shared to dedicated
* An optional LAN device in the VM host that provides physical network connectivity for the vswitch. If no LAN device is specified, the vswitch is a local switch that acts as a high-speed LAN connection between VM guests.

The screen for creating vswitches is not shown in this example scenario.

After creating the `intranet` vswitch, the next step in the wizard adds a virtual network device to the VM guest that will rely on the vswitch. Figure 6-7 shows the interface for adding a net-

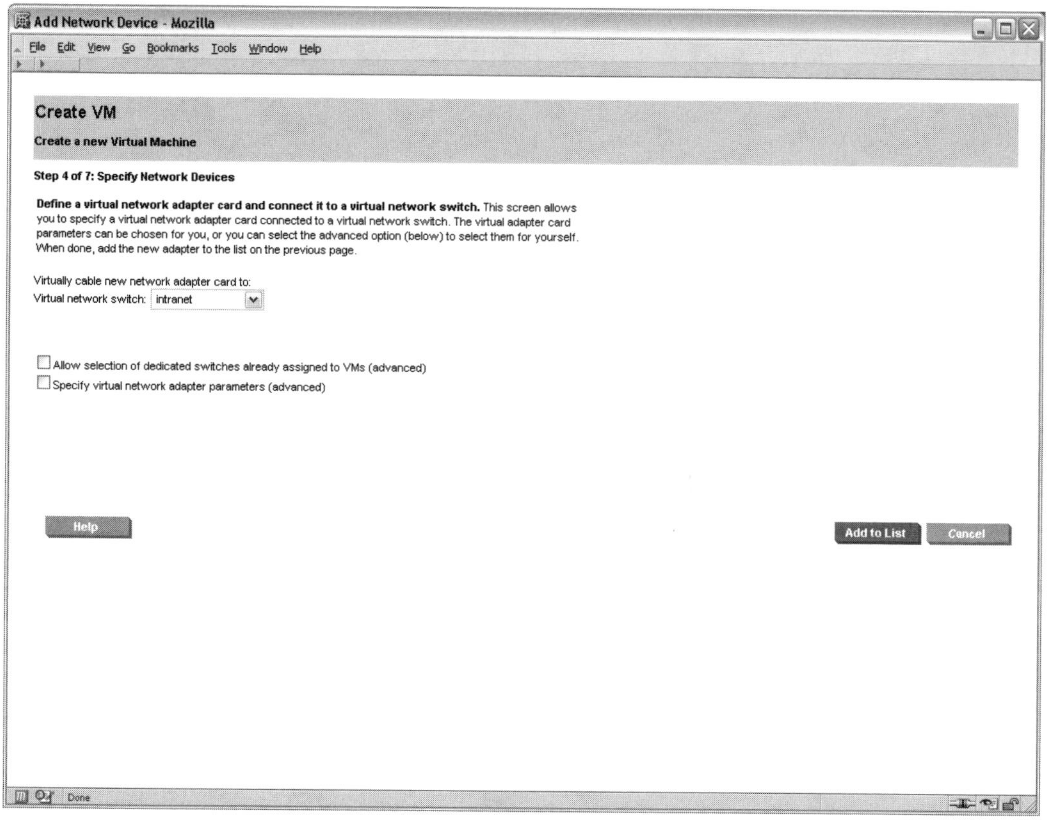

Figure 6-7 Add Network Device to Virtual Machine

work device in the Create VM Guest wizard. In this case, the newly created intranet vswitch is selected from the list of available vswitches. Multiple network adapters can be added to a VM guest, in which case this process is repeated as necessary. However, in this scenario, each VM guest will be connected to only one network.

After configuring the networking devices for the VM guest, storage devices must be assigned. The interface for adding storage devices is shown in Figure 6-8. This screen allows physical and logical storage to be mapped to virtual devices in the VM guest. For this scenario, the physical disk device /dev/rdsk/c1t6d0 is being mapped to a virtual disk device for the rex05 VM. As a result of this mapping, the rex05 VM will have complete and exclusive access to the physical disk device. However, the VM will have a virtualized device path, as shown in Table 6-3. The benefit of this mapping is that the configuration within each of the VM guests can be identical, regardless of the physical storage devices that are backing the virtual storage devices. This consistency affords numerous system administration efficiencies because the management of each VM guest is repeatable and predictable.

Figure 6-8 Add Disk Device to Virtual Machine

After configuring the storage devices for the VM, the administrators for the VM guest are configured. Note the administrator's screen is not shown in this example. The root user on the VM host always has full control to boot, shut down, remove, and administer all of the VM guests. However, other non-root users and groups can be configured with administrative privileges. In this scenario, only the root user will be allowed to perform administration tasks on the rex05 VM. When adding non-root administrators for a VM guest, the configured administrators are allowed to perform administrative duties only from the VM host for the allowed VM guests. These administrative privileges do not extend into the VM guest operating system. If that is required, the user or group must be granted the appropriate permissions from within the VM guest's operating system. The purpose for having non-root administrators on the VM host is to allow non-root users to perform certain administrative duties on a subset of the VM guests.

At this point, the necessary steps required to create the rex05 VM guest are complete. The final screen in the wizard is a summary of the VM guest that will be created. The summary screen is not shown, but it contains the information that has been supplied for the creation of the VM guest. The processor entitlements, memory allocation, networking devices, and storage devices that have been specified for the VM guest are shown in the various tabs of the summary screen. All of the tabs on the summary screen should be carefully reviewed to ensure that the settings were input properly.

In addition to the configuration options for the VM guest, one of the tabs in the summary screen shows a preview of the command that will be executed on the VM host to create the VM guest. This screen is useful to assist in learning the proper syntax and usage of the Integrity Virtual Machines command-line interfaces. Pressing the finish button on the summary screen results in the creation of the VM guest.

Booting the Virtual Machine

The final step required to complete the creation of the VM guest is installing an operating system. Integrity Virtual Machines provides a simulated firmware interface shell, specifically the Extensible Firmware Interface (EFI), which is used to install an operating system either over the network or from DVD media in the same way it would be done on a physical Integrity platform.

Viewing the Virtual Machine

The status and configuration of Integrity Virtual Machines can be viewed from the VM management GUI or from the VM command-line interfaces. Figure 6-9 shows the configuration for the rex05 VM guest. It displays the overall status and configuration of the VM guest as well as graphical views illustrating the mapping of physical networking and storage devices to the virtual networking and virtual storage counterparts.

In addition to the graphical status information, the Integrity Virtual Machines command-line interface can be used to view the status of VM guests. The output shown in Listing 6-1 is the textual status and configuration of the rex05 VM.

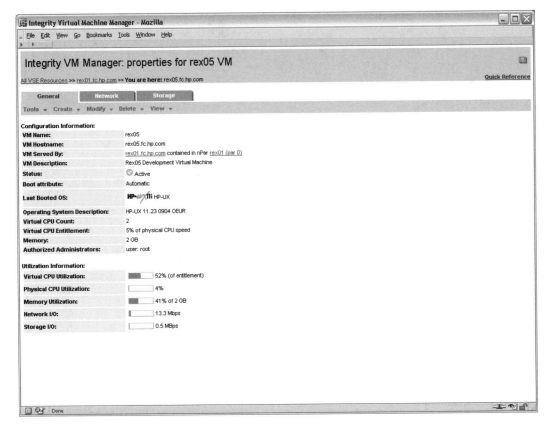

Figure 6-9 Virtual Machine Guest Details

Listing 6-1 Virtual Machine Command Line Status

```
# hpvmstatus -V
[Virtual Machines]
Virtual Machine Name    : rex05
Virtual Machine UUID    : 9c39a408-60c9-11d9-84a2-000e7fed810c
Virtual Machine ID      : 4
Virtual Machine Label   : Development VM for Web Application
VM's Model Name         : server Integrity Virtual Machine
VM's Serial Number      : VM00448001
Operating System        : HPUX
OS Version Number       : B.11.23
State                   : Up
Boot type               : Unknown
Console type            : vt100-plus
Number of virtual CPUs  : 2
Number of devices       : 1
Number of networks      : 1
Memory                  : 1 GB
```

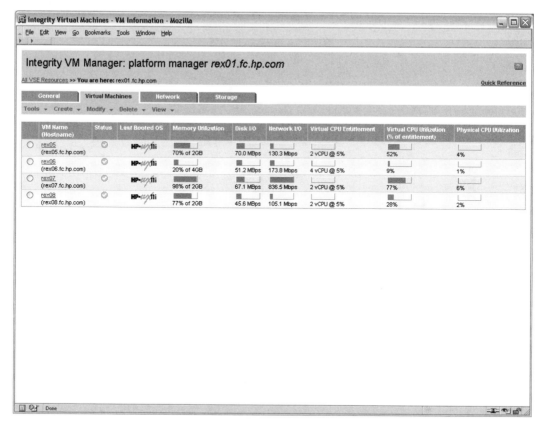

Figure 6-10 Integrity Virtual Machines Guest General Information

At this point, additional VM guests can be created and booted. This example scenario does not walk through the steps for creating the additional VM guests. The remaining screens in this example illustrate the visualization capabilities of the VM management GUI on a VM host with several VM guests running.

Viewing Integrity Virtual Machines Configuration

The configuration of Integrity Virtual Machines can be viewed using the command-line interface or through the VM management application. Figure 6-10 shows the high-level configuration and status of the VM guests that have been created within the rex01 VM host. Notice that the virtual CPU entitlements and the virtual CPU utilization metrics are shown in this summary view, along with memory, network I/O bandwidth, and disk I/O bandwidth utilization information.

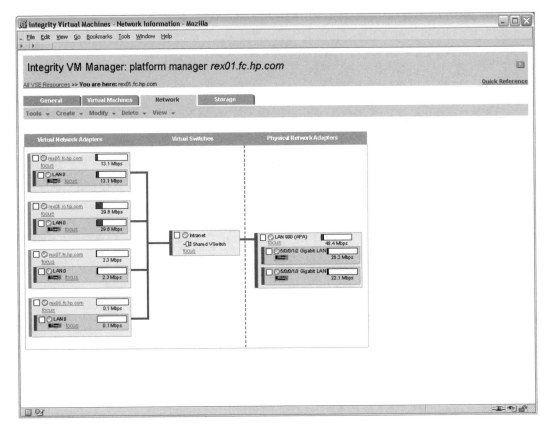

Figure 6-11 Integrity Virtual Machines Guest Network Configuration

The networking view of the virtual machine management application is shown in Figure 6-11. This view graphically illustrates mapping of virtual network resources in the VM guests to the physical network devices in the VM host. This view serves as a vital resource when troubleshooting network performance issues because the utilization of each virtual network device can be visually traced back to the physical networking interface and vice versa. The network tab also makes evident which VM guests are using each of the virtual switches and which VMs have exclusive access to network devices in the VM host.

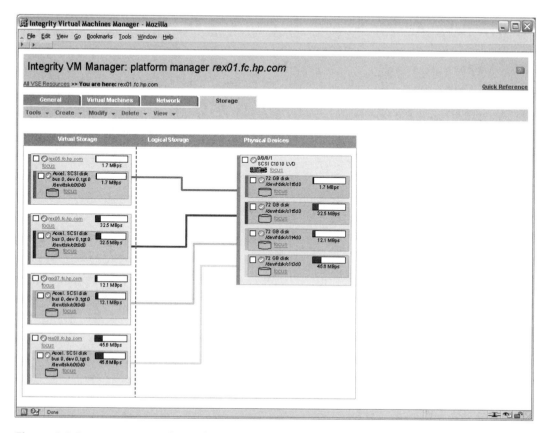

Figure 6-12 Integrity Virtual Machines Guest Storage Configuration

Figure 6-12 is the final graphical view in the virtual machine management application. Akin to the network tab, this tab graphically displays each virtual storage device configured for the VM guests and their associated physical devices in the VM host. This view makes it easy to make configuration decisions and troubleshoot storage issues, especially when multiple physical storage devices are connected to the VM host through the same physical storage adapter. In such a configuration, extremely high storage traffic by a VM guest could create a situation in which another VM guest experiences degraded storage performance.

These views provide a tremendous amount of information and troubleshooting capabilities for VM guests. This level of detail is vital in an environment where physical resources are virtualized and shared between multiple operating systems.

Summary

Many changes have occurred in operating system and computer hardware technology since the Compatible Time Share System was developed in the early 1960s. The CTSS operating system formed the foundation for time-sharing systems that are prevalent today. In many ways, Integrity Virtual Machines take the fundamental ideas developed decades ago on the CTSS and provide a virtualized platform for running multiple operating systems simultaneously on the same hardware. Just as the CTSS allowed a single hardware platform to be used by multiple users at the same time, Integrity Virtual Machines allows a single hardware platform to host multiple operating systems. The result is dramatically higher system utilization and greater workload isolation. Additionally, VMs using Integrity Virtual Machines can more easily be migrated from one hardware platform to another without modification because the resources are virtualized.

This chapter began with an architectural overview of Integrity Virtual Machines and the most common terminology the software uses. Then an example scenario was discussed that demonstrated the administration of Integrity Virtual Machines. The example showed the power and flexibility in creating virtual machines that are capable of sharing CPU, networking, and storage resources.

Integrity Virtual Machines fulfills a crucial role in HP's Virtual Server Environment. The ability to run workloads in isolated environments with the flexibility to migrate VMs from one hardware platform to another is extremely powerful. When combined with the full suite of products in HP's Virtual Server Environment such Global Workload Manager, the end result is a highly available virtualized computing platform that results in a high degree of resource sharing and utilization.

7

Secure Resource Partitions

Chapter Overview

Most the partitioning technologies in HP's Virtual Server Environment have one thing in common. They require a distinct operating system to be configured and maintained for every partition. Regardless of whether nPartitions, virtual partitions, or virtual machines are being employed, the technology requires a separate operating system. While this is certainly acceptable and often desired to ensure that applications retain a high level of isolation, it is not always necessary. In some situations it is perfectly acceptable for multiple applications to coexist within the same operating system. When users stack multiple applications in a single operating system, the first question they typically ask is, "How do I ensure that one application won't starve the others during times of peak resource utilization?" Secure Resource Partitions are the answer to this question.

Secure Resource Partitions (SRPs) allow multiple workloads to be hosted within a single operating system while retaining both resource and security isolation. Each SRP is assigned a subset of the operating system's CPU, memory, and disk I/O resources. In addition, workloads running within a SRP can be completely isolated from a security standpoint to ensure that an errant workload has no effect on the others within the operating system image. One of the major benefits of SRPs is that workloads are guaranteed access to a subset of the operating system's hardware without requiring a distinct operating system. For example, if five instances of a database are needed, a single operating system can be configured with SRPs and each instance can be associated with a unique SRP. The SRPs are isolated from the standpoint of security and resource utilization.

This chapter begins with an overview of the SRP technology. A description of the two CPU allocation managers, the fair share scheduler (FSS) and processor sets (PSETs) is provided. Following the SRP overview, the fundamental terminology relating to SRPs is detailed. Finally, an example scenario is covered that uses SRPs within a virtual partition environment. Each SRP is configured to run an instance of an Oracle database and provide resource isolation within each virtual partition.

Secure Resource Partitions Overview

Secure Resource Partitions enable the resources under the control of a single operating system to be further divided into secure compartments for the purposes of running workloads. Figure 7-1 shows a set of workloads running in separate operating systems on separate hardware platforms. While this environment is highly isolated, not all workloads require that level of isolation. In addition, computing environments such as those shown in Figure 7-1 typically experience lower resource utilization because none of the hardware resources are shared. When a workload is not busy, the hardware is left idle.

Secure Resource Partitions rely on features of the HP-UX kernel to provide resource and security isolation between workloads. Figure 7-2 demonstrates the consolidation of Workloads A, B, and C to a single server platform. In this environment, each workload is isolated in a Secure Resource Partition. The SRP guarantees that a specified amount of system resources will be available for each workload when needed. In addition, each SRP is isolated from a security standpoint with the result that no workload is able to affect another workload either intentionally or unintentionally. The consolidated environment results in higher resource utilization because resources that aren't needed by Workload A, for example, can be used by Workload B. In addition, the environment shown in Figure 7-2 requires a single operating system, as opposed to a distinct

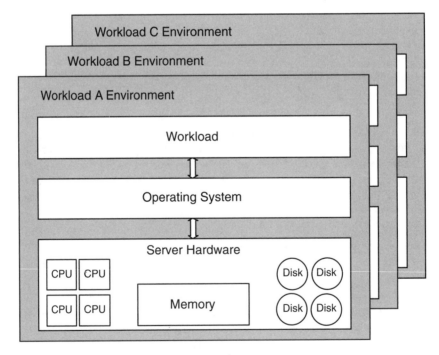

Figure 7-1 Workloads Running in Isolation

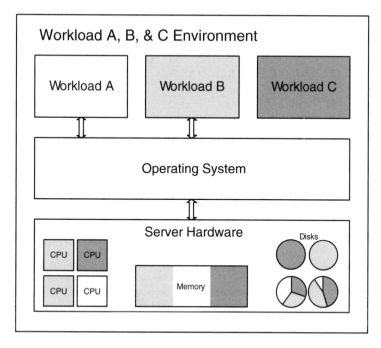

Figure 7-2 Consolidated Workloads Running in Secure Resource Partitions

operating system for each workload; this results in lower maintenance time. Finally, SRPs provide the ability to overprovision a system with workloads that have peaks that are not aligned.

SRPs also offer the ability to install, configure, and maintain a single application with multiple instances running in each of the SRPs. Applications such as databases work well in this type of environment. This saves administration costs; it is necessary to maintain only one instance of the application. In addition, application licensing costs will likely be decreased because applications are typically priced based on the number of CPUs. Using SRPs results in a lower requirement for hardware resources and has the result of achieving higher utilization of resources.

Secure Resource Partitions offer the ability to control several areas of a system. These controls can be enabled and disabled independently and there is no requirement that all of these controls be used when SRPs are employed. The following system attributes can be controlled and managed with SRPs based on the requirements of the workloads.

- security compartment isolation (available starting with HP-UX 11i v2)
- CPU allocation in either whole or partial CPU increments
- memory allocation
- disk I/O bandwidth allocation

The fundamental technology behind SRPs is the Process Resource Manager product (PRM). PRM has been available on HP-UX for many years and continues to increase its capabilities. The CPU, memory, and disk I/O bandwidth resource controls are all handled through PRM. The security-isolation aspect of SRPs is available through integration of PRM with the HP-UX Security Containment product.

The HP-UX Security Containment product contains several features designed to provide a highly secure operating environment that does not require users to modify applications. The secure compartment feature within the HP-UX Security Containment product provides security isolation between workloads that prevents workloads running under a single operating system from affecting one another. The integration of secure compartments and PRM is not illustrated in the example scenario presented in this chapter; however, several tools are provided with the PRM product to facilitate the integration with secure compartments. See the *HP Process Resource Manager User's Guide* version C.03.00 for details on integrating PRM and HP-UX Security Containment.

note

> The HP-UX Security Containment product is available beginning with HP-UX 11i v2.

Secure Resource Partitions Terminology

There are several important terms relating to SRPs. These terms are used throughout the remainder of the chapter and in SRP documentation.

Application Manager: the operating system process that is responsible for ensuring that all processes are running in the proper PRM group. The application manager polls the PRM configuration file and the process table and moves processes to the appropriate PRM group as needed.

CPU Manager: the technology used to schedule processes on CPUs. FSS, PSETs, or a combination of the two can be used as the CPU manager.

Fair Share Scheduler (FSS): the process scheduler used for PRM groups that schedules processes to run according to the entitlement of each group. FSS guarantees that each workload receives its entitled share of the processors. A major benefit of using FSS is the ability to allocate CPU resources on sub-CPU granularity.

Processor Sets (PSETs): a subset of the active processors on a server. When using PSETs as the CPU manager for a PRM group, CPU granularity is limited to whole CPUs. Processes running in a PRM group with PSETs as the CPU manager will be scheduled with the standard HP-UX time-share scheduler, not the fair share scheduler.

Entitlement: the guaranteed amount of system resources an SRP will receive when the overall system utilization is at 100% and the workload within each PRM group is utilizing its full allocation of system resources. In situations where a workload is not busy, its resources may be used by other SRPs, and vice versa. As a result, actual resource utilization may be higher or lower than the entitlement, depending on each workload's demands, but the entitlement is a minimum guaranteed amount of system resources if they are needed. Entitlements apply only to FSS groups.

Shares: units of CPU, memory, and disk I/O bandwidth allocated for PRM groups. The allocated number of shares is the minimum entitlement for the resources in a group. The number of shares allocated in the system are totaled and each SRP receives the appropriate percentage of resources based on the number of shares it has been allocated. For example, consider the situation where one PRM group is allocated 20 CPU shares, a second group is allocated 40 shares, a third group is allocated 40 shares, and a final group is allocated 100 shares. In this case there is a total of 200 CPU shares allocated. The first group's entitlement is 10% (20/200), the second and third groups' entitlements are 20% (40/200), and the final group's entitlement is 50% (100/200).

CPU Capping: a resource control put in place to ensure that each PRM group consumes no more CPU resources than allowed. CPU capping can be useful in situations where increased performance due to resource sharing may set false expectations for application performance. For example, users could become accustomed to high levels of application performance and become dissatisfied when the performance returns to normal levels. Using this control may result in lower system utilization because resources not being consumed by a PRM group cannot be shared, which results in idle hardware.

Security Compartment: a restriction placed around an application (processes, executables, data files, and communication channels) that prevents access to resources outside the compartment. The overall design philosophy of security compartments is similar to that of a submarine. When a submarine sustains damage to a portion of the vessel, catastrophic damage is generally avoided because the effects of the damage are restricted to the compartment directly compromised. Security compartments are designed in much the same way, providing isolation between applications that prevents security breaches from causing damage beyond the compartment directly compromised.

Disk I/O Bandwidth Manager: a kernel module that monitors HP Logical Volume Manager (LVM) volume groups and VERITAS Volume Manager (VxVM) disk groups. The I/O requests are rearranged by the kernel monitor to ensure that disk bandwidth entitlements are met.

Memory Manager: a process running on the operating system that is responsible for ensuring PRM groups are granted their entitled memory. The memory manager also supports memory capping.

Memory Capping: an upper bound on the memory entitlement that ensures that each PRM group consumes no more memory than allowed.

PRM Group: a collection of users and applications that can contain secure compartments and are allocated CPU, memory, and disk bandwidth entitlements. PRM groups have a name and an ID. Two PRM groups are created by default: the PRM_SYS group that contains the system processes has an ID of 0 and the OTHERS PRM group has an ID of 1.

System Group: the PRM group that contains all system processes by default. All processes started by root are placed in the system group. The system group is commonly referred to as the PRM_SYS group.

Others Group: the PRM group that contains all of the processes started by users who have not been explicitly associated with a PRM group. The others group is simply referred to as OTHERS.

Example Secure Resource Partitions Scenario

This example scenario walks through the process of configuring SRPs within two different vPars. Each of the vPars is running within a single nPartition. Two SRPs will be created within each of the vPars and each SRP will contain an instance of an Oracle database.

Table 7-1 shows the initial configuration of the system. In this example, the zoo21 and zoo19 virtual partitions reside within a two-cell, eight-CPU nPartition. The nPartition has a total of 8 GB of memory. The zoo21 virtual partition contains two databases instances, the HR and the Payroll databases. The zoo19 virtual partition also contains two database instances, the Finance and Sales databases.

The system's current configuration as shown in Table 7-1 does not allow resource controls on the individual databases. In this example, the HR database is expected to be three times as busy as the Payroll database. However, nothing in the current implementation ensures that the HR

Table 7-1 Initial System Configuration

Database Instance	Contained in	CPUs Num	Amount of Memory
hr_db	zoo21 (vPar)	4	2048 MB
payroll_db	zoo21 (vPar)		
finance_db	zoo19 (vPar)	4	2048 MB
sales_db	zoo19 (vPar)		

database has access to the required resources when they are needed. One solution would be to create another virtual partition for each of the database instances, but the result would be twice the number of operating system instances to install, configure, and maintain. In addition, the database application is able to run multiple instances within a single operating system with little concern of affecting the other database instances. The primary aspects to consider when stacking similar applications such as database instances are in the area of coordinating maintenance widows and application availability. The former requires up-front planning and coordination for scheduling hardware and software maintenance. The risks associated application availability in a consolidated environment can be mitigated by employing HP Serviceguard as described in Chapter 16, "Serviceguard."

Another common area of concern when consolidating applications is resource contention. To remedy this problem, Secure Resource Partitions will be implemented to ensure that each instance of the database receives a fair share of resources. Table 7-2 shows the final resource allocation for each of the database instances. In the zoo21 vPar, PSET PRM groups are used to guarantee CPU resource allocation. In the zoo19 vPar, FSS PRM groups are used to ensure proper CPU resource allocation. In addition, the PRM memory manager will be enabled in the zoo19 vPar to ensure that each PRM group has adequate memory available and that each of the instances receives their required memory. CPU capping will also be enabled in the zoo19 implementation of PRM.

Configuring PRM Processor Set Groups

The first step in configuring the PRM software is ensuring that the software is properly installed. The PRM software is bundled in the HP-UX 11i Enterprise Operating Environment. The following command shows the products that constitute the PRM software. The three components

Table 7-2 Final System Configuration

SRP Group Name	Contained In	Num CPUs	CPU Manager	Security Compart-ment	Memory Manager	Memory Capping	CPU Entitlement	CPU Capping
hr_db	zoo21 (vPar)	4	Yes (Psets)	No	No	No	3 CPUs	No
payroll_db	zoo21 (vPar)		Yes (Psets)	No	No	No	1 CPU	No
finance_db	zoo19 (vPar)	4	Yes (FSS)	No	Yes (60%)	Yes (80%)	60%	Yes
sales_db	zoo19 (vPar)		Yes (FSS)	No	Yes (40%)	Yes (60%)	40%	Yes

of PRM are the kernel infrastructure, the PRM user-level library, and the actual PRM product. The following command can be used to verify that the software is installed:

```
# swlist -l product ¦ grep "Process Resource Manager"
  PRM-Sw-Krn      C.01.01 Process Resource Manager PRM-Sw-Krn
                          product
  PRM-Sw-Lib      C.02.02 Process Resource Manager PRM-Sw-Lib
                          product
  Proc-Resrc-Mgr C.02.02 Process Resource Manager Proc-Resrc-Mgr
                          Product
```

After verifying the PRM software is properly installed, the PRM configuration process can be initiated. PRM allows a configuration file to be edited either directly or through a graphical user interface (GUI). For the entirety of this scenario, the PRM GUI will be used to create the configuration file. The generated configuration file will be shown after the configuration process is complete.

The PRM GUI is located in /opt/prm/bin/xprm. The initial PRM screen is shown in Figure 7-3. The name of the system is shown on the left-hand side and the default configuration file is

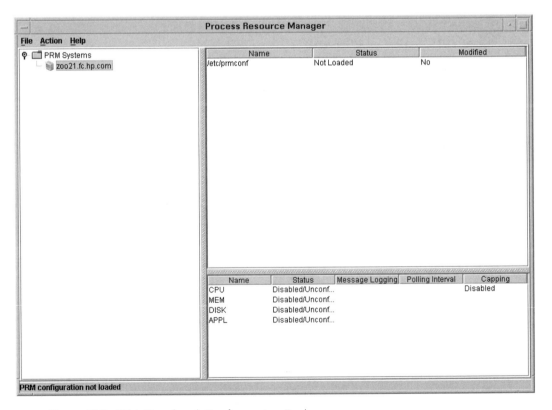

Figure 7-3 PRM Graphical Configuration Tool

shown on the upper-right-hand side. Notice that the status of the configuration file shows it is not currently loaded. On the lower-right-hand side, each of the PRM managers are listed along with their respective status values.

In order to create the desired configuration, select the default configuration file, /etc/ prmconf. Then select the Action menu and choose the Edit menu. This opens a forms-based editor for configuring PRM groups, as shown in Figure 7-4.

The first PRM group to be created is the hr_db group. This group will be allocated three CPUs in a PSET. To create the group, specify the name in the Group field. Select the PSET checkbox. Finally, specify three CPUs in the Number of CPUs field. Add the PRM group to the configuration by pressing the Add button.

The second PRM group is the payroll_db group. As shown in Table 7-1, there are four CPUs in the zoo21 vPar. Three of the CPUs have been allocated to the hr_db PRM PSET group. This leaves one processor in the default PSET that must always have at least one processor. As a result, all processes other than those belonging to the hr_db PRM group will run in the default PSET. Actually, the configuration of PRM groups could stop here because the hr_db will be allocated 3 CPUs and the payroll_db instance will be restricted to the single processor in the default PSET. However, the payroll_db group will be competing with all the other processes on the system, including login shells, cron jobs, and system daemons. In order to ensure that the

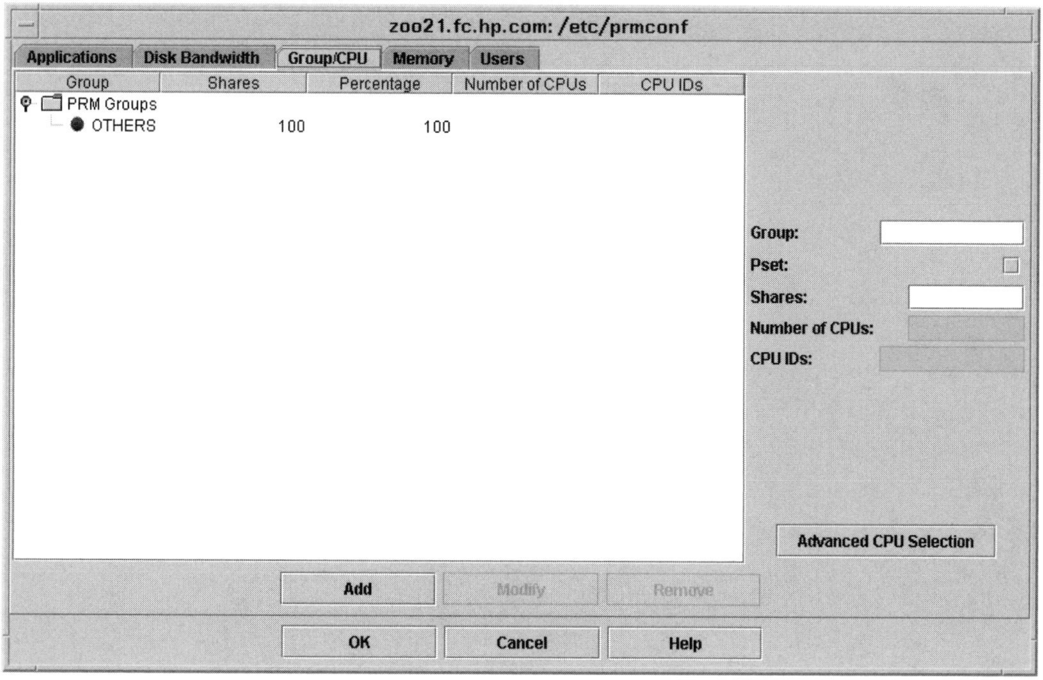

Figure 7-4 Secure Resource Partition Configuration Editor

payroll_db receives a majority of the CPU resources in the default PRM group, a fair share scheduler group will be created within the default PSET. The payroll_db FSS group will be allocated 90 percent of the CPU resources in the default PSET. This is achieved by specifying the name in the Group field and specifying the value 900 in the Shares field. Next, 100 shares are allocated to the OTHERS group. This creates the desired 90% allocation to the payroll_db group; the remaining 10% is for all the other processes on the system.

The final PRM group configuration is shown in Figure 7-5. Notice that the hr_db group has 75% of the systems resources with three CPUs. The payroll_db group has been allocated 22.5% of the system and the OTHERS group has been allocated 2.5% of the system. The payroll_db and the OTHERS group are sharing the default PSET. The PRM_SYS group is not explicitly listed in the configuration, but the PRM software will create the group automatically. The PRM_SYS group will be allocated a percentage of the resources in the default PSET to ensure that system processes receive the resources they need; the actual utilization is typically low for processes in the PRM_SYS group.

Having completed the PRM group and CPU configuration, the PRM applications must be specified. The PRM application manager uses application groups to determine to which group processes should be associated. To configure the PRM applications, select the Applications tab in the PRM configuration editor, as shown in Figure 7-6. For each of the PRM groups, an application record is defined. An application record consists of the application name that is the full path

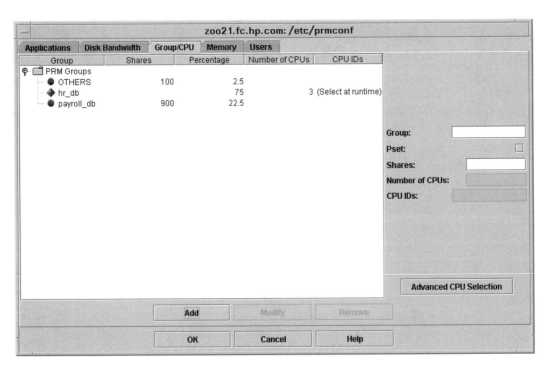

Figure 7-5 Final PRM Group Configuration

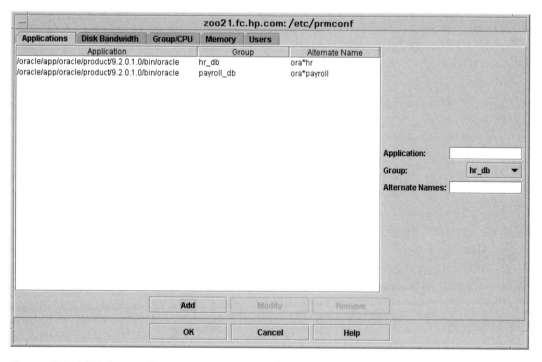

Figure 7-6 PRM Secure Resource Partition Applications

to the executable, the group to associate with the application, and a set of alternate names. The alternate name list is especially important for applications such as Oracle databases because the database processes rename themselves upon startup according to the name of the instance that is specified in the ORACLE_SID environment variable. When the application manager is assigning processes to PRM groups, special checks are performed to ensure that the executable matching the alternate name is really the same executable as specified in the application field. For example, a shell script whose name matches the regular expression for a PRM group's alternate name will not be moved to the PRM group even though the name of shell script matches the regular expression. This check ensures that only the desired applications are running within each PRM group.

To configure application records, specify the absolute path of the executable in the Application field. Wildcard characters are allowed in the filename portion of the application name. This is useful when all of the executables in a given directory should be associated with a specific PRM group. Use the Group field to select the PRM group as configured in Figure 7-5. Finally, specify alternate names in the Alternate Names field. These steps are performed for the hr_db and payroll_db database instances. Notice that the Application field is identical for both groups; the Alternate Name field is the distinguishing factor that appropriately assigns the processes to their PRM groups.

The PRM configuration is now complete, but the file has not been saved. If you press the OK button on the dialog box shown in Figure 7-6, the application returns to the original PRM dialog shown in Figure 7-3. The configuration will have a status of Not Loaded and the Modified field will indicate Yes. Save the PRM configuration by selecting Configuration File from the Action menu and then selecting the Save menu item.

After saving the PRM configuration, you can view it from the command line using the prmlist command or by viewing the configuration file directly with a text editor. Listing 7-1 shows the output of the prmlist command.

Listing 7-1   PRM Configuration with prmlist

```
# /opt/prm/bin/prmlist

PRM configured from file:  /etc/prmconf
File last modified:        Wed Oct  6 20:06:32 2004

PRM Group                     PRMID   CPU Entitlement
- - - - - - - - - - - - - - - - - - - - - - - - - - - - - - - - - -
OTHERS                          1           2.50%
hr_db                          65          75.00%
payroll_db                      2          22.50%

PRM User        Initial Group     Alternate Group(s)

- - - - - - - - - - - - - - - - - - - - - - - - - - - - - - - - - -

adm             OTHERS
bin             OTHERS
daemon          OTHERS
hpdb            OTHERS
lp              OTHERS
nobody          OTHERS
nuucp           OTHERS
root            (PRM_SYS)
smbnull         OTHERS
sys             OTHERS
uucp            OTHERS
webadmin        OTHERS
www             OTHERS

PRM Application                Assigned Group Alternate Name(s)
- - - - - - - - - - - - - - - - - - - - - - - - - - - - - - - - - -

/oracle/app/oracle/product/9.2 hr_db          ora*hr

/oracle/app/oracle/product/9.2 payroll_db     ora*payroll
```

Listing 7-2 shows the resulting PRM configuration file. Notice that the PRM group records for the hr_db and payroll_db groups are present with their respective configuration settings. The application records are also listed as configured. No disk I/O bandwidth, memory, or user records have been configured.

Listing 7-2   PRM Configuration File

```
# cat /etc/prmconf
#
# Group/CPU records
#
OTHERS:1:100::
hr_db:PSET:::3:
payroll_db:2:900::
#
# Memory records
#
#
# Application records
#
/oracle/app/oracle/product/9.2.0.1.0/bin/oracle::::hr_db,ora*hr
/oracle/app/oracle/product/9.2.0.1.0/bin/oracle::::payroll_db,ora*payroll
#
# Disk bandwidth records
#
#
# User records
#
```

At this point the PRM configuration is complete, but none of the PRM managers are enabled. Listing 7-3 shows the process listing for all processes matching the executable names of the database instances. Notice that the second column, PRMID, is blank for all of the processes.

The ps command accepts a special option, -P that displays the PRMID column. Because PRM is not yet enabled, the command displays a warning message that makes it clear PRM is not configured. Several columns have been removed from the ps command's output in this chapter for formatting purposes.

Listing 7-3   Process Listing before Enabling PRM

```
# ps -efP | grep -e ora.*payroll -e COMMAND
ps: Process Resource Manager is not configured
    UID   PRMID    PID  PPID  TIME COMMAND
  oracle      -   3768     1  0:00 ora_d000_payroll
  oracle      -   3756     1  1:44 ora_ckpt_payroll
  oracle      -   3760     1  0:00 ora_reco_payroll
  oracle      -   3754     1  0:41 ora_lgwr_payroll
  oracle      -   3752     1  0:35 ora_dbw0_payroll
  oracle      -   3758     1  0:55 ora_smon_payroll
  oracle      -   3766     1  0:01 ora_s000_payroll
  oracle      -   3762     1  1:03 ora_cjq0_payroll
  oracle      -   3764     1  4:48 ora_qmn0_payroll
  oracle      -   3750     1  0:24 ora_pmon_payroll
```

```
# ps -efP ¦ grep -e ora.*hr -e COMMAND
ps: Process Resource Manager is not configured
    UID   PRMID    PID  PPID   TIME COMMAND
 oracle       -   3718     1   1:32 ora_ckpt_hr
 oracle       -   3730     1   0:00 ora_d000_hr
 oracle       -   3732     1   0:00 ora_d001_hr
 oracle       -   3714     1   0:37 ora_dbw0_hr
 oracle       -   3726     1   4:22 ora_qmn0_hr
 oracle       -   3712     1   0:21 ora_pmon_hr
 oracle       -   3720     1   0:55 ora_smon_hr
 oracle       -   3728     1   0:32 ora_s000_hr
 oracle       -   3716     1   0:40 ora_lgwr_hr
 oracle       -   3722     1   0:00 ora_reco_hr
 oracle       -   3724     1   0:57 ora_cjq0_hr
```

Loading the PRM Configuration

To load a saved PRM configuration, select Configuration File from the Action menu of the main PRM GUI shown in Figure 7-3 and then select Load, moving processes to assigned group. This step creates PSETs and moves all processes to their respective PRM groups. Loading the configuration does enable the PRM resource managers. Listing 7-4 shows the process listing after the processes have been moved. The second column, PRMID, illustrates the processes associated with each database instance having been assigned the appropriate PRM group.

important

It is important to use the ps command as shown to ensure that the application name and alternate name fields are specified correctly. If the processes do not have the correct PRMID, then the processes have not been properly placed in their groups and none of the PRM resource controls will be effective.

Listing 7-4 Process Listing before Enabling PRM

```
# ps -efP ¦ grep -e ora.*hr -e COMMAND
    UID   PRMID    PID  PPID   TIME COMMAND
 oracle   hr_db   3718     1   1:32 ora_ckpt_hr
 oracle   hr_db   3730     1   0:00 ora_d000_hr
 oracle   hr_db   3732     1   0:00 ora_d001_hr
 oracle   hr_db   3714     1   0:37 ora_dbw0_hr
 oracle   hr_db   3726     1   4:23 ora_qmn0_hr
 oracle   hr_db   3712     1   0:21 ora_pmon_hr
 oracle   hr_db   3720     1   0:55 ora_smon_hr
 oracle   hr_db   3728     1   0:32 ora_s000_hr
 oracle   hr_db   3716     1   0:40 ora_lgwr_hr
```

```
   oracle  hr_db     3722      1  0:00 ora_reco_hr
   oracle  hr_db     3724      1  0:58 ora_cjq0_hr
# ps -efP | grep -e ora.*payroll -e COMMAND
      UID  PRMID        PID   PPID  TIME COMMAND
   oracle  payroll_db  3768      1  0:00 ora_d000_payroll
   oracle  payroll_db  3756      1  1:44 ora_ckpt_payroll
   oracle  payroll_db  3760      1  0:00 ora_reco_payroll
   oracle  payroll_db  3754      1  0:41 ora_lgwr_payroll
   oracle  payroll_db  3752      1  0:35 ora_dbw0_payroll
   oracle  payroll_db  3758      1  0:55 ora_smon_payroll
   oracle  payroll_db  3766      1  0:01 ora_s000_payroll
   oracle  payroll_db  3762      1  1:03 ora_cjq0_payroll
   oracle  payroll_db  3764      1  4:49 ora_qmn0_payroll
   oracle  payroll_db  3750      1  0:24 ora_pmon_payroll
```

GlancePlus is used throughout this chapter to monitor the applications and PRM groups. The GlancePlus parameter file located in /var/opt/perf/parm can be modified to include application entries for each of the instances of the database as shown in Listing 7-5.

Listing 7-5 GlancePlus Parameter File Defining Database Applications

```
# cat /var/opt/perf/parm
[...]

application = payroll_db
file = ora*payroll

application = hr_db
file = ora*hr

application = other_user_root
user = root
```

After starting GlancePlus, select Application List from the Reports menu. Figure 7-7 shows the resulting report. Notice that both the hr_db and payroll_db are consuming roughly the same amount of CPU resources because the PRM resource managers are not yet enabled.

In addition to the textual reports, GlancePlus offers CPU graphs. Select Application CPU Graphs from the Reports menu of the Application Lists window to see graphical CPU consumption. Figure 7-8 shows a graph of CPU use for each of the database instances. Again, each of the database instances is consuming roughly the same amount of CPU resources.

Enabling PRM Processor Set CPU Manager

You will need to enable the PRM CPU manager to enforce the resource entitlements. Using the PRM configuration editor, select the CPU manager from the lower-right-hand corner, as shown in Figure 7-9. Then select Resource Managers from the Actions menu. Finally, select Enable

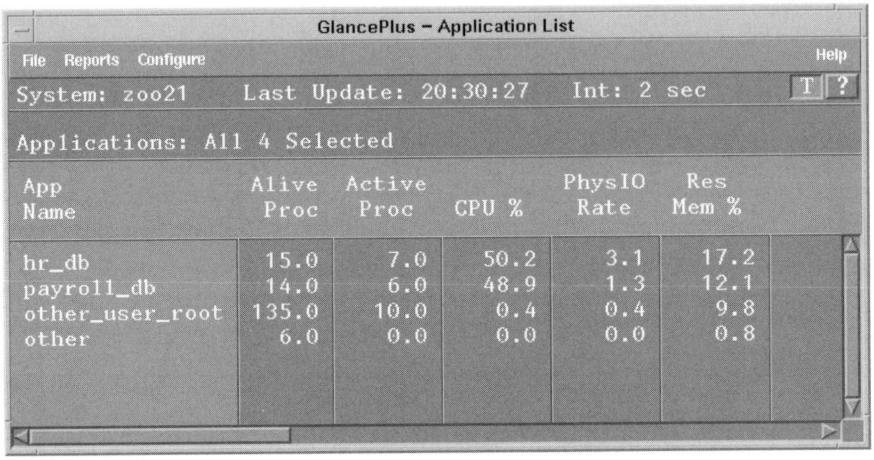

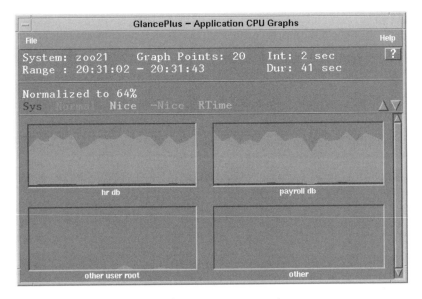

Figure 7-7 GlancePlus Application List before Enabling PRM

Resource Manager. Follow the same steps to enable the application manager, shown in the lower-right-hand corner as APPL. After these two steps are complete, PRM is fully enabled for this PRM configuration. Existing processes are being controlled with the PRM CPU manager and new processes will be moved to their appropriate PRM groups.

Figure 7-8 GlancePlus Application CPU Graphs

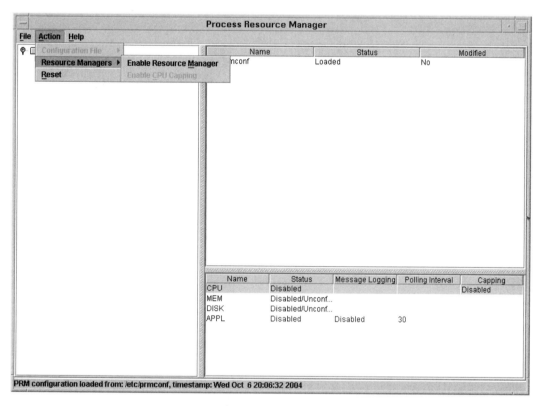

Figure 7-9 Enabling PRM CPU Manager

Viewing PRM Processor Set Group Resource Utilization

After PRM has been enabled, the Application List in GlancePlus shown in Figure 7-10 will demonstrate that PRM is properly restricting CPU consumption based on the configured entitlements. The hr_db database instance is now receiving approximately 75% of the system's CPU resources and the payroll_db database instance is receiving approximately 25%. The payroll_db, other_user_root, and other applications listed in Figure 7-10 are all in the default PSET, sharing a single processor. The hr_db application has exclusive access to the second PSET, which has three processors.

Another tool that can be used to monitor PRM groups is the prmmonitor command. This command provides textual output of resource consumption of the PRM groups. Listing 7-6 shows the output of the command. The -s command-line option displays the default PRM groups, PRM_SYS and OTHERS, in the output. The 5 option at the end of the command is the sample period's time in seconds. At every sample period, a new section of output is displayed showing the current resource consumption and the status of the PRM managers.

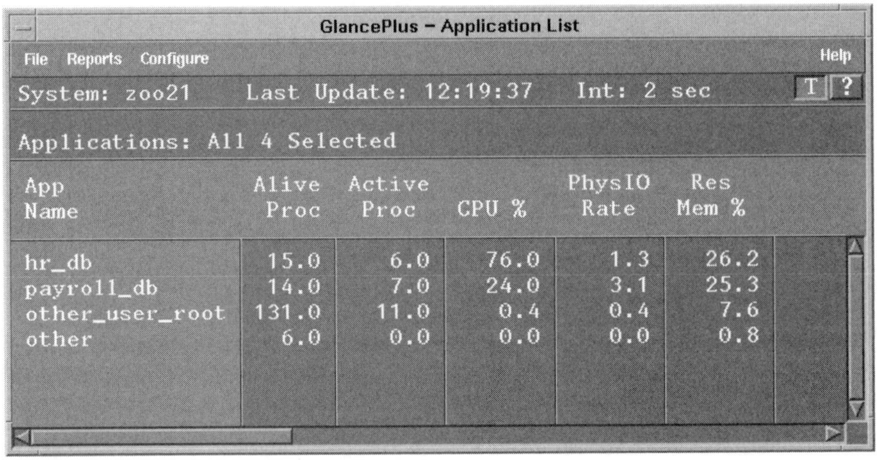

Figure 7-10 Glance Plus Application List after Enabling PRM CPU Manager

---

Listing 7-6 PRM Monitor Command Output

```
# /opt/prm/bin/prmmonitor -s 5

PRM configured from file:  /etc/prmconf
File last modified:        Wed Oct  6 20:06:32 2004

HP-UX zoo21 B.11.11 U 9000/800    10/09/04

Sat Oct  9 12:33:12 2004    Sample:  5 seconds
CPU scheduler state:  Enabled
                                          CPU        CPU
PRM Group                   PRMID    Entitlement     Used
_____
(PRM_SYS)                     0                     0.40%
OTHERS                        1         2.50%       0.00%
payroll_db                    2        22.50%      24.60%
hr_db                        65        75.00%      70.70%

PRM application manager state:  Enabled  (polling interval:
30 seconds)



Sat Oct  9 12:33:17 2004    Sample:  5 seconds
CPU scheduler state:  Enabled
                                          CPU        CPU
PRM Group                   PRMID    Entitlement     Used
_____
(PRM_SYS)                     0                     1.35%
OTHERS                        1         2.50%       0.00%
```

```
payroll_db                            2        22.50%   23.65%
hr_db                                65        75.00%   73.15%

PRM application manager state:  Enabled  (polling interval:
30 seconds)
```

The configuration of PRM is complete for the zoo21 vPar. Each instance of the database has been allocated a subset of the operating system's resources. Using various monitoring tools, the configuration has been verified to be working as expected. Now the PRM groups must be configured for the zoo19 vPar.

Configuring PRM Fair Share Scheduler Groups

The second portion of this example scenario demonstrates the configuration of fair share scheduler PRM groups in the zoo19 virtual partition. Two instances of the Oracle database are running in the zoo19 vPar, the finance_db and the sales_db. As shown in Table 7-2, the finance_db instance will be allocated 60% of the system's CPU resources and the sales_db will be allocated the remaining 40%. In addition, memory groups will be created to ensure that each database has adequate memory.

PRM fair share schedule groups are configured in much the same way as PSET PRM groups using the PRM configuration editor, /opt/prm/bin/xprm. When executed, the initial screen similar to the one in Figure 7-3 is displayed. From the initial screen, select the default configuration file /etc/prmconf and then select Edit from the Action menu. The PRM configuration editor similar to the one in Figure 7-4 is displayed.

Using the PRM configuration editor, specify the name of the group in the Group field and input the number of shares in the Shares field. These two steps are performed for both the finance_db and the sales_db. Assign the finance_db 60 shares and the sales_db 40 shares. Modify the OTHERS group so it is allocated 1 share. The PRM software automatically allocates shares to the PRM_SYS group by default, even though it is not shown in the list. The complete PRM Group configuration is shown in Figure 7-11.

Configuration of the PRM FSS CPU groups is complete. The next step is to configure the application records. The application records are configured identically, regardless of whether PRM FSS or PSET groups are used. Figure 7-12 shows the final application records for the finance_db and sales_db groups.

Unlike the PSET groups created in the zoo21 vPar, memory groups will be configured for the PRM groups in zoo19. Configuration and activation of the memory groups ensures that each application is allocated sufficient memory during peak utilization. The Memory tab of the PRM configuration editor allows memory groups to be defined.

Figure 7-13 shows the initial screen for specifying memory resource groups. The first step in configuring memory resource groups is to select the Add all missing button near the bottom of the screen.

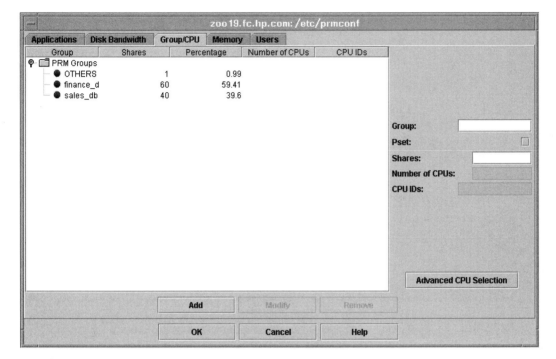

Figure 7-11 PRM Configuration Editor with FSS Groups Defined

important

When using memory resource groups, you must define a memory group for every PRM CPU group. Using the Add all missing feature ensures that a memory group exists for every PRM group.

Figure 7-14 shows the memory groups as added when the Add all missing feature is used. Notice that each group is allocated 1 share, meaning equal allocation between the groups. Since equal allocation is generally not what you intend, select each of the finance_db and sales_db records. When a record is selected, the fields on the right side of the screen are populated and can be edited. Modify the finance_db so it is allocated 60 shares and has a cap of 80 percent. Then modify the sales_db so it is allocated 40 shares with a cap of 60 percent. The memory caps specify the upper bound of memory consumption for each of the PRM groups. When applications reach their memory cap, they will be suppressed.

The memory shares and caps are used in this example to illustrate their configuration. Choosing the proper values for the memory allocation and caps requires an analysis of the workload and an understanding of its memory requirements.

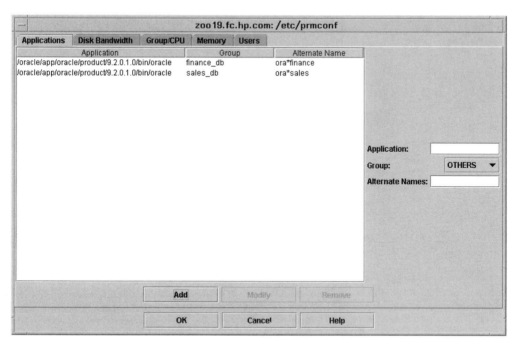

Figure 7-12 PRM Configuration Editor with Application Groups Defined

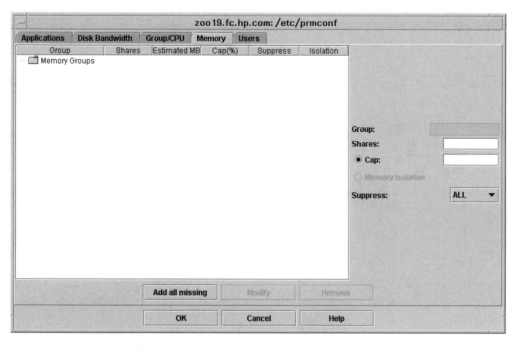

Figure 7-13 PRM Configuration Editor for Memory Resource Groups

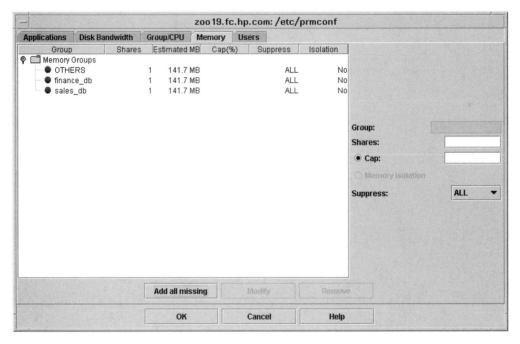

Figure 7-14 PRM Configuration Editor after Adding Missing Groups

Figure 7-15 shows the final configuration of the PRM memory groups. Notice that the finance_db application has been assigned 60 shares with a cap of 80%. The sales_db has been allocated 40 shares with a cap of 60%.

note

> The sum of the Estimated MB fields in Figure 7-15 is much less than the physical memory available on the system. In this example, the zoo19 vPar is allocated 2GB of memory, but the sum of the Estimated MB fields is roughly 400MB. The disparity exists because PRM removes kernel memory, locked memory, and shared memory from the estimated values.

The configuration of the PRM groups for zoo19 is complete. Select the OK button to return to the main PRM configuration screen. To save the configuration, select Configuration File from the Action menu and select Save.

The resulting PRM configuration file is shown in Listing 7-7. Notice that the memory records start with the characters "#!". These lines are not comments, they are actual configuration settings.

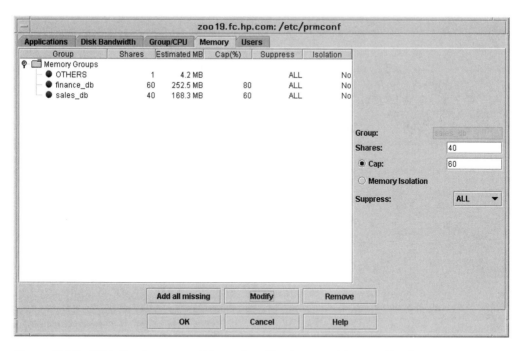

Figure 7-15 PRM Configuration Editor after Configuring Memory Entitlements

Listing 7-7 PRM Configuration File

```
# cat /etc/prmconf
#
# Group/CPU records
#
OTHERS:1:1::
finance_db:2:60::
sales_db:3:40::
#
# Memory records
#
#!PRM_MEM:1:1::::
#!PRM_MEM:2:60:80:::
#!PRM_MEM:3:40:60:::
#
# Application records
#
/oracle/app/oracle/product/9.2.0.1.0/bin/oracle:::: finance_db,ora*finance
/oracle/app/oracle/product/9.2.0.1.0/bin/oracle:::: sales_db,ora*sales
#
# Disk bandwidth records
```

```
#
#
# User records
```

At this point the configuration file has been saved but the applications have not been moved to their application groups, and none of the PRM resource managers are running. Once again, the GlancePlus parameter file can be updated as shown in Listing 7-8 to track the primary workloads running within zoo19.

Listing 7-8 GlancePlus Parameter File Defining Database Applications

```
# cat /var/opt/perf/parm
[...]
application = sales_db
file = ora*sales

application = finance_db
file = ora*finance

application = other_user_root
user = root
```

Figure 7-16 shows that the two database instances are consuming almost identical amounts of CPU and memory resources.

Figure 7-17 shows the Application CPU Graphs in GlancePlus. This view shows that although the workloads are varying in CPU consumption, the average of the two is close to equal.

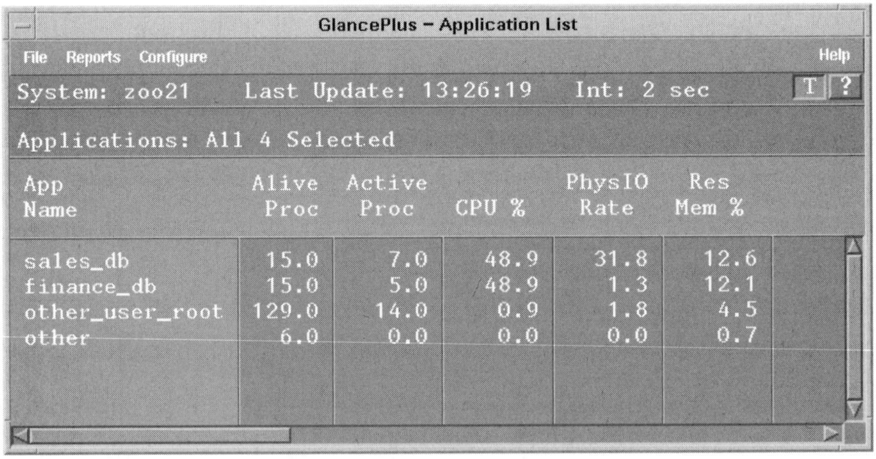

```
                    GlancePlus — Application List
 File  Reports  Configure                                    Help
 System: zoo21      Last Update: 13:26:19    Int: 2 sec    T  ?

 Applications: All 4 Selected

 App            Alive   Active              PhysIO   Res
 Name           Proc    Proc     CPU %      Rate     Mem %

 sales_db       15.0     7.0     48.9       31.8     12.6
 finance_db     15.0     5.0     48.9        1.3     12.1
 other_user_root 129.0  14.0      0.9        1.8      4.5
 other           6.0     0.0      0.0        0.0      0.7
```

Figure 7-16 GlancePlus Application List before Enabling PRM

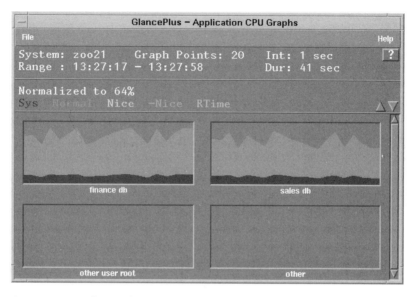

Figure 7-17 GlancePlus Application CPU Graphs before Enabling PRM

Loading the PRM Configuration

The next step in the configuration process is to load the configuration. From the main PRM configuration screen, select Configuration File from the Action menu and then select Load, moving processes to assigned groups. This step moves all processes to their assigned groups but does not enable the CPU, application, or memory managers.

After loading the configuration, use the ps command to verify that the processes have been assigned to the proper groups. The PRMID column of Listing 7-9 shows each of the processes associated with the workloads is assigned to the proper PRM groups.

Listing 7-9 Process Listing after Enabling PRM

```
# ps -efP ¦ grep -e ora.*sales -e COMMAND
    UID   PRMID     PID   PPID  TIME COMMAND
  oracle  sales_db  28014 28012 1:46 oraclesales
  oracle  sales_db  28015 28012 1:46 oraclesales
  oracle  sales_db  28016 28012 1:46 oraclesales
  oracle  sales_db  27049     1 0:00 ora_d001_sales
  oracle  sales_db  28013 28012 1:46 oraclesales
  oracle  sales_db  27037     1 0:01 ora_smon_sales
  oracle  sales_db  27045     1 0:00 ora_s000_sales
  oracle  sales_db  27029     1 0:00 ora_pmon_sales
  oracle  sales_db  27031     1 0:03 ora_dbw0_sales
  oracle  sales_db  27033     1 0:05 ora_lgwr_sales
```

```
oracle   sales_db   27043     1 0:04 ora_qmn0_sales
oracle   sales_db   27035     1 0:01 ora_ckpt_sales
oracle   sales_db   27039     1 0:00 ora_reco_sales
oracle   sales_db   27041     1 0:01 ora_cjq0_sales
oracle   sales_db   27047     1 0:00 ora_d000_sales

# ps -efP | grep -e ora.*finance -e COMMAND
     UID   PRMID       PID   PPID   TIME COMMAND
oracle   finance_db   28056 28054 1:34 oraclefinance
oracle   finance_db   26897     1 0:03 ora_dbw0_finance
oracle   finance_db   26903     1 0:01 ora_smon_finance
oracle   finance_db   28058 28054 1:34 oraclefinance
oracle   finance_db   28057 28054 1:34 oraclefinance
oracle   finance_db   28055 28054 1:33 oraclefinance
oracle   finance_db   26915     1 0:00 ora_d001_finance
oracle   finance_db   26913     1 0:00 ora_d000_finance
oracle   finance_db   26895     1 0:00 ora_pmon_finance
oracle   finance_db   26899     1 0:05 ora_lgwr_finance
oracle   finance_db   26907     1 0:01 ora_cjq0_finance
oracle   finance_db   26905     1 0:00 ora_reco_finance
oracle   finance_db   26911     1 0:00 ora_s000_finance
oracle   finance_db   26901     1 0:02 ora_ckpt_finance
oracle   finance_db   26909     1 0:04 ora_qmn0_finance
```

Enabling PRM Fair Share Schedule Groups

The final step in activating the PRM configuration is to enable the PRM managers. The following actions must be taken from the main PRM configuration screen shown in Figure 7-9.

1. Enable the CPU manager by selecting the CPU line in the lower-right-hand corner of the screen. Then select Resource Managers from the Action menu and select Enable Resource Manager.

2. Enable CPU capping by selecting Resource Managers from the Action menu and then selecting Enable CPU Capping.

3. Enable the memory manager by selecting the MEM line in the lower-right-hand corner of the screen. Then select Resource Managers from the Action menu and select Enable Resource Manager.

4. Enable the application manager by selecting the APPL line in the lower-right-hand corner of the screen. Then select Resource Managers from the Action menu and select Enable Resource Manager.

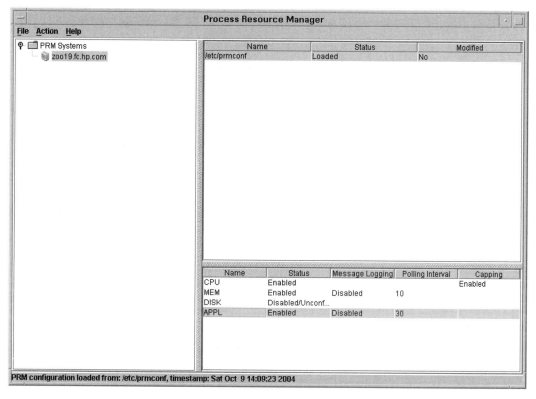

Figure 7-18 Final PRM Configuration and Status after Enabling PRM

When these steps have been performed, PRM actively monitors the system and controls resource utilization. Figure 7-18 shows the final PRM configuration screen with all of the configured PRM resource managers enabled.

Monitoring PRM Fair Share Scheduler Groups

The PRM groups have been configured and enabled as is evident in Figure 7-19, which shows the GlancePlus Application List. Notice that the finance_db is now receiving over 60% of the system's resource while the sales_db is receiving roughly 34% of the system's resources.

In addition to the GlancePlus Application List, views are available within GlancePlus specifically for monitoring PRM groups. Selecting PRM Group List from the Reports menu of the main GlancePlus screen provides a view similar to the Application List but does not require

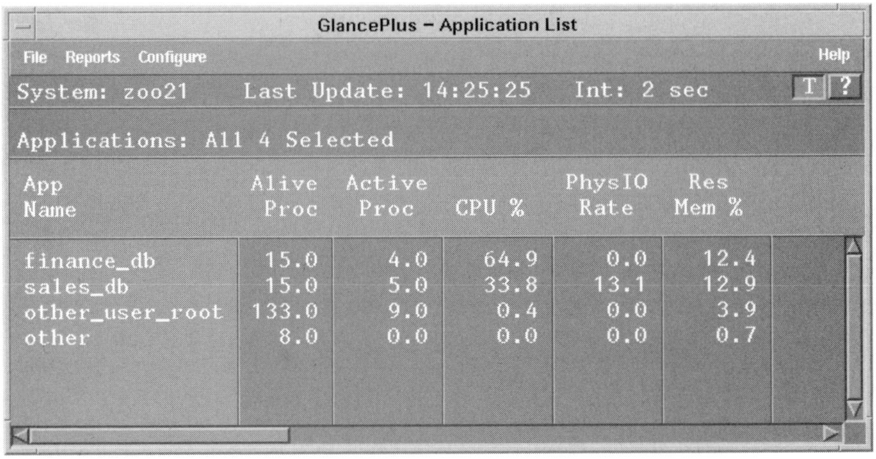

Figure 7-19 GlancePlus Application List after Enabling PRM

modifications to the GlancePlus parameter file. The PRM Group List in GlancePlus is shown in Figure 7-20.

Using the PRM-specific reports and graphs has the added benefit of showing the default PRM groups PRM_SYS and OTHERS. The PRM CPU Graphs shown in Figure 7-21 confirms the expected amounts of CPU consumption for each of the PRM groups.

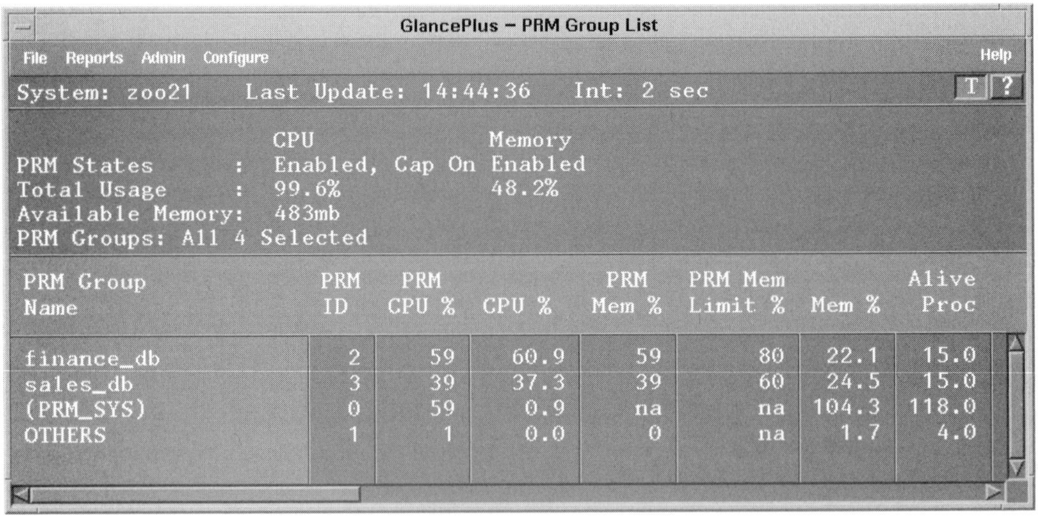

Figure 7-20 GlancePlus PRM Group List

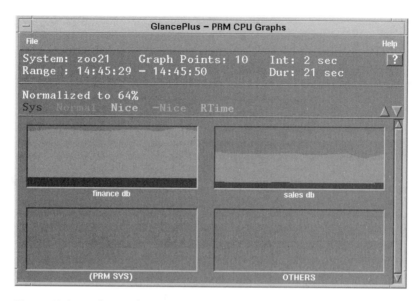

Figure 7-21 GlancePlus PRM CPU Graphs

Viewing the Effects of CPU Capping

The PRM configuration on zoo19 has CPU capping enabled. In some situations this is desired in order to guarantee that an application receives no more than its share of the system. In fact, users of the workload may like the increased performance when a workload is using more than its share of the system and may become dissatisfied when the system is busy and the workload is receiving only its allocated share of the system.

However, in other cases, CPU capping may not be required. Figure 7-22 shows the two database workloads. Currently the finance_db is idle, but the sales_db is consuming about 36% of the system. In this case, the sales_db is consuming all of its CPU resources and could use more resources if they were available.

For illustration purposes, CPU capping will be disabled in the zoo19 PRM configuration. In the PRM configuration editor, select the CPU manager in the lower-right-hand corner of the screen. Then select Resource Managers from the Action menu. Finally, select Disable CPU Capping. Figure 7-23 shows the resulting resource consumption. The sales_db is now consuming 88% of the system. This is allowed because CPU capping has been disabled and the finance_db application is not using its allotment of CPU resources. When the finance_db application becomes busy, the CPU allocations will go back to their configured entitlements.

It should be clear from this illustration that CPU capping may result in decreased system utilization when idle resources are not being shared.

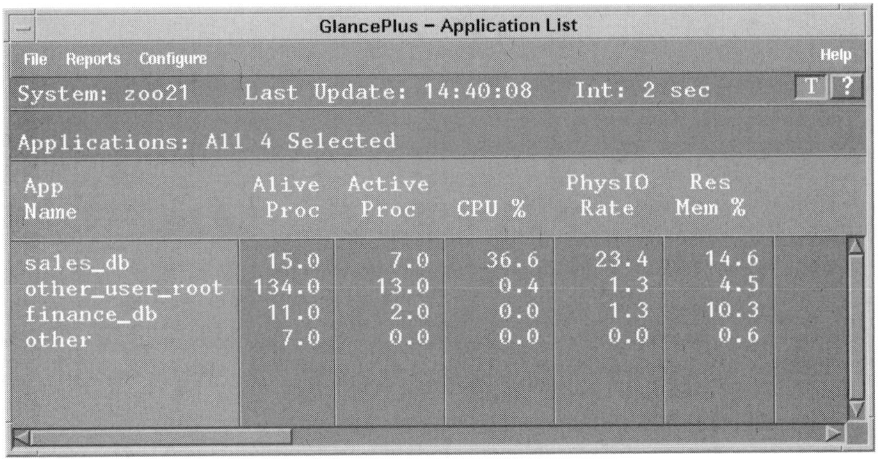

Figure 7-22 GlancePlus Application List with PRM CPU Capping Enabled

Disk I/O Bandwidth Management

PRM also offers a disk I/O bandwidth resource manager. It monitors the I/O requests in the kernel for LVM volume groups and VxVM disk groups. The I/O requests are reprioritized in the kernel to ensure that disk bandwidth entitlements are met. The configuration of the disk manager is not covered in this book, but its usage and configuration is very similar to that of the other PRM managers.

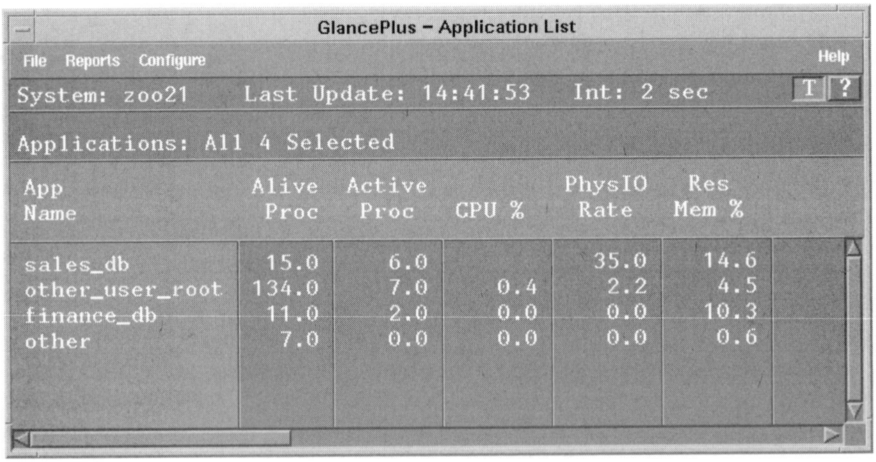

Figure 7-23 GlancePlus Application List with PRM CPU Capping Disabled

Summary

Secure Resource Partitions rely on the HP Process Resource Manager product and provide a tremendous amount of flexibility and control in environments where operating system isolation is not required. Each SRP is guaranteed a portion of a system's resources and is isolated from a security standpoint. The sub-CPU granularity provided by SRPs allows fine control over resource allocation. Using SRPs makes possible high system utilization and lower maintenance costs as fewer operating systems and applications must be installed, configured, and maintained.

SRP configurations can use any combination of the CPU manager, the memory manager, the disk I/O bandwidth manager, and secure compartments. The CPU manager is responsible for ensuring that CPU entitlements are being met by scheduling processes according to workload demands and SRP entitlements. The memory manager allows memory resources to be controlled and even capped to ensure that each workload has the necessary memory available when it is required. The disk I/O bandwidth manager rearranges I/O requests to meet the requested entitlements of each SRP. Secure compartments protect workloads from other processes on the system.

The example scenario in this chapter demonstrates the use of SRPs in an nPartition that contains virtual partitions. The virtual partitions are divided into SRPs and each SRP is running a separate instance of a database. Each instance of the database is guaranteed an amount of the operating system's resources but is able to share resources when they are available. This configuration illustrates the power and flexibility offered through combinations of the partitioning technologies in HP's Virtual Server Environment.

8

Overview of HP's Utility Pricing Solutions

HP's Utility Pricing solutions for the HP 9000 and Integrity servers consists of a set of solutions that makes it possible to acquire servers and server components and only pay for what you use.

At first glance it might not be obvious why Utility Pricing Solutions are considered part of the Virtual Server Environment—that is, until you consider that these solutions are tightly integrated with the rest of the VSE, including the partitioning continuum and workload management. All of these solutions allow you to instantly activate additional capacity to respond to changes in the demand on workloads. Since this dynamism is a major driving force of the rest of the VSE, these solutions fit in very nicely.

Utility Pricing Solutions

There are two distinct types of Utility Pricing Solutions. The first is a set of Instant Capacity solutions and the other is the utility computing solution called Pay per use.

The Instant Capacity solutions allow you to purchase a system that has more capacity than is required when the system is purchased. You then have the ability to activate and pay for the capacity when you need it. In other words, Instant Capacity is all about simplifying the upgrade process. It was originally designed as a way to reduce the lead time for CPU upgrades. The idea was that if the system is shipped with the upgrades already installed (but inactive), the customer could activate the additional capacity instantly. Since the customer doesn't pay for the bulk of the cost of the upgrade until they activate the CPUs, this program has cost characteristics that are similar to a standard purchase and installation of additional CPUs. However, it can be done instantly and without shutting down the system.

Effectively this gives you instant access to capacity upgrades while deferring the cost of the upgrades until you actually need them. This is useful if you know that the system you are purchasing will require an upgrade at some time in the future but that the system will be underutilized until then.

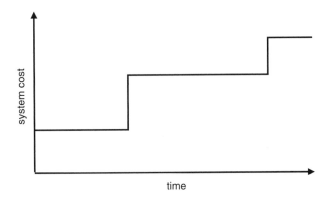

Figure 8-1 The Overall Cost of a System as Instant Capacity Resources Are Activated

Currently, Instant Capacity can be obtained for one or more CPUs or cell boards. This program requires you to purchase what is called a right-to-access (RTA) license for the inactive resources. The up-front cost of the RTA license is a fraction of the full cost of the resources. However, this amount can be applied to the cost of the permanent activation of the resource later.

Figure 8-1 shows how the cost of the system increases over time as you activate additional capacity.

You can see in this graph that the capacity can be added gradually if you have a steady increase in load. You can also increase the capacity in larger increments if you have larger, more-sudden increases in load, like the addition of new workloads or migration of a large number of users onto the system.

There is another Instant Capacity solution, called Temporary Instant Capacity. The key to this is that you can activate Instant Capacity CPU resources for short periods of time and then deactivate them when they are no longer needed. Figure 8-2 shows a contrasting view of costs over time with Temporary Instant Capacity.

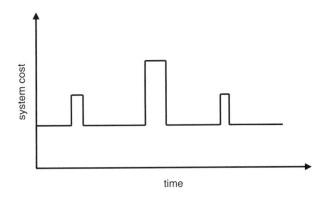

Figure 8-2 The Cost of a System as Temporary Instant Capacity Resources Are Activated and Deactivated

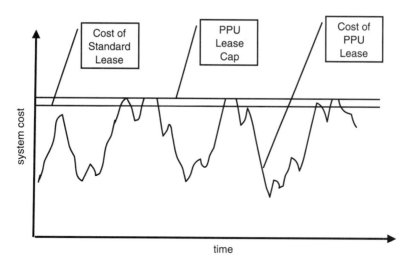

Figure 8-3 The Lease Cost of a Pay Per Use System Compared to a Standard Lease

In this case you can see that the costs increase only during the short periods of time that you actually need to the resources to be active. In addition, if you have longer-term increases in load, you can activate one or more of the CPUs permanently.

The last of the Utility Pricing Solutions is called Pay per use (PPU). The overall time-varying cost aspects of Pay per use are similar to Temporary Instant Capacity, but PPU is a leasing model. You are leasing the system from HP Financial Services (HPFS), but the lease payment varies from one month to the next depending on the utilization of the server. Figure 8-3 shows how the PPU cost varies over the life of a lease.

This graph shows that with a standard lease you would pay for all of the resources of the system every month. With a PPU lease, you would have a lower payment in any month where the system is lightly used. You might also pay slightly more than a standard lease if the system is heavily used over the course of the month. The key is that as long as the system isn't heavily used every month, you will end up paying less. In fact, as will be described later, you are guaranteed not to pay any more than a standard lease over the life of a PPU lease.

The remainder of this chapter will provide more detail about each of these solutions, including the program requirements for each of them.

CPU Instant Capacity

The first Utility Pricing Solution that HP delivered was CPU Instant Capacity. This provides the ability to acquire a system with extra CPU capacity for future upgrades. The CPUs are physically present in the system but are inactive so they don't participate in process scheduling by the operating system.

This section focuses primarily on the permanent activation of Instant Capacity CPUs. We will cover temporary activation in the next section.

CPU Instant Capacity Use Model

The use model for Instant Capacity is really quite simple. The goal of Instant Capacity is allow you to defer the cost of an upgrade you know you will need in the future. This upgrade could be needed because:

* You are expecting an increase in the number of users for the application the server is being purchased for

* The server is being purchased for a consolidation environment and the applications will be migrated to the new server gradually over the course of a year or more

* You expect to be deploying new applications on the server in the future

As part of the acquisition process for the server, you will work with your HP Sales technical consultant or authorized partner to ensure that there is sufficient spare capacity on the system to meet the needs of expected upgrades. The norm in the past was to pay the full cost of these resources from the beginning. Using Instant Capacity in this environment is an improvement because:

* The bulk of the cost of the extra resources needed for the new workloads is deferred.

* Capacity planning becomes easier because even if you overestimate the need for resources, you will have extra resources to apply to other workloads. Essentially, the cost of overestimating is lower because you only pay a fraction of the cost for the unused capacity.

One thing to note is that the CPUs can be activated while the system is on line. To take advantage of this you will need to ensure that the extra CPUs are physically located in the nPars where they will be activated. Once you have determined how many Instant Capacity CPUs you want, you purchase what is called a right-to-access (RTA) license for the CPUs. When you need to upgrade the system, you simply send a purchase order to HP for the balance of the cost of those CPUs. HP will respond with information about how to access the Utility Pricing portal to get a right-to-use (RTU) codeword that can be used to license the additional CPUs. Once you have applied the codeword to any HP-UX partition in the system, you can then use the `icod_modify` command to activate processors in the relevant partition.

CPU Instant Capacity Requirements

The Instant Capacity program is a combination of a financial services agreement and the technology to implement it. The general principles of the program include the following:

- Customer purchases the RTA license for the Instant Capacity processors when the system is purchased.

- Customer must maintain the Instant Capacity software running on all the HP-UX partitions on the system or HP will assume that all of the resources assigned to the partition are active.

- Customer must agree to migrate to newer versions of the Instant Capacity software when they are released.

- The customer can assign a system contact that will receive e-mails from HP when there is a change in the status of a CPU or a compliance exception has occurred.

- If the system is moved to another location, then you need to notify HP ahead of time. Generally speaking, HP won't have any issues as long as the system isn't being moved to a different country.

Some other benefits of the Instant Capacity program include:

- There is no need to purchase HP support or software (OE) licensing for the additional CPU until it is activated.

- Instant Capacity CPUs can be factory or field installed.

- There is no premium for purchasing the CPU via Instant Capacity. The RTA cost paid up front is applied to the cost of the CPU when it is activated. In addition, if the cost of the CPU decreases between the time the system is acquired and when you activate the CPU, you pay the reduced cost.

- Instant Capacity CPUs are used as part of the Dynamic Processor Resilience feature of HP systems. If the system detects intermittent errors on a CPU, it will take it off line to ensure that it doesn't cause the system or partition to crash. If there are available Instant Capacity CPUs on the system, it will activate one of those CPUs at no cost to you to keep the system at full capacity.

Using Instant Capacity CPUs to Do Processor Load-Balancing between nPars

An interesting feature of Instant Capacity is that the number of inactive CPUs is measured across the entire complex in a cell-based server. In other words, if you have a complex that has been split up into multiple hard partitions, it doesn't matter which partition the inactive CPUs are in. This is easier to explain using an example. Figure 8-4 shows a server complex with four cells, split into two nPartitions with two cells each and a total of four inactive Instant Capacity processors.

In this picture you see that the system has been partitioned into two electrically isolated nPartitions. Each partition has two cells with a total of eight physical CPUs. However, there are two inactive CPUs in each partition, so these are really six CPU partitions, with a total of twelve active CPUs in the complex.

One other very important feature here is that these Instant Capacity CPUs can be activated and deactivated without requiring a reboot of any of the partitions. So if the workload in partition nPar1 experiences a spike in load, you can deactivate CPUs in nPar2 and activate the other two CPUs that are already physically present in nPar1. This is depicted in Figure 8-5.

As you can see in this picture, there are still twelve active processors on the system. However, we now have eight active CPUs in nPar1 and only four active CPUs in nPar2. This makes it possible to satisfy the spike in load on the workloads running in nPar1 and the extra CPUs do not sit idle in nPar1 when they are not needed.

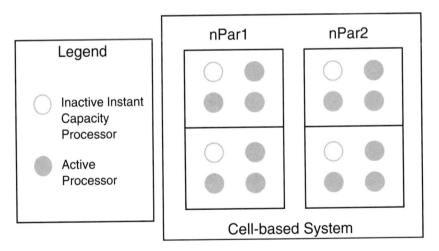

Figure 8-4 A Cell-Based Server with Two nPartitions and Instant Capacity Processors

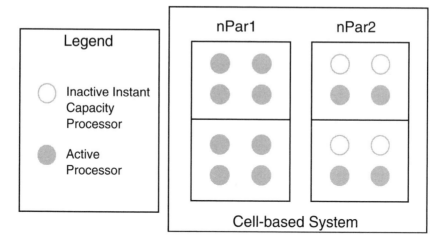

Figure 8-5 Using Instant Capacity Processors to Increase CPU Capacity in nPar1

Of course, this can go the other way also. Suppose the workload in nPar1 is no longer busy and the workload in nPar2 experiences a spike. Figure 8-6 shows nPar2 with eight active CPUs.

This makes it possible to satisfy the performance requirements in nPar2 with the same number of active CPUs on the system.

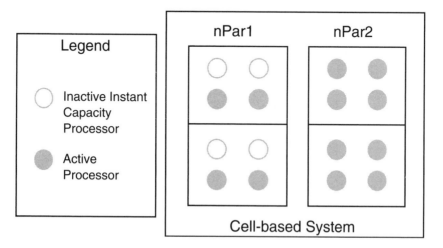

Figure 8-6 Using Instant Capacity Processors to Increase CPU Capacity in nPar2

If you think about this, Instant Capacity allows you to:

* Scale each of these nPars from four CPUs to eight CPUs
* One CPU at a time
* While both partitions remain up and running
* While maintaining the electrical isolation between the partitions
* Without incurring any cost for activating the Instant Capacity CPUs

If you are purchasing a cell-based system and plan to do consolidation by carving the system up into multiple nPartitions, you really should consider purchasing the system with some Instant Capacity resources so you can get this flexibility. This effectively makes it possible to share the spare capacity between the partitions rather than having it sit idle in one partition when it could be used in another. If you are considering getting permanent licenses for all the CPUs, this will reduce the cost of the system and give you additional flexibility for allocating resources to the workloads that need them.

Several important considerations:

* This does require the system to have inactive Instant Capacity CPUs.
* The partition you want to activate the CPU in must have an available inactive CPU physically present.

The key to this last point is that you should ensure that each of the nPars has enough physical CPUs in the partition to satisfy the maximum amount of capacity that might be required for the workloads running there. Of course, if you guess wrong, you can always reconfigure your nPartitions to add additional cells to the partition, but this will require a reboot, so it is preferable to have some extra capacity there in the form of Instant Capacity CPUs.

Using Instant Capacity CPUs to Do Processor Load-Balancing between Separate Servers

A new capability provided on top of Instant Capacity is the ability to migrate the licenses between systems. This is effectively the same type of functionality as described above, but you now have the ability to do this across physically separate systems. This provides an additional capability to ensure that you don't have idle processors on one system when there are workloads on another that can use them. A few key points about this new capability:

* The Instant Capacity Share Group is a new concept from HP. This is a group of systems over which you want to be able to migrate Instant Capacity licenses. There will be restrictions on the members of each group.

- A management software component is responsible for managing the migration of licenses between servers. This software runs on any system local to the servers in the group and can manage multiple groups.

- The mechanism for deactivating and activating processors is the same as when moving between nPars.

- This capability is provided as a separate product at an additional cost.

Although there is an additional cost for this capability, this will probably be more than off-set by the savings you will realize because you won't have to purchase permanent licenses for capacity that is only needed for short periods of time.

CPU Temporary Instant Capacity

Once you have Instant Capacity processors in your system, another solution allows you to access this additional capacity. With Temporary Instant Capacity you can turn these CPUs on for short periods of time to respond to unexpected spikes in load.

note

> Each system purchased with Instant Capacity will automatically be provided with a license for 5 days of Temporary Instant Capacity. This is intended to provide the ability to instantly activate a processor while going through the acquisition process for a permanent license. You can also add standard Temporary Capacity licenses to this initial bank if you want.

CPU Temporary Instant Capacity Use Model

Temporary Instant Capacity (TiCAP) is really just an alternative method for activating Instant Capacity processors that are already in your system. The process for accessing these looks like this:

- Ensure there are enough physical CPUs in each nPar to accommodate the maximum load that is expected for the workloads running there. When you are acquiring the system, purchase some number of them as inactive Instant Capacity processors. You should ensure that you have permanently active CPUs that are sufficient to cover the load for the majority of each day or month. The rest can be Instant Capacity CPUs.

- Purchase a Temporary Instant Capacity license. This license entitles you to activate the Instant Capacity CPUs for 30 CPU days, which is equivalent to 720 CPU hours, or 43,200 CPU minutes.

- Pull the Temporary Instant Capacity license codeword from the HP Utility Pricing portal and apply it to your system. This sets up a bank of CPU minutes on the system. You can now activate and deactivate the Instant Capacity CPUs any time you wish.

- The Temporary Instant Capacity license works much like a bank debit card or a prepaid phone card. When you activate a CPU, it starts deducting minutes from your bank. When you deactivate the CPU, it stops deducting.

- You can activate multiple CPUs with a single Temporary Instant Capacity license, but it will deduct time from your bank for each CPU that you have activated.

- When your balance drops below a configurable threshold, which defaults to five CPU days, The TiCAP software sends an e-mail to the system contact to warn them that they may want to consider either permanently activating one or more CPUs or purchasing an additional Temporary Instant Capacity license.

- If the balance goes to zero, you will no longer be able to activate processors. However, the currently active processors will remain active until you reboot a partition. If you have a negative balance in your Temporary Instant Capacity account on the system, the software will notify you that you are out of compliance. If you choose to do a permanent activation of a CPU, the negative TiCAP balance is wiped out. If you purchase another Temporary Instant Capacity license, the negative balance is deducted from the amount of minutes you add when you apply the codeword to the system.

Some of the key benefits of this approach include:

- A single Temporary Instant Capacity license gives you the ability to activate any number of CPUs. If you have an nPar with 30 inactive processors, you can activate all 30 of them. This will deduct time from your bank for each CPU, but this is a very nice level of flexibility. For the cost of one TiCAP license, you can activate 30 CPUs to respond to an unexpected demand.

- The system has the same amount of capacity you would have purchased to cover peak load and some amount of room for growth.

- The system costs less because you only need to pay for roughly 25% of the cost of the Instant Capacity CPUs.

- You can maintain much higher utilization of your active capacity because you know you have spare capacity that can be instantly activated in the event of an infrequent or unexpected spike in load.

- This provides a very simple capacity-planning metric to use when additional permanent capacity should be activated. If you find you are frequently activating your TiCAP CPUs and needing to renew your 30-day licenses regularly, you might want to consider adding more permanent capacity. We describe a formula in the next chapter that will help you decide if you should get more Temporary Instant Capacity or permanently activate a CPU.

Temporary Instant Capacity Requirements

There are only a few requirements for Temporary Instant Capacity that are above and beyond the standard CPU Instant Capacity requirements. You still have to satisfy all the requirements for standard Instant Capacity, including the purchasing of a right-to-access license for the Instant Capacity CPUs. The additional requirements include:

- Older versions of Instant Capacity required you to set up each partition on the system to send a daily e-mail to HP. Although this requirement has been removed starting with the version 7 release, you can still use it if you want to be able to use the portal to get usage information across all of your Instant Capacity systems. The e-mail is encrypted and sent once each day, every time there is startup or shutdown of a partition, and every time there is an activation or deactivation of a component. This also allows you to get usage and remaining capacity information from the Utility Pricing portal. There is no need for the system to be able to accept incoming e-mail, but it must be able to send outgoing e-mail.

- You need to purchase a Temporary Instant Capacity license. You can actually purchase as many of these as you think you will need depending on your consumption requirements and how much lead time you need to process purchases. You can choose to consume the initial 5 days of Temporary Capacity that is provided with your Instant Capacity licenses, but keep in mind that this will reduce your ability to activate processors while waiting for a permanent license.

- When your Temporary Instant Capacity balance drops to zero, you must either deactivate all Instant Capacity processors or purchase another TiCAP license. The system will not automatically deactivate processors on line, but they will be deactivated upon the next reboot. If a negative balance builds, it will be deducted from the next license added to the system. Alternatively, if you purchase one or more of the Instant Capacity processors for permanent activation, any negative balance will be erased.

If you have a system with Instant Capacity processors in it, you would be well served to investigate purchasing a Temporary Instant Capacity license. You will gain a tremendous amount of flexibility for a remarkably low cost.

Cell Board Instant Capacity

The Cell board Instant Capacity solution offers you a way to have extra cell boards on a system without having to pay the full cost of those resources when the system is acquired.

Cell Board Instant Capacity Use Model

The use model for Cell board Instant Capacity is much the same as it is for Instant Capacity for CPUs. The only major differences include:

* The cell will also contain memory, so the codeword you get to activate the cell will include the code for the cell, the memory on the cell, and potentially one or more of the CPUs on the cell.

* Until a future release of HP-UX, the cell cannot be activated on line. You will have to apply the codeword, assign the cell to a partition (if it isn't already in one), set the cell's Use on Next Boot flag to "y," and then reboot the partition.

Cell Board Instant Capacity Requirements

There are a couple of extra requirements for Cell board Instant Capacity. These include:

* All of the memory on the cell must be activated when the cell is activated.

* At least one CPU must be active on every cell in a partition. It is possible to activate the cell board and memory without getting additional CPUs by deactivating a CPU somewhere else on the system. This is a way to increase the amount of memory to a partition without having to add additional CPUs. This will also provide more flexibility in the future because you can now use Temporary Instant Capacity or the Instant Capacity CPU rebalancing capability to increase the capacity of this partition if an unexpected load occurs on the partition.

Pay Per Use Utility Computing

Pay per use (PPU) is a very different model than Instant Capacity. All of the Instant Capacity offerings are technologies that allow you to purchase resources, either permanently or temporarily, on systems that you have purchased. Pay per use is a leasing model. Instead of purchasing the system from HP, you are leasing it. The key difference between a PPU lease and a standard lease is that the PPU lease payment will vary from month to month depending on the usage of the system for the previous month. The PPU lease payment has two components. The first is the base payment, which is roughly half the cost of a standard lease. The other component is the variable portion of the payment.

PPU Use Model

Since Pay per use (PPU) is a lease model from HP Financial Services, it does require that you use HPFS to lease the system. Once the system is installed on your site, PPU metering software on each partition in the system monitors CPU utilization. This software passes this data on to the PPU meter for forwarding to HP. HP uses the data to populate the PPU portal and for billing purposes.

There are two different models for determining the utilization of the system—Active CPU and Percent CPU.

Before we get into a discussion of these current PPU options, a little history lesson is in order. There have been some fairly significant changes in the PPU program starting with version 7 of the PPU software. In order to avoid confusing existing customers, we provide a brief description of the previous models.

Legacy PPU Solutions

The original PPU program was built on top of Instant Capacity capabilities in the systems and was called the Active CPU utilization model. The key difference was Active CPU required each partition to send an encrypted e-mail to HP when CPUs were activated and deactivated. HP used this information to determine how many CPU hours were consumed each day, which it then aggregated to produce a monthly utilization for billing purposes.

The Active CPU model uses a method very similar to Temporary Instant Capacity to determine utilization. You have the ability to activate CPUs when you need them and deactivate them when you don't need them. The metering software monitors the activation status of the CPUs over the course of the day to determine what the average utilization is. As an example, let's say that we have a system with 12 physical CPUs; four are active as a base, which is all that is used during nighttime hours (7:00 PM to 7:00 AM). Then at 7:00 AM we activate an additional four CPUs to cover the morning rush. At 10:00 AM we turn off two of these CPUs because the morning rush is over by then. The next rush comes at 1:00 PM, so we reactivate those two CPUs then and turn them back off at 2:00 PM. The final rush of the day is between 4:00 PM and 7:00 PM. To determine the average utilization, we need to add up the number of CPUs active for each hour and then average it over the day. Using the above description, we have:

- four CPUs for twelve hours (7:00 PM to 7:00 AM) = 48 hours
- eight CPUs for seven hours (7:00 AM to 10:00 AM, 1:00 PM to 2:00 PM, 4:00 PM to 7:00 PM) = 56 hours
- six CPUs for the remaining five hours = 30 hours

These all add up to 134 CPU hours; divided by 24 hours in the day, this equals an average of 5.58 CPUs per hour. Even though you have a peak capacity of eight CPUs for a significant part of the normal workday, you are only being charged for 5.58.

Subsequent releases of PPU provided a number of enhancements to this solution. The most significant of these was the introduction of the Percent CPU model, which included the use of a hardware PPU meter at the customer site. In this model, all of the CPUs are always active and the utilization of these CPUs is measured every five minutes. The meter uses a secure protocol to communicate with each of up to 100 partitions to collect the data. It then aggregates the data and sends it to HP via HTTPS or encrypted e-mail. The five-minute interval data for each CPU is averaged for the full 24 hours of each day. Then all the CPUs are averaged together to find the systems overall daily average. These values are then averaged one more time across all of the days of the month to determine the monthly average that your payment is based upon. One nice advantage of the meter is that no production partitions are required to support outgoing e-mail. All communication from the production systems remains inside your firewall. The only device that is required to have access to the Internet is the meter itself. There are two options for communication between the meter and HP. The first is HTTPS, which is a secure web protocol, and the other is encrypted e-mail. When using HTTPS, the data is sent to HP every five minutes as it is received. If e-mail is used, the data is encrypted and sent to HP once each day.

Current PPU Solutions

The current program, starting with Release 7 of the PPU software, always uses the meter, even for Active CPU Pay-per-use models. Essentially, both programs now work the way the prior Percent CPU model worked, but with several key enhancements. These include:

- New PPU commands activate and deactivate CPUs to ensure that they don't get used by the system and that they will contribute a 0% utilization to the average.
- It is now possible to deactivate CPUs in the Percent CPU model. This ensures that those CPUs contribute a 0% utilization rate to the average utilization of the system while they are inactive.
- Active CPU can now be calculated using data from the meter. The data collected can be used to identify when CPUs are activated and deactivated so that this data can be used to determine the active CPU count throughout the day.

Figure 8-7 shows the infrastructure for getting the information to HP and how HP uses it.

This figure shows a simplified architecture of the PPU data collection system. The major components of this infrastructure include:

- Metering software that runs on each partition on the PPU systems. This software monitors the utilization of the system.
- A PPU meter that is used to collect and aggregate the metering data from up to 100 partitions. Prior to version 7 of PPU, the meter was only used for Percent CPU PPU. For Active CPU metering, the data was sent directly from the

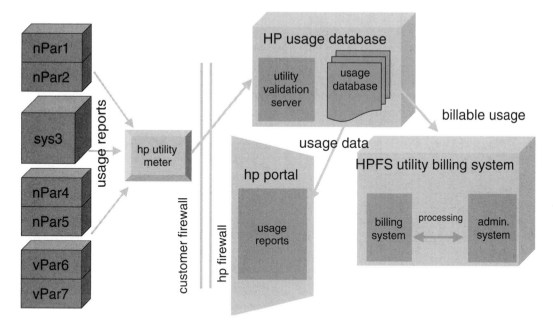

Figure 8-7 The Infrastructure Behind Pay Per Use

partitions themselves to the HP usage database. Starting with version 7, the meter is used for both Active CPU and Percent CPU measurements.

- The usage database includes facilities to decrypt the messages sent for customer systems and then store this data in the database.
- Once the data is in the database, you can view the data about your systems from the secure portal.
- This data is also used by the billing system to determine the variable portion of your payment which is used when generating your monthly PPU invoice.

Several interesting data points about this program:

- The maximum monthly PPU payment is 105% of a standard lease. In order to get over 100% of a standard lease, the system would need to be running at a very high average utilization rate (currently over 70%).
- The maximum cumulative cost over the life of the PPU lease is 100% of the standard lease. In other words, if you pay the 105% consistently, you will eventually pay the full cost of the lease early and you will then have no payments for the remainder of the lease. Of course, you would have to make the maximum payment from the start of the lease through 34.2 months of a 36-month lease for this to happen, so you are much more likely to save money than to prepay the lease.

We will discuss this in more detail in the next chapter, but the bottom line here is that if you are leasing a system, you can't lose by going with PPU rather than a standard lease. We find that some customers have a hard time getting budgeting approval for a varying monthly payment. A trick would be to budget based on the maximum payment and then decide what you are going to do with the savings in the months that it is lower than that.

PPU Requirements

The key program requirements for Pay per use include:

* You must enter into a PPU leasing contract with HP Financial Services.
* You are required to maintain the PPU monitoring software on each partition on your PPU systems.
* You are required to upgrade to newer versions of the PPU monitoring software when they become available.
* You are required to maintain either e-mail or HTTPS connectivity between the meter and HP.
* If you are using Active Capacity, you are responsible for activating and deactivating CPUs when capacity is needed. However, you can automate this using either Workload Manager or Global Workload Manager, which will be discussed in Part 3 of this book.

Summary

This chapter focused on the Utility Pricing solutions that are available for HP 9000 and Integrity servers. These are integrated with the other Virtual Server Environment solutions to provide additional flexibility and opportunity for cost savings.

The Instant Capacity and Temporary Instant Capacity solutions are useful for systems that have been purchased from HP or an authorized partner. These provide the ability to acquire a system with additional capacity built in which can then be activated either temporarily or permanently, depending on your needs.

The Pay-per-use solution is an alternative leasing model whereby the monthly lease payment varies based on the average CPU utilization of the server in the prior month.

All of these solutions provide the ability to acquire a system that is over-provisioned without having to pay for resources you don't end up needing.

Making the Most of Utility Pricing Solutions

Chapter Overview

Let's not beat around the bush—if the server you are purchasing supports any of these solutions, get them. The benefits far outweigh the tradeoffs. That said, these solutions aren't perfect, and there are some tradeoffs that may be show-stoppers in some customer environments—but these should be rare. The vast majority of customers who purchase HP systems will pay less in the long run if they use one or more of these Utility Pricing Solutions.

We will describe in this chapter specifically why we make these statements. Each of the solutions available for HP 9000 and Integrity servers has its own benefits and tradeoffs, which we will describe. We will also identify the sweet spots—the places where you get the most bang for the buck with each of these solutions.

These programs are remarkably beneficial for the customer. Of course, it is possible that HP will alter these programs to make them less forgiving, but the way they are currently set up, they heavily favor the customer. So for the time being, you should not purchase a system that doesn't have one of these solutions. Don't pay more than you have to.

One last note before we get started. Each of these solutions is actually a "program." What this means is there are people involved in many different disciplines that make these products work. All of the solutions described in the other parts of this book are software or hardware products. The programs we describe in this part of the book are creative ways of purchasing HP 9000 and Integrity servers. In each case, HP is putting systems and software on your site that are at least partially owned by HP. Therefore, these programs involve HP Financial Services, Marketing, Sales, HP IT, and Engineering. We mention this because some of the software components may have unexpected features, but there is usually logic behind them when you consider the breadth of the impact on HP.

Instant Capacity

The first solution we consider is Instant Capacity. HP was the first to introduce the concept of Instant Capacity to the industry. The idea was to dramatically reduce the time it takes for a customer to upgrade their systems. Prior to Instant Capacity, the process a customer went through to upgrade a system with additional processors took several months and required that the system be brought down while the new processors were installed. With Instant Capacity, the process has been reduced to a matter of minutes at most and the new processors can be brought on line while the system is running and under load.

Because of the way that Instant Capacity was implemented, there are a few other benefits that are compelling features in and of themselves. These include the ability to migrate capacity between nPars and the simplification of the capacity planning process.

Another solution in the Instant Capacity space is Cell board Instant Capacity. This allows you to have whole cell boards, including CPUs and memory, available for activation.

Key Benefits

We will focus first on CPU Instant Capacity because it has a number of benefits above and beyond what you gain with Cell board Instant Capacity. A number of indispensable benefits come with CPU Instant Capacity. These include:

* The ability to flex the active capacity of nPartitions
* The ability to flex the active capacity of a group of separate servers
* The ability to defer the cost of planned upgrades
* Simplification of the capacity planning process
* Very inexpensive spare capacity
* Component price protection—if the price drops before you activate, you get the lower price

We covered the ability to flex nPartitions in Chapter 8. Instant Capacity processors can be activated and deactivated while the system is on line and under load. Also, HP measures the number of active processors across the entire cell-based complex, regardless of how many nPartitions are active. The combination of these gives you the ability to adjust the active capacity between electrically isolated nPartitions one CPU at a time while all the partitions continue to run and service application workloads. This is done by deactivating a processor in one partition and activating an available Instant Capacity processor in another. Because the total number of active processors never increases, this can be done with no additional cost. This is a feature that you don't want to do without.

The same thing goes for the new capability for doing this across separate servers. In this case there is an additional cost for this product, but the savings you will get by a reduction in the need for permanently active processors will far outweigh this cost.

The next benefit is the one that started the Instant Capacity program in the first place—the ability to defer the cost of upgrades until you need them. You can purchase a system with all the capacity you will ever need, but you can defer the cost of some of that capacity until you really need it. If you know you will be adding users to an application or adding additional applications to the server but those increases are not scheduled for a year or more, it might be worthwhile to delay the cost of that capacity. This is especially true when you consider the next key benefit.

One rather obscure benefit of Instant Capacity is that it can dramatically simplify your capacity-planning processes. We see many IT organizations go through a capacity-planning process that looks something like this:

1. Make an educated guess as to the peak load they expect an application to experience. If this is an existing application that is being rehosted, the IT organization may have existing data to base this estimate on.

2. Estimate how much resource it will take to satisfy the peak load on the new system.

3. Add in some amount for expected growth over the life of the new system.

4. Multiply the result by some constant (which is often two) to make up for the uncertainty in the first three steps. The real issue here is that the penalty for being low is much more severe than the penalty for being high. If the system turns out to be too small, you will have to get another larger server and go through another application migration.

The end result of this, of course, is that the system ends up being woefully underutilized. Now let's consider doing this with Instant Capacity processors. You can still go through the steps above, but you can purchase the system with the active capacity you came up with in step 2. Then you can acquire the rest of the processors as Instant Capacity. If you end up needing them, the system can be upgraded very easily and very quickly. With the included Temporary Instant Capacity, which we will talk about next, you can instantly activate the capacity while you go through the process of acquiring and applying the permanent licenses. If you don't end up needing them, you get the next benefit—lower cost.

Instant Capacity processors will cost you a fraction of the cost of a permanent processor. This gets you a right-to-access (RTA) license for the CPU. Some may say you are paying for a portion of CPUs you aren't using. Keep in mind that these processors are effectively your spare capacity. If you didn't have Instant Capacity, you would have purchased these CPUs at full price. The real benefit here is that HP is paying for the majority of your spare capacity!

The final benefit is that you still get price protection if the price of the Instant Capacity components drops from the time you acquire the system to the time you activate the capacity. As an example, let's say you acquire a system and the cost of a processor is $10,000 (this is not the real price—just a nice round number for this example). If you pay $2,500 up front to get the RTA license and then activate the processor 18 months later and the current price is now $7,500, you will only need to pay $5,000 (the current price minus the original RTA cost) to get the permanent right-to-use (RTU) license for that processor.

Now let's briefly discuss the key benefits of cell-board Instant Capacity. Because cell-board Instant Capacity includes memory, the activation of a cell board cannot be done while the partition is on line. This capability is planned for a future release of HP-UX. Even today, cell-board Instant Capacity includes all the benefits of CPU capacity *except* the ability to migrate capacity between partitions while they are on line. All of the remaining benefits mentioned above would still be available to you. The other key benefit of cell-board Instant Capacity is that it includes memory. Most workloads that need additional capacity for growth will need both memory and CPU. If all you have is CPU Instant Capacity, you will need to load the system up with all the memory that will be needed when the system is at peak capacity. This is probably okay if you are using the CPUs for short-term spikes in load, but if the spare capacity is for longer-term growth, you will probably want to include one or more complete cell boards in your Instant Capacity allocation.

Key Tradeoffs

There are a few tradeoffs of Instant Capacity that you should be aware of. As we have hinted before, the benefits normally will far outweigh these tradeoffs, but the tradeoffs still exist.

A clarification of an issue that may or may not have been clear from the discussion on using Instant Capacity to flex nPars is the fact that this flexing requires available Instant Capacity processors in the partition you want to activate additional capacity. Each partition must be sized for the maximum capacity that will be required. You would then want permanent licenses for the "normal" load and the rest could be Instant Capacity. One thing to consider is that without this ability you would have had to purchase 100% of all the CPUs, while now you are only paying for a fraction of the spare capacity.

One other tradeoff of the flexing is that HP-UX is the only operating system that supports Instant Capacity. None of the other operating systems available for Integrity servers is capable of supporting activation and deactivation of CPUs, so all partitions on the system that will have inactive components need to be running HP-UX.

Another consideration is that the newest versions of Instant Capacity take advantage of a free short-term Temporary Instant Capacity (TiCAP) license to make them instant. When the program was first started, it was possible for the customer to activate a CPU on the system and pay for it later. This was possible because the Instant Capacity software would send an e-mail to HP when the activation occurred. A large number of customers could not use this program because it required their production systems to be able to send e-mail. In order to eliminate the need for e-mail, the software was changed to require a codeword in order to license a CPU for activation. This requires that you send a purchase order to HP and then get a codeword from the Utility Pricing portal. For most companies this will take at least a few days. In order to address this, HP is now providing a short-term Temporary Instant Capacity license at no extra charge with every Instant Capacity server. This allows you to activate the Instant Capacity CPU instantly and should provide enough time to get through the acquisition process and get the permanent license codeword applied to the system. The amount of time provided at no charge is a factor of the number of Instant Capacity CPUs ordered with the system.

The last tradeoff is the fact that until there is a future release of HP-UX, cell-board instant capacity requires a reboot of the partition after it has been brought on line and configured in a partition. The process would be to obtain the RTU codeword for the cell, apply the codeword to the system, assign it to a partition, and then reboot the partition. You would need to ensure you perform a "reboot for reconfiguration" that will ensure that any changes to the partition configuration would be applied before the operating system is booted.

Instant Capacity Sweet Spots

Most of the sweet spots in Instant Capacity are related to the flexibility it brings and the fact that the up-front cost of that flexibility is a fraction of what you would pay if you didn't have Instant Capacity. The reason this is important is that workloads do not have constant demand. This is true whether you run a single workload on a small system or whether you run many workloads on a larger system. You will always need spare capacity to meet peak demand. However, for most workloads the peak utilization is three to five times the average. If you are to have any hope at all of getting the average utilization of a server above 30% you will have to either flex your partitions to allow sharing of spare capacity or you will need to implement something that allows you to temporarily activate capacity when it is needed. To illustrate this, Figure 9-1 shows the actual utilization of a real production server with a consolidated workload.

The average utilization of this server is somewhere in the 20-CPU range. If this system used Instant Capacity and Temporary Instant Capacity, the number of permanent CPUs could be set at 28 CPUs and it would take a long time to consume a whole 30-CPU-day TiCAP license. This would mean that average utilization would be 20/28, or 71%. And there would still be plenty of capacity if a spike required more than the 28 CPUs.

The fact that Instant Capacity allows you to flex the capacity of nPars one CPU at a time while the partitions are running and under load and while maintaining electrical isolation between your mission critical workloads is a really sweet spot. nPartitions are sized the same as if they were being set up without Instant Capacity—in other words, they should each have enough physical capacity to handle the peak loads expected for that partition. However, rather than getting all the capacity as permanent capacity, the user only needs to purchase enough permanent capacity to handle slightly more than the average load that will be placed on the application for the first year. HP will pay for most of the rest.

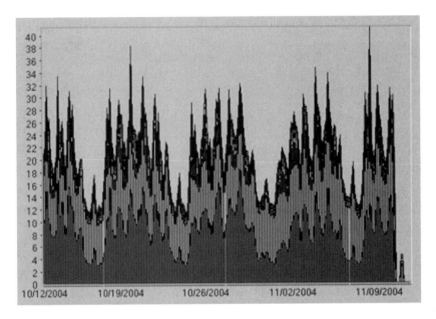

Figure 9-1 CPU Utilization over the Course of a Month for a Consolidated Server

Sweet Spot #1: Use Instant Capacity to Flex nPartitions

Users who want to set up a system with multiple nPars will almost always want to have Instant Capacity to allow them to flex those partitions so that spare capacity can be shared between nPars.

The new capability for sharing Instant Capacity licenses across servers means that it is possible to provide this flexing over an even larger set of workloads. The more workloads that share the capacity, the more likely it is that some of them will be idle while others are busy. This increases utilization and lowers cost. This allows users to group development and test servers with production servers. If production gets a peak, it is possible to migrate capacity from a development or test server to production. This can be done while maintaining completely separate servers for these environments.

Sweet Spot #2: Use Instant Capacity to Flex Servers

The ability to migrate Instant Capacity licenses between servers can provide even more ability to balance the CPU capacity across an environment. This is particularly useful for failover servers.

The small initial cost of Instant Capacity and the speed with which it can be brought on line provides a very nice opportunity for an inexpensive cushion of spare capacity.

Sweet Spot #3: Use Instant Capacity as Inexpensive Spare Capacity

> The fact that HP is paying for most of the cost of your spare capacity is a benefit that you should take advantage of unless there is a compelling reason not to do so.

Another nice sweet spot of Instant Capacity is the fact that it simplifies capacity planning for consolidation environments. Instant Capacity makes it possible to load a system with inexpensive spare capacity that gets activated only when needed; for example, when a new workload is placed on a consolidated server. If you have overestimated what will be needed, you will have extra capacity that you have previously activated when the next application is deployed. This will reduce the amount of new capacity you need to activate for that workload. And if you ever underestimate, additional capacity can be brought on line instantly.

Sweet Spot #4: Use Instant Capacity to Simplify Capacity Planning for Consolidation

> Spare capacity can be brought on line instantly without requiring a reboot, which dramatically simplifies capacity planning. The cost of underestimating is much smaller than the cost of acquiring a whole new system.

This is especially nice for systems that will be used for a consolidation environment. This is because companies rarely load all the applications on a new system all at once. Typically they purchase a large system and install a small number of workloads first and then load up the system with new workloads over the course of time, sometimes over more than a year. (You might not even need as much as you thought you did when you originally purchased the system.)

One area where the standard CPU Instant Capacity won't help is when you need to activate additional memory. This can't be done on line until a future version of HP-UX, but this memory is still something you will need if you expect your workloads to grow over time. Cell board Instant Capacity provides this.

Sweet Spot #5: Include Cell Board Instant Capacity to Provide Spare Capacity for Memory

> Most workloads as they grow will require additional CPU and Memory resources. Including one or more cell boards in your Instant Capacity allocation will allow for the growth in memory requirements.

Cell board Instant Capacity is especially useful for a consolidated environment. It is possible to purchase a large system with capacity to handle a large number of workloads and dole out the resources as new projects require capacity. When you use Instant Capacity, HP has been paying for the majority of the cost of that capacity while you were waiting for the project to get started. When the project is ready, you activate the additional capacity required, create a new nPar and install the OS and applications for the partition. This can dramatically reduce the time required get a project up and running. Instant Capacity also makes it possible to adjust the size of the partition if it is not clear what resources the new project will require.

Sweet Spot #6: Use Cell-Board Instant Capacity for Quick Startup of New Consolidated Workloads

Cell-board Instant Capacity can be used by IT organizations to ensure they have plenty of capacity on site for new projects that arrive over time.

Temporary Instant Capacity

It was a bit of a challenge to separate this section from the previous one because the benefits are tightly coupled. Temporary Instant Capacity relies on the fact that Instant Capacity is available. One of the reasons it makes sense to separate them is the fact that there may be some benefits of TiCAP that would lead you to want Instant Capacity in the first place.

Key Benefits

Given that Temporary Instant Capacity requires CPU Instant Capacity, we will focus here on the additional benefits you get by purchasing TiCAP licenses for your Instant Capacity CPUs. These include:

- Instant turn-on capability for Instant Capacity processors
- The ability to activate capacity for short periods of time
- It can be used on systems that were purchased as capital equipment rather than leased

In order to remove the need for e-mail to be sent to HP from the system, Instant Capacity now requires a codeword before you can permanently turn on a CPU. This means that Temporary Instant Capacity is required to instantly activate a processor. To resolve this, HP is now providing a balance of Temporary Instant Capacity with each Instant Capacity CPU purchased. This makes it possible to temporarily activate the CPU and acquire the codeword to permanently activate it later.

Temporary Instant Capacity gives users the ability to react to short-term spikes in load on applications. These spikes can be expected or unexpected. They can be the result of more users on an application or a failover. The important thing is that rather than having to purchase the spare capacity up front that is needed for these spikes, you can use TiCAP to react to them when they are needed. This reduces the up-front cost of the system, increases the average utilization of the system, and still provides the spare capacity required for these spikes in load.

Temporary Instant Capacity is a utility pricing alternative to pay per use that supports systems that have been purchased as capital equipment rather than leased. It also provides more control over your costs because you decide when to purchase capacity and how much.

Key Tradeoffs

This will be a really short section. There were a couple tradeoffs in this section, but they have all been addressed by version 8 of Instant Capacity. Version 8 eliminates the need for e-mail from the server and the new Multi-Complex Instant Capacity solution allows a shared pool of Temporary Instant Capacity.

Temporary Instant Capacity Sweet Spots

There are several situations where Temporary Instant Capacity is really useful: reacting to short-term spikes in load and managing capacity on a failover system.

Variations in load are often significant—the load during a peak time on a weekday, or during overnight batch processing can be an order of magnitude larger than the load over the weekend. The average utilization of a system can't possibly get over 30%–40% unless a workload management tool is used to share spare capacity or some solution is implemented to activate capacity when the spikes occur. This is the sweet spot of TiCAP: you can comfortably run a system at a high level of average utilization because you know that additional CPUs can be activated instantly when one of those spikes occurs.

Sweet Spot #1: Use Temporary Instant Capacity to React to Short-Term Spikes in Load

Temporary Instant Capacity gives you the ability to instantly react to expected or unexpected spikes in load. This allows you to run your system at a higher level of average utilization while still maintaining a comfortable surplus of capacity.

The second sweet spot for Temporary Instant Capacity is that it provides a low-cost failover server. It is common for companies to set up clusters so that production applications will failover onto a server that is running a lower-priority workload—such as batch, development, or production testing. Often those lower-priority workloads don't need anywhere near the capacity required for the production workload. The combination of Instant Capacity and Temporary Instant Capacity makes it possible to purchase a system with sufficient capacity for the production workload but have permanently active capacity that is sufficient for the lower-priority workload. The rest is inactive Instant Capacity. Then, when a failover occurs you can turn on whatever capacity is required for the production workload at the time of the failover. If the load is light when the failover occurs, you may need to activate only a small number of processors, but if the load is heavy, you will still have the capacity required. This is the perfect opportunity to let HP to pay for most of your spare capacity. In this case, you will rarely use that capacity—at least that is the hope.

Sweet Spot #2: Inexpensive Failover

Temporary Instant Capacity makes it possible to lower the cost of a failover system. Simply activate the capacity required only when the failover occurs and deactivate it when the workload migrates back to its primary server.

One other sweet spot for Temporary Instant Capacity is when a customer would really love to get a PPU utility solution but for whatever reason can't lease a system. The combination of Instant Capacity and TiCAP provides a very similar flexible cost structure, but the bulk of the system is purchased and can be depreciated as a standard capital asset. This has the added advantage that you have full control over the utility costs. You choose when to purchase Temporary Capacity, how much to purchase, and when to consume it.

Sweet Spot #3: Utility Pricing without Having to Lease the System

Temporary Instant Capacity makes it possible to pay for only the capacity you use. This provides much of the benefit of PPU, but it can be implemented on a capital asset.

Deciding When to Permanently Activate an Instant Capacity CPU

This discussion is in the Temporary Instant Capacity section because we are specifically addressing the issue of how to determine when to do a permanent activation based on how much TiCAP you are consuming. This question isn't as simple as it might seem. At first glance, it would make sense that if you are consuming 30 CPU days of TiCAP in less than 30 days, you should activate a CPU permanently. The reason this isn't the right answer is that TiCAP gives you the ability to activate any number of CPUs, whereas the permanent activation only gives you one. Therefore, if every time you activate a CPU, you activate 10 of them (maybe because this is being used for failover only), then activating a single permanent CPU will reduce your consumption of Temporary Instant Capacity by only 10%. This meager savings probably wouldn't be offset by the cost of the permanent activation for quite some time.

So, the key issue is return on investment. How long will it take for the Temporary Instant Capacity savings to recoup the cost of the permanent activation? You will need three data points for this:

- The percentage of time in each day there was at least one Temporary CPU active over the last month or more. The key is that you ignore CPUs 2 through N—all you care about is the first one. This is because this is the only CPU you will stop paying for when you permanently activate one.

- The cost of permanently activating a CPU—all you care about here is what has not yet been paid. The initial cost for the RTA license is a sunk cost and therefore should not be considered for this decision. Also consider that the remaining cost will probably go down as the cost of the CPU goes down over time. You will need to get the current cost from your HP sales representative or authorized partner.

- The cost of a 30-CPU-day TiCAP license—divided by 30 so you can have daily costs.

This is the formula:

Permanent activation cost / (Daily TiCAP cost * percentage used by first CPU)

This formula yields the number of days it will take for the savings in Temporary Instant Capacity to pay for the permanent activation. As an example using fictitious numbers, let us assume that the permanent activation cost is $1,000 and the TiCAP cost for 30 days is $300 (which means $10 per day). We could use the percent utilization to determine how long it will take to recoup our investment in a permanent license. If the average utilization of the first CPU is 100%, which means that the CPU is always on, it would take 1000/(10 * 100%) = 100 days. So the investment would be recouped in roughly 3 months. Now, if the average utilization of the first CPU was 10%, it would take 1,000/(10 * 10%) = 1,000 days. This is almost 3 years.

Armed with this information, you can decide what level of return on investment is sufficient for your organization and determine when to activate a permanent CPU based on levels of utilization.

Pay Per Use

As was mentioned in the last chapter, Pay per use (PPU) is different than Instant Capacity and Temporary Instant Capacity because it is actually an alternative lease program in which your payment to HP varies depending on how busy the system is over the course of each month.

Key Benefits

The key benefit of a PPU lease is that virtually all customers will save money compared to a standard lease. In the PPU Program, there is a base payment and a variable payment each month. The base payment is usually roughly half of the cost of a standard lease. The variable payment is based on average utilization over the course of the previous month.

The key things to consider when investigating PPU are that the maximum monthly payment is 105% of a standard lease and even if you have a number of months where you reach that 105% ceiling, you are guaranteed not to pay more than a standard lease over the life of the lease. One other key consideration is that you would have to run a system at over 70% average utilization to exceed the standard lease payment for any month. So consider this question: How many systems do you have that have an average utilization over 70% for an entire month? This includes nights, weekends, and holidays. Clearly, if you have systems that are consistently that busy, Pay per use wouldn't be a good fit. Industry averages are in the 30% range. For these systems, PPU would represent a significant savings.

Key Tradeoffs

The key tradeoffs of the PPU a program include the fact that it is a lease and that you will need to have budgeting flexibility to handle the variability of monthly lease payments.

The first item is pretty straightforward — if leasing a system is a problem, Temporary Instant Capacity has many of the benefits of PPU but can be used on a system that is a capital purchase.

The variable budgeting issue is another of those nontechnical problems that can, nonetheless, make this solution a nonstarter for some companies.

Another tradeoff is that the PPU program requires outbound communication to be sent from the PPU meter to HP from inside your firewall. The communication between the PPU software running on each partition and the utility meter is secure and is all done behind your firewall. The meter can send the utilization data to HP via e-mail or an SSL connection. Many customers choose the e-mail connection because it can be secured at the firewall to be outbound only. So no hole is required in the firewall to make that work. However, HP typically recommends using the HTTPS connection because it provides more reliable connectivity and can be used for auto patching of the utility meter.

Pay Per Use Sweet Spots

The sweet spot for PPU occurs any time you are leasing a system. Since you are guaranteed not to pay more than a standard lease and you have an opportunity to save in any month the system isn't heavily used, there is really no financial risk to choosing this option.

The more you look at it, the clearer it becomes. If you are going to lease a system anyway, you are almost guaranteed to save money with Pay per use. Since you are guaranteed not to pay more than the standard lease, you really shouldn't lease a system that isn't PPU.

Sweet Spot #1: Cost of PPU Will Not Exceed Cost of a Traditional Lease

> Because the program carries a guarantee that you will not pay more than a standard lease over the life of the lease, you can't go wrong with PPU.

Another sweet spot is where you have bursty workloads. If you have workloads that have very high peaks, but those peaks are short in duration, PPU can provide significant savings. This is because the 5-minute data is averaged every day for every CPU. All the CPUs are averaged together to get a daily average for the whole server. Then this data is averaged a third time for the whole month. All this averaging means that short-term peaks in load are smoothed out of the result. This means that you can have a system capable of handling a very high peak load but you will only need to pay for the much lower average.

Sweet Spot #2: PPU Benefits Companies with Bursty Workloads

> Because PPU uses several levels of averaging, short-term peaks in workloads are smoothed out.

Choosing between Active CPU and Percent CPU Pay Per Use

There are two things to consider here, the PPU cost of the system and the cost of software for the applications you will run on the system. The PPU version 7 release brought the ability to activate and deactivate CPUs even when using the Percent CPU metric. Any CPUs you turn off will contribute 0% utilization to the average that is calculated for the system. The key difference between Percent CPU and Active CPU is that with Percent CPU you pay for the actual utilization of the active CPUs. With Active CPU, you would pay for 100% of active CPUs, whether they were being used or not. This may make Percent CPU seem like an obvious choice, except that the per-CPU cost for Active CPU is lower than it is for Percent CPU—precisely to make up for the fact that active CPUs are rarely running at 100%.

If you are using a workload manager to maintain a particular utilization level, you can expect that it will keep the same number of CPUs active in either case. Therefore, you should compare the pricing of Active CPU and Percent CPU to see which one provides you the best option. Both will be better than a standard lease, but there may be a slight advantage of one compared to the other.

The other consideration is the cost of the software running on the system. If you are using software that is priced on a per-CPU basis, you will want to work with your software vendor to determine if they will support your purchasing licenses for only the number of CPUs that you plan to activate for the software. An example would be a PPU system or partition with 16 CPUs that would use only 12 active CPUs. It is possible that the software vendor would allow you to purchase a 12-CPU license for the software. You would be obligated to pay for additional licenses should you activate more than the 12 CPUs that you have licensed, but if this doesn't happen until many months later, you have deferred that cost until you needed it. This should work for either Active CPU or Percent CPU since both have the capability to turn off CPUs, but you should verify that the software vendor supports both.

ISV Considerations

Independent Software Vendors (ISVs) are increasingly moving toward more flexible technologies. The market is moving in this direction in a big way, and the ISVs have lagged behind the hardware vendors. There are really two things to consider when determining how well an ISV application will support these technologies. The first is whether the ISV applications can run normally in an environment where resources can be turned on and off in a utility fashion and the second is whether ISVs will provide pricing options that will make using these solutions even more beneficial.

ISV Support

This is virtually the same topic as we covered in Chapter 3—how well do ISV applications run in an environment where resources are being activated and deactivated as needed? The resource-allocation mechanisms are exactly the same as we described in Chapter 3. In other words, the CPU process scheduler handles CPUs coming and going, so the applications do not need to do anything special to run in this environment.

Some ISVs may balk at the idea of removing a CPU from the products control. They will say things like "that could dramatically impact the performance of the application." Well, yes, reducing the amount of CPU available to an application will likely reduce its performance. However, this can't impact the ability of the application to run, because the process scheduler will still run those threads, they are just running on fewer CPUs. So the only impact on the application will be performance. Now you have to ask the question why you are removing the CPU from this application. The only reasons you would be doing this are because you either have a higher-priority application that needs it or the application is not using the CPU effectively. In the former case, you are obviously willing to accept a performance impact on this lower-priority application to speed up a higher-priority one. In the latter case, the application is running much faster than it needs to so either the performance won't be impacted or the impact will still be within the boundaries of acceptable performance objectives. This is particularly important in this case because you are paying extra for performance that is exceeding your goals when you use these Utility Pricing Solutions.

ISV Licensing Options

Some ISVs are looking into supporting HP's Utility Pricing Solutions. As these solutions have become more mainstream, ISVs have become more willing to consider creative licensing programs to support them. That said, as of this writing, none of the ISVs have standard programs that support Utility Pricing. You will need to work with your ISVs to get them to support your specific needs.

One very important thing to note, though, is that even if your ISV doesn't support these Utility Pricing Solutions, this is not a reason to not to use them! If you configure a system or partition for a peak of 16 CPUs, the most you will have to pay for your software is a 16-CPU license. If you don't use Utility Pricing, you will pay full price for the hardware and full price for the software. If you use one of these solutions, you may still pay full price for your software, but the hardware will cost you less, so the overall solution will still cost you less.

Sizing an nPar When You Are Using Utility Pricing Solutions

For pay per use, the answer is fairly simple. You can size the system for your expected peak and you will only pay for the amount you are actually using.

For Instant Capacity, you will want to purchase permanent capacity for the bulk of the normal load but use Temporary Instant Capacity for the highest of the peaks. If you have data about the utilization of your servers, you can use this data to determine how much spare capacity is needed for your workloads. The more data you have the better. If you have hourly or shorter-interval data you can determine what your peaks are and how long they last. The trick is to configure the nPar to have enough total capacity to handle the peaks but use Instant Capacity processors for the highest of the peaks.

Let's use an example. The normal load on a system requires seven CPUs on average and fluctuates between 5 and 10 for all but one hour per day and goes up to 12 during that hour. For this system you could size the nPar so that there is sufficient capacity for the peak, plus, say, 30% growth and still get the nPar into two cells using dual-core processors. To summarize:

- Minimum is 5 CPUs
- Maximum is 12 CPUs, not only for 1 hour per day
- We could provide a 30% cushion on the max ($12 \times 1.3 = 15.6$) and still get the capacity into a 2 cell nPar

So the nPar now has two cells with eight CPUs each, but six of your CPUs are inactive Instant Capacity processors. The six Instant Capacity processors carry an up-front cost of less than two CPUs, so your cost is less than 12 CPUs instead of the 16 you would have paid for without Instant Capacity. So what happens when you need the extra two CPUs of capacity for one hour per day? You use Temporary Instant Capacity for that.

Now let's consider the cost of the TiCAP. One 30-CPU-day TiCAP license is equivalent to 720 CPU hours. If you are using an average of two CPU hours per weekday, that is 10 per week. This means that a single TiCAP license will last you 72 weeks or almost sixteen months!

Summary

We have described each of the Utility Pricing Solutions and why they will almost assuredly save you money. They key difference between the Pay per use and Instant Capacity programs are that PPU is a lease and Instant Capacity is for a capital purchase. We hope you have learned why these solutions provide benefits that far outweigh any tradeoffs.

10

Instant Capacity

Chapter Overview

Planning for and purchasing new hardware is an arduous task. There is often a balance between over-provisioning current computing requirements based on expected growth and buying excess capacity that is under utilized. This balancing act is further complicated by the rapidly changing demands on the datacenter. New applications are regularly being added, and often new hardware is required in a short timeframe. HP's response to this problem is Instant Capacity.

HP's Instant Capacity solution allows a server to be purchased without initially paying the full price of the system. Using Instant Capacity, a subset of the hardware components are initially inactive. When the hardware is required, a license is purchased for the components and they are available for immediate activation. This enables the user to gradually purchase a server over time as workload demands increase and new applications are added to the datacenter.

This chapter begins with an overview of the Instant Capacity technology. The fundamental terminology relating to Instant Capacity is covered, followed by an example that applies Instant Capacity codewords for Instant Capacity cells, memory, and CPUs. This chapter does not discuss Temporary Instant Capacity. Temporary Instant Capacity is covered in Chapter 11, "Temporary Instant Capacity."

Instant Capacity Overview

HP's Instant Capacity offering allows an nPartition server to be purchased with unlicensed hardware components that include cells, CPUs, and memory. Having unlicensed hardware components in the server from the time of purchase makes it possible to immediately increase compute resources without procuring additional servers, allocating floor space, and performing the other tasks associated with new hardware acquisitions. Instead, when the unlicensed components are required by workloads, a right-to-use (RTU) license is purchased. A codeword is then applied to the system and the hardware is available for immediate activation.

When a right-to-use license is purchased for a cell, the license also contains a right-to-use license for zero or more CPUs, all of the memory, and all of the I/O associated with the cell. This flexibility allows a cell and all of its memory and I/O to be activated while leaving a portion of CPUs unlicensed. At a later time, another RTU license can be purchased that allows a portion of the remaining CPUs to be activated.

The version of Instant Capacity discussed in this book is supported only on HP nPartition servers with at least one nPartition running the HP-UX operating system. In nPartitions running Linux, Microsoft Windows, or OpenVMS, HP assumes all of the processors are active. Consequently, sufficient hardware must be licensed for all of the hardware in nPartitions running Linux, Microsoft Windows, or OpenVMS.

The licensing of Instant Capacity components is on a complex-wide basis. The number of licensed cells, the amount of active memory, and number of active processors is not considered solely on a per-nPartition basis. Therefore, a CPU can be deactivated in one nPartition and a CPU can be activated in a separate nPartition without changing the number of licensed CPUs in the complex. Chapter 15, "Workload Manager," demonstrates the use of Instant Capacity technology for the purpose of migrating CPU resources between nPartitions to meet service-level objectives without purchasing additional Instant Capacity components. The number of unlicensed components is maintained in the firmware on the management processor of each nPartition server. When a right-to-use license is purchased and a codeword is applied, the number of unlicensed components stored in firmware is updated. The Instant Capacity data stored in firmware is then used by the Instant Capacity software to determine whether unlicensed components may be activated and whether the system is in compliance.

Figure 10-1 shows the process of activating unlicensed CPUs. The figure depicts the case where the Instant Capacity CPUs are located in a licensed cell that is active. The CPUs are initially inactive, or deactivated. A codeword is then applied using the `icod_modify` command. Applying the codeword licenses one or more CPUs for use, but it does *not* activate any CPUs. CPUs can then be activated immediately with a separate command, or if applications running within an OS do not appropriately account for dynamic CPU additions, the activation of Instant Capacity CPUs can be deferred until the next reboot.

Instant Capacity cells are generally assigned to an nPartition, but the Use on Next Boot flags for the cells are set to No. The cells remain inactive when the nPartition is booted. Because the cells are inactive, the memory and I/O associated with the cells is also inactive. The nPartition configuration tools `parmgr`, `parmodify`, and `parcreate` can be used to change the Use on Next Boot flag as described in Chapter 4, "nPartition Servers"; the operation will be allowed only after a codeword has been applied that licenses the cell. After applying a codeword, the Use on Next Boot flag must be changed and a reboot for reconfiguration must be performed on the nPartition to activate the cell.

In Figure 10-2, the process of activating an Instant Capacity cell is illustrated. Initially the cell is assigned to an nPartition but the cell is inactive because the cell's Use on Next Boot flag is set to No. When a codeword is applied, the cell, zero or more CPUs, all of the cell's memory, and

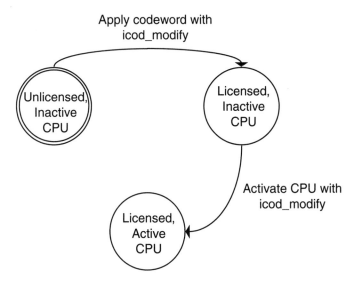

Figure 10-1 Activation Process of Instant Capacity CPUs

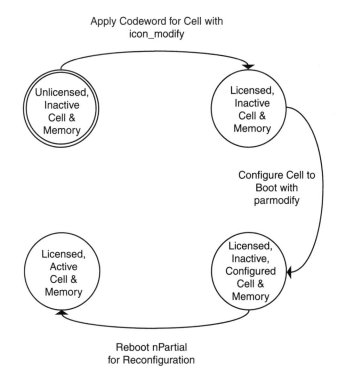

Figure 10-2 Activation Process of Instant Capacity Cells

all of the cell's I/O can be activated. It is not necessary to license all of the CPUs to activate a cell. In fact, an Instant Capacity cell can be activated without licensing any of its CPUs.

Activating Partial Instant Capacity Cells in new nPartitions

An important subtlety should be understood when activating Instant Capacity cells that are to be assigned to a new nPartition. HP does not require all of the CPUs on a cell to be licensed in order to activate an Instant Capacity cell. However, at the time a cell is activated and used to create a *new* nPartition, there must be an adequate number of licensed CPUs to account for the total number of CPUs on the cell. The available CPU licenses can come from the application of a codeword, or CPUs in other HP-UX nPartitions can be temporarily deactivated. After the nPartition is created and the HP-UX operating system is installed, the number of active CPUs can be decreased using the Instant Capacity software. When an nPartition is created, there is no way for the Instant Capacity software to know whether Microsoft Windows, Linux, OpenVMS, or HP-UX will be installed on the nPartition. If an operating system other than HP-UX is installed, all of the CPUs in the nPartition will be active. Therefore, the Instant Capacity software assumes the maximum number of CPUs will be activated when new nPartitions are created.

In summary, when planning for the creation of nPartitions using newly licensed Instant Capacity cells, keep in mind that the Instant Capacity software requires licenses for all of the CPUs on the cells assigned to the nPartition. After HP-UX is installed, the Instant Capacity Software can be used to deactivate those CPUs that are not required in the newly created nPartition.

After applying a codeword for the cell and CPUs, the cell must be configured to boot with the nPartition. This is done with either parmgr or the parmodify command by setting the Use on Next Boot flag to Yes. Setting the Use on Next Boot flag does not immediately activate the cell. A reboot for reconfiguration must be performed on the nPartition in order for the cell to be activated. In this case, the icod_modify command is used to apply the codeword, but it is not used to activate resources. Instead, the parmodify command indirectly causes hardware resources to become active after the reboot for reconfiguration is performed.

Instant Capacity Terminology

Instant Capacity Codeword is an encoded string of letters and numbers describing a change in the Instant Capacity state of the system. The most common codeword is a right-to-use license for unlicensed components. Codewords may also dispense Temporary Instant Capacity as described in Chapter 11, "Temporary Instant Capacity." Codewords are available from the Instant Capacity portal after purchasing licenses for one or more Instant Capacity components. A single Instant Capacity codeword can contain RTU licenses for any number of unlicensed cells, memory, and CPUs.

Unlicensed Cell is a cell within an nPartition server that has not been licensed for use. Unlicensed cells must be inactive at all times and can be activated only after purchasing a RTU license and applying a codeword. An unlicensed cell can be inactive because its Use on Next Boot flag is set to No or because it has not been assigned to an nPartition.

Unlicensed Memory is an amount of memory in a complex that is not licensed. Unlicensed memory is the sum of all the memory on inactive cells. Memory can be activated or deactivated only by activating or deactivating the cell containing the memory. There is no mechanism to activate or deactivate memory independent of the cell containing the memory and a subset of the memory on a cell cannot be activated or deactivated.

Unlicensed Processors are processors in a complex that have not been licensed for use. The overall number of unlicensed processors is maintained complex-wide basis by the management processor.

Inactive Processor is a processor that is not in use by any operating system. A processor may be inactive because it is contained within an inactive cell or because the Instant Capacity software has deactivated the processor to keep the system in compliance with the Instant Capacity contract. One of the major benefits of using Instant Capacity is the ability to immediately activate inactive processors. Inactive processors that are contained in active cells can be immediately activated after purchasing a right-to-use license and applying an appropriate Instant Capacity Codeword. No reboot of the operating system is required. Inactive processors are also referred to as deactivated processors.

Exception status is a flag that indicates whether the system is in compliance with the number of unlicensed Instant Capacity components.

Audit Snapshot is a string of letters and numbers used for periodic auditing purposes. An audit snapshot is available within a system snapshot report from the Instant Capacity command-line interfaces and is required when requesting an Instant Capacity codeword from the portal. An audit snapshot can also be entered into the HP Instant Capacity portal for reporting purposes.

Example Instant Capacity Scenario

The remainder of this chapter will focus on an example scenario. This example will revisit the scenario described in Chapter 4, "nPartition Servers." In the scenario, the nPartition server was configured with two cells in the rex01 nPartition and two absent cells. The scenario walked through the process of physically adding two new cells to the server. One of the new cells was added to the existing rex01 nPartition and the second new cell was used to create a new nPartition, rex02.

In this example scenario, instead of starting with two empty cells slots, unlicensed Instant Capacity components are present in the system. One Instant Capacity cell contains 4GB of unlicensed memory and eight unlicensed CPUs. Table 10-1 provides a representation of the initial server configuration. Notice the unlicensed cell, cab0, cell3, is inactive.

Table 10-2 shows the configuration of the complex after the example scenario. The unlicensed cell will be licensed along with 4GB of memory and six CPUs. The cell that was initially inactive, cab0, cell3, will be active in the newly created rex02 nPartition. This configuration leaves two processors inactive in the rex02 nPartition. Chapter 11, "Temporary Instant Capacity," will describe the process for activating these two processors on a temporary basis as business conditions demand. Additionally, Chapter 15, "Workload Manager," will describe how these two Instant Capacity processors can be used for dynamic CPU allocation across separate nPartitions.

Table 10-1 Initial Complex Configuration

nPartition Name	Active CPUs	Cells	Num CPUs	Cell Status	I/O Chassis	Total Memory	Active Memory
rex01	8	cab0, cell0	4	Active	cab0, bay0, chassis0	4GB	4GB
		cab0, cell1	4	Active	cab0, bay0, chassis1	4GB	4GB
		cab0, cell2	4	Active	cab8, bay0, chassis0	4GB	4GB
		cab0, cell3	4	Inactive	cab8, bay0, chassis1	4GB	0GB

Table 10-2 Final Complex Configuration

nPartition Name	Active CPUs	Cells	I/O Chassis	Cell Status	Num CPUs	Total Memory	Active Memory
rex01	12	cab0, cell0	cab0, bay0, chassis0	Active	4	4GB	4GB
		cab0, cell1	cab0, bay0, chassis1	Active	4	4GB	4GB
		cab0, cell2	cab8, bay0, chassis0	Active	4	4GB	4GB
rex02	2	cab0, cell3	cab8, bay0, chassis1	Active	4	4GB	4GB

Viewing Status of the Instant Capacity System

Figure 10-3 provides a graphical view from Partition Manager of the initial system configuration. Eight of the CPUs in the rex01 nPartition are not active; four of these inactive CPUs are on the inactive cell, cab0, cell3. Additionally, four CPUs are inactive on the three remaining active cells. Specific CPUs are not labeled as Instant Capacity CPUs because Instant Capacity does not consider specific CPUs to be Instant Capacity components. The Instant Capacity software only ensures that the proper amount of resources is inactive.

The initial Instant Capacity status of the system is shown in Listing 10-1. Several fields have been highlighted in the output. The first is the Exception status. If the system were not in compliance with the number of expected inactive components, a message would be displayed in this field indicating why the system is not in compliance.

note

> The Instant Capacity software used in this example scenario refers to unlicensed components as "iCOD" components. The software is being updated to simply refer to Instant Capacity components as unlicensed components.

The Active processors field indicates how many processors are currently active in the local nPartition. The four CPUs in cab0, cell 3 are inactive, as are four of the twelve CPUs in the rex01 nPartition. Instant Capacity determines which CPUs are activated and deactivated using an algorithm that is not published. Therefore, the system administrator does not need to choose the specific CPUs to be activated and deactivated.

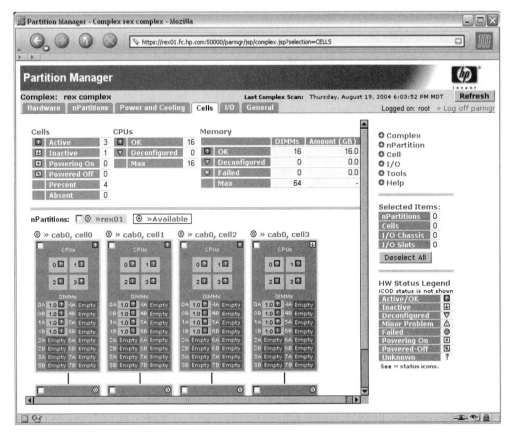

Figure 10-3 Initial nPartition Configuration

As described in Table 10-2, the output in Listing 10-1 shows the unlicensed cell, eight unlicensed processors, and 4GB of unlicensed memory. Along with each of these values, the quantity of actual inactive components is also provided. This allows a quick comparison to ensure that at least the required numbers of components are inactive.

Listing 10-1 Initial Instant Capacity Status

```
# icod_stat
Software version:        B.06.03
System ID:               rex01
Serial number:           USE4416CNL
Product number:          AB240A
Unique ID:               ad2b3532-abd9-11d8-a988-7877a7f45c12
System contact e-mail:   Not set
From e-mail:             Set to the default ('adm')
Asset reporting:         on
Exception status:        No exception
```

```
Local Hard Partition Information
-------------------------------
Total processors:                               16
Intended Active processors:                      8
Active processors:                               8
Licensed processors that can be activated:       0
Processors that can be activated if licensed:    4
Processors that cannot immediately be activated: 4

Global iCOD Information
-----------------------
iCOD cells:                                      1
Actual inactive cells:                           1
iCOD processors:                                 8
Actual inactive processors:                      8
iCOD Memory:                                     4.0 GB
Actual inactive Memory:                          4.0 GB
Temporary capacity available:                    0 days,
                                                 0 hours,
                                                 0 minutes
Processors using temporary capacity:             0
Projected temporary capacity expiration:         N/A

Allocation of iCOD Resources Among Partitions
---------------------------------------------------------------
nPar  Inactive  Inactive     Inactive
ID    Cells     Memory       CPUs      nPar Name
====  ========  ===========  ========  ======================
  0       1          4.0 GB      8      rex01 (local)
N/A       0          0.0 GB      0      Unassigned Cells

iCOD Partition Configuration Information
---------------------------------------------------------------
      Intended  Actual            Compatible
nPar  Active    Active   Total    Software
ID    CPUs      CPUs     CPUs     Installed   nPar Name
====  ========  ======   =====    ==========  ====================
  0       8        8       16       Yes       rex01 (local)
```

Listing 10-1 shows that the System contact e-mail value is not set for this system. This field is the e-mail address for the system administrator, system contact, or other individual who is responsible for ensuring that the system remains compliant with the number of unlicensed components. Before applying a codeword or performing Instant Capacity configuration changes, HP recommends that users set the System contact e-mail address. E-mail messages are sent to the address supplied in this field when Instant Capacity configuration changes are made and when the system is not in compliance with the Instant Capacity contract. The system contact is configured using the following command:

```
# icod_modify -c bryanj@rex01
```

```
The contact e-mail address has been set to bryanj@rex01.
```

Applying an Instant Capacity Codeword

Activation of Instant Capacity components requires an Instant Capacity RTU license contained in a codeword. RTU codewords are available from the Instant Capacity portal after a license has been purchased for the components. The icod_stat -s command is issued to gather the information required for obtaining a codeword. Listing 10-2 shows an Instant Capacity system snapshot of rex01 that contains an audit snapshot in the last line.

Listing 10-2 Instant Capacity System Snapshot Report

```
# icod_stat -s
Product number: AB240A
Serial number:  USE4416CNL
Audit snapshot:
vYXAJWC.v5ngfaK.688cwTP.BwHjXzs.sMekFUR.4dc9jsC.0uy2N25.
GR2RUf4.dGnVi8T.VeQ2
```

In addition to the information found in the icod_stat -s output in the system snapshot report, the following pieces of information are necessary to acquire an Instant Capacity codeword:

- An HP sales order number from the purchase of the right-to-use license
- The number of cells being licensed
- The number of CPUs being licensed
- The amount of memory being licensed

Instant Capacity codewords affect the entire complex. Notice that there are no requirements to specify nPartition configuration information, such as the nPartition to be created, the specific cell to be activated, or exact CPUs to be activated. Instead, the codewords are applied at the complex level and the system administrator is able to activate the licensed resources as necessary.

Figure 10-4 shows an example screen of the Instant Capacity portal which is located at **http://www.hp.com/go/icod/portal**. The *Create codeword* screen in the portal provides an interface for entering the system and order information and will respond with an Instant Capacity codeword.

Listing 10-3 demonstrates the application of an Instant Capacity codeword. The icod_ modify command is used to apply the codeword. In this case, the RTU codeword allows one cell, 4 GB of memory, and six CPUs to be activated. The application of the codeword does *not* activate any resources. Additional commands must be issued to take advantage of the newly licensed Instant Capacity components.

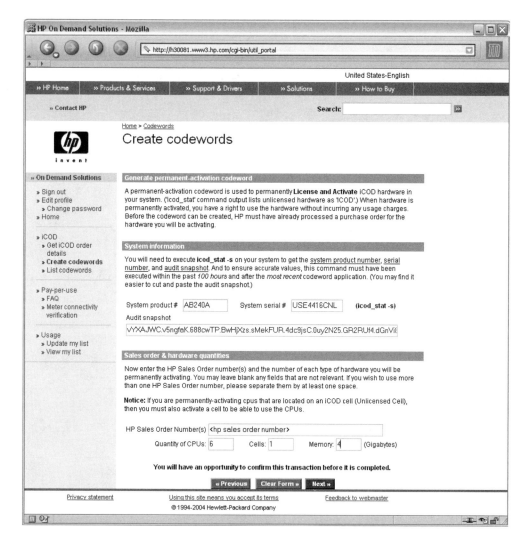

Figure 10-4 Example Instant Capacity Portal Screen for Creating a Codeword

note

> Application of an Instant Capacity codeword does not activate any resources.
> Further steps must be taken to activate the desired hardware components.

Listing 10-3   Application of Instant Capacity Right-to-Use Codeword

```
# icod_modify -C \
> BE7hzjK.Rx4yA3v.XHLL4GY.gjrQbQx-DKWGyRt.EyaVJaf.6jXpDCn.qqFNf8
The following valid codeword has been applied to the complex:

    Right-to-Use Codeword
    6 CPUs
    1 Cells
    4.0 GB of Memory

Execute the icod_stat(1M) command to see the results of the
application of this codeword.

NOTE:    Application of Right-to-Use codewords does not result
         in the activation of components.  Components must be
         activated separately.
```

Listing 10-4 shows the status of the system following the application of the codeword. There are now zero unlicensed cells, two unlicensed CPUs, and no unlicensed memory in the complex. The listing shows there has not been any change in the number of active cells, processors, or memory. Also shown in the output is the change to the System contact e-mail as a result of the icod_modify command shown previously.

Listing 10-4   Instant Capacity Status after Application of Right-to-Use Codeword

```
# icod_stat
Software version:        B.06.03
System ID:               rex01
Serial number:           USE4416CNL
Product number:          AB240A
Unique ID:               ad2b3532-abd9-11d8-a988-7877a7f45c12
System contact e-mail:   bryanj@rex01
From e-mail:             Set to the default ('adm')
Asset reporting:         on
Exception status:        No exception

Local Hard Partition Information
--------------------------------
Total processors:                                  16
Intended Active processors:                         8
Active processors:                                  8
Licensed processors that can be activated:          4
Processors that can be activated if licensed:       0
Processors that cannot immediately be activated:    4
```

```
Global iCOD Information
---------------------
iCOD cells:                              0
Actual inactive cells:                   1
iCOD processors:                         2
Actual inactive processors:              8
iCOD Memory:                             0.0 GB
Actual inactive Memory:                  4.0 GB
Temporary capacity available:            0 days,
                                         0 hours,
                                         0 minutes

Processors using temporary capacity:     0
Projected temporary capacity expiration: N/A

[...]
```

Creating a New nPartition

The hardware components can now be activated as a result of applying the Instant Capacity codeword. The inactive cell, cab0, cell3, will be removed from the rex01 nPartition. It will then be used to create a new nPartition, rex02. The following two commands perform these tasks:

```
# parmodify -p 0 -d 3
# parcreate -c 3::: -P rex02
Partition Created. The partition number is: 1
```

The parcreate command would not have been allowed if the RTU codeword had not been applied. All nPartition configuration changes are validated with the Instant Capacity software, so the order in which codewords are applied and configuration changes are made is important.

When creating a new nPartition, the Instant Capacity software is consulted to ensure that the change will not take the system out of compliance. During the validation setup, the Instant Capacity software assumes that all of the CPUs on a cell will be activated. The difference between the number of Actual inactive processors and the number of iCOD processors must be equal or greater than the number of CPUs on the cells being added to the nPartition. In this case, there are eight inactive processors and two Instant Capacity CPUs. This leaves a total of six inactive licensed CPUs. The cell contains four CPUs, so the operation to create a new nPartition is permitted.

The Instant Capacity status of the server after creating the rex02 nPartition is shown in Listing 10-5. This command was executed from the rex01 nPartition. Notice the rex02 nPartition shown in the two tables near the end of the output. The Intended Active CPUs column shows how many CPUs the Instant Capacity software is assuming will be active in the nPartition when it is booted. Since the intention is to have only two CPUs active in rex02, the icod_modify command must be used after HP-UX is installed to deactivate two of the CPUs.

Listing 10-5 Instant Capacity Status after Creating New nPartition

```
# icod_stat
[...]

Global iCOD Information
------------------------
iCOD cells:                            0
Actual inactive cells:                 1
iCOD processors:                       2
Actual inactive processors:            8
iCOD Memory:                           0.0 GB
Actual inactive Memory:                4.0 GB
Temporary capacity available:          0 days,
                                       0 hours,
                                       0 minutes

Processors using temporary capacity:   0
Projected temporary capacity expiration:   N/A

Allocation of iCOD Resources Among Partitions
-------------------------------------------------------------------------
nPar   Inactive  Inactive     Inactive
ID     Cells     Memory       CPUs      nPar Name
====   ========  ===========  ========  ======================
  0       0          0.0 GB       4      rex01 (local)
  1       1          4.0 GB       4      rex02
N/A       0          0.0 GB       0      Unassigned Cells

iCOD Partition Configuration Information
-----------------------------------------------------------------------
       Intended  Actual            Compatible
nPar   Active    Active   Total    Software
ID     CPUs      CPUs     CPUs     Installed    nPar Name
====   ========  ======   =====    ==========   ====================
  0       8         8       12        Yes        rex01 (local)
  1       4         0        4        No         rex02
```

Viewing Status of Complex from Newly Created nPartition

The rex02 nPartition has been created and an operating system has been installed. The process of installing the HP-UX operating system is not shown, as the only important consideration is to ensure that the Instant Capacity software is installed along with HP-UX on the nPartition.

The final nPartition configuration is shown in Figure 10-5. The two nPartitions are active and are running HP-UX. Additionally, both nPartitions have the Instant Capacity software installed and configured.

The Instant Capacity status of the complex from the rex02 nPartition is shown in Listing 10-6. Of particular interest are the fields showing the intended number of active CPUs. Since no

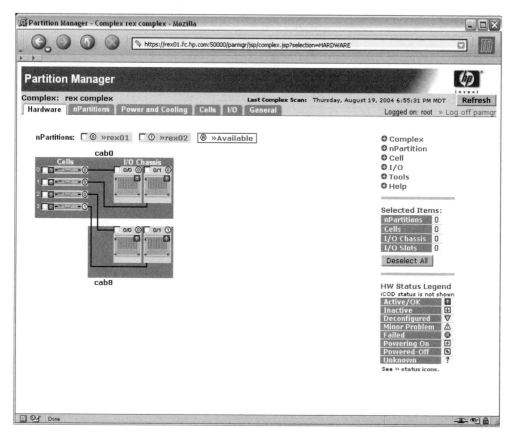

Figure 10-5 Final nPartition Configuration

configuration changes have been performed to adjust the number of intended active CPUs in rex02, the Instant Capacity software assumes that the maximum number of CPUs will be activated.

Listing 10-6 Instant Capacity Status on rex02 nPartition

```
# icod_stat
Software version:      B.06.01
System ID:             rex02
Serial number:         USE4416CNL
Product number:        AB240A
Unique ID:             ad2b3532-abd9-11d8-a988-7877a7f45c12
System contact e-mail: bryanj@rex01
From e-mail:           Set to the default ('adm')
Asset reporting:       on
Exception status:      No exception
```

```
Local Hard Partition Information
-------------------------------
Total processors:                           4
Intended Active processors:                 4
Active processors:                          4
Licensed processors that can be activated:  0
Processors that can be activated if licensed:  0
Processors that cannot immediately be activated: 0

Global iCOD Information
-----------------------
iCOD cells:                                 0
Actual inactive cells:                      0
iCOD processors:                            2
Actual inactive processors:                 4
iCOD Memory:                                0.0 GB
Actual inactive Memory:                     0.0 GB
Temporary capacity available:               0 days,
                                            0 hours,
                                            0 minutes

Processors using temporary capacity:        0
Projected temporary capacity expiration:    N/A

Allocation of iCOD Resources Among Partitions
----------------------------------------------------------------
nPar  Inactive  Inactive      Inactive
ID    Cells     Memory        CPUs       nPar Name
====  ========  ===========   ========   ======================
  0      0         0.0 GB         4       rex01
  1      0         0.0 GB         0       rex02 (local)
N/A      0         0.0 GB         0       Unassigned Cells

iCOD Partition Configuration Information
----------------------------------------------------------------
      Intended  Actual          Compatible
nPar  Active    Active   Total  Software
ID    CPUs      CPUs     CPUs   Installed   nPar Name
====  ========  ======   =====  ==========  ====================
  0      8         8       12     Yes        rex01
  1      4         4        4     Yes        rex02 (local)
```

Deactivating Two CPUs

Two of the four CPUs in the rex02 nPartition must now be deactivated. This is done by using the following icod_modify command on the rex02 nPartition. This command sets the intended number of active processors to two.

```
# icod_modify -s 2 \
> "Setting intended number of active processors to 2":"Bryan Jacquot"

2 processors are intended to be active and are currently active.
```

The second line of the command is optional and provides a descriptive comment for the change. This comment is logged in the Instant Capacity log file and is also sent in an e-mail to the Instant Capacity system contact. The final field in the command is the name of the administrator performing the change. The `icod_modify` command must be issued by the `root` user, and therefore a field is available to provide clarity in who was authenticated as root and issued the command.

The command shown deactivates two CPUs immediately. If the applications running in the nPartition were not able to handle the dynamic removal of CPUs, the change could have been deferred until the next reboot by adding the `-D` command line option.

It is important to remember the Instant Capacity codewords are applied at the complex level, regardless of the nPartition in the complex where the command is executed. In this example, the RTU codeword allowed six CPUs to be activated, among other things. The codeword was applied on rex01, but it did not specify which CPUs could be activated. The command that deactivated two CPUs in the rex02 nPartition applies to the nPartition where the command is executed. This command is not a complex-wide change; instead, the Instant Capacity software ensures that only two CPUs are activated in the rex02 nPartition. Other than applying Instant Capacity codewords, the `icod_modify` command affects the local nPartition where it is executed.

The status of the system after deactivating the CPUs is shown in Listing 10-7. Notice that there are now two active processors and that the intended number of active processors is also two. The number of intended active processors will persist across reboots.

Listing 10-7 Instant Capacity Status after Deactivating Two Processors in rex02

```
# icod_stat
[...]

Local Hard Partition Information
--------------------------------
Total processors:                             4
Intended Active processors:                   2
Active processors:                            2
Licensed processors that can be activated:    2
Processors that can be activated if licensed: 0
Processors that cannot immediately be activated: 0

Global iCOD Information
-----------------------
iCOD cells:                                   0
Actual inactive cells:                        0
iCOD processors:                              2
Actual inactive processors:                   6
iCOD Memory:                                  0.0 GB
Actual inactive Memory:                       0.0 GB
Temporary capacity available:                 0 days,
                                              0 hours,
                                              0 minutes
Processors using temporary capacity:          0
Projected temporary capacity expiration:      N/A

[...]
```

When Instant Capacity processors are activated or deactivated, the system contact is sent an e-mail message. Listing 10-8 shows the e-mail that was sent after the two processors in rex02 were deactivated. The e-mail notifications can be enabled or disabled using the `icod_notify` command.

Listing 10-8   Email Notification for CPU Deactivation

```
Date: Thu, 19 Aug 2004 19:38:32 -0600 (MDT)
To: bryanj@rex01
Subject: iCOD Configuration Change Notification

A configuration change has been made to the following system:
      rex02

One or more processors were deactivated.

Details of the change include:

Time of change:                      08/19/04 19:38:32
Previous number of active processors: 4
Current number of active processors:  2
Number of processors to be active after reboot: 2

Description of change: Setting intended number of active
                       processors to 2
Person making change:  Bryan Jacquot
System contact e-mail: bryanj@rex01

If you are the system contact and do not want to receive this
type of notification in the future, it can be disabled by
executing the following command on the system in question:
    /usr/sbin/icod_notify -n off
To turn notification on, execute:
    /usr/sbin/icod_notify -n on
```

Activating Remaining Processors

The initial codeword applied to the complex provided a RTU license for six additional CPUs. Two of those processors have been consumed in the rex02 nPartition. The four deactivated CPUs in the rex01 nPartition can now be activated. The following command achieves this objective:

```
# icod_modify -a 4 \
> "Activating remaining 4 licensed CPUs":"Bryan Jacquot"

12 processors are intended to be active and are currently active.
```

Listing 10-9 shows the final Instant Capacity status of the complex. There are two inactive CPUs and two Instant Capacity CPUs, and the system is in compliance with the Instant Capacity contract.

Listing 10-9 Final Instant Capacity Status with Two Instant Capacity CPUs

```
# icod_stat
[...]

Local Hard Partition Information
--------------------------------
Total processors:                                12
Intended Active processors:                      12
Active processors:                               12
Licensed processors that can be activated:       0
Processors that can be activated if licensed:    0
Processors that cannot immediately be activated: 0

Global iCOD Information
-----------------------
iCOD cells:                                      0
Actual inactive cells:                           0
iCOD processors:                                 2
Actual inactive processors:                      2
iCOD Memory:                                     0.0 GB
Actual inactive Memory:                          0.0 GB
Temporary capacity available:                    0 days,
                                                 0 hours,
                                                 0 minutes
Processors using temporary capacity:             0
Projected temporary capacity expiration:         N/A

[...]
```

Viewing the Instant Capacity Log Files

The Instant Capacity commands log configuration changes on the system where the changes are made. The application of the Instant Capacity codeword, the activation of the four CPUs on rex01, and the deactivation of the two CPUs on rex02 are shown in Listing 10-10.

These log files are not aggregated between the nPartitions in the complex automatically. Therefore, HP recommends that the clocks in each nPartition be synchronized to allow aggregation of the log files using external tools.

Listing 10-10 Instant Capacity Log File Entries

```
<rex01:/var/adm/icod.log>
Date:                       08/19/04 19:32:04
Log Type:                   Right-to-Use codeword applied
Processors:                 6
Cells:                      1
Memory (GB):                4.000

Date:                       08/19/04 19:46:10
Log Type:                   Configuration Change
Total processors:           12
Active processors:          12
Intended Active CPUs:       12
Description:                Activating remaining 4
                            licensed CPUs
Changed by:                 Bryan Jacquot

<rex02:/var/adm/icod.log>

Date:                       08/19/04 19:38:32
Log Type:                   Configuration Change
Total processors:           4
Active processors:          2
Intended Active CPUs:       2
Description:                Setting intended number
                            of active processors to 2
Changed by:                 Bryan Jacquot
```

Migrating Instant Capacity CPUs between nPartitions

The Instant Capacity infrastructure enables more than just activation of Instant Capacity components after they are licensed. Using the Instant Capacity software, CPUs can be activated and deactivated dynamically provided the system is not taken out of compliance. As a result, nPartitions can be dynamically sized based on workload utilization requirements. Listing 10-11 shows a script that could be used to migrate Instant Capacity CPUs between two nPartitions. In the example scenario, the two CPUs in the rex01 nPartition can be dynamically deactivated and two CPUs can be dynamically activated in the rex02 nPartition. This allows a workload to retain the hardware and electrical isolation inherent with nPartitions but provides dynamic CPU migration capabilities similar to vPars. When Instant Capacity is used for dynamic CPU migration, the CPUs are not being moved from one nPartition to another; instead, the CPUs are being activated and deactivated in such a way as to never have more CPUs active than are licensed. The only restriction relating to the migration of Instant Capacity CPUs is the system must not be taken out of compliance. Therefore, CPUs must be deactivated in the source nPartition before they are activated in the destination nPartition.

Listing 10-11 Script for Migrating Instant Capacity CPUs

```
#!/usr/bin/sh
# ***************************************************************
# Migrate Instant Capacity CPUs
# --------------------------------------------------------------
#
# Usage:
#  migrate_icod_cpus -s <source nPar> -d <dest nPar> -c <count>
#
# Description:
#
# This script will move <count> CPUs from <source nPar> to
# <dest nPar>.  The source and destination parameters are the
# hostnames of the nPartitions.  ssh is used to remotely
# execute the commands on the respective nPartitions.  This
# script assumes trust relationships have been established
# between the node running this script and the source and
# destination nPartitions.
#
# This script is for illustration purposes only.
#
# ***************************************************************


#
# Initialize variables
#
SOURCE=""
DEST=""
COUNT=""
USAGE="migrate_icod_cpus -s <source nPar> -d <dest nPar> \
-c <count>"

#
# Parse the command line arguments, see getopt(1) for usage
# details.
#
set -- $(getopt c:d:s: $*)

if [ $? -ne 0 ]; then
  print -u2 "$USAGE"
  exit 1
fi

while [ $# -gt 0 ]; do
  case "$1" in
  '-c')
    COUNT=$2
    shift 2
    ;;
  '-d')
    DEST=$2
    shift 2
    ;;
  '-s')
```

```
    SOURCE=$2
    shift 2
    ;;
  --)
    break        # this is the end of parameters
    ;;
  esac
done

#
# Ensure all of the required parameters were specified
#

if [ -z "$SOURCE" -o -z "$DEST" -o -z "$COUNT" ]; then
  print -u2 "ERROR: Missing required argument(s)"
  print -u2 "$USAGE"
  exit 1
fi

ssh root@$SOURCE "/usr/sbin/icod_modify -d $COUNT" || exit $?

ssh root@$DEST "/usr/sbin/icod_modify -a $COUNT"

exit $?
```

The `migrate_icod_cpus` script demonstrates an isolated yet flexible computing environment. Each nPartition retains hardware isolation but has CPU flexibility attributes that are typically available only from environments with lower levels of isolation. Given the availability of two Instant Capacity CPUs in the rex complex, the number of active CPUs in each nPartition can vary based on workload demands.

The `migrate_icod_cpus` script is not practical for a production environment. It does not ensure that the number of licensed CPUs are always active. For example, if the destination nPartition happens to be down, two licensed CPUs will be left inactive after they are deactivated in the source nPartition. Chapter 15, "Workload Manager," describes a mechanism to robustly migrate Instant Capacity CPUs based on workload demands.

Summary

Instant Capacity fulfills a vital role in HP's Virtual Server Environment. Instant Capacity eases the process of planning for new workloads by allowing a system to be purchased over time as computing requirements increase.

After purchasing a right-to-use license for Instant Capacity hardware resources, an Instant Capacity codeword is applied to the system. Instant Capacity codewords can contain licenses for cells, CPUs, and memory. After a codeword has been applied, the resources can be instantly activated. The use of Instant Capacity provides a powerful level of flexibility by allowing CPUs to be deactivated in one nPartition and activated in another. Thus, a workload can have both hardware isolation and dynamic CPU migration capabilities. All of these features ease the planning and purchasing of new hardware.

11

Temporary Instant Capacity

Chapter Overview

Many data centers are built with redundancy and failover mechanisms that can handle serious disaster situations. In most cases, HP Serviceguard has been configured to failover a workload to a separate system should a problem occur with the primary hardware or software. While redundant hardware configurations do provide robust computing environments, it is costly to maintain hardware that is grossly underutilized while waiting for a failover to occur. One of HP's solutions to this problem is the Temporary Instant Capacity program. Like the Instant Capacity program, Temporary Instant Capacity allows users to purchase a system without licensing all of the hardware at the time of the initial purchase. This provides a great deal of flexibility to handle situations, such as a way to temporarily activate unlicensed hardware when a Serviceguard failover occurs. After the primary hardware and software environment has been restored, the unlicensed components can be deactivated. The Temporary Instant Capacity that has been purchased is consumed only when it's needed.

As part of HP's Virtual Server Environment, Temporary Instant Capacity enables hardware resources to be instantly activated only when they are needed. Using Temporary Instant Capacity allows unlicensed CPUs to be deactivated when they are not needed. In contrast, Instant Capacity right-to-use licenses are permanent; when a license is applied, it permanently activates resources.

This chapter provides an overview of Temporary Instant Capacity along with some of the fundamental Temporary Instant Capacity terminology. The bulk of the chapter discusses an example scenario that picks up where the example in Chapter 10, "Instant Capacity," left off. The scenario describes the process of activating and deactivating unlicensed CPUs in an environment where a testing nPartition is serving as a Serviceguard failover for a production workload.

Temporary Instant Capacity Overview

Temporary Instant Capacity allows a computing environment to flex as the workloads demand. The demands may be a result of a Serviceguard failover, cyclical peaks in workload usage, or a variety of other reasons. Regardless of the reason, Temporary Instant Capacity provides a way to pay for hardware when it is needed, not when it is acquired.

Temporary Instant Capacity is a feature of Instant Capacity. As shown in Figure 11-1, users can activate unlicensed CPUs using the Temporary Instant Capacity software. A Temporary Instant Capacity codeword must be applied to provide Temporary Instant Capacity. When the user activates the CPUs using a special Temporary Instant Capacity option for the `icod_mod-ify` command, the software debits time from the Temporary Instant Capacity balance. When the user deactivates the CPU, debiting from the Temporary Instant Capacity balance stops. When the Temporary Instant Capacity balance is depleted, HP requires the CPUs to be deactivated. However, to prevent the possible disruption of an application, the Temporary Instant Capacity software does not automatically deactivate unlicensed CPUs. Instead, they must be manually deactivated by the user. Unlicensed CPUs that are active after the Temporary Instant Capacity balance is depleted causes a negative balance to accrue that must be paid for by purchasing and applying further codewords.

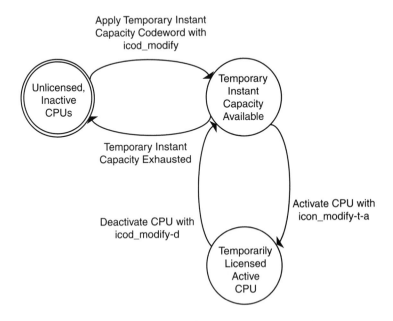

Figure 11-1 Usage Diagram of Temporary Instant Capacity

important

> When the Temporary Instant Capacity balance is depleted, it does not result in CPUs being automatically deactivated. Instead, the Temporary Instant Capacity balance will begin accruing a negative balance that must be reconciled by purchasing and applying further codewords.

When the Temporary Instant Capacity balance is depleted and the CPUs have been manually deactivated, additional Temporary Instant Capacity codewords can be purchased and applied to re-enable the use of the unlicensed CPUs.

Temporary Instant Capacity Terminology

Temporary Instant Capacity Codeword: an encoded string of letters and numbers that contains an amount of Temporary Instant Capacity. Temporary Instant Capacity codewords are available from the Instant Capacity portal after the user purchases some amount of Temporary Instant Capacity.

Temporary capacity available: the amount of Temporary Instant Capacity CPU time available for the complex. This time is tracked in CPU minutes.

CPU Minutes: the number of minutes available for Temporary Instant Capacity activation. For example, if 1,000 CPU minutes are available, one CPU can be activated for 1,000 minutes; two CPUs can be activated for 500 minutes each, or four CPUs can be activated for 250 minutes. CPU minutes are purchased in increments of 30 CPU days and are tracked on a per-second basis. Temporary Instant Capacity is decremented only in 30-minute blocks.

Example Temporary Instant Capacity Scenario

The Temporary Instant Capacity example scenario picks up from where the example from Chapter 10, "Instant Capacity," left off. The rex02 nPartition has two unlicensed CPUs that have been deactivated. This scenario describes how to activate these two CPUs using Temporary Instant Capacity in a situation where the rex02 testing nPartition is serving as a Serviceguard failover node for a production workload. Only when the Serviceguard package is active on the rex02 nPartition should Temporary Instant Capacity CPUs be activated. This scenario will not cover the process of setting up the Serviceguard cluster, nor will it discuss the steps required to automatically activate Temporary Instant Capacity CPUs based on activation of a Serviceguard package. Those two processes are covered in Chapter 16, "Serviceguard," and Chapter 15, "Workload Manager," respectively.

The software used to activate, deactivate, and monitor Temporary Instant Capacity is the same software used to manage Instant Capacity. All deactivated CPUs within nPartitions running HP-UX can be activated using Temporary Instant Capacity. Most of the commands shown in this example are identical to those shown in Chapter 10, "Instant Capacity." There are three primary differences between managing Temporary Instant Capacity and Instant Capacity.

- Temporary Instant Capacity requires e-mail connectivity from complexes using Temporary Instant Capacity to HP for the purpose of asset reporting.
- Temporary Instant Capacity codewords contain only temporary capacity. When the user requests a Temporary Instant Capacity codeword, he or she does not need to request the number of CPUs, cells, and the amount of memory. The only piece of information required is the number of CPU days the user wants to purchase.
- Temporary Instant Capacity requires additional command-line arguments when the user is activating processors.

Configuring E-mail Connectivity

The version of Temporary Instant Capacity used in this chapter requires e-mail connectivity to HP for asset reporting. Configuring and sending asset reports by e-mail consists of the following steps.

1. *Set the From e-mail address.*

   The From e-mail address is the address used in e-mail asset reports sent to HP. The default address is adm@<fully qualified domain name of the system>. If the default address is not correct or monitored, the `icod_modify` command should be used to change the value. The domain name in the From e-mail address field must be resolvable by the domain name system (DNS), otherwise HP will not receive the asset report. The value of this field is displayed by the `icod_stat` command. The following command illustrates setting the From e-mail address.

   ```
   # icod_modify -f bryanj@rex01.fc.hp.com

   The from e-mail address for all iCOD correspondence to HP
   has been set to bryanj@rex01.fc.hp.com.
   ```

2. *Enable asset reporting.*

   Asset reporting is enabled by default, but the current setting should be verified with `icod_stat`. If asset reporting is found to be off, it should be enabled with the following command:

```
# icod_notify -a on
Asset report e-mail generation has been turned on.
```

3. *Configure Sendmail.*

   Entire books have been written about Sendmail configuration; therefore, the specifics of configuring HP-UX to send e-mail will not be discussed in this context. See the "Installing and Administering Internet Services" guide referenced in Appendix A for details on configuring Sendmail.

4. *Test e-mail connectivity.*

   E-mail connectivity with HP should be tested using the icod_notify command. The command will send an asset report to HP, to the root user on the partition, and to the e-mail address specified on the command line. In response to the asset report, HP will send a message to the specified e-mail address confirming e-mail connectivity.

```
# icod_notify bryanj@rex01.fc.hp.com

Asset report e-mail was sent to HP with a request for a reply.
The response will be sent to the specified e-mail address:
bryanj@rex01
```

Viewing the Initial Status

Once e-mail asset reports are being sent to HP, the next step is to view the configuration of the complex. Listing 11-1 shows the initial Temporary Instant Capacity status of the complex. Initially, there is zero temporary capacity available on the system. However, two unlicensed CPUs in the rex02 nPartition are inactive. These two unlicensed CPUs will be used as Temporary Instant Capacity when a Serviceguard failover occurs to the nPartition.

Listing 11-1 Initial Instant Capacity and Temporary Instant Capacity Configuration

```
# icod_stat
Software version:        B.06.01
System ID:               rex02
Serial number:           USE4416CNL
Product number:          AB240A
Unique ID:               ad2b3532-abd9-11d8-a988-7877a7f45c12
System contact e-mail:   bryanj@rex01
From e-mail:             bryanj@rex01.fc.hp.com
Asset reporting:         on
Exception status:        No exception
```

```
Local Hard Partition Information
- - - - - - - - - - - - - - - - - - - - - - - - - - - - - - -
Total processors:                               4
Intended Active processors:                     4
Active processors:                              2
Licensed processors that can be activated:      0
Processors that can be activated if licensed:   2
Processors that cannot immediately be activated: 0

Global iCOD Information
- - - - - - - - - - - - - - - - -
iCOD cells:                                     0
Actual inactive cells:                          0
iCOD processors:                                2
Actual inactive processors:                     2
iCOD Memory:                                    0.0 GB
Actual inactive Memory:                         0.0 GB
Temporary capacity available:                   0 days,
                                                0 hours,
                                                0 minutes

Processors using temporary capacity:            0
Projected temporary capacity expiration:        N/A

Allocation of iCOD Resources Among Partitions
- - - - - - - - - - - - - - - - - - - - - - - - - - - - - - - - - - - - - - - - - - - - - - - - -
nPar  Inactive  Inactive     Inactive
ID    Cells     Memory       CPUs      nPar Name
====  ========  ===========  ========  =======================
  0      0         0.0 GB        0      rex01
  1      0         0.0 GB        2      rex02 (local)
 N/A     0         0.0 GB        0      Unassigned Cells

iCOD Partition Configuration Information
- - - - - - - - - - - - - - - - - - - - - - - - - - - - - - - - - - - - - - - - - - - - - - - - -
        Intended  Actual           Compatible
nPar    Active    Active   Total   Software
ID      CPUs      CPUs     CPUs    Installed   nPar Name
====    ========  ======   =====   ==========  ====================
  0       12        12      12       Yes       rex01
  1        4         2       4        No       rex02 (local)
```

Acquiring a Temporary Instant Capacity Codeword

Temporary Instant Capacity can be purchased in increments of 30 CPU days. After you have purchased Temporary Instant Capacity, go to the Instant Capacity portal to acquire a codeword. The Instant Capacity portal at **http://www.hp.com/go/icod/portal** requires the following information for a Temporary Instant Capacity codeword:

- Product number
- Serial number
- Audit snapshot
- HP sales order number
- Number of Temporary Instant Capacity CPU days

Like Instant Capacity, the amount of temporary capacity is tracked at the complex level. As a result, Temporary Instant Capacity can be used in any nPartition running HP-UX in the complex, even simultaneously in multiple nPartitions. The product number, serial number, and audit snapshot are available from the `icod_stat` command. Listing 11-2 shows the command displaying the system snapshot that is required when you acquire a Temporary Instant Capacity codeword.

Listing 11-2 Instant Capacity System Snapshot

```
# icod_stat -s
Product number: AB240A
Serial number:  USE4416CNL
Audit snapshot:
mFXkeaT.txEdPkq.P2VKsFM.dD5ztet.fVfBXt7.8VTqT5g.ALWjhdm.
KMHQ1TF.J3AXaMg.qhP2
```

Once you have the `icod_stat` system snapshot, you can use the Instant Capacity portal to acquire the Temporary Instant Capacity codeword. Figure 11-2 shows an example screen from the Instant Capacity portal on the Create codewords page. Notice that the screen is different from the Instant Capacity right-to-use codeword page shown in Chapter 10, "Instant Capacity," as the number of CPUs, cells, and memory is not required for Temporary Instant Capacity. Instead, the number of CPU days is required.

Applying the Temporary Instant Capacity Codeword

After you have received a Temporary Instant Capacity codeword from the portal, the next step is to apply the codeword to the system. The `icod_modify` command applies the Temporary Instant Capacity codeword with the `-C` argument. The Temporary Instant Capacity codeword applied in this example contains 90 CPU days of CPU time. This can be consumed by one CPU that is active for 90 days, two CPUs active for 45 days, or any other combination of CPUs and time. Temporary Instant Capacity does not need to be consumed in a continuous block of time and is debited only while unlicensed CPUs are active. When the unlicensed CPUs are deactivated, the Temporary Instant Capacity balance does not change.

Figure 11-2 Temporary Instant Capacity Codeword Portal

```
# icod_modify \
> -C XJ64Fa4.nsAFEiG.hJE9603.Nz3L0Xg-FH5G5eu.YB1wiL3.LFQDjWT.p5efEz7
The following valid codeword has been applied to the complex:

    Temporary Capacity Codeword
    90 days, 0 hours, 0 minutes

Execute the icod_stat(1M) command to see the results
    of the application of this codeword.
```

Listing 11-3 shows the status of the system after you have applied the codeword. There are now 90 days of temporary capacity on the system. At this point, unlicensed CPUs in any nPartition in the complex running HP-UX may be activated as temporary capacity.

Listing 11-3 Temporary Instant Capacity Status after Applying Codeword

```
# icod_stat
[...]

Global iCOD Information
-----------------------
iCOD cells:                               0
Actual inactive cells:                    0
iCOD processors:                          2
Actual inactive processors:               2
iCOD Memory:                              0.0 GB
Actual inactive Memory:                   0.0 GB
Temporary capacity available:             90 days,
                                          0 hours,
                                          0 minutes

Processors using temporary capacity:      0
Projected temporary capacity expiration:  N/A
[...]
```

Activating Temporary Instant Capacity

To activate unlicensed CPUs you will need to specify a special argument in the icod_modify command. As shown in the following command, the –t option is required when you activate unlicensed CPUs that are intended to consume Temporary Instant Capacity. If you intend to defer activation of the CPUs until the next reboot, the -D argument should be added to the command.

important

> Always specify the -t option when activating temporary capacity. Failure to specify the option will cause the command to fail and zero CPUs will be activated. Only when the -t option is specified will the Temporary Instant Capacity software allow the unlicensed processors to be activated and begin debiting Temporary Instant Capacity.

The following command also shows a description of the activation of unlicensed CPUs. This field is logged in the Instant Capacity log file and is sent via e-mail to the system contact when the CPUs are activated. The final field in the command is the full name of the administrator activating the command. The icod_modify command must be executed by root, so this field allows an administrator to provide clarity about exactly who activated the processors.

```
# icod_modify -t -a 2 \
> "Activating two Temporary Capacity \
> CPUs for failover testing":\
> "Bryan Jacquot"

4 processors are intended to be active and are currently active.

Processors using temporary capacity:            2
Projected temporary capacity expiration:        10/09/04
                                                19:00:00
```

After the unlicensed CPUs have been activated, an e-mail is sent to the system contact for the nPartition. Remember, this field is configured using the icod_modify command. Listing 11-4 shows the e-mail that is sent to the system contact when the temporary capacity is activated.

Listing 11-4 Email Notification for Temporary Instant Capacity Processor Activation

```
Date: Wed, 25 Aug 2004 19:00:20 -0600 (MDT)
To: bryanj@rex01
Subject: iCOD Configuration Change Notification

A configuration change has been made to the following system:
        rex02

One or more processors were activated.

Details of the change include:

Time of change:                    08/25/04 19:00:20
Previous number of active processors: 2
Current number of active processors:  4
Number of processors to be active after reboot: 4

Description of change: Activating two Temporary Capacity
CPUs for failover testing
Person making change:  Bryan Jacquot
System contact e-mail: bryanj@rex01

If you are the system contact and do not want to receive this
type of notification in the future, it can be disabled by
executing the following command on the system in question:
    /usr/sbin/icod_notify -n off
To turn notification on, execute:
    /usr/sbin/icod_notify -n on
```

The status of the complex after activating the unlicensed CPUs is shown in Listing 11-5. This command was executed approximately 30 minutes after the temporary capacity was activated. Temporary Instant Capacity software does not continuously monitor temporary capacity. Instead, Temporary Instant Capacity is debited every 30 minutes. If the `icod_stat` command had been executed immediately after the activation of the CPUs, the output would have most likely stated that the full 90 days of temporary capacity was available. Since there are two active CPUs consuming temporary capacity, after approximately 30 minutes of clock time, a total of one CPU hour of temporary capacity has been consumed. Therefore, the Temporary Instant Capacity software reports that 89 days and 23 hours remain.

note

Temporary Instant Capacity accounting is not performed continuously. Instead, the Temporary Instant Capacity software periodically wakes up and takes a snapshot of the system and then goes back to sleep. Executing the `icod_stat` command every minute will not result in immediate updating of the temporary capacity available.

Listing 11-5 Temporary Instant Capacity Status after Activating Processors

```
# icod_stat
[...]

Local Hard Partition Information
--------------------------------
Total processors:                            4
Intended Active processors:                  4
Active processors:                           4
Licensed processors that can be activated:   0
Processors that can be activated if licensed: 0
Processors that cannot immediately be activated: 0

Global iCOD Information
-----------------------
iCOD cells:                                  0
Actual inactive cells:                       0
iCOD processors:                             2
Actual inactive processors:                  0
iCOD Memory:                                 0.0 GB
Actual inactive Memory:                      0.0 GB
Temporary capacity available:                89 days,
                                             23 hours,
                                             0 minutes

Processors using temporary capacity:         2
Projected temporary capacity expiration:     10/09/04
                                             19:00:00

[...]
```

Deactivating Temporary Instant Capacity

Temporary capacity is deactivated in much the same way it is activated. The `icod_modify` command is used along with options to deactivate processors. In this example, testing of Temporary Instant Capacity with the Serviceguard failover has been completed, so both unlicensed processors will be deactivated. Notice that no special option is required when deactivating CPUs. Instead, as soon as the number of active CPUs is less than or equal to the number of licensed CPUs, the Temporary Instant Capacity software stops debiting the Temporary Instant Capacity balance.

The -D option can be provided in the command to deactivate processors if the change should be deferred until the next reboot. This feature is especially useful when applications running in an nPartition have not been designed to accommodate a dynamic environment in which CPUs are instantly deactivated. Using the -D option causes Temporary Instant Capacity to be debited until the reboot is performed. Therefore, the reboot should be performed in a timely fashion to avoid unnecessary use of Temporary Instant Capacity.

In the following command, the -d (lower case) command line option causes the specified number of CPUs to be instantly deactivated. Since the -D (upper case) command line option was not appended to the command, the CPUs are instantly deactivated instead of the deactivation being deferred until the next reboot.

```
# icod_modify -d 2 \
> "Testing deactivation of Temporary \
> Capacity CPUs after failover \
> is restored":\
> "Bryan Jacquot"


2 processors are intended to be active and are currently active.

Processors using temporary capacity:          0
Projected temporary capacity expiration:      N/A
```

Viewing the Temporary Instant Capacity Log File

Both Instant Capacity and Temporary Instant Capacity share the same log file. Listing 11-6 shows the log file with the application of the Temporary Instant Capacity codeword, followed by the debit to the temporary capacity. Finally, the log file shows the deactivation of the unlicensed CPUs.

In this scenario, the Temporary Instant Capacity codeword was applied on the rex02 nPartition and the unlicensed CPUs were activated in the rex02 nPartition. However, the Temporary Instant Capacity codeword does not need be applied to the same nPartition where temporary capacity will be used. Temporary Instant Capacity codewords apply to the entire complex, so unlicensed CPUs could have been activated in any nPartition running HP-UX in the complex.

Listing 11-6 Temporary Instant Capacity Log File

```
< /var/adm/icod.log >

Date:                           08/25/04 18:58:20
Log Type:                       Temporary capacity codeword
                                applied
Temporary capacity added:       90 days, 0 hours, 0 minutes

Date:                           08/25/04 19:00:20
Log Type:                       Configuration Change
Total processors:               4
Active processors:              4
Intended Active CPUs:           4
Description:                    Activating two Temporary
                                Capacity CPUs for failover
                                testing
Changed by:                     Bryan Jacquot

Date:                           08/25/04 19:30:34
Log Type:                       Temporary capacity debit
Temporary capacity CPUs:        2
CPU minutes debited:            60
Temporary capacity available:   89 days, 23 hours, 0 minutes

Date:                           08/25/04 19:35:43
Log Type:                       Configuration Change
Total processors:               4
Active processors:              2
Intended Active CPUs:           2
Description:                    Testing deactivation of
                                Temporary Capacity CPUs
                                after failover is restored
Changed by:                     Bryan Jacquot
```

Summary

The version of Temporary Instant Capacity illustrated in this chapter in HP's Virtual Server Environment provides a means for resources to be instantly activated when needed and deactivated when the resources are no longer needed. This functionality provides cost savings while meeting the demands of workloads in the datacenter.

Temporary Instant Capacity requires a system with e-mail connectivity to HP for asset reporting. However, this requirement has been removed in the latest version of the software. After configuring e-mail connectivity, a Temporary Instant Capacity codeword must be purchased and acquired. These codewords are purchased in blocks of 30 CPU days. Once a codeword is retrieved from the Instant Capacity portal, it is applied to the complex and Temporary Instant Capacity is immediately available for use.

Whether the situation is a Serviceguard failover or an unexpected peak in demand, unlicensed CPUs can be instantly activated to meet the needs of the workloads. When temporary capacity is no longer needed, the CPUs can be instantly deactivated. HP's Virtual Server Environment provides integration between Workload Manager and Temporary Instant Capacity to automate the process of activating and deactivating unlicensed CPUs as shown in Chapter 15, "Workload Manager." This combination of technologies provides a dynamic and robust computing environment without the typical costs of fully redundant hardware configurations.

Temporary Instant Capacity can be used in many environments for many purposes. Serviceguard failover situations, unexpected peaks in system utilization, and cyclical peaks in workload utilization can all be handled by the Temporary Instant Capacity solution.

12

Pay Per Use

Chapter Overview

What do your power bill, your water bill, and your computer hardware bill all have in common? Answer: all three of these utilities can be billed based on the amount of resources you consume. This seems normal for your water bill and power bill, but paying for computer hardware based on usage? HP's Pay per use (PPU) solution enables customers to lease computer hardware with a variable payment based on actual use of the system.

HP's Virtual Server Environment combined with the PPU solution delivers the ability to treat a data center as a utility. When the workloads demand greater computing resources, the resources are ready and waiting. When the demand for resources decreases, the PPU solution tracks the decline and the lease payment reflects the levels of demand and utilization.

PPU is a very simple technology from a system administration point of view. During the initial configuration of the system, software must be installed and configured. After those steps are complete, the PPU software needs very little, if any, administrator attention. The only exception to this rule is the CPU capping feature, which sets the maximum number of CPUs that should be active. This chapter begins with an overview of the PPU product and then walks through the process of configuring a PPU system to ensure proper utilization reporting.

Pay Per Use Overview

Two types of PPU metrics can be used for billing purposes. PPU can either be based on the *percent utilization* of the CPUs or on the number of *active CPUs*. When the percent utilization method is used, all CPUs are active. The PPU software tracks the utilization of the CPUs and the monthly lease payment reflects the actual level of use. In contrast, the active CPU method bases the monthly lease payment on the number of active CPUs, not the utilization of those CPUs.

Like Instant Capacity and Temporary Instant Capacity, when more CPU resources are required, they can be instantly activated. When the resources are no longer needed, they can be deactivated. In both the percent utilization and active CPU methods of reporting, the PPU software tracks the amount of CPU resources consumed and reports the utilization to the HP utility meter.

The HP utility meter is a hardware system that is configured by an HP service representative. The meter must have connectivity to the Internet and HP servers. One utility meter can collect usage data for a maximum of approximately 100 partitions or storage devices. From a PPU administration perspective, the only piece of information the HP utility meter needs is the hostname or IP address. There are no administration tasks that must be performed on the HP utility meter after the meter has been initially set up and configured.

A common concern when customers consider using PPU is the possibility that the lease payment will be much higher than expected due to unforeseen peaks in workload demands. In order to prevent unexpected leaps in resource utilization and the associated costs, PPU allows the system to be configured with CPU capping. When a customer uses CPU capping, the maximum number of CPUs that can be active on each partition is fixed. This results in a hard upper boundary on the amount of resources that can be consumed, thus ensuring the payment is within a bounded range.

Pay per use is supported on HP 9000 and HP Integrity nPartition servers running either HP-UX or Microsoft Windows operating systems. The Pay per use solution has the following requirements that must be met for each partition in the complex.

- PPU software must be installed on every partition. This includes installing the software on every HP Virtual Partition running within nPartitions.
- PPU software must have network connectivity to the PPU utility meter.
- PPU software must be configured to communicate with the PPU utility meter.

The following example scenario walks through the process of ensuring that these requirements are met for an HP-UX nPartition participating in PPU. It also describes the initial steps of configuring a Microsoft Windows nPartition for PPU.

Example Pay Per Use Scenario

This example scenario walks through the process of configuring HP-UX and Microsoft Windows nPartitions to use PPU. It assumes that the HP utility meter has been set up and configured, as HP service representatives or authorized HP partners are responsible for installing and maintaining the meter. In the HP-UX portion of this scenario, the active CPU metric is being utilized. Notice that none of the commands specify the type of metric being tracked; instead, the metric is specified in the contract and is available on the PPU portal. Pay Per Use for Microsoft Windows only supports the percent utilization billing model.

remember

> The steps covered in this scenario must be performed on every partition in the complex. If these steps are not taken, HP may assume that you are using 100% of your CPUs in partitions that are not properly configured.

The steps covered in the HP-UX portion of this example are executed on an HP 9000 Superdome with 16 cells. There are 14 nPartitions configured in the complex. The zoo3 nPartition used throughout the scenario contains a single cell that has four CPUs. The Microsoft Windows portion of this example is executed on an HP Integrity rx8620 with four cells. There are four nPartitions configured in the complex. The rex03 nPartition contains a single cell that has four CPUs.

Ensuring That Software Is Installed

The first step in configuring a PPU system is to install the PPU software on every partition in the complex. If the software is not currently installed, it can be downloaded from **http://www. hp.com/go/softwaredepot**. The HP-UX product number for PPU is T2351AA. For Microsoft Windows, the software is included in the SmartComponent, WMINParProvider64PPU.msi.

In HP-UX, the PPU software is installed using the Software Distributor HP-UX installation tools. (The steps required to install the software are not shown in this example.) After the installation is complete, the swlist command can be used to ensure that the software is installed on the partition.

```
# swlist ¦ grep T2351AA
  T2351AA      B.07.00          HP-UX Pay Per Use (PPU)
```

In order to verify that the PPU software in installed on Microsoft Windows partitions, select Run from the Start menu. Enter services.msc. in the Run dialog. The resulting services console is shown in Figure 12-1. Notice the HP Pay per use service is listed, the status is shown as Started, and the startup type is configured to be Automatic.

After ensuring that the PPU software is properly installed and running on every partition, the next step is to configure the Pay per use software with the utility meter that will be used to track utilization data. The ppuconfig command is used for all of the PPU configuration tasks and operates the same on both HP-UX and Microsoft Windows with the exception of the command's path. The command is located in /usr/sbin on HP-UX and C:\Program Files (x86) \Hewlett-Packard\ppu on Microsoft Windows.

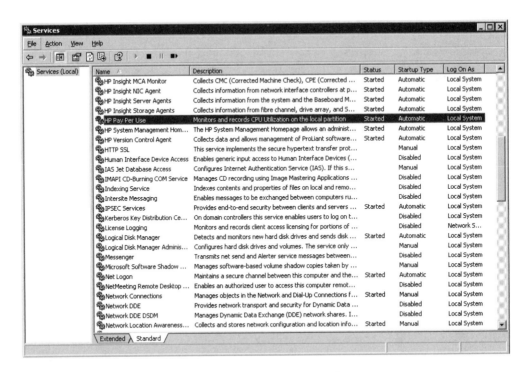

Figure 12-1 HP Pay Per Use Service for Microsoft Windows

Configuring the Pay Per Use Software on HP-UX Partitions

The next step is to configure the PPU software so it can communicate with the HP utility meter. You must provide either the hostname or IP address for the meter to the PPU software. The following HP-UX command configures the PPU software to use the utility meter with the hostname `ppumeter.fc.hp.com`.

```
# /usr/sbin/ppuconfig -m ppumeter.fc.hp.com
The utility meter IP/hostname is set to 'ppumeter.fc.hp.com'.
Pay Per Use daemon (ppud) started.
```

Executing the command as shown configures the PPU software so it can communicate with the HP utility meter and starts the PPU daemon, ppud. The PPU daemon is added to inittab and the daemon automatically starts after every reboot and restarts the process if it is stopped. All HP-UX PPU partitions must have the ppud daemon running at all times. When the daemon is not running, utilization data is not gathered and sent to the utility meter. As a result, HP may assume 100% CPU utilization for the partitions.

Configuring the Pay Per Use Software on Microsoft Windows Partitions

Configuring the Pay per use meter on Microsoft Windows partitions is similar to the configuration process for HP-UX with one primary difference: the ppuconfig command is located in a different place. The following Microsoft Windows command configures the PPU software to use the utility meter with the hostname ppumeter.fc.hp.com.

```
C:\Program Files (x86)\Hewlett-Packard\ppu> ppuconfig -m ppumeter.fc.hp.com
```

If the PPU service is running and the meter is reachable, this command does not emit any output.

Viewing the Initial Configuration

Since the ppuconfig command is used the same on HP-UX and Microsoft Windows, the remainder of this example scenario will illustrate the commands only on HP-UX.

The initial HP-UX configuration of the PPU software on the zoo3 nPartition is shown in Listing 12-1. Notice that all of the CPUs are active in this nPartition. The listing also shows that the utility meter is to be configured as shown in the previous step. The default system identifier is the partition's hostname. If a more descriptive identifier is desired, it can be manually configured as shown in the next step.

Listing 12-1   Initial HP-UX Pay Per Use Configuration

```
# /usr/sbin/ppuconfig

Utility Meter IP/Hostname:                    ppumeter.fc.hp.com
System Identifier:                            zoo3
CPUs to be active at next reboot (CPU Cap):   all
CPUs that can be activated without a reboot:  0
Active CPUs:                                  4
```

Performing Additional Configuration and Testing Steps

The PPU software offers the flexibility to configure the system identifier if the hostname is not appropriate. In some organizations, the hostname is an attribute that is considered to be private information. In other organizations, a more descriptive label is desired for proper tracking. In this example, the system identifier will be configured so it contains the model number, the asset number, and the physical location of the system.

```
# /usr/sbin/ppuconfig -s \
> "Model: SD64000, Asset: HP123456789, Location: FC3LE3"
The system ID is set to
'Model: SD64000, Asset: HP123456789, Location: FC3LE3'.
```

After setting the system identifier, the CPU cap will be set for this nPartition. Instead of leaving all four CPUs active in the nPartition, one of them will be deactivated. The ppuconfig command is used to set the CPU cap. The -r option in the command makes the change immediately. Without the -r option, the CPU would not have been deactivated until the next reboot of the nPartition.

note

CPU capping is supported only on HP-UX.

```
# /usr/sbin/ppuconfig -c 3 -r
The CPU cap is set to 3.
3 processors are now active.
```

The final step is to test the connectivity with the utility meter. When this command is executed, the PPU software sends a usage report to the utility meter and verifies round-trip communication.

```
# /usr/sbin/ppuconfig -t
Round trip communication with the utility meter succeeded.
```

The final PPU configuration is shown in Listing 12-2. Notice that the number of active CPUs is now three and one CPU can be immediately activated. When the workloads in the zoo3 nPartition demand more CPU resources and the costs of activating the fourth CPU are acceptable, the CPU can be instantly activated using the ppuconfig command.

Viewing the Final Configuration

Listing 12-2 Final Pay Per Use Configuration

```
# /usr/sbin/ppuconfig

Utility Meter IP/Hostname:                    ppumeter.fc.hp.com
System Identifier: Model: SD64000, Asset: HP123456789,
                   Location: FC3LE3
CPUs to be active at next reboot (CPU Cap):  3
CPUs that can be activated without a reboot: 1
Active CPUs:                                 3
```

Viewing the Utilization Reports

If the partitions in the complex have all been configured with the PPU software and connectivity to the utility meter is set up properly, usage reports will be available on the PPU portal. The PPU portal is available at **http://www.hp.com/go/payperuse**. The PPU reports are available two days after actual use occurs. Figure 12-2 shows an example usage report for a system participating in the active CPU PPU solution. This is a sample utilization report; it is not from the zoo3 or rex03 nPartitions discussed in the example scenario.

An example summary percent utilization PPU report is show in Figure 12-3. This report is for a single day. It shows the partition ID, the uptime over the selected 24-hour period, the percent usage, the number of CPUs, and the measurement status. A similar report is available for every partition in the PPU server. Selecting the link in the right-most column provides additional utilization details broken down in five-minute intervals.

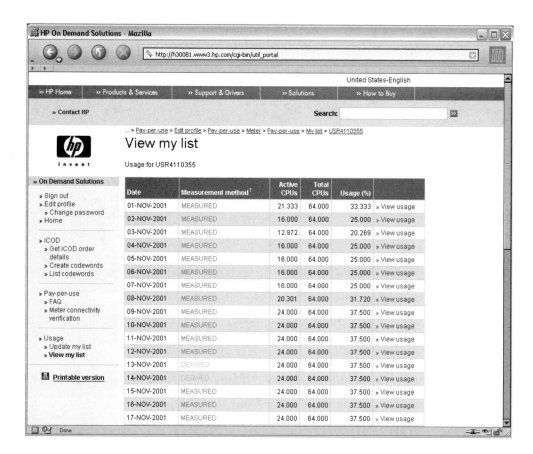

Figure 12-2 Pay Per Use Portal Active CPU Summary Report

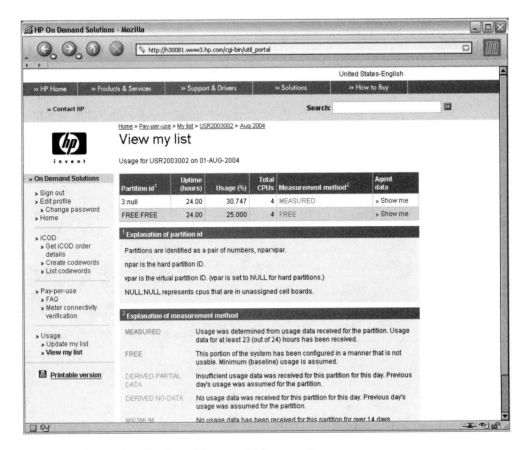

Figure 12-3 Pay Per Use Portal Percent Utilization Summary

In addition to the summary information shown in Figure 12-3, detailed utilization data is also available from the PPU portal. Figure 12-4 shows a detailed CPU utilization usage report for each CPU on a five-minute basis. The average of the data shown in the detailed report is used to calculate the monthly payment for the PPU server.

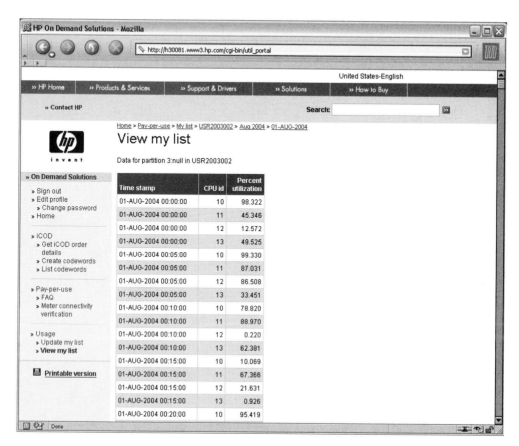

Figure 12-4 Pay Per Use Portal Detailed Percent Utilization Report

Summary

The PPU solution in HP's Virtual Server Environment eases some of the pain associated with ca-pacity planning and over-provisioning. Instead of purchasing a system that is bigger than needed to handle the peak workload demands, the system can be leased with monthly payments that are based on the actual utilization of the system, like the billing systems water and electricity com-panies use.

PPU requires users to load special software on every partition in the server. Each partition must have network connectivity to the HP utility meter and must be configured to send usage reports to the meter. The PPU software allows the system identifier to be customized for reporting purposes. In addition, a CPU cap can be configured to control the maximum resource availability and associated payments.

Once the initial system configuration is complete, PPU is very lightweight solution for system administrators. A periodic check of the PPU portal will ensure that all partitions are reporting utilization data appropriately.

13

Overview of Virtual Server Environment Management and High Availability Tools

Chapter Overview

The Virtual Server Environment is HP's answer to the need for increased utilization and application isolation on large servers. Partitioning Solutions isolate applications on a large server while still allowing the partitions to share resources. Utility Pricing Solutions provide the ability to add resources to a server when it is convenient and remove them when they are no longer needed. And finally, management tools simplify the management and maintenance of this dynamic environment.

One of the side effects of virtualization and the flexibility that these technologies provide is that management of the VSE can be more challenging. You now have resources freely moving between partitions, workloads moving between systems in high-availability clusters and even virtual machines flexing and moving between physical systems.

HP has developed a new set of integrated management tools, called HP Integrity Essentials, to simplify the management of this adaptive environment. These include visualization and configuration, automation, and capacity planning.

Visualization refers to the ability see where all your workloads are running and what resources they are consuming. Configuration is the ability to create or modify the configuration of each of the VSE technologies. HP has put these together because the visualization and configuration of each of these products naturally go together. Each of the products in the VSE has a configuration interface.

- The Integrity Essentials Virtualization Manager is a new product that pulls together the visualization of all the VSE technologies. The configuration of all of the partition and management functions is being embedded in this product, in some cases by providing seamless integration points with the existing configuration tools, such as Partition Manager and the Integrity Virtual Machine Manager.

- Each partitioning product in the VSE portfolio has its own configuration inter-face that can also be run independently. It is likely that this will continue to be the case for the foreseeable future. However, we will focus on the visualization and configuration management product in this book because that is the future direction of the integration of the visualization aspect of management. The goal is for you to be able to use this product to monitor all of the core VSE partition-ing and management technologies.

Automation refers to the ability to automate reconfiguration operations so you don't need ad-ministration staff dedicated to monitoring the environment and making decisions about when something needs to done and how to do it. There are four management products in this space.

- Workload Manager is the original automatic resource-balancing tool. It gives you the ability to reallocate resources in a Virtual Server Environment using service-level objectives for each of your workloads.

- Serviceguard is the leading high-availability solution in the industry. It monitors the health of systems and applications and will automatically restart an application on another server when any service-affecting failure occurs. It can also be used to reduce any downtime incurred for maintenance activities by allowing the work-load to be manually moved to an alternate server while the maintenance is done. Over time, there will be increasing levels of integration of the Serviceguard Man-ager graphical user interface product with the rest of the VSE management suite.

- Global Workload Manager (gWLM) is the newest member of this group. It has many of the same automation features as the original Workload Manager product but provides them in a simpler package designed to support the IT as a service model.

- Systems Insight Manager (SIM) is the management platform on which most of the HP systems management tools are integrating, including the new VSE man-agement suite.

Capacity planning in the context of VSE management is the ability to get reports that will give you valuable guidance about how to take advantage of the VSE technologies for your specific workloads. The key product in this area is capacity advisor.

- Capacity Advisor allows you to analyze data about your workloads to provide guidance about where to put new workloads and how to configure your resource-allocation policies for optimum resource allocation. It does this while taking into account flexing characteristics of the different partitioning solutions as well as Serviceguard cluster configurations and gWLM polices assigned to the workloads. This product will also be tightly integrated in the VSE management suite.

We will provide more details on all of these products later in this chapter and through the rest of this part of the book.

VSE Visualization and Configuration

Arguably the most important aspect of managing an adaptive infrastructure is the ability to visualize what is running where and what resources are being consumed by all your workloads. In order to meet this need, HP has developed an integrated set of visualization and configuration utilities that allow you to traverse the hierarchy of partitions throughout your Virtual Server Environment and get and set performance and configuration information no matter where you are in the user interface. This suite is intergrated into the HP Integrity Essentials Virtualization Manager.

note

> This section provides an overview only of the VSE visualization and configuration capabilities. More details, and some usage examples, will be provided in Chapter 17, "VSE Management Suite."

Visualizing Your Virtual Server Environment

The Systems Insight Manager (SIM) provides a single management solution for systems-level management of all supported operating systems on the full range of HP servers, from Proliant Blades to HP 9000 and Integrity Superdomes. Within the HP Systems Insight Manager interface a new set of capabilities called Integrity Essentials, allows you to visualize your VSE technologies. This section will provide screenshots and descriptions of how to navigate through the menus and links in Virtualization Manager to get access to the information you need to understand how your systems and the hierarchy of partitions are configured and how resources are being allocated to the various partitions and virtual machines.

Hierarchical Partition Views

The first view you will often want to see is a view of all the systems that have VSE technologies. This is available under the System tab. This view shows the hierarchy of partitions on each of those nodes and a snapshot of the resource utilization of each partition. An example of this view is shown in Figure 13-1.

This view is color-coded for the types of partitions, and the blocks are nested to show the hierarchy of partitions. There are also one or more links in each box that will allow you to navigate to all of the relevant management views for that partition.

Another thing to notice in Figure 13-1 is that a number of VSE-specific links and menus are available in the HP SIM screen when the VSE management tools are installed. The first thing you will notice is the navigation pane on the left-hand side has a number of items under All VSE Resources. These items are categorizations of the nodes in your datacenter that are using VSE technologies. You also have the ability to create your own categories to list groupings of systems

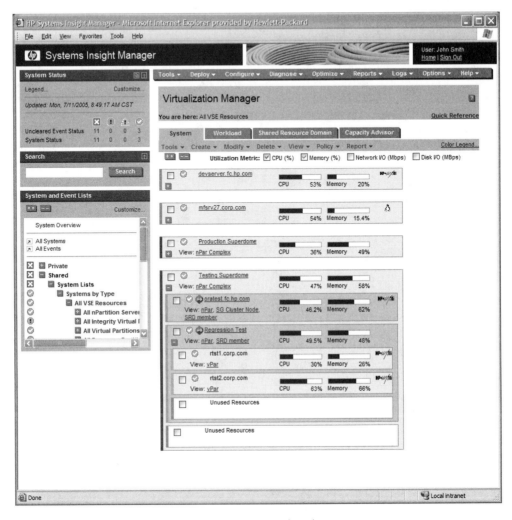

Figure 13-1 VSE Virtualization Manager Hierarchical Partition View

that are relevant to you. For example, if you have a set of partitions or systems that support a particular application, you can create a grouping and place those systems in it. When you select that link, the view in Figure 13-1 will appear but will have only the systems and partitions that are associated with the grouping that you created. In addition, the menu below the tabs has VSE-specific management functions. The links in this menu will be active or inactive depending on the types of partitions you select in the main panel.

Workload View

Another top-level view is the Workload View. A workload is any grouping of processes or applications that provide a unique business function. A simplification of this would be all the processes running in a particular partition. The Workload View allows you to view the workloads running on your VSE infrastructure independent of where they are running. Effectively, this gives a snapshot of the health of all your critical workloads and provides links to management views that are appropriate for the workload and the type of partition it is running in. An example of this view is shown in Figure 13-2.

This view provides a performance snapshot of each workload and status and location information. It also provides links to the workload detail view and the partition configuration details view.

As you navigate around the System and Workload Views, you will find many places where you can click links to drill down into more details or into a configuration view for any of the partition types. The rest of this section shows some of the views available and how to get to them.

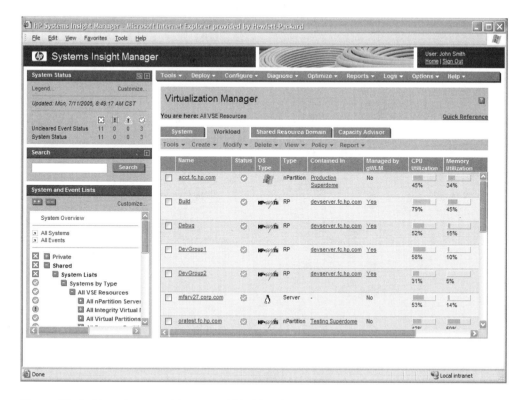

Figure 13-2 Virtualization Manager Workload List View

nPars Complex Detail View

From either of the primary views, you can navigate your way to the complex detail view by selecting the link for the partition you want to view. Figure 13-3 shows the complex detail view being launched from the System View. If you have used the Partition Manager, you will recognize this screen. The Partition Manager screens have been integrated into Virtualization Manager.

The complex detail view provides a color-coded graphical representation of the nPartitions on the complex you selected. From here you can see which cells are in each nPar and the connectivity to each I/O chassis. You can drill down from this view to get more details on any of these items by clicking on them.

In the complex detail view you will also see menu items in the right-hand side menu that will allow you to configure whatever is selected in the view. From the complex view, you can create or modify nPars on the complex using these menu items.

vPars Detail View

If a partition is a vPar and you select the link for the vPar, you will drill down to the detail view of the Virtual Partition. An example of this screen is shown in Figure 13-4.

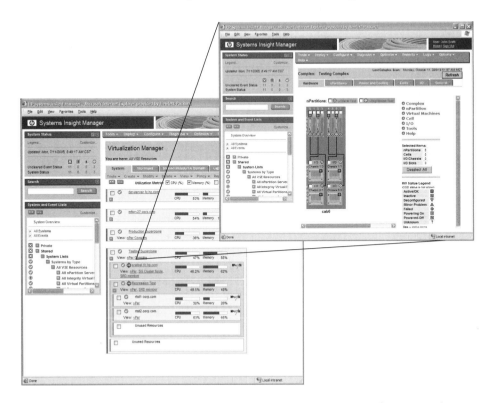

Figure 13-3 Partition Manager Complex Detail View Launched from Virtualization Manager

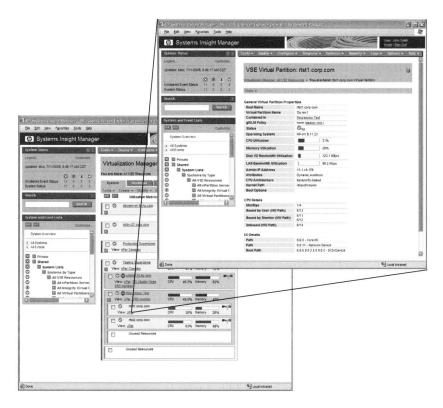

Figure 13-4 Virtual Partition Detail View

This view provides vPar configuration and resource utilization details for the vPar that you selected.

VM Detail View

As with the other partition types, a link will bring up the detail view of the Integrity Virtual Machine. An example of this view is shown in Figure 13-5.

This view provides VM configuration details and information about the current resource utilization. One nice feature of this view is the mapping of virtual resources inside the VM to the

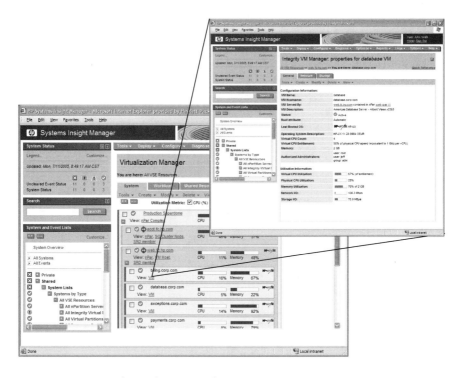

Figure 13-5 Virtual Machine Detail View

physical resources that are being used by the virtual components. This can be accessed by clicking the Network or Storage tabs in the VM detail screen. An example is shown in Figure 13-6.

This can be very helpful when you are trying to diagnose performance issues inside a VM. Selecting the "focus" link on the physical components will show all of the virtual devices that are sharing that physical device.

Secure Resource Partitions Detail View

In the future release, it will be possible to drill down to the Secure Resource Partitions detail view from the partition hierarchy. An example of this view is shown in Figure 13-7.

This view provides an overview of the configuration and current status of the Secure Resource Partition. Secure Resource Partitions can be created by Process Resource Manager, Workload Manager or Global Workload Manager. Initially, gWLM secure resource partitions will be shown here, but the others will be supported in future releases.

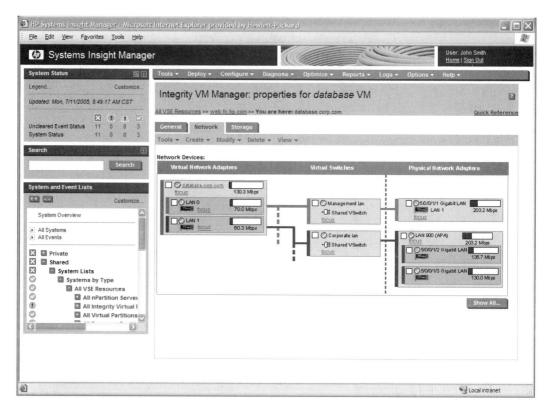

Figure 13-6 VM Network Detail View

Instant Capacity/Temporary Capacity/Pay Per Use Detail Views

A later release of the Virtualization Manager product will also provide a view that shows any complex that has unlicensed Instant Capacity resources. In addition, you will be able to identify and get utilization information from systems that have been leased under the Pay per use utility pricing program.

Workload Management and High Availability Integration

The workload management and high-availability solutions are automation tools that integrate with the other partitioning technologies. Because the automation is happening in the background, the integration in the user interface is that the visualization screens allow you to see the

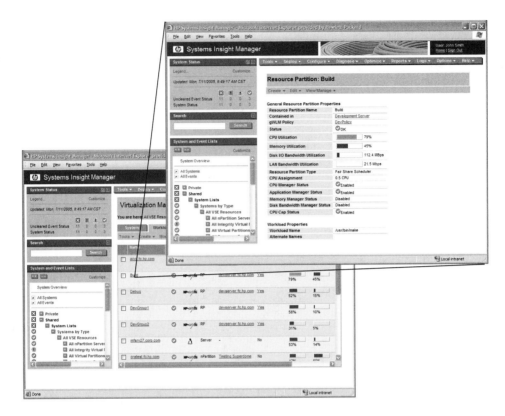

Figure 13-7 Secure Resource Partition Property Page

results of what the automation tools are doing. You also have one-click drill-down links that allow you to see and influence what these automation products are doing.

As an example, as gWLM is moving a CPU from one vPar to another, you can see the number of CPUs in each vPar change. If you want to see more information about how or why gWLM is moving the CPUs, you can navigate to the relevant gWLM screen using either the menus on top of the screen or the drill-down links. You can also get to these screens from the Optimize menu in Systems Insight Manager. An example of accessing the gWLM shared resource domain (SRD) view from the SRD member link is shown in Figure 13-8.

You will also be able to access menus for Workload Manager and Serviceguard Manager, although those menu items will launch the WLM or Serviceguard Manager GUI. You will see tighter integration with these tools in the future.

As you may have already noticed, you have the ability to get to the configuration utilities for all the VSE management tools, including gWLM, Capacity Advisor, Serviceguard Manager, Workload Manager, and Process Resource Manager via the menu items and drill-down links available on each of the screens.

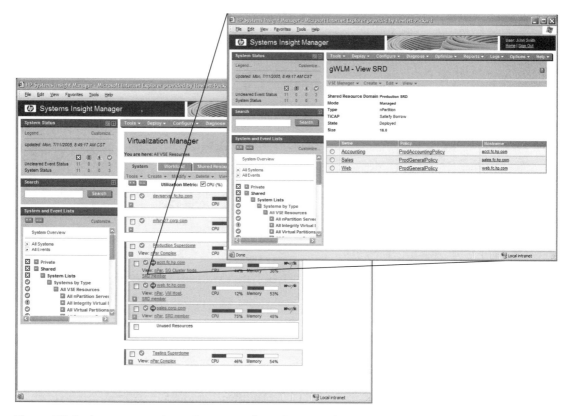

Figure 13-8 Accessing gWLM SRD View from the Virtualization Manager

VSE Management Suite Architecture

The VSE management tools have been integrated to use a manager-agent model. The user interfaces of the tools run from a central management server. Each product will use one or more agents that are running on the managed nodes in the infrastructure.

Management Station Architecture

A key design goal of these products was to provide a unified look and feel for the user. This is accomplished by providing a central set of user interface screens in the Virtualization Manager that then provide links to the other products' screens as needed. A very high-level view of the architecture of the management tools on the Central Management Server (CMS) is provided in Figure 13-9.

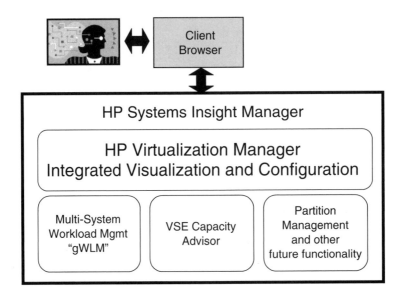

Figure 13-9 High-Level Architecture of the Central Management Server

All of these products run under the HP Systems Insight Manager. The visualization and configuration functions are a key component of SIM. This is how all the tools can provide a seamless look and feel. Each of the other products has its own user interface screens as appropriate, but they are accessed from a unified visualization interface.

Managed-Node Architecture

Each of the management tools relies on one or more components that are running on the managed nodes. These are typically referred to as "agents." The CMS and the agents use multiple interfaces, but this detail is hidden by the user interface. A high-level view of the agent architecture is shown in Figure 13-10.

The CMS applications may access the agents via Web-Based Enterprise Management (WBEM) or other protocols depending on what information is required. These agents will then access the underlying partition or management product via their standard Application Programming Interfaces (APIs). Effectively, the agents are a means of access to the functionality provided by the other products running on the managed nodes.

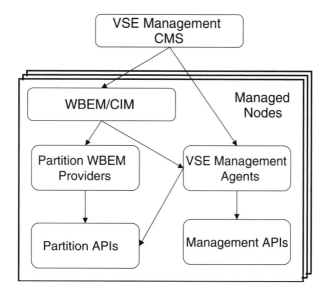

Figure 13-10 Managed-Node Agent Architecture

HP-UX Workload Manager

HP introduced the Workload Manager (WLM) product in early 2000. It focuses on simplifying the application of shared resources to the workloads that need them. It does this by monitoring the workloads that are running on a consolidated server and reallocating unused resources to workloads that are experiencing an increase in load and need more resources.

The original goal was to provide for automatic reconfiguration of Resource Partitions. At the time, resource partitioning through the Process Resource Manager product was the only partitioning technology available on HP-UX and HP had not yet introduced its Utility Pricing products.

A lot has changed in the five years since then. Now four partitioning products and three Utility Pricing products are integrated with the Workload Manager. (HP has also introduced the new Global Workload Manager, but we have more on that later in this chapter.) WLM is described as the "intelligent policy engine" behind the Virtual Server Environment. Users specify service-level objectives for each workload and WLM allocates resources using any of the flexing technologies that happen to be available on the system.

note

> This section only provides an overview of the HP-UX Workload Manager. More details and some usage examples will be provided in Chapter 15, "Workload Manager."

WLM and the Virtual Server Environment

The key thing to understand about Workload Manager is that it is an automation tool—nothing more, nothing less. All of the flexibility that WLM takes advantage of is inherent in the underlying VSE technology. There is nothing you can do with WLM that you couldn't do manually by using the standard interfaces of the other VSE products. However, doing these tasks manually would be exceptionally complex and time consuming.

You would have to set up performance or utilization monitors for all of your partitions and applications. You would then need to have someone watching those monitors 24 hours a day looking for which applications are experiencing increases in load. When they saw one, they would have to find another application or partition that was underutilized and then determine how to reallocate resources. They would have to know the commands required to reallocate the resources from the idle partition to the busy one, which would be different depending on what partitioning technology was being used on the various systems. This also assumes that this could all be done before the spike in load for the application subsides.

The remainder of this section will discuss how WLM integrates with each of the other VSE technologies and some more-advanced WLM capabilities.

Partitions

The WLM product integrates with all of the partitioning solutions available on HP's high-end and midrange servers.

note

> Although nPars and Integrity VMs either already or will support Windows, OpenVMS, and Linux, WLM is an HP-UX only product. If you want to do workload management of partitions running other operating systems on Integrity servers, you should skip to later in this chapter and read the section on Global Workload Manager.

nPars with Instant Capacity

As you may recall from Part 1 of this book, nPartitions are fully electrically isolated from each other. Since WLM is a tool for automating the migration of resources between partitions, it needs to do so between electrically isolated partitions. This clearly can't be done if you are sharing the same physical CPUs, so we use Instant Capacity CPUs.

In Part 2 we described how it is possible to migrate an Instant Capacity right-to-use (RTU) license from one nPar to another. This is the capability that WLM relies on to apply the available active CPU capacity to the partition that has the heaviest load. Figure 13-11 shows a summary of the diagrams shown back in Chapter 8.

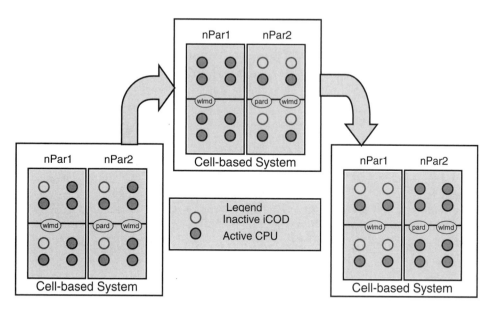

Figure 13-11 WLM Migrating Instant Capacity RTU Licenses between nPars

As you can see in Figure 13-11, a daemon (wlmd) is running in each partition and one global daemon (wlmpard—labeled pard in the figure) is running in each complex. The wlmd daemon is responsible for allocating resources to the workloads inside the partition when there is more than one workload. It is also responsible for passing data to the wlmpard daemon that describes the resources required to satisfy the workloads running in the partition. The wlmpard daemon uses this information to determine if there is a need to adjust the active capacity in any of the nPars. If so, it deactivates a processor in an idle partition and activates a processor in a busy one. The result is that the CPUs are always active in the partition that can use them. They will never run idle in one partition if they could be used by another.

In Figure 13-11, the workload in nPar1 gets busy, so WLM deactivates CPUs in nPar2 and activates CPUs in nPar1. This provides the maximum capacity of eight CPUs to the workloads in nPar1 while they are busy. Then the workloads in nPar1 become idle and the workloads in nPar2 get busy. WLM can then deactivate CPUs in nPar1 and activate them in nPar2 to ensure that the CPUs are available for the workloads that need them.

This provides the ability to flex each partition from four CPUs to eight CPUs, one CPU at a time, while both partitions are running and while maintaining full electrical isolation between the partitions. WLM allows you to do this automatically.

A key consideration in making this work is that you want to ensure that each nPar has sufficient physical CPUs in the partition to meet the peak needs of all the workloads running there.

Chapters 8 and 9 discuss how to optimize the number of active and inactive CPUs available in each partition. The nice thing is that the inactive CPUs only cost a fraction of the cost of active CPUs. Effectively, HP is paying for most of the cost of your spare capacity.

Virtual Partitions

HP's virtual partitions (vPars) product has supported the migration of CPUs from one vPar to another since it was first released. WLM released a version that supported the automatic movement of these CPUs about a month later.

Migrating CPUs between vPars provides similar benefits to those we saw with nPars but with one major difference. Because there is no physical isolation between the CPUs in the partitions, it is possible to deallocate a CPU from one partition and allocate the exact same physical CPU to another partition. It is not necessary to have idle Instant Capacity to do this. Figure 13-12 shows how this works for vPars.

The WLM configuration for vPars is similar to that for nPars. In Figure 13-12, you see where the eight physical CPUs on the system are allocated to the different partitions as the loads on the workloads vary over time. In the first box, both vPars have four CPUs. When the load increases on the workload running in vPar1, WLM moves two CPUs from vPar2 and apply them to vPar1. Later, when the load on vPar1 decreases and vPar2 becomes busy, WLM migrates the CPUs back to vPar2; the box on the right shows six CPUs in the partition. This can all be done in real time while both of these partitions are under load.

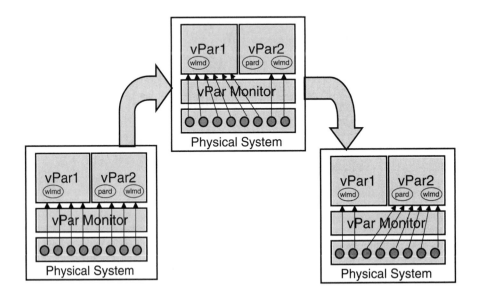

Figure 13-12 WLM Migrating CPUs between vPars

Secure Resource Partitions

Secure Resource Partitions (SRPs) was the first flexible partitioning technology that WLM supported. In fact, it was the only partitioning technology available on HP-UX platforms when WLM was first introduced.

SRPs allow you to run multiple workloads in a single copy of HP-UX and isolate them from each other from both a resource perspective and a security perspective. Figure 13-13 shows how SRPs work.

WLM works with Secure Resource Partitions to move the boundaries of how much CPU each partition gets as the loads on each of the applications vary over time. If Application A gets a spike in demand, WLM will pull CPU resources from idle workloads in the other partitions and allocate them to partition 0. If you are using FSS CPU controls for these partitions, then WLM can allocate them in sub-CPU granularity increments. If you are using PSETs, then it will do this with whole-CPU granularity. You can also combine FSS and PSET partitions in the same configuration. For example, consider if Partition 0 and Partition 1 are FSS partitions and Partition 2 is a PSET. If application C requires additional resources, it will need a whole CPU. If there are sufficient idle shares in Partitions 0 and 1 to add up to a whole CPU, WLM will shrink those partitions and add a CPU to Partition 2.

WLM Memory Controls for Secure Resource Partitions

Additionally, because Secure Resource Partitions is currently the only partitioning technology that supports online migration of memory between partitions, WLM also supports this feature.

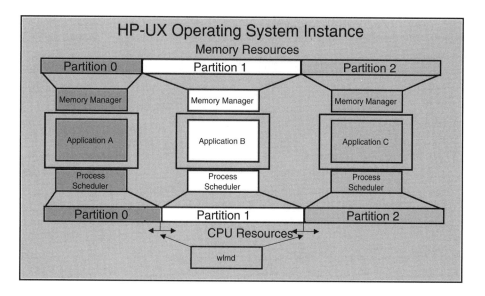

Figure 13-13 WLM Reallocation of CPU Shares among Secure Resource Partitions

However, because the method of reallocating memory between partitions is paging, this is not something that you would want to do at every WLM interval. Therefore, WLM has implemented a way to reallocate memory when workloads activate or deactivate. This is most useful for Serviceguard packages. Effectively, when a package fails over and activates on a node where WLM is running, it will reallocate the memory to ensure that the new workload gets an appropriate share of the memory. It will do this for CPU allocations as well, of course.

Utility Pricing

There are three Utility Pricing technologies. Instant Capacity provides the ability to permanently activate capacity that is available on the system. You can also activate this spare capacity with a Temporary Instant Capacity license, which allows you to activate Instant Capacity for short periods of time. Finally, there is Pay per use, which allows you to lease a system from HP and pay only for the capacity that you use each month.

WLM integrates with all of these. However, because WLM is primarily intended to reallocate resources to meet real-time workload demands, is integration with standard permanent activation Instant Capacity is only to reassign Instant Capacity RTU licenses between nPars, which was described in the previous section. In this section we will describe how WLM integrates with Temporary Instant Capacity and Pay per use. Both of these technologies allow users to instantly activate and deactivate spare capacity when the workloads on a system require it.

Temporary Instant Capacity

As was described in Chapter 8, "HP's Utility Pricing Solutions," it is possible to take advantage of available Instant Capacity processors by activating them for short periods of time using Temporary Capacity. WLM's integration with this is fairly simple—if there are not enough CPUs active on the system to meet the needs of the workloads running there, and Instant Capacity CPUs are available, and there is Temporary Capacity licensed on the system, WLM will activate additional Temporary Instant Capacity CPUs to meet the demand. You also have the ability to specify that only high priority workloads can activate these processors using the `icod_thresh_priority` keyword in the configuration file.

One of the nicest features of this is that WLM will only activate processors after it has made all available attempts to reallocate CPUs that are already active. Only then will it consider activating additional capacity. In other words, if there are idle resources in any of the other Secure Resource Partitions, vPars or nPars on the system, it will reallocate those resources before it will activate any additional Temporary Instant Capacity CPUs.

Pay Per Use

Since PPU systems are leased and the lease cost varies based on the utilization of the server, customers are typically less concerned about increasing the utilization of the server and more concerned with controlling utility costs. As a result, there is often a smaller number of workloads and partitions on PPU systems than on other servers that WLM manages. The key feature that WLM provides on a PPU system is that it will ensure that the capacity is used efficiently, which, in turn, ensures that your monthly payments are as low as they can be while still meeting the service-level objectives of the workloads running there.

There are two types of PPU, Active CPU and Percent CPU. WLM is most useful in ensuring that idle CPUs are deactivated, which is very similar to how it manages Temporary Instant Capacity. Both Percent CPU and Active CPU PPU now allow you to activate only the CPUs you need for your workloads and keep the rest inactive. The payment you make at the end of the month is based in part on how many CPUs were active throughout the course of the month. WLM's normal operation is to allocate the minimum amount of CPU required. It monitors the workloads running on the system and activates an additional CPU if additional resources are needed. When idle CPUs are active, it turns them off. It effectively minimizes the amount of time the CPUs are on, and thereby your cost, because it turns CPUs on as soon as they are needed and turns them off as soon as they become idle.

Other VSE Management Tools

WLM is also integrated with the other VSE management tools. The level of integration varies depending on the product and tends to focus on what would be the most useful to real customers.

Serviceguard

Since Serviceguard is a high-availability tool, the integration of WLM with Serviceguard is focused on ensuring that a workload will get the appropriate amount of resources when it fails over onto a WLM-managed system. This is depicted in Figure 13-14.

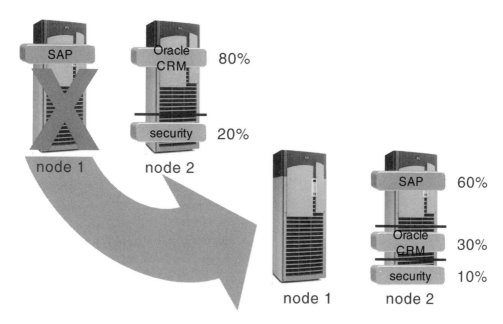

Figure 13-14 WLM Reallocation of CPU Resources after a Serviceguard Failover

As you can see, when the system is running its normal workloads, the Oracle CRM instance gets 80% of the resources of node 2. However, the SAP instance running on the other server is higher priority than the CRM database. Therefore, when the SAP instance fails over onto node 2, WLM reallocates the resources of node 2 to ensure that the SAP instance gets a larger share of the system.

One key feature of the WLM integration with Serviceguard is that WLM does active monitoring of the workload after the failover. The reason this is important is that if the workload is not busy when the failover occurs, it will migrate the resources back to the other workloads, even if they are lower priority. It will ensure that the SAP instance gets the resources it needs, but if SAP is idle when the failover occurs (e.g. in the middle of the night), then WLM will let the other workloads use the resources rather than letting them go to waste.

Integrity Essentials Virtualization Manager

Earlier in this chapter we discussed the new Virtualization Manager. This product enables customers to visualize where their workloads are running, what resources these workloads are consuming, and what other workloads they are sharing resources with.

The integration of the Virtualization Manager with Workload Manager is focused on configuration. In this initial release, the Virtualization Manager will launch the WLM graphical user interface when you select a workload or partition where WLM is being used to control resource allocation.

Advanced WLM Features

The WLM product has some very sophisticated features. However, you should be aware of what you are getting into before implementing them. A basic WLM configuration can be set up and deployed very quickly. When you start getting fancy, there may be some unintended side effect that you hadn't considered. This is why we typically recommend that you start off simply and expand your configuration into some of these more-sophisticated features after you are more familiar with how the product works.

Hierarchical Arbitration

A new feature of the 3.0 release of Workload Manager is the ability to stack partitions in any combination and take advantage of all of the flexing characteristics available for all of them. This also includes the ability to activate and deactivate Temporary Instant Capacity or PPU processors if they are available. HP has pulled in all resource allocation functionality that was not related to SRPs into the global arbiter daemon. This daemon is now the central coordination point for all nPar, vPar, Temporary Instant Capacity, and PPU reallocation functions. Figure 13-15 shows what is possible with this new global arbiter.

Figure 13-15 illustrates a Serviceguard failover and WLM's reallocation of resources. The first thing to happen is a failure of the application in secure resource partition 2.1.2. Serviceguard sees this and restarts the package on secure resource partition 1.1.2. WLM sees this happen and immediately reallocates resources between the secure resource partitions inside the

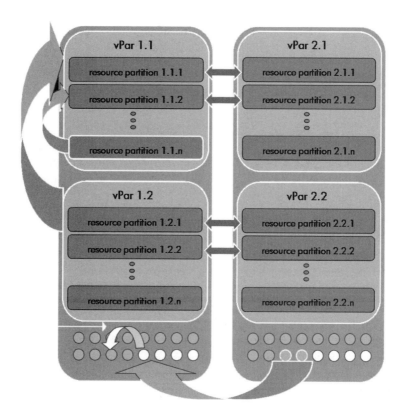

Figure 13-15 WLM Managing nPars, vPars, Secure Resource Partitions, and Temporary Instant Capacity Resources to meet the Demands of a Serviceguard Failover

vPar. If there are not enough resources in the vPar to satisfy the requirements of the workload when the failover occurs, it will assess the resource requirements of all of the workloads across the entire system. It will reallocate Instant Capacity resources across the nPars, assign those resources to vPar 1.1, and apply them to secure resource partition 1.1.2. If there are not enough resources to satisfy all the workloads even after reallocating them across the entire system, it will activate the Instant Capacity CPUs on the nPar using a Temporary Instant Capacity license if one is available.

The important thing to consider here is that WLM will minimize the cost of Temporary Instant Capacity by first applying idle resources in any of the other partitions before resorting to activating the Instant Capacity processors. This is a very nice combination of features, but it requires a sophisticated system configuration. We recommend that you start with one or two of these features and build up the configuration of the others over time.

Metric-Based Goals

WLM was the first goal-based workload manager available in the Unix market. It allows you to allocate the resource entitlement of a workload based on an arbitrary application metric, such as the application's response time.

The concept is quite simple, actually. WLM monitors the response time of the application at every interval. When the response time exceeds the goal you have set, it adds some amount of additional CPU in proportion to how far off from the goal the actual value of the metric is. It then waits for another interval to see what impact this had. If the response time is still above the goal, more CPU is added again. This process is repeated until the actual response time drops below the goal that is defined. When the load on the application drops and the response time drops significantly below the goal, some of the CPU is returned to the free pool so it can be allocated to other workloads that need it.

Configuring WLM to use metrics is quite simple. The use of metric-based goals is considered to be an advanced feature because it requires a user to have quite a bit more knowledge about the application being controlled. Some of the issues include:

* You need to have access to some useful metric about the application. This can be response time, queue length, or the number of users or processes.

* You need to have a metric that fluctuates in relation to the application's need for resources. If adding CPU to the application doesn't improve the value of the metric, it isn't a good candidate for a goal.

* Sometimes these metrics vary much more quickly than WLM can react. For example, when a request queue length is used and the requests are typically handled in a very short time, the instantaneous queue length might not be a good indication of the ongoing load on the application. It would do little good for WLM to add a CPU to a workload because of a high queue length if the application can flush the queue in less than one second. In this case, an exponentially degrading average of the queue length can be used (which WLM will do for you if you use the cntl_smooth option). Another option would be to use the value of the change in the queue length rather than the value of the actual queue length. If the queue length is increasing, it is likely that the application needs more resources.

Although there are ways to work around all of these issues, it requires a much more detailed understanding of the application and how it reacts to changes in the amount of CPU available.

ISV Toolkits

HP provides a number of toolkits that simplify the data-collection process for some major independent software vendor (ISV) applications. Table 13-1 lists the toolkits that come with WLM. Many of these toolkits will be supported in future versions of gWLM as well.

These are shipped with the WLM product and are also available for download from software.hp.com. Although these toolkits simplify the collection of detailed performance data from these applications, you will still need to develop an understanding of how the application and these metrics react to changes in resources.

Table 13-1 WLM ISV Toolkits

Toolkit	How It Works
Oracle	Allows you to specify an application-specific query. Allows you to use this query as a measure of the response time of the database. Alternatively you can use the query to pull data out of the database and use that as a metric. This is useful for other applications, such as SAP, that store their own response-time data in the Oracle database.
WebLogic	Uses the standard JMX management interface to pull the queue length and size of the free thread pool out of a WebLogic instance.
Apache	Will run a URL fetch through the Apache instance and time how long it takes for the server to respond. This is useful for getting response time for any CGI program or even a J2EE server that uses Apache as its front end.
Job Duration/SAS	Managing batch jobs is very different than managing a application with a long-running server. The thing you want to control is how long it takes to finish the job. This toolkit monitors jobs and tracks how much CPU is required to complete them. You can then specify how long you want the job to take, and WLM will set its entitlement to ensure that it gets enough CPU to complete in the specified time.
	There is an extension specific to SAS that allows you to instrument your SAS job with a macro that reports how far along the job is at each step. The job-duration toolkit uses this to determine if this specific run of the job is taking more or less time than normal and adjusts the CPU to meet the job duration goal specified.
SNMP	Allows you to define any SNMP variable by its object identifier. It will query this variable at every WLM interval and feed the value into WLM.

High Availability with HP Serviceguard

The Serviceguard name is used to describe a set of high-availability and disaster-tolerant solutions. These are all based on the Serviceguard HA product but provide different features depending on the goals of the solution. We will provide a very brief overview of why you might need a high-availability solution, then we will cover the products.

note

> This section only provides an overview of the Serviceguard suite. More details, and some usage examples, will be provided in Chapter 16, "Serviceguard."

High Availability and Disaster Tolerance

In this section we will provide a brief overview of what high availability is, how it is different than disaster tolerance, and why these solutions are as important as they are.

Why Are High Availability and Disaster Tolerance Important?

There are many sources for information about how costly a major service outage can be. The cost of a failure varies based on the industry and the nature of the application. A large number of factors impact the true cost of a failure. These include:

- tarnished company reputation and customer loyalty
- lost opportunities and revenue
- idle or unproductive labor
- cost of restoration
- penalties
- litigation
- loss of stock value
- loss of critical data

It is likely that you already know which applications in your environment are the ones that are likely to cause the company to have serious financial problems. The type of high availability or disaster tolerance you might want to implement will often depend on the cost of implementing the failover technology compared to the likely cost of a failure. We will describe the various options you have so you can make an educated decision.

High Availability vs. Disaster Tolerance

High availability typically requires providing redundancy within a data center to maintain service when there are hardware or software failures. This can also help minimize the damage done by human errors, which account for about 40% of all application failures. Service can normally be restored in only a few minutes.

Disaster tolerance involves providing redundancy between separate data centers so that the service can be restored quickly in the event of a major disaster, which might include a fire, a flood, an earthquake, or terrorism. Service can typically be restored in from tens of minutes to a few hours.

There is a third solution, sometimes called disaster recovery. This typically involves sending staff to separate facility with backup tapes. The disaster recovery facility might have spare equipment or may have systems that are used for lower-priority work, so they can be repurposed in the event of a disaster. Service recovery using this method can take days to weeks, depending on how similar the spare systems are to the original production systems.

Components of High-Availability Technology

Many components are necessary to provide a highly available infrastructure. Some are hardware, some are software, some are architecture, and some are processes. Some examples of the components include:

- Single-system high-availability components: this involves purchasing systems, storage and network equipment that have high availability built in through the use of redundant internal components and online addition and replacement of components.

- Multisystem availability: This includes clustering, load balancing, rapid failover, and recovery. This is what the Serviceguard product provides.

- High availability through manageability: it is also possible to provide some level of high availability by ensuring that you are notified very quickly when a failure occurs and having manual processes in place that can quickly bring the service back on line. This will never be as fast as it could be if it were automated, but is often better than nothing.

- Disaster tolerance: this generally involves providing data replication between separate sites to ensure that if a disaster were to impact the main production site there would be an up-to-date copy of the data that could be brought up in a short period of time. This is what the Serviceguard Extended Campus Cluster, Metrocluster, and Continentalcluster products provide.

Now let's take a look at the anatomy of a Serviceguard cluster.

HP High-Availability Solutions

Installing high-availability software on a system is not sufficient to get high availability. It is also important that the hardware be configured to allow for a failure. This involves setting up redundant paths to all your mission-critical data and applications.

Serviceguard Concepts

A number of critical concepts will help you understand the rest of this section. These include:

- *Cluster*: A cluster is a set of systems over which you will run your application packages. Multiple systems are configured into what is called a Serviceguard cluster. These systems must have connectivity to shared networks and storage to ensure that the packages can fail over from one system in the cluster to another.

- *Package*: A Serviceguard package consists of the application processes and system resources necessary to allow the application to run. This includes the disks containing the data for the application and the network IP address that users access the application with.

- *Service*: In Serviceguard terminology, a service can be one or more of the processes of the application, any service required by the package, and/or monitoring utilities that are watching the application. Serviceguard will monitor any process that is configured as a service and will attempt to restart the process if it exits. If the restart fails the configured number of times, the package will be failed over to another server.

- *Data network*: These networks allow users to connect to the application. The cluster will be configured with one or more data networks. It is generally recommended in a high-availability architecture that there be dual network interfaces on each system that use different network infrastructures. This ensures that a single card failure doesn't cause an application failover.

- *Heartbeat network*: A special network in a Serviceguard configuration that is used exclusively to allow the nodes in the cluster to monitor each other. This is how Serviceguard determines when a failure occurs that requires a restart of the application packages on another system in the cluster.

- *Relocatable package IP Address*: These are the addresses that allow users to connect to the application. Each package can have one or more relocatable IP addresses. When a failover occurs, the address of the package is moved to the new system so that users can connect to the application without having to know that it is running on a new system.

- *Shared storage*: Any storage used by the application must be available to each system in the cluster that you want to run the application on. When a failover occurs, the storage is disconnected from the primary system and then connected to the failover system before the application is started on the new node.

- *Cluster lock disk/cluster lock logical unit number (LUN)*: one serious concern in a clustered environment is ensuring that the multiple systems that have connectivity to any shared disk don't all think they own the data. If this were to occur, it would be possible for the data to become corrupted. The risk in a Serviceguard environment is that a false failover can happen where the two systems could lose network connectivity but not storage connectivity. In this case, if Serviceguard started the application on the failover node while the original node was still writing to the disk storage, data corruption might occur. Serviceguard has a number of functions that were designed to ensure this doesn't happen. The cluster lock is one of these functions. This will be described in more detail later in this section.

- *Quorum server*: as an alternative to the cluster lock disk or cluster lock LUN, it is also possible to run a quorum server to accomplish the same function. A single quorum server can support up to 50 different clusters and up to 100 different servers. Also, the cluster lock disk is only supported on clusters of two to four nodes. The disk/LUN solution doesn't require a separate server, so it is often used for two-node failover clusters. It is impractical to have shared connectivity to the cluster lock disk/LUN from larger clusters, but performance is the primary reason that the quorum server is required on clusters larger than four nodes.

Hardware Architecture

High availability generally involves redundancy. The more redundant components you have, the higher the availability you will be able to achieve. Clearly, there is a point of diminishing returns. Figure 13-16 shows the architecture of a reasonable middle ground.

In this example, each system has dual network connections for data and a separate heartbeat LAN that also provides connectivity to the quorum server. In addition, each system has dual fiber-channel cards, each of which is connected to a separate fiber-channel switch, each of which is then connected to one or more storage devices. The key to this is that no one failure will cause a failover. It would take two components, both of which are matched and on the same system, before a failover would occur. Even then, since all the nodes in the cluster are connected to the same storage and networks, any of the other nodes can take over for the failed system.

Software Architecture

Now lets talk about the Serviceguard product. The key features of the Serviceguard cluster product include:

- Each Serviceguard cluster can have up to 16 nodes in it.
- Serviceguard is designed for use when all nodes are in a single datacenter.
- Serviceguard provides for automatic failover of up to 150 application packages, 900 services, and 200 relocatable package IP addresses per cluster.
- Disks can be connected to the systems in the cluster using either SCSI or fibre channel.

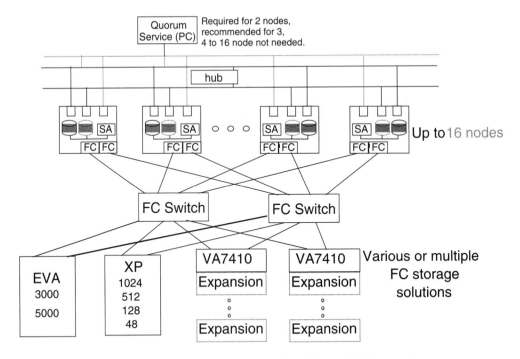

Figure 13-16 An Example of the Architecture of High-Availability Hardware

- The cluster requires a single IP subnet for heartbeat networks, which can be Ethernet, fiber distributed data interface (FDDI), or Token Ring.
- Serviceguard uses LVM or VxVM to manage disk volumes.
- A cluster lock disk is required for clusters with two nodes, but it is optional for clusters with three or four nodes.
- Alternatively, you can use a quorum server in place of a cluster lock disk to support clusters with up to 16 nodes.

We will discuss some of these features in more detail later when we describe the hardware and software architectures of a Serviceguard cluster.

One other thing to consider when designing your cluster is how you want the applications to behave after they have failed over, particularly whether you want to have idle hardware that is able to accept the workload without any performance impact. There are three primary cluster types:

- *Active-Standby*: this is where you have a hot standby node that is not running any packages. This model usually involves a matched pair of servers so that you can ensure that the failover node is ready to accept a failover at any time with no performance impact on the production workload. This doubles the hardware cost of the solution.

- *Active-Active*: this is where each of the nodes in the cluster has one or more packages running on it at all times. When a failover occurs, the package startup scripts on the failover node can shut down the other packages running there (if they are test or development workloads, for example). Optionally, additional resources could be made available by using some of the other VSE solutions and a workload management tool.

- *Rolling Standby*: this is where you have a multinode cluster in an n+1 configuration such that there is always one node in the cluster that is not running any packages. When a failover occurs, the standby node becomes the primary node for whatever workload fails over. When the failing node comes back up, it becomes the new standby node. This provides much of the benefit of an active-standby configuration but at a more reasonable cost.

Protecting Against Split Brain

One serious concern in a clustered environment is ensuring that the applications that can run on multiple systems don't start up on more than one system at a time. This is a phenomenon called "split brain" in which a cluster breaks up into multiple smaller clusters, each of which thinks the rest of the cluster has failed. Figure 13-17 shows how this can occur.

This picture shows that the network connectivity to two of the nodes in the cluster is lost. However, there is no loss of connectivity to the storage. Therefore, node C thinks that node A has failed and starts the failover process. This includes connecting to the disks for A and starting the package. If this were to occur, then both of these nodes would be running the application and both would be connected to the same storage. This could cause data corruption. The Serviceguard product goes to great lengths to ensure that this can never happen.

The first thing Serviceguard does is attempt to reform the cluster whenever it detects a failure. This must happen before any packages are failed over. This reformation will fail unless the cluster has at least half of the systems that were in the original cluster. Since no two portions of the cluster will both be able to get more than half the nodes in the original cluster, there is no way that Serviceguard can reform more than one cluster. This resolves the split-brain problem

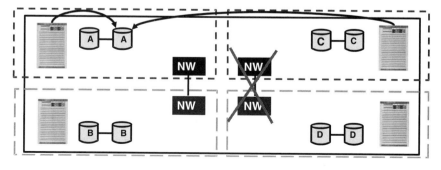

Figure 13-17 How a Split-Brain Cluster Could Corrupt Data

for all but one special case where a cluster splits up into two equal halves. Serviceguard uses several mechanisms as tie-breakers to avoid this situation. The first is a cluster lock disk on HP-UX and a cluster lock LUN on Linux. These are used for smaller clusters. For larger clusters this is managed using a quorum server. In both cases the disk, LUN, or quorum server is connected to all of the nodes in the cluster. If the cluster reforms and has exactly half of the nodes from the original cluster, it will attempt to acquire the cluster lock. If it succeeds, it will reform the cluster and start any packages that were on the nodes that are no longer in the cluster. If it is unable to get the lock, it shuts down any packages and disconnects them from the shared storage. This ensures that no two nodes are ever connected to the shared storage at the same time.

Serviceguard Manager

Serviceguard also has a management utility called Serviceguard Manager. This is a Java graphical user interface for managing your Serviceguard clusters. Figure 13-18 shows some screenshots of Serviceguard Manager.

In this figure you can see that the left-hand pane shows a list of clusters and the right-hand pane provides status details of whichever cluster you have selected on the left. The details pane shows the cluster, the nodes in the cluster, and the packages running on each node. You can also

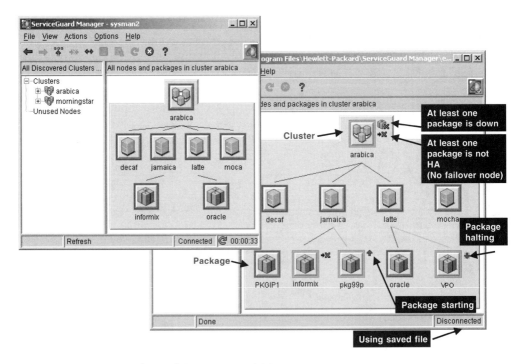

Figure 13-18 Screenshots of Serviceguard Manager

see the status of each node and each package. There are mini-icons next to packages whenever something of interest is happening with that package, such as package shutdown or startup or the lack of an available active failover node for the package.

From the GUI you can perform virtually any operation you might want on a cluster. Some examples include:

- start or halt a cluster
- start or halt a node in a cluster
- start or halt a package
- move a package from one node in the cluster to another
- edit a package or cluster configuration

Serviceguard Manager works by connecting to a daemon called the object manager that is configured to monitor one or more clusters. You connect to the object manager by logging in from Serviceguard Manager. You can control who is allowed to log in to the object manager by editing the /etc/cmclnodelist file on the node running the object manager.

As you saw earlier in this chapter, this GUI has been integrated with the new VSE management suite. In the first release of the Virtualization Manager, the integration provides a context-sensitive launch of the current Serviceguard Manager product. This integration will become tighter in future releases.

HP Disaster-Tolerant Solutions

High-availability clusters are intended to provide nearly immediate recovery from a single point of failure. These are achieved through redundant hardware and Serviceguard software to recover from component or node failures and are typically implemented in a single datacenter. For truly mission-critical applications where any sustained outage poses a significant risk to the business, it is important to guard against multiple points of failure as well.

Disaster-tolerant clusters are capable of restoring service even after multiple failures or massive single failures in the primary datacenter. These solutions replicate the application data and provide the ability to move the application to an entirely different datacenter in a different part of the building, a different part of the city, or another city. The distance between the datacenters is dependent on the types of disasters you are trying to guard against and the technology used to replicate the data between the datacenters.

We will discuss three types of disaster-tolerant clusters in this section:

- *Extended Distance Cluster*: These clusters can be from a mile or two to up to 100km depending on the technology used to connect the datacenters for data replication.
- *Metrocluster*: A Metrocluster is similar to an Extended Distance Cluster, but it includes a fault-tolerant disk array and a third site as a cluster arbitrator.
- *Continentalcluster*: A Continentalcluster involves two separate clusters in geographically dispersed locations that can be unlimited distances apart.

Extended Distance Cluster

An Extended Distance Cluster, sometimes called an Extended Campus Cluster, runs a cluster across multiple datacenters with high-speed networking between them. The distance between the datacenters is dependent on the technology used for data replication. Table 13-2 lists the technologies and the distances they support.

It is possible to set up a two-datacenter solution or a three-datacenter solution. The key difference between these is that the two-datacenter solution is implemented with dual cluster lock disks and the three-datacenter solution uses a quorum server in the third datacenter.

Two-Datacenter Extended Distance Cluster

Because the two-datacenter solution requires the use of dual cluster lock disks, the size of the cluster is limited to a maximum of four nodes. In addition, the cluster must be split evenly; you can have a two-node cluster or a four-node cluster. Figure 13-19 shows the layout of a two-site cluster.

You must have at least two network paths and it is recommended that you have three different network paths between the datacenters to ensure continuous access to the two cluster lock disks should there be a network failure. Application data is mirrored between the two primary datacenters and you must ensure that the mirrored copies are in different datacenters.

Three-Datacenter Extended Distance Cluster

The three-datacenter solution is architecturally very similar to the two-datacenter solution. The third site serves as a tie-breaker in case connectivity is lost between the other two sites. Figure 13-20 shows the layout of a three-site cluster.

Table 13-2 Supported Distance Between Datacenters is Dependent on the Networking Technology

Type of Link	Maximum Distance Supported
Fast/Wide SCSI	25 meters
Gigabit Ethernet Twisted Pair	50 meters
Short Wave FibreChannel	500 meters
Long Wave FibreChannel	10 kilometers
FDDI Networking	50 kilometers
Finisar Gigabit Interface Converters	80 kilometers
Dense Wave Division Multiplexing (DWDM)	100 kilometers

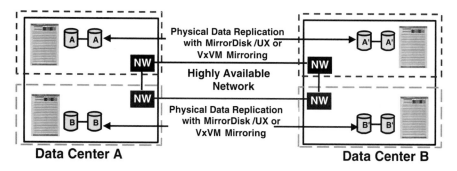

Figure 13-19 A Two-Site Extended Distance Serviceguard Cluster

The third site can either run two nodes that are part of the cluster, called arbitrator nodes, or a quorum server. The two arbitrator nodes are part of the cluster but can't be sharing the disks in either of the primary datacenters. They are cluster members that are not running any packages or they can be running packages that failover locally but not to either of the other datacenters. Or the third site could be running a quorum server. This brings several advantages—more nodes and lower overhead. Since the arbitrator nodes are cluster members that can't be running any packages, the maximum size of the cluster would be 14, or seven nodes in each datacenter. In addition, the overhead of the cluster quorum server is quite low and could be run on a small Linux server or a server that is running other workloads.

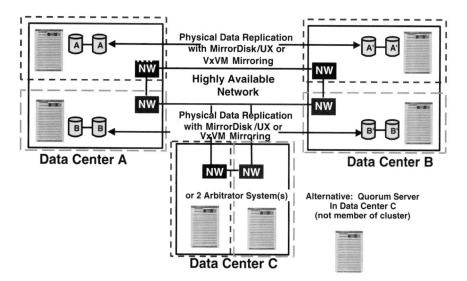

Figure 13-20 A Three-Site Extended Distance Serviceguard Cluster

Metrocluster

The main difference between an Extended Distance Cluster and a Metrocluster is that the data replication between the two primary sites is handled by an EMC Symmetrix, HP XP, or EVA disk array. Figure 13-21 provides an example architecture for a Metrocluster.

Notice in this figure the existence of the CA/SRDF Link is the primary difference between this architecture and the Extended Distance Cluster.

There are two Metrocluster products, Metrocluster/CA for HP disk arrays and Metrocluster/SRDF for EMC. The "CA" in "Metrocluster/CA" stands for "continuous access," which is a data replication product available with the XP and EVA disk arrays from HP. The "SRDF" in "Metrocluster/SRDF" stands for "Symmetrix remote data facility," which is the data-replication product available from EMC for the EMC Symmetrix disk arrays.

The Metrocluster/CA product is a set of scripts and utilities that simplifies the integration of the CA functionality with the Extended Distance Cluster. The Metrocluster/SRDF product is a similar set of utilities designed to assist in integrating the EMC SRDF product.

For more information on how to set up either of these products, see the "Designing Disaster Tolerant High Availability Clusters" document available on http://docs.hp.com.

Continentalclusters

Datacenters that are more than 100 kilometers away require a very different architecture. The primary difference between an Extended Distance Cluster and a Continental Cluster is that with the Extended Distance Cluster you have a single cluster with nodes in multiple datacenters. With the Continentalcluster there are two separate clusters. The solution is to allow one cluster to take over

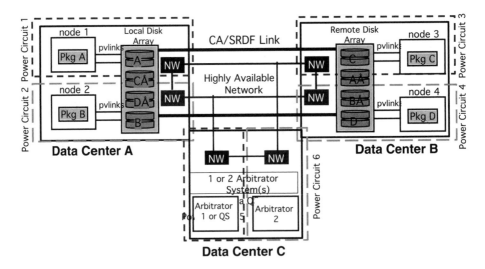

Figure 13-21 An Example Three-Site Serviceguard Metrocluster

operation of the critical packages in the other cluster in the event of a disaster that takes down an entire cluster. The Continentalclusters product is a set of utilities to monitor geographically remote clusters and a command to start critical packages on the recovery cluster if the primary cluster is lost.

An example of the architecture of Continentalclusters is shown in Figure 13-22.

As you can see in Figure 13-22, there are two distinct clusters running in separate data-centers connected by a wide-area network (WAN). Although the figure shows an active-standby configuration, it is not necessary for the recovery cluster to be idle. A supported configuration is where both clusters are running packages under normal circumstances and each cluster is monitoring the health of the other cluster. Continentalclusters use physical or logical data repli-cation using disk arrays, just like Metroclusters.

Because of the higher likelihood that a spurious network error will cause a false alarm, Con-tinentalclusters does not automate the failover. However, the product does provide a single com-mand to initiate the failover manually. The process of failover would include:

1. Continentalclusters detects a failure of the remote cluster: Each cluster monitors the health of the other cluster and generates alarms when a failure occurs.

2. Continentalclusters sends a notification of the failure. This can be done through a text log, e-mail, an SNMP trap, or an OPCmsg (for OpenView Operations).

3. You verify that the cluster has failed. It is critical that you ensure that the appli-cations are not running on both clusters at the same time. This would involve contacting the WAN service provider, speaking with operation staff at the pri-mary site, and discussing options with application owners.

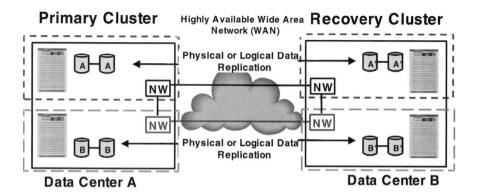

Figure 13-22 An Example Serviceguard Continental Cluster

4. You issue the recovery command. The `cmrecovercl` command will halt the data replication between the clusters and start all the recovery packages on the local cluster.

One thing to consider with Continentalclusters is that because the two clusters are physically distinct and managed separately, you will need to have administration processes in place to ensure that the versions of the applications on the primary and recovery clusters are kept in sync so that when a recovery is required, there aren't any surprises. This is true of all high-availability clusters, but it may be more of a challenge in this case because of the distance between the datacenters supported by Continentalclusters.

Global Workload Manager

HP has had great success with the Workload Manager product. They have learned much about how customers use the product and how they want to manage the sharing of resources. In addition, a new type of customer environment has emerged which has unique needs: IT as a service. This is a fast-growing trend in the industry because it makes it possible for IT organizations to take better advantage of the virtualization technologies that are now available. Some specific requirements that service providers and IT organizations that act like service providers are concerned about include:

* They need to manage larger numbers of servers, so they need ease of use and the ability to create a small set of standard policies and use them over and over. This is much like a level of service with a web site hosting provider—one plan might get 500MB of space and a second might get 1GB.

* The IT organization does not know what the priorities of the applications are, so they need to allow sharing of resources where all workloads are at the same priority.

* The IT organization needs to be able to guarantee a certain level of resources when a system is under heavy load.

* The IT organization will need a way to measure how much resource each workload uses so that they can charge the business units for their actual usage.

* The IT organization needs to be able to manage a large number of servers from a central location.

In order to meet these requirements, HP developed the new Global Workload Manager (gWLM) product, which is tightly integrated into the VSE management suite of products. It provides many of the same features as the WLM product, but does so from a central management server. Also, in order to simplify the product, the most important customer use cases are very easy to implement.

note

This section only provides an overview of the Global Workload Manager product. More details, and some usage examples, will be provided in Chapter 19, "Global Workload Manager."

gWLM Concepts

The gWLM product introduces a few simple concepts that allow you to understand how the product works. These are:

- *Workload*: a set of processes that together make up some functionality that is useful to the business.

- *Compartment*: gWLM compartments can be partitions or a system if that system has Temporary Instant Capacity or PPU to make it flexible.

- *Shared Resource Domain (SRD)*: the set of compartments over which you can share resources. The set of partitions that are allowable here will depend on the technologies you are using to allocate resources to your workloads. For example, a set of nPars on a system can be an SRD if there are Instant Capacity processors available so the active capacity can be reallocated to the different nPars as demand varies.

- *Policy*: defines how resources should be allocated to the workload. Each workload is assigned a policy.

- *Mode*: the mode of operation that gWLM should use when managing a particular SRD. It is possible to run gWLM in either advisory or managed mode. Running gWLM in advisory mode means that it will monitor each of your workloads and your compartments and make recommendations about how much resource each workload needs at any time, but it won't reallocate resources. Managed mode will cause gWLM to automatically act upon the recommendations.

A gWLM home page within Systems Insight Manager provides a very simple interface for doing whatever you might want to do with gWLM. This is shown in Figure 13-23.

This view is intended to provide a new user with a stepping-off point to get started with managing systems with gWLM. All of the links shown here can also be accessed by selecting the appropriate menu item from the gWLM menu.

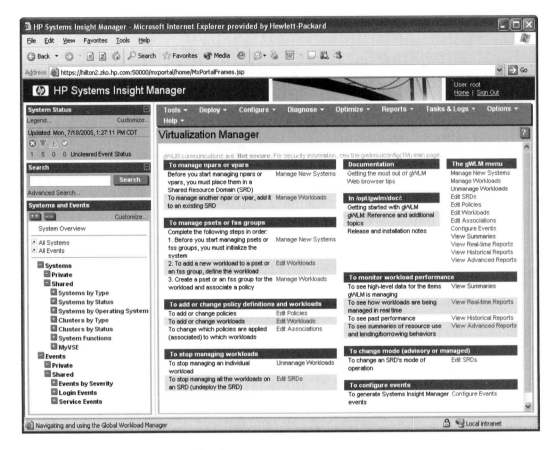

Figure 13-23 The Global Workload Manager Home Page

Compartment Types

The 2.0 release of gWLM will support a larger number of compartment types. These include:

- *Secure Resource Partitions*: FSS- or PSET-based resource partitions with optional security compartments. gWLM will allocate sub-CPU granularity to FSS-based secure resource partitions or whole-CPU granularity to PSET-based partitions.

- *Virtual Partitions (vPars)*: gWLM provides the ability to reallocate CPUs between different vPars on the same system or nPar.

- *nPars with Instant Capacity*: If a system has Instant Capacity processors, gWLM can be used to reallocate the active CPUs between the nPars on the system.

- *Integrity VMs*: gWLM is able to reallocate the amount of physical CPU that is allocated to each Virtual CPU in Integrity VMs.

* *Utility Systems*: Any system with Temporary Instant Capacity or Pay per use processors can use gWLM to control the activation and deactivation of those utility processors.

* *Linux Processor Sets*: gWLM supports the reallocation of CPUs between processors sets on a Integrity system or nPar running Linux. This does, however, require that the Linux distribution is running a 2.6 or above version of the Linux kernel. This was the kernel version where processor sets were added.

In addition to flexing these compartments, gWLM will also automate the activation and deactivation of Utility Pricing technologies.

* *Temporary Instant Capacity*: gWLM activates Instant Capacity Processors using Temporary Instant Capacity on any system that has them if they are needed to satisfy defined policies.

The gWLM 2.0 product will also be supported on OpenVMS, which has some very similar flexing technologies. These include:

* *Galaxy*: this is similar to HP-UX vPars.

* *Processor Affinity*: This is similar to Processor Sets, which gWLM already supports on both HP-UX and Linux.

* *Class Scheduler*: This is similar to the FSS groups that are available on HP-UX and the Class-based Kernel Resource Management (CKRM) scheduler that is available in some Linux distributions.

Policy Types

A policy is how you describe to gWLM how it should determine when the workload needs more or less resources. The policy types supported with the 2.0 version of gWLM will include:

* *Fixed*: A fixed policy is used when the entitlement should stay the same regardless of what may be happening on the system.

* *OwnBorrow*: This is a new policy type that is unique to gWLM. Each workload will "own" a certain amount of resources. This amount is guaranteed to be available if the workload needs it. However, if the workload is idle, some of these resources may be loaned out to other workloads that are busy. In exchange, this workload may be able to borrow resources from other idle workloads if it needs more than its "owned" value. This allows workloads to share idle resources but have a certain amount that will always be available if they need them.

* *Utilization*: This policy allows you to set a minimum and a maximum entitlement for the workload as well as a utilization target. When the utilization of the resource is below the target, gWLM will remove resources from the compartment and allow a busy workload to use them. When the utilization is above the target, gWLM will attempt to allocate additional resources to satisfy this workload when it is busy.

- *Custom*: The custom policy allows you to create an OwnBorrow type of control, but to use a custom metric rather than the default CPU uilizations.

gWLM Features and Benefits

The gWLM product has a number of key features. The most obvious is that it allows you to manage how resources are allocated to different workloads running in the infrastructure. In addition, it provides monitoring functionality that allows you to see how resources are being allocated. It also integrates with other VSE or ISV applications.

Resource Management

Arguably the most compelling feature of gWLM is its ability to automate the assignment of resources in your VSE to the workloads that need them in real time. Much like the original WLM product, gWLM provides automation capabilities on top of all the other flexing technologies available in the VSE.

One nice side effect of the way gWLM implements policies is that they are independent of the flexing technology used. This allows the same policy to apply to workloads that are running on nPars with Instant Capacity and to Linux PSETs at the same time.

Integrity Virtual Machines

Allocation of CPU resources to Integrity Virtual Machines is very different than nPars and vPars. This is because CPU resources are allocated in sub-CPU granularity. CPUs are not moved from one partition to another; instead, you simply increase one VM's share of the resource by decreasing another VM's share. This is illustrated in Figure 13-24.

What you see in Figure 13-24 is two VMs running on a four-CPU Integrity system or partition. Each VM shows four virtual CPUs in its operating system. However, those CPUs are actually sharing the four physical CPUs with the other VM.

In the first block, both VMs virtual CPUs are getting about 50% of a physical CPU. When the workload in VM2 gets busy, WLM reallocates the physical CPU shares to give VM2 a 75% entitlement. Conversely, when the workload in VM1 gets busy, WLM will reallocate the shares to give VM1 a 75% entitlement. Inside the VMs, the change in entitlement is completely transparent. The only noticeable change is that the virtual CPUs are running slower or faster depending on how busy the VM is.

Monitoring

Because gWLM is making its resource allocations without any operator intervention, it is critical that administrators have the ability to see what it is doing. For this, gWLM has both real-time and historical monitoring reports. Figure 13-25 shows one of the real-time reports.

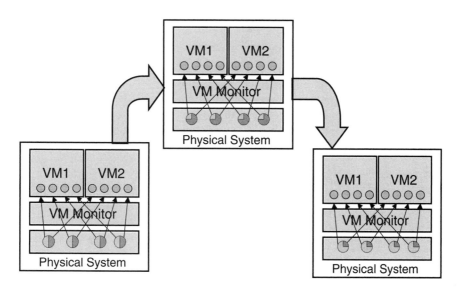

Figure 13-24 gWLM Reallocation of CPU Shares between Integrity Virtual Machines

This graph shows the target and actual utilization in the workload compartment, along with the resource allocation based on that utilization. As you can see, when the actual utilization exceeds the target, gWLM responds by increasing the amount of CPU allocated to the workload. Conversely, when the actual utilization drops below the target, gWLM will take some of the CPU allocation away and apply it to other workloads on the system.

Because gWLM is collecting data for allocation and reporting purposes, it stores the data in a database so that historical reports can be provided as well. The following historical reports will be available with the 2.0 version of gWLM.

* Workload Resource Audit Report
* Top Borrowers Report

The first of these reports provides data that can be used to help a business unit understand how its workloads consumed resources over the course of a month. The second will help an IT organization determine if certain workloads are consistently borrowing idle resources from other workloads. This may warrant a change in policy to increase the owned value for the workload.

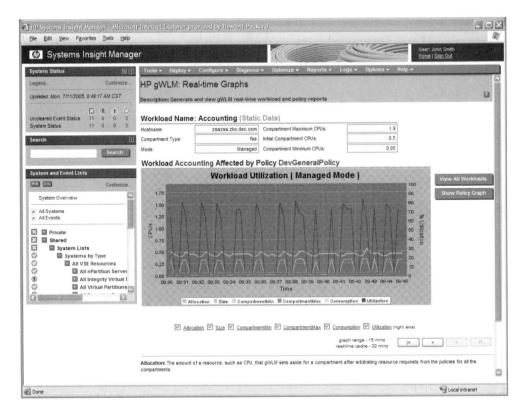

Figure 13-25 The gWLM Real-Time Workload Report

gWLM Architecture

The gWLM product was the first VSE management suite product introduced. It follows the standard manager-agent model of the rest of the VSE management suite. Figure 13-26 provides a high-level view of the architecture of gWLM.

The central management server runs the gWLM console. This is the same system you are running HP Systems Insight Manager on. The console has the user interface screens that are integrated with HP SIM and some daemon functions. The console also holds the databases for configuration and performance data.

The agent will run on every operating system image you want to manage with gWLM. If you have a system with only one OS image but you want to manage multiple workloads using secure resource partitions, you will run one agent on that OS image.

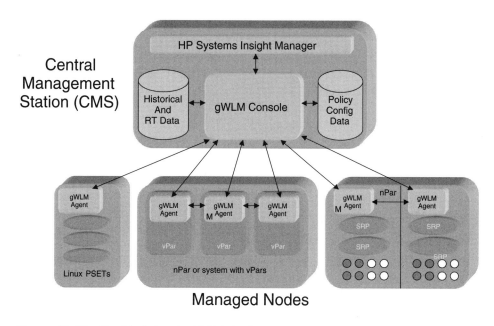

Figure 13-26 The High Level gWLM Architecture

If you have a system with partitions running separate OS images, like vPars, nPars, or VMs, you will run an agent on each of those partitions. On those systems the various agents will negotiate with each other to elect a master. The master is responsible for resource arbitration and managing the migration of resources between the partitions. Each agent collects information about the utilization and workload performance of local workloads and passes this information to the master. The local agent will send all this information to the master for arbitration. Once the master has determined how the resources should be allocated, it sends commands back to the other agents to allocate or deallocate local resources.

Capacity Advisor

Although many benefits can be gained from taking full advantage of virtualization and automation in the VSE, it tends to require specialized management tools. Capacity planning is a good example. The very dynamic nature of the VSE environment makes traditional capacity-planning tools ineffective.

In response to this, HP has developed a capacity-planning tool called Capacity Advisor that is specifically designed to predict how the flexibility and automation inherent in the VSE will impact the running of your workloads. It can also be used to make recommendations on how to take advantage of some of these VSE technologies.

note

> This section only provides an overview of the Capacity Advisor product. More details, and some usage examples, will be provided in Chapter 18, "Capacity Advisor."

Capacity Planning in the VSE

The flexibility and automation available in the VSE pose some unique challenges. These include:

- partitions that can flex automatically or manually
- Utility Pricing solutions that allow idle resources to be brought online for short periods of time to meet peaks in demand for resources
- flexing that can be automated based on the utilization of resources in the partition or on the actual real-time performance of the workload
- workloads that can be manually or automatically migrated between physical systems

Let's explore these issues in a bit more detail before getting into how the Capacity Advisor tool deals with them.

Flexible Partitions

A partition is an isolated environment in which you can run a workload without the fear that other workloads running on that server will impact it. Four different types of partitions are available on high-end HP platforms as part of the Virtual Server Environment. They each have unique flexing characteristics.

- *nPartitions*: nPars are fully electrically isolated partitions. Therefore, you are not allowed to share any resources. The mechanism used for flexing nPars is Instant Capacity processors. By loading up each partition with sufficient physical processors to meet the peak demand, you can use Instant Capacity to turn them off when they are not needed and activate them when the workload gets busy. nPars can be flexed only if they have Instant Capacity processors, and the tool needs to understand how many of them are available in each nPar. It also needs to realize that this migration may take longer than some other flexing operations because it is important to ensure that a CPU is deallocated in one nPar first and then allocated to the other.

- *Virtual Partitions*: vPars allows you to migrate CPUs between partitions while on line, and there are plans to support online memory migration as well. For capacity-planning, the tool needs to know that the same physical CPU can be moved from one vPar to another as long as both vPars are in the same nPar.

- *Integrity VMs*: Resources are allocated to VMs in very granular shares. Therefore, a capacity-planning tool will need more-detailed data about workload resource consumption.

- *Secure Resource Partitions*: Secure Resource Partitions also provide share-based resource controls. As of the first release of the VSE management suite, secure resource partitions are the only partitioning technology that supports online memory migration. Others will come shortly, but this is a unique feature that capacity advisor needs to be able to react to.

These are just a few examples of how a capacity-planning tool needs to adapt to the capabilities of the Virtual Server Environment.

Utility Pricing Solutions

For Capacity Advisor, the most interesting Utility Pricing technologies are Temporary Instant Capacity and Pay per use. Both of these allow you to allocate resources when a workload needs them. For the purposes of capacity planning, a tool needs to know if these resources are available and if there are business rules for when these resources can be activated. These will impact the ability of Capacity Advisor to simulate the use of these resources.

gWLM Automation

The fact that the flexing of resources in the VSE can be automated also impacts capacity planning. Capacity Advisor understands how gWLM policies are implemented and uses this information to adjust its simulations based on the policy that is defined. You can also have it rerun a simulation with a different policy to understand how the workload would have reacted if the other policy had been applied.

Serviceguard Failover

Since workloads in a Serviceguard cluster can be manually or automatically migrated from one physical system to another, it is important that a capacity-planning tool know what systems and partitions each workload might be running in. This information will be important when determining what peak resources might be needed in case of a failover.

Capacity Advisor Features

The first release of Capacity Advisor will focus on a few key uses. These will be expanded over time, but it is important to get the infrastructure in place and solve the most compelling capacity-planning problems customers will have with the VSE. These are:

- simulation of movement of a movement from one system to another
- simulation of the activation of additional resources on one or more partitions on a system
- trending of resource consumption
- simulation of changes in load on a workload

One of the unique features of the VSE is that workloads can be manually or automatically moved from one system to another. The goal of Capacity Advisor is to simulate the workload running on the other system so that before you initiate the move you can assess whether there will be resource contention issues. Another use for this is where you have a new workload and need to find a system in the infrastructure where it can run. Capacity Advisor will provide features to create a load profile based on data from a similar workload. You can then run a simulation to assess the impact of running this workload in a flexible partition on one or more systems in your existing infrastructure.

Another nice feature of the VSE is the ability to reallocate resources between partitions and to allocate additional resources using Temporary Capacity or PPU. Capacity Advisor will allow you to simulate the impact of a change in the available resources in a partition or system. You can use this to determine if the change you are considering will result in any performance issues due to resource contention.

The third item above is basic capacity planning. The tool will allow you to analyze historical resource consumption data and determine when or if you will run into resource contention issues with your workloads.

The fourth item in the list above is the case where you are expecting a change in the load on an application and want to simulate what impact that change will have on the partition and system where the load is running. Capacity Advisor will allow you to adjust the data pattern. For example, if you are expecting to double the number of users for a particular application, you can run a simulation with the values for that application at double their historical rate. This will show if there will be any potential contention on the system.

A number of core features are required to make these uses possible. These include:

- the ability to collect historical data for workloads in the infrastructure
- the ability to graph historical data
- the ability to create an estimated demand profile for a workload that has not yet been deployed or to insert an expected change to a workload's demand profile
- the ability to define a set of scenarios over which you can run your simulations
- the ability to create a baseline for the resource consumption profile of a workload

The first item above is probably an obvious one. Capacity Advisor will allow you to collect data from several sources. It has its own data-collection mechanism in the VSE workload utilization WBEM provider. This is the same provider that the visualization and configuration management product uses to display real-time performance data in the big-picture views. However, Capacity Advisor pulls this data at configurable intervals and stores it in a database so it can do all the other things it does. In order to limit the amount of duplicate data that is being collected from your various systems, Capacity Advisor can also import data being collected by the OpenView Performance Agent. One nice feature of the utilization WBEM provider is that it allows you to define a workload as an arbitrary set of processes running on the system. That way if you have multiple applications running in a single partition, you can view each application's resource consumption independently.

Graphing is another obvious requirement. You have collected all this data and you want to see what it looks like! Capacity Advisor will provide a large number of graphical reports — everything from a simple view of the data for a workload to the trending of the workload to the stacking of multiple workloads on a system or partition.

The third item above is needed to allow you to simulate the addition of a new workload to a VSE-based system. You need to be able to create a "phantom" load that you would expect the new workload to look like so that you can assess what impact it will have on the system or systems you plan to run the new workload on. A variation on this is the ability to simulate the impact of an expected change to the load on an application. This will give you the ability to see the impact on a workload of the doubling of the number of users, for example.

Capacity Advisor runs all of its reports and simulations based on what is called a "scenario." The best way to think of a scenario is that it is a collection of workload data and constraints that will be used to run simulations. An example would be that you want to move a workload to another system but aren't sure which system would be the best fit. The scenario would contain the data for the workload and the constraints for where that workload is allowed to run. Capacity Advisor can then show you what other systems or partitions meet the constraints and allow you to choose which one you want to simulate. The product will then run a simulation of what the resource consumption profile would be on the target system if you were to move the workload there.

The last feature is important to ensure that any simulations you are running are based on appropriate data. Many workloads will experience abnormal resource consumption profiles at certain times. These may be due to special promotions, month-end processing patterns, or unexpected failovers, among other things. Therefore, you want to create a baseline profile for the application that allows you to exclude any abnormalities in the application's resource consumption. This can be used to detect when the workload is not behaving normally, or it could be used to ensure that you are basing future resource allocation decisions on "normal" usage patterns rather than idiosyncrasies.

Capacity Advisor Architecture

Like the other products in the VSE management suite, Capacity Advisor will have a component that runs on the central management server (CMS) and one that runs on the remote managed nodes. One difference, though, is that the agent running on the remote node is generally quite simple. This is because its only function is to collect data about the workloads running on each OS image. In fact, even the data collection is done on the CMS; the agent is simply providing access to the data from the network. Most of the functionality of this product is in how it allows you to use the data it collects.

CMS Architecture

The architecture of the CMS portion of Capacity Advisor consists of a database, a user interface, a simulation engine, and both a scenario and a historical database. Figure 13-27 provides a high level view of this architecture.

The user interacts with Capacity Advisor through the Systems Insight Manager interface. The user interface portions of Capacity Advisor consist of a scenario editor, which you use to define the constraints for the simulations you want to run, and the report generator, which takes the output of the simulation engine and provides a human-readable report.

Data Collection Architecture

Capacity advisor needs data. There are two ways to get data into the database and there will be more in future releases. The current options are:

* Use Capacity Advisor data collection using the HP utilization WBEM provider
* Use OpenView Performance Agent data available on the managed nodes

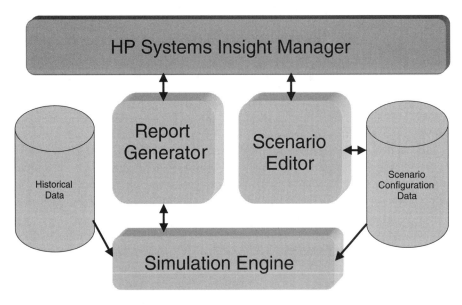

Figure 13-27 The Architecture of the CMS Portion of Capacity Advisor

The first item is where Capacity Advisor will collect data on your behalf from the utilization WBEM provider that is available on the remote partitions.

Another common data source for HP customers is the OpenView Performance Agent. This tool collects a tremendous amount of data for performance analysis and troubleshooting. Capacity Advisor needs only a small subset of this data. Therefore, it provides a utility that will allow you to pull this data into the Capacity Advisor database.

A future release will allow gWLM to use resource consumption data. This will be an important integration point for the VSE Management suite: data collected by one tool will be available to other tools.

Figure 13-28 provides an architectural view of the data-collection infrastructure of Capacity Advisor.

The data loader portion of this architecture is used by all the collection mechanisms. This is a reusable component that can be used to collect data from virtually any source and get it into Capacity Advisor database. You notice though, that the data does need to be cleaned up and converted into the correct format before the loader will accept it.

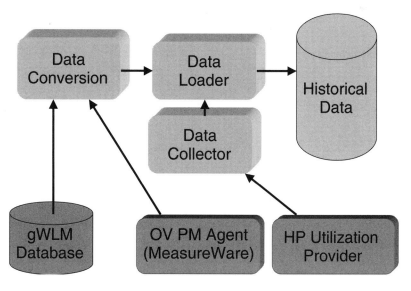

Figure 13-28 Architecture of the CMS Portion of Capacity Advisor

Summary

Management of an environment as dynamic as the Virtual Server Environment requires a specialized set of tools. HP has recognized this and is providing a tightly integrated suite of tools that can provide the ability to monitor, visualize, configure, safeguard, automate, and plan for this dynamism. This suite makes it possible to take full advantage of the many benefits of virtualization with the VSE.

This chapter has provided an overview of each of the management tools that are part of the Virtual Server Environment. Later chapters in this section will provide you with guidance in how to best take advantage of these tools and will provide detailed descriptions of each tool and examples of how to use them to solve real problems.

14

Making the Most of Virtual Server Environment Management and High Availability Tools

Chapter Overview

This chapter will cover the Virtual Server Environment management and high availability tools in the same order as in the last chapter. We will start with the Integrity Essentials Virtualization Manager and then cover Workload Management Serviceguard, and finally the new VSE Capacity Advisor product.

Integrity Essentials Virtualization Manager

This product is the core of the new VSE management suite of products; it provides the integration point for all the other products described in this chapter. It provides discovery, visualization, monitoring, and configuration of other VSE technologies. It makes it possible to manage the VSE without requiring the user to have detailed knowledge of what other tools or products are being used.

Key Benefits

There are a few key benefits of this product, and they are big ones.

- It helps you visualize the partitioning hierarchy that has been deployed on your systems.
- It provides a logical mapping between workloads and the systems and partitions they are running on.
- It provides a single point of management.

The first thing that you will see when you point your browser at the VSE management suite portal is a big-picture view of all of your servers and workloads that are using VSE technologies. The partition big-picture view allows you to see a hierarchical view of all the partitions on all your servers. This also provides a high-level view of the status of each of your partitions. Because of the ability of VMs to move around and the ability you have to make different combinations of partitions on each of your servers, this is truly a critical view.

The big-picture view of your workloads provides a list of all of your workloads and tells where they are running and their status. In addition, both of these views can be customized for each user so they can get a view of only the partitions and/or workloads they are responsible for.

The other key feature is that this product serves as the launching point for accessing whatever functionality you might want from any of the VSE management tools. By selecting a workload or partition you can:

- View information about the workloads running in the partitions or the partitions the workloads are running in
- Get real-time or historical performance reports about the partitions or workloads
- Get or modify the configuration of VSE technologies
- Get or modify information about the Global Workload Manager (gWLM) policies defined for the workloads
- Activate or deactivate gWLM policies for the workloads
- Get capacity-planning reports about the workloads or partitions

This is only a subset of the functionality, but you get the idea. The Virtualization Manager doesn't provide all this functionality, but it is the component that makes it all easy to understand and use.

Key Tradeoffs

There are also a few tradeoffs. Generally speaking, these tradeoffs are due to the fact that this is a new product. Some of the configuration tools for underlying VSE technologies will be tightly integrated from the start and others will have only visualization or launch capabilities and tighter integration will be provided in future releases. Examples of this include:

- Initial support for vPars is visualization only, configuration is done using the command line tools
- Initial support for secure resource partitions created in Process Resource Manager and Workload Manager is through the context sensitive launch of the GUI's for those products.
- Initial support for Serviceguard is visualization and launch

The first tradeoff is that the first release of the Virtualization Manager will have limited support for some of the VSE technologies. These include:

- *Virtual Partitions*: the Virtualization Manager will discover and allow you to view the configuration of existing vPars, but you will need to use the vPars command-line utilities for configuration operations. Over time, it will support some of the simpler reconfiguration tasks, such as moving a CPU from one vPar to another.
- *Secure Resource Partitions*: If you have created the secure resource partitions using Process Resource Manager or Workload Manager, you will have view-only capabilities in Virtualization Manager. The first release of the Virtualization Manager will provide the ability to launch those GUIs from the partition view. A later release will discover secure resource partitions and allow you to view current resource consumption, but you will need to use Process Resource Manager or Workload Manager to create or modify the configuration of the secure resource partitions. Since Global Workload Manager is tightly integrated with the Virtualization Manager, you will have links and menu items available so you can view, create, or modify these secure resource partitions from the Virtualization Manager GUI. Over time, support for secure resource partitions created by Process Resource Manager and Workload Manager will be added.
- *Workload Manager*: A number of Workload Manager menu items are available from the Virtualization Manager GUI, but these will simply provide a context-sensitive launch of the Workload Manager GUI.
- *Serviceguard*: Support for Serviceguard Manager will be phased in over time. The initial release will support visualization of clusters and context-sensitive launches of the Serviceguard Manager GUI. Subsequent releases will provide tighter integration. Right away, you will be able to view the nodes and/or partitions that are part of each of your Serviceguard clusters in the Virtualization Manager. You will also be able to see a status of the nodes and the packages in each cluster. However, when

you want to modify the configuration or initiate a package move, you will need to use the Serviceguard command-line utilities or launch the Serviceguard manager. This integration will be improved in future releases.

Sweet Spots

The Virtualization Manager is designed to provide the central point of management for a large number of technologies. Visualization alone is a significant benefit when you have an environment as dynamic as what is available in the VSE. The real sweet spots for this product are:

* any time you have multiple types of partitions on a single system
* any time you are using multiple management tools

If you are using different types of partitions on each of your servers, the Virtualization Manager will be indispensable. This is especially true if you have combinations of partitions—such as VMs inside of nPars, for example.

Sweet Spot #1: The Virtualization Manager Manages a Hierarchy of Partitions

The Virtualization Manager will be indispensable if you have multiple types of partitions in your infrastructure. This will be even more important if you have multiple types of partitions on each system.

Another key sweet spot of the Virtualization Manager is that it provides you with a consolidated management view of all your workloads, regardless of which types of partitions they are running in and what management and automation tools you are using for them.

Sweet Spot #2: The Virtualization Manager Provides Consolidated Views of Workloads

Over time it will be likely that you will be using different combinations of VSE capabilities and management tools on different servers. The Virtualization Manager will provide a single workload view that provides access to all the management functionality required for each workload, regardless of what other tools are in use.

If you are using any of the other VSE management tools, the Virtualization Manager provides a common look and feel, as well as the launch point for the functionality of all the other tools. In fact, HP viewed this as so important that you can't get gWLM or Capacity Advisor without the Virtualization Manager.

Sweet Spot #3: The Visualization and Configuration Management Tool Provides Access to the Features of Global Workload Manager and Capacity Advisor

> The Virtualization Manager is the integration point for all the VSE management tools and provides the context for accessing the functionality for all those tools.

Tips

> If you are in a sizable datacenter, the left-hand side of Systems Insight Manager will tend to accumulate a large number of servers. We recommend you use SIM system lists to create groups that make sense for how you manage your systems. These lists can be organized any way you want — you can even have groups for each of your administrators that have only the systems that that administrator is concerned about.

A nice feature of the Virtualization Manager is the ability to create a custom workload, which can be any combination of processes running in a partition. It does not have to be managed by PRM, WLM or gWLM. This is used only for monitoring. The custom workload configuration can be used to instruct the utilization WBEM provider to collect resource consumption statistics for an application running on a partition even if it is in a consolidated environment with other applications. This data can also be used with Capacity Advisor.

Workload Manager

The descriptions of the sweet spots of Workload Manager cover both the HP-UX Workload Manager and Global Workload Manager. This is because although they have very different architectures and user interfaces, they are attempting to solve the same basic problem—controlled sharing of resources between workloads running on a shared infrastructure. They both accomplish this by flexing the size of the partitions running the workloads or by activating and deactivating Utility Pricing resources in the partitions running the workloads.

Key Benefits

A number of key benefits can be gained from the use of HP's workload management products. These include:

- *Automation*: These products automate the reallocation of resources between partitions that can share resources.
- *Increased Utilization*: These products give you strict control over how shared resources are allocated to competing workloads. This makes it easier to increase the utilization of the system while still ensuring that each workload gets the resources that it needs.
- *Optimization*: These products ensure that resources get applied to the highest-priority workloads while also allowing idle resources to be applied to lower-priority workloads. This ensures that resources don't go idle if they can be used by another workload.
- *Utility Pricing cost control*: Workload management ensures that utility resources are only on when they are needed, thereby minimizing your utility costs.
- *Consistent Performance:* These products make it possible to maintain consistent performance as loads vary and can also ensure applications don't overperform on systems that are overprovisioned for consolidation.

Both Workload Manager and Global Workload Manager are automation tools. All of the flexing done by these tools could be done manually using the underlying partitioning or Utility Pricing tools. However, performing these functions manually would require a tremendous amount of time and effort. You would have to:

1. Monitor all of your workloads 24 hours a day, 7 days a week

2. Detect when a workload needs additional resources

3. Survey the rest of the environment to determine if there are available resources that could be moved to the workload

4. Remember and run the commands required to deallocate the resources that are idle

5. Remember and run the commands to allocate them to the workload that needs them

6. Ensure that all the commands were executed in the right order in a hierarchical configuration (for example where Instant Capacity processors are being moved between nPars and subsequently allocated to one or more VMs)

And you would need to do all of this before the load spike subsided. Clearly this would require an inordinate amount of some very talented administrator's time. If you really want to take advantage of the flexing characteristics of the Virtual Server Environment, you will need to use workload management tools to automate these tasks.

The second major benefit of workload management tools is that they give you tight control over how resources get shared by competing workloads. This gives you the ability to run both high- and low-priority workloads on a system to increase the overall utilization of the system while ensuring that the high-priority workloads will get the resources they need when they get busy. A good example is when you have a development or test workload running on a server that is also the target for the failover of a production workload. With workload management, the development or test workload can continue to run after the failover, but its resources may get constrained to make resources available to the production workload.

Optimization in this context means that resources are applied to the highest-priority workloads and are not allowed to go to waste if there is a workload that can use them. The example from above fits here also. When you run both high- and low-priority workloads on a system, workload management will ensure that the high-priority workloads get preferential access to resources. This can allow you to run a system at a high level of utilization and still ensure that the high-priority applications will get the resources they need when they get a spike in load. The idea here is that you have low-priority workloads that will consume resources you would normally allow to go to waste to ensure that there is no performance impact on high-priority workloads when they get busy.

Another benefit is Utility Pricing solutions. Since these workload management products are designed to minimize wasted resources, they will ensure that if resources are idle, they will be turned off. This will minimize your costs because the resources will be activated the moment they are needed and deactivated the moment they are idle.

The last benefit is that these products control the performance of applications. The result is that the performance of applications will be consistent regardless of how heavy the load is on the application. Another interesting use case for this are when a system has been provisioned to run many workloads, but may only have a few initially. These products can be used to provide planned performance even when the system is only running a subset of the workloads that are planned for the system.

Key Tradeoffs

There are some tradeoffs that you will have to accept if you want to get the advantages above. The first is that a side effect of running workload management is that it may impact the raw performance of applications when compared to running them on an uncontrolled environment. Since you will be running multiple workloads, the overall throughput of your highest-priority workloads will be increased, but in order to accomplish this, the amount of resources allocated to each workload needs to be constrained so that idle resources can be applied to other workloads that can use them. Workload management is designed to optimize the running of multiple workloads.

Another tradeoff for gWLM is that it requires Java on each of the managed partitions. Java Virtual Machines are generally available and shipped with virtually all major operating systems. However, some customers prefer not to run Java on their production systems—typically because of manageability concerns. If you are one of these customers, you can still use Workload Manager—its daemons are standard HP-UX executables.

One tradeoff for WLM is that it supports only HP-UX. The 2.0 version of the gWLM product supports HP-UX, Linux, and OpenVMS on HP Integrity servers.

Sweet Spots

Both Workload Manager and Global Workload Manager are automation tools. They provide a way to take advantage of the flexibility of the VSE to allocate resources to the applications that need them in real time. The sweet spots for this take place when automation can provide significant benefits. These include:

- increased utilization
- automatic allocation of resources to workloads
- reduced costs of Utility Pricing solutions
- automated allocation of resources upon a failover

One of the primary benefits of the VSE is the ability to increase utilization by sharing resources between multiple workloads on a system. HP's workload management products make this much more accessible because they give you control over how the resources get shared.

Sweet Spot #1: Workload Management Improves Utilization

Workload management improves utilization by ensuring that idle resources do not go to waste if other workloads on the system can use them.

Attempting to manually manage the reallocation of resources between workloads would be somewhere between difficult and impossible.

Sweet Spot #2: Workload Management Automates Sharing of Resources between Multiple Workloads

> It would be very difficult to manage the reallocation of resources manually. If you want dynamic reallocation of resources, automation is not really optional.

Workload management will minimize the cost of a Utility Pricing solution. The cost of Temporary Capacity and Pay per use will vary based on the amount of resources being consumed by your workloads. HP's workload management products are specifically designed to provide only enough resources to each workload to satisfy their needs in real time. If resources are idle, the products will deactivate them. This will ensure that you are not paying for resources that you are not using. Even if you have Percent Utilization PPU, you can take advantage of WLM. In the second part of the book we described the fact that PPU version 7 now supports the ability to deactivate CPUs to ensure that you get some CPUs with 0% utilization. These workload management products can be used to manage how many CPUs are active at any time to minimize your utility costs even for Percent Utilization PPU.

Sweet Spot #3: Workload Management Will Minimize the Cost of your Utility Pricing Solution

> Because these workload management tools will deactivate any CPUs that are idle, you will not be paying for resources that you are not using.

The last sweet spot is using workload management to give you automatic allocation of resources upon a failover. This gives you the ability to make productive use of your failover environment for the 99+ percent of the time that it is not needed for the production workload.

Sweet Spot #4: Workload Management Will Automate Reallocation of Resources upon Failover

> These tools can automatically react to a failover to ensure that your highest-priority applications get the resources they need. This combined with Temporary Capacity can provide a low-cost failover environment that automatically responds to a failover by activating additional resources.

Choosing between Workload Manager and Global Workload Manager

The primary difference between WLM and gWLM is the fact that WLM is configured one system and one partition at a time. gWLM has a central management server that manages the policies and the data collected by many nodes in the infrastructure. There are some differences in their support for specific technology features, but these will disappear over time.

The short answer here is that you should use gWLM if it meets your needs. gWLM has some very nice benefits over WLM; it has been specifically designed to allow a central IT organization to manage a large number of servers on behalf of its business units.

Some features of WLM will be added to gWLM over time. For example, early releases of gWLM had support for secure resource partitions, but only for the CPU controls. The ability to configure and even flex the other resources will be added over time.

The key tradeoffs you will have with WLM when compared to gWLM is that WLM does not support the central management server. You need to configure each system separately. Interestingly, this may also be an advantage for some customers that have a small number of systems to manage and don't want to create a central management server to manage them. The other big tradeoff, of course, is that WLM will not support Integrity Virtual Machines or operating systems other than HP-UX. If you want to autoflex VMs, you will need to use the gWLM product.

The bottom line is that if you have a small number of systems with a small number of workloads (which don't require VM support), then WLM may be a good choice. If you are a central IT organization that wants to manage a larger number of systems, gWLM is the best choice.

Tips

Some general tips apply to workload management in general and some are specific to WLM or gWLM because the use models of the two products are very different.

General Workload Management Tips

Keep it Simple

The most common problem customers have with either of these tools is that they attempt to be too ambitious the first time they use them. Get your feet wet by creating a simple configuration with CPU utilization goals or gWLM's OwnBorrow policies. After you have become comfortable with how the product manages resources, you can branch out to performance goals and custom metrics for gWLM policies.

Create a mixture of performance-sensitive and -insensitive applications to maximize resource utilization

By putting performance-sensitive production applications in the same shared-resource domain as batch or test/development workloads that can absorb (some) performance impact, you can increase the utilization on a server fairly significantly. This is because the insensitive applications can consume a large amount of resources while the performance sensitive production applications are relatively idle and they can be scaled back when they are very busy.

Have Business Units Project Utilization in Probability Ranges

Projections of the load on new applications are notoriously inaccurate. That's because it is very hard to predict what the load might be before an application is deployed. Application owners tend to overestimate the expected load to ensure that the system isn't undersized. However, this leads to massive over-provisioning. A trick is to have the business units project the load by probability distribution. Determine what the worst-case and "most likely" load would be. This way you can ensure that there are sufficient aggregate spare resources (which are sharable) to handle the worst case but you can size the partition for the most likely.

Use Headroom to Handle Bursty Loads

One concept that is true for both WLM and gWLM is that they are using data from the last interval to predict the resource requirements for the next interval. If you have very bursty loads, the tendency is to attempt to create very short intervals to speed up the reaction of these products to the bursts. The problem with this is that it can cause uneven fluctuations in resources. The real issue is that the bursts need to be handled by the resources that were allocated from data in the previous interval. Both of these products provide "headroom" built into the entitlements. That is, they actually deliberately assign slightly more resources than are really required to meet the expected demand. The trick to handling bursty loads is to increase the amount of headroom so that if a burst happens sufficient resources are already available to handle most or all of the burst.

HP-UX Workload Manager

Here are some tips specific to the HP-UX Workload Manager product.

Use the GUI

The GUI is a fairly new feature of WLM, and it has been enhanced several times in the last few releases. It really is a nice tool—use it. One recommendation, though, is that you set the preferences for the graph view to 5 or 10 minutes. All of the data for your graphs is stored in memory on your desktop. If you leave it set for a long time, it will load lots of data into memory, which may impact the performance of your desktop.

Use the Configuration Wizard

The WLM configuration wizard provides a very simple step-by-step approach to almost all of the common WLM configurations. One tradeoff is that the wizard can't read in a configuration file and reconstruct the path you went down to create it. Therefore, another recommendation is that you keep the wizard running (don't hit the Finish button) while you are testing your configurations. That way if you want to tweak the configuration, you can simply go back to the wizard and hit the Back button to change the configuration.

Putting wlmpard in a Serviceguard Package

The wlmpard daemon reallocates resources across different operating system images on a system. Many customers ask if this daemon is highly available. The answer is that it, by itself, is not, but it has been designed to support Serviceguard as a packaging mechanism. Because wlmpard manages multiple OS images on a single system, it is normally running on one of the partitions on the system. Actually, prior to version 3.0 this was a requirement. Starting with version 3.0 of WLM, you can have wlmpard run on a separate node so you can put it into a package in the same cluster the other workloads are running in.

Global Workload Manager

Familiarize Yourself with OwnBorrow Policies

We have found that gWLM's OwnBorrow policies are the ones that most customers get excited about. It will help to familiarize yourself with these and then create a number of them that you can then deploy to many workloads on your various systems.

Use the Command Line to Move gWLM Policies between CMS Nodes

If you have multiple gWLM central management servers, you can use the command-line utilities to dump configuration data out of one and upload it to another. This is particularly useful if you have created a standard set of policy definitions and don't want to enter them again manually.

Serviceguard

Serviceguard is actually a whole suite of products. However, they are all based on the standard Serviceguard high-availability product. The Extended Campus Cluster, Metrocluster, and Continentalcluster products are actually utilities on top of Serviceguard that allow you to expand the distances between the nodes in a cluster or connect multiple clusters.

Key Benefits

Serviceguard products are high availability. As such, they focus on reducing the amount of downtime taken from a failure of one type or another. The key benefits include:

* maximizes service uptime and data integrity for your critical applications
* allows the movement of applications to systems with excess capacity while simplifying the administration, management, and monitoring of cluster configurations

* minimization of downtime due to scheduled maintenance activities
* functionality for virtually any type of unexpected failure

The most obvious benefit of using one or more of the Serviceguard products is they can maximize uptime by dramatically reducing the amount of downtime you take from an unexpected failure. This is because you have automation that will detect a failure and start migrating the workload in as little as five seconds. There is no way you could do this manually. In addition, a major design principle of these products is ensuring data integrity. A great deal of effort has gone into building features that will ensure that failures will not lead to data corruption.

The second benefit has been available all along, but has recently become more interesting to customers. This is the fact that you can use the Serviceguard product to proactively migrate applications in response to performance issues or resource contention.

The third benefit is one that people sometimes don't consider, but we find that most customers just love it. This is the ability to manually migrate an application over to a failover node so that the application can remain running while the primary system is down for maintenance. This effectively reduces the downtime for maintenance windows from hours to minutes.

The last benefit is that these products can work for system failures, application failures, natural disasters, and human errors. The last of these is the most common. System failures are handled by the standard Serviceguard heartbeat mechanisms. If a node stops talking to the cluster, it will automatically be taken out of the cluster and its packages will be started on an alternate server. You can also implement application monitors that watch for process failures. You can even create application monitors that run dummy transactions into the application to verify that it is responding. If any of these monitors detect that the application is not working correctly, a failover will be initiated to bring the application back on line. For natural disasters, you can implement Metroclusters or Continentalclusters. These will guard against different levels of disaster. The Metrocluster will guard against most localized disasters, such as weather, power outages, or even terrorist attacks. If you have truly mission-critical applications that must be brought back on line quickly even in the event of a catastrophic failure, you can use Continentalclusters to spread the cluster out to unlimited distances. This would cover you for disasters that take out whole cities—things like hurricanes or the U.S. East Coast power outage that occurred in 2003.

Key Tradeoffs

There are a few tradeoffs of high availability in general. These include:

* it can be expensive to maintain
* it requires application monitors
* it requires redundant hardware and software

The first is the most significant one, of course. True high availability requires redundant hardware on each system, redundant network and storage infrastructure, and extra systems to take over in case there are multiple failures in any of these areas and the applications need to be failed over to a redundant server. All of this adds cost over and above what would be required to run the application in a non-high-availability environment. In addition, the cost escalates quickly with the need for more availability as you approach disaster tolerance. The data-replication hardware, software, and network infrastructure will add to those costs. We will discuss below the key question of "How much high availability is enough" when we discuss the sweet-spot configurations for high-availability and disaster-tolerant clusters.

About 40% of the failures in production environments are related to failures in the application software itself. Some software failures are very easy to detect in a generic fashion. A simple example is where the software processes fail to run. However, most software failures don't result in the processes stopping. Application hangs or memory leaks are examples that would not be obvious from outside the application. Detection of these types of problems requires that you provide a way to monitor the application. A number of high-availability reference architectures and toolkits provide this type of monitoring for major ISV applications. Most customers will also have custom applications. The key here is that you will want to have application monitors for any applications that you consider mission-critical. A good example of a monitor would be a process that periodically runs a dummy query transaction into the application to verify that it is responding to requests.

The last item above is the fact that to provide true high availability, you will want to create a hardware and software infrastructure with lots of redundancy. The goal is to remove all single points of failure at every level of the architecture. This means providing dual network interfaces, each connected to a separate network. You will want dual I/O cards, connected to separate storage area network infrastructures. These types of precautions ensure that a single card failure will not have an impact on the availability of the applications. It would actually take multiple failures of the same type to require Serviceguard to rehost the application. For example, both network cards would have to fail on a node before a failover would be required. This is a very nice high-availability feature, but, as we mentioned above, it has a cost. In addition, you will need to provide a failover environment capable of hosting the applications. The failover environment will need to have sufficient resources to satisfy the load on the production application when a failover occurs. In these days of trying to increase the utilization of our production environments, this requires that we have significant amounts of spare capacity laying around waiting for a failover to occur. We described in Part 2 of this book how to use Utility Pricing solutions to provide spare capacity for these environments but still allow you to increase your utilization.

Sweet Spots

The key question for Serviceguard is this: How much high availability are you willing to pay for? The cost of redundant hardware and software can be significant. However, if you focus on a few of these key sweet-spot configurations, you can get a great deal of high availability for a reasonable cost.

The first sweet spot is also one of the most common Serviceguard configurations, a two-node active-active cluster. In this configuration, you have two nodes running normal application loads and each workload is configured to fail over to the other server. The fact that both nodes are running applications means that you would need to have the two servers whether you do the high availability or not. Therefore, the added cost of making this high availability is relatively small. You would need to set up redundant links to network and I/O, and you would probably want to provision more resources for the cases when both workloads need to run on the same system. You should consider Instant Capacity for the excess resource requirements.

Sweet Spot #1: Serviceguard In a Two-Node Active-Active Cluster

> The incremental cost for high availability when configuring two existing nodes in an active-active cluster is relatively low.

Another thing to consider is whether you are willing to accept a performance impact on your production applications when there is a failure situation. Since most systems run at a low level of utilization most of the time anyway, you may be able to rely on the available resources on the target systems to handle the new workload without a significant performance impact. However, if this is not acceptable, a nice sweet spot configuration is the rolling failover cluster. This is where you have four or five systems in a cluster where one of them is always idle. When a failure occurs on any of the other systems, the workloads running there can fail over onto the idle system and there will be no performance impact on any of the workloads. The only time you would have a potential for a performance impact would be when multiple systems or workloads failed at the same time. Two things to consider here are that this should happen very rarely and that if you use workload management the available resources on all the other nodes in the cluster should be sufficient to minimize the performance impact. Another thing to consider is that multiple failures at the same time may constitute a disaster and you may want to fail over to the disaster-tolerance site if you have one.

Sweet Spot #2: Serviceguard Allows You to Create n+1 Clusters to Minimize the Performance Impact of a Failover

> An n+1 cluster is a low-cost solution that would ensure that there is no performance impact unless you have multiple failures at the same time.

In the third sweet spot, if you have multiple datacenters in the same city, using Metrocluster will reduce the likelihood that a localized major failure, such as a power outage or fire, will take down your entire cluster. This requires that you use SAN storage and utilize the storage array's data replication, but you should probably be doing that anyway.

Sweet Spot #3: Metrocluster Provides a Reasonable Cost Disaster-Tolerance Solution

> Metrocluster can provide disaster tolerance for all but the most significant of disasters.

For your truly mission-critical workloads, you should take advantage of Continentalcluster also. This allows you to run two separate clusters in different parts of the country or different countries and allow one of the clusters to take over for the other in the case where most or all of a datacenter is taken out for whatever reason. The additional cost of this could be minimized by running other workloads on the systems in the disaster-tolerance site. The development or test workloads could be shut down or, if you have workload management, their resources could be minimized upon a failover.

Sweet Spot #4: Continentalcluster Handles Truly Mission-Critical Workloads

> If a major disaster that took out an entire cluster would open the company up to a risk of going out of business, it's just not worth the risk. You can reduce the cost here by picking only truly mission-critical workloads and by running development or test workloads on your disaster-tolerance systems during normal operations.

Putting these last three sweet spots together, you get a configuration like that in Figure 14-1.

In this configuration you have a three-datacenter Metrocluster with at least two sites in different suburbs of the same city. Should a serious disaster take out both of these sites, Continentalcluster will allow the mission-critical production workloads from this cluster to fail over to a disaster-tolerance site in a different city. Also, we could configure the Metrocluster as an n+1 cluster at each of the primary sites and the disaster-tolerance site as an n+2 cluster to minimize any potential performance impacts of either of these failovers. This configuration would provide us with the following benefits:

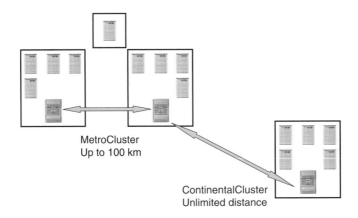

MetroCluster
Up to 100 km

ContinentalCluster
Unlimited distance

Figure 14-1 Combining Metrocluster and Continentalcluster

- A single system or workload failure would recover automatically in a matter of seconds to minutes.

- A localized major failure that took out only one of the primary datacenters would be recovered automatically in a matter of minutes.

- Should both of the primary datacenters fail as a result of a large-scale disaster, you could recover the production workloads in just a few hours.

- The performance impact of any of these failures is minimized because idle resources are available in each of the datacenters that could handle the failover.

- The costs of idle resources are minimized because there are workloads running on 9 of the 14 nodes during normal operations. These costs can be further reduced by using these idle systems to run development or test workloads during normal operations or using Instant Capacity.

Tips

You should test your high-availability or disaster-tolerance solution at least monthly. It would be a shame to go to the expense and trouble of setting up a high-availability or disaster-tolerant configuration only to have it fail when you finally need it. One way to do this would be to schedule routine maintenance on each of your systems once a month and activate the failover before you do it. This will ensure that the workload will successfully make it over to the failover node and back — and it will also give you a convenient maintenance window for doing hardware or software maintenance each month. This will also minimize your downtime during the maintenance windows because you can do this maintenance while the production workload is running on the failover node.

Serviceguard has a feature called Service Management. This was originally intended to be used to monitor the normal running of the application processes and other services required by the application on the system. If those processes exit, the service manager will attempt to restart them — if that fails, it will failover the package. This feature can also be used to provide a way for you to control the failover of a package. You simply create a script or process that monitors the status of the workload and exits if the workload is having problems — any problem that you want to test for. This can be whether the performance of the workload is acceptable, whether there is access to some other system or resource that is required by the workload, or even whether the workload is responding to a synthetic request you send it. When this monitor exits, Serviceguard will initiate a failover of the package to the failover node.

Capacity Planning with Capacity Advisor

Another place where the flexibility of the VSE can introduce new challenges is capacity planning. Most capacity-planning tools are designed to assess resource consumption trends, determine when additional resources will be needed, and determine what size a new system will need to be to support a workload. Clearly, when the size of the system or the partition running the workload can vary based on the load on the application, it is no longer necessary to size a server or partition for the peak of the workload. More accurately, the size of the server becomes an aggregate size based on the set of applications that will be running there and when each of them peaks.

To address this, HP has introduced the Capacity Advisor product as part of the VSE management suite. This product is intended to address the same set of problems as traditional capacity-planning products but to do it with knowledge of the flexing characteristics of the underlying VSE technologies.

Key Benefits

The key benefits that you will see with Capacity Advisor include:

- in-depth knowledge of the flexing capabilities of each of the VSE technologies
- ability to take advantage of data collected by other tools
- ability to do what-if analyses based on potential reconfigurations of the VSE technologies you may be considering
- ability to provide guidance in how to best take advantage of VSE technologies

The most significant of these is the first one. There are many capacity-planning tools out there, but none of them have a detailed understanding of the impact the flexing characteristics of each of the partitioning or Utility Pricing technologies will have on the real capacity requirements of your workloads.

The fact that Capacity Advisor can input data from the OpenView Performance Agent and will be able to input data from other data sources in the future, means that you can reduce the amount of data you are collecting. Rather than collecting another set of data, Capacity Advisor can simply adapt the data from these other tools.

Each of the VSE technologies can be reconfigured based on the needs of the workloads running on a system. This can mean changing the size of a partition or even moving a workload from one system to another. Capacity Advisor makes it possible for you to simulate any of these changes to understand what the impact would be before you actually do it.

The last item in the list above alludes to the fact that you can use Capacity Advisor to simulate changes to the environment that allow you to optimize how resources are used. By taking advantage of flexing or moving workloads around to take better advantage of available resources, you may be able to reduce the need to purchase additional systems.

Key Tradeoffs

This is a new product. Therefore, the tradeoffs center on the fact that the first release will provide only the most compelling capacity-planning features for users of a VSE. The focus for this product is to provide basic capacity planning that will take the flexibility of the VSE into consideration in its simulation algorithms.

Sweet Spots

Some of the sweet spots for Capacity Advisor are really by association with the other VSE Products. For example, the fact that partitions can flex means that you can run a system at higher utilization and still be sure you have enough resources to handle any expected or unexpected spikes in demand. The sweet spots for this product include:

- increasing the comfort level of customers regarding high utilization
- moving an app onto a VSE system
- moving an app between systems in a VSE

The level of flexibility that is available in the VSE has been around for a few years, but it is still new to many customers. The idea of using this capability to drive up utilization introduces the risk that multiple applications will peak at the same time and there will not be enough resources for all of them. This makes some customers uncomfortable. Capacity Advisor can help with this by giving the customer the ability to assess the resource consumption patterns of various combinations of applications to help find the right balance between increasing utilization and risking performance problems due to multiple applications peaking at the same time.

Sweet Spot #1: Capacity Advisor Increases Utilization Comfortably

Capacity Advisor simulations can increase your comfort level that your systems will not run out of resources, even if multiple applications peak at the same time.

Another sweet spot for Capacity Advisor is when you are considering moving an application off an existing platform onto a server that is using VSE technologies. Capacity Advisor can help you determine what VSE system to put the new application on and help you understand how to configure the resource minimums and maximums and even the gWLM policies for the workload on the new system.

Sweet Spot #2: Capacity Advisor Simulates Moving an Application into the VSE

> At some point you will need to move applications from static systems or partitions into a flexible VSE environment. Capacity Advisor will help you understand where to put the application and how to configure the VSE to handle it.

The third item is a variation on the second—Capacity Advisor can be used to simulate the movement of a workload between systems on a VSE. The benefits are similar, but this feature also helps you see what level of resources will be freed up on the original platform to see if there is room for some other application to be placed there.

Sweet Spot #4: Capacity Advisor Can Rebalance Your VSE

> It is possible that you will deploy a number of workloads within a set of VSE systems and the result will be an uneven load. Capacity Advisor can help you determine how to rebalance the workloads to better load the various systems in the environment.

Summary

The VSE management suite of tools provide a very broad set of features. These tools provide many features that may appeal to different sets of customers. This chapter has concentrated on providing some guidance on features that provide the most compelling benefits for the largest number of customers.

The remaining chapters in this section will provide details about how to use many of the features of these products.

15

Workload Manager

Chapter Overview

The 1909 Ford Model T is widely known as the first automobile produced on an assembly line. The vehicle had a wooden dashboard with brass trim, leather upholstery, and a speedometer. Some models were even equipped with windshields. Since the initial introduction of the Model T, countless safety and convenience features have been added to automobiles. Technologies such as intermittent wipers and cruise control are now standard features in most automobiles. Intermittent wipers allow a driver to focus on the road instead of having to repeatedly turn the wipers on and off. Similarly, cruise control gives drivers the ability to set the speed of the vehicle and focus on driving instead of having to consciously keep the vehicle at a fixed speed.

The Workload Manager product in HP's Virtual Server Environment offers advances in computing technologies analogous to the features that have been added to the original Model T. Figuratively speaking, WLM adds intermittent wipers, cruise control, and other automation capabilities to computing environments. Like intermittent wipers, Workload Manager provides automated resource allocation so that administrators don't need to monitor workloads and perform manual adjustments. Like cruise control, Workload Manager allows system administrators to configure the desired response time and adjusts the throttle to ensure that resources are provided to the workload to maintain the desired response time.

This chapter begins with an architectural overview of the Workload Manager (WLM) product and its capabilities. The fundamental terminology regarding Workload Manager is covered next. Then a detailed scenario involving the integration of Workload Manager and virtual partitions (vPars) is described. In the scenario, Workload Manager is configured to migrate CPUs between two virtual partitions based on the resource utilization within each vPar. A second example scenario is covered that demonstrates Workload Manger's integration with Serviceguard. In the second scenario, Workload Manager is utilized in a Serviceguard failover environment to ensure that a workload that has failed over to an adoptive node receives the resources necessary to sustain the workload. In situations where the adoptive node does not have adequate CPU resources, Workload Manager activates unlicensed Temporary Instant Capacity CPUs to ensure that the production workload meets its service-level objectives (SLOs).

Overview of Workload Manager Architecture

Workload Manager provides an intelligent policy engine that monitors workloads running in a Virtual Server Environment and dynamically adjusts resource allocation to ensure that workloads are meeting their service-level objectives. The architecture of WLM relies on several building blocks that are used according to the technologies that have been chosen to manage resources. The Workload Manager product was originally designed to reallocate resources between Secure Resource Partitions using Process Resource Manager (PRM). As a result, the most critical component of WLM is the wlmd daemon. This daemon is responsible for collecting data for workloads running on the system, determining the level of resources required to meet the SLOs for each workload, and then reconfiguring the Secure Resource Partitions to better meet all of the SLOs in the environment. The internal architecture of wlmd is shown in Figure 15-1. The major internal components of wlmd include:

> *Controllers*: WLM initializes a workload controller for every SLO. The controllers are responsible for taking in whatever data is being used to drive resource entitlements based on the defined goal for the SLO, determining how well the workload is currently satisfying its goal, and then deciding whether a resource adjustment is required to help the workload better meet the goal. The controller then passes the new entitlement request to the arbiter.

> *The Arbiter*: The resource arbiter is responsible for taking in all the resource requests from all of the controllers and deciding which requests will be granted. If there are sufficient resources to satisfy all requests, each workload gets the requested resources. If there is not enough to go around, the arbiter uses the priorities on the SLOs to determine the entitlements. The highest-priority SLOs will get their requests filled before lower-priority SLOs.

Figure 15-1 also shows that there are different types of controllers depending on the type of goal defined for the workload. WLM supports the following types of controllers.

> *Metric Data Collector* is used when a specific goal has been defined, such as "response time must stay below five seconds." In this case, an external process or script must provide the response-time metric to the controller. The controller will base its entitlement request on how well the actual response time compares to the goal.

> *Usage Data Collector* is a simple CPU utilization goal. In this case there is no need for a data collector because WLM collects the data itself. The controller will request more CPU resources if the utilization in the partition is high (greater than 75% by

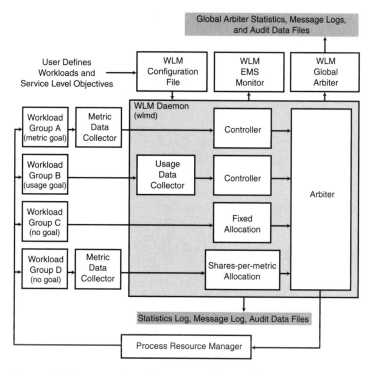

Figure 15-1 Internal Architecture of the wlmd Daemon

default). If the utilization is low (below 50% by default) then the controller will give back some of the resources and allow another workload to use them.

Fixed Allocation also requires no external data sources. In this case, the controller will always request the same resource entitlement. The arbiter will satisfy the request as long as there is enough left over after satisfying higher-priority SLOs.

Shares-per-metric sets the requests and entitlements based on the value of an external metric. The shares-per-metric controller could be used with a metric such as "the number of users" or possibly "the number of processes" if the workload is batch oriented. With this controller, the entitlement request could be some number of shares for each process or user. This allows the entitlement to increase when a workload gets busy, but it is not necessarily a direct measurement of the actual performance of the workload.

Finally, Figure 15-1 shows the linkage between the WLM arbiter to the PRM infrastructure. This linkage is used to reconfigure Secure Resource Partitions after the WLM arbiter has determined new entitlements. This information is also passed to the global arbiter in a multipartition configuration, which is discussed next.

Architecture of Workload Manager's Multipartition Mode

WLM also supports a multipartition mode. In this mode multiple nPartitions or virtual partitions can share resources with WLM acting as the arbiter between multiple partitions. When WLM is running in the multipartition mode, two additional daemons, wlmpard and wlmparc, arbitrate across the partitions. Figure 15-2 shows how these additional daemons are used.

The wlmpard daemon is the global arbiter. This daemon accepts the entitlement requests from the wlmd daemons in each of the partitions and determines if there is any need to reallocate CPU resources between the partitions. When it sees the need to reallocate resources, it sends requests to the wlmparc daemons running in each partition to either deallocate or allocate resources.

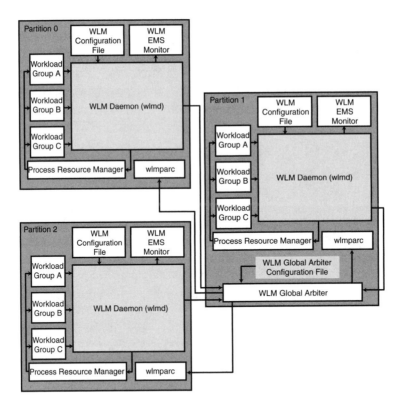

Figure 15-2 Architecture of WLM when Managing Resources across Multiple Operating Systems

Remote User Interface Architecture

The previous architectural discussions have focused on the WLM collectors and daemons. The last architectural feature of interest is WLM's remote GUI. The architecture of the remote user interface is shown in Figure 15-3.

The WLM GUI is a Java application that can run on the managed system or on any Windows, HP-UX, or Linux system that has the Java Runtime Environment version 1.4.2 or higher. On the managed nodes, an additional communications daemon, wlmcomd, is required. The GUI connects to the remote wlmcomd daemons via secure sockets layer (SSL); and once it establishes the connection, the data that is passed between the GUI and the partition is encoded in XML. This lightweight communication protocol makes it possible to run the GUI on a desktop connected to the systems via a low-speed connection with very little performance degradation.

The WLM GUI also allows users to create a partition set, which consists of an arbitrary group of partitions that are running wlmcomd. After the partition set has been defined, WLM's monitoring and management functions are greatly enhanced. Since the partitions need not reside within the same system, the partitions that host a multi-tier application, for example, can be defined in a partition set. WLM creates a single graph that monitors the resource utilization of all the instances in the application.

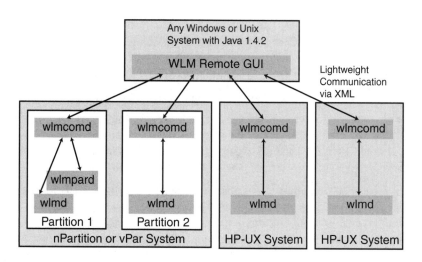

Figure 15-3 Architecture of the WLM Remote Graphical User Interface

Workload Manager Configuration Options

WLM can be configured through a graphical user interface or by directly editing the configuration files. There are two configuration options when using the GUI. The first option is the WLM wizard, `wlmcw`. The WLM wizard continues to evolve and starting in version 3.0 it supports template-based configurations. The templates provide a step-by-step configuration of the most common configuration choices. The following templates are supported in the WLM wizard in version 3.0:

Utility Pricing PPU: provides configuration assistance for a single nPar wlmd and wlmpard configuration that minimizes the Pay per use cost of a system by ensuring that CPUs are turned off when they are idle.

Secure Resource Partitions: provides configuration assistance for multiple workloads running in a single OS image. It enables configuration of SLOs for each workload and allows the configuration of each workload to be isolated in a security compartment.

Multipartitions: provide configuration assistance for either CPUs between nPartitions using Instant Capacity or reallocation of CPUs between vPars. In these configurations, there is a single workload in each OS image and CPU utilization will be used to determine when more CPU resources are needed.

The second configuration option is a form-based configuration editor GUI, `wlmgui`. The WLM GUI allows users to load and edit an existing configuration or create a new configuration. HP highly recommends that users start with a simple configuration until they become comfortable with how WLM allocates resources. At that point, the users can use the WLM GUI to tweak individual configuration parameters to tune the configuration.

Workload Manager Terminology

A few key concepts should be understood before diving into the example WLM scenarios. These terms are used throughout the remainder of this chapter and throughout the WLM product documentation.

Service-Level Objectives: measurable goals used to ensure that workloads receive the necessary resources. SLOs specify which partition the workload is running in, a goal that defines how WLM should determine when to reallocate resources, a priority that indicates the relative priority of the workload, and optional conditions. These conditions further customize the SLOs by, indicating what circumstances should be in effect in order for the SLO to apply. Conditions can be the time of day, day of week, day of month or any event that can be detected on the system, such as a Serviceguard failover. Each workload must have at least one SLO.

Priority: the relative importance of an SLO. Each SLO has an associated priority that is used to allocate resources. The workload with the highest priority will be allocated resources until it is able to meet its SLO. Multiple workloads may have the same priority, in which case they are treated equally when WLM allocates excess resources. The use of priorities may cause lower-priority workloads to receive very little, if any, resources. Therefore, configuration of the SLO priority should be thoroughly considered, as the consequences on a low-priority workload can be dramatic when a high-priority workload is busy.

Entitlement: the minimum allocation of CPU, memory, or disk bandwidth resources a workload receives. Depending on the resource type, the entitlement may be specified in shares, in percentages, or in absolute units.

Workload: a set of processes that is monitored and managed as a group. The definition of a workload may vary depending on the technology being used to allocate resources. If Secure Resource Partitions are being used to isolate multiple workloads within a single OS instance, then it is necessary to define which processes belong to each Secure Resource Partition. This is done by identifying the executables that belong to a particular application and/or a list of users. If the workload is all the processes on an OS instance using vPars, nPars, Temporary Instant Capacity, or Pay per use to reallocate resources, then there is no need to define the details of the processes or users for the workload.

Goals: a measure of workload performance or resource utilization. Goals can be defined in a number of ways. The easiest to configure are CPU utilization goals. These require no special data about the application and can be used for any workload. Alternatively, real-time metrics such as response time, queue length, number of users connected, or number of processes can be used in a goal. For example, if response-time data is already being collected for the application, a goal can be configured that specifies the response time should stay below five seconds. If the response time goes above this value, WLM will allocate additional CPU resources until the response time drops back down below the goal.

Workload Manager and Virtual Partitions Scenario

The first example scenario illustrates the use of WLM across two vPars, migrating CPUs between them as the workloads demand. This scenario is an extension of the scenario described in Chapter 7, "Secure Resource Partitions." In this scenario, instead of fixed-size virtual partitions that use PRM to allocate the resources to each of the Secure Resource Partitions, Workload Manager is used to migrate CPUs between the two virtual partitions based on the demands of the workloads. Table 15-1 shows the high-level configuration of each of the Secure Resource Partitions and the virtual partitions that contain them.

Table 15-1 Virtual Partition and Secure Resource Partition Configurations

Workload Group Name	Contained in	Priority	Minimum Number of CPUs	Maximum Number of CPUs
hr_db	zoo21 (vPar)	10	1	7
payroll_db	zoo21 (vPar)	20		
finance_db	zoo19 (vPar)	12	1	7
sales_db	zoo19 (vPar)	15		

Overview of WLM and Virtual Partition Scenario

This example scenario consists of the following steps.

1. *Configure WLM on the First Virtual Partition*

   This step involves using the WLM configuration wizard to define the workloads and service-level objectives for the two database workloads that will run on the first vPar, zoo21. All of the configuration steps in this section are performed from within the zoo21 vPar.

2. *View the WLM Configuration*

   The output of the WLM configuration wizard is a configuration file. This step examines the resulting configuration file.

3. *Create the WLM Partitions Configuration File*

   The WLM partitions configuration file is manually created in this step from a template provided by the WLM software. This step involves copying the template and defining a partition set for the two vPars, zoo19 and zoo21.

4. *Start Workload Manager on the First Virtual Partition*

   This step validates the syntax of the WLM configuration file and the WLM partition configuration file. In addition, both the wlmd and wlmpard daemons are started.

5   *Configure the Second Virtual Partition*

With the first vPar configured and the daemons running, the second vPar is ready for configuration. The configuration of the zoo19 vPar is so similar to that of zoo21 that the configuration file is simply copied over and modified slightly. The WLM configuration of the zoo19 vPar does not require the configuration of the WLM partitions file since that process is only required once for each partition set.

6.   *Start Workload Manager on the Second Virtual Partition*

This step validates the syntax of the WLM configuration file and starts the wlmd daemon on the second vPar, zoo19.

7.   *Monitor Workloads with Workload Manager*

Configuration of WLM is complete at this step and the workloads can be easily monitored with WLM. This step shows the WLM tools available for monitoring workloads that are being managed by WLM.

Configuring WLM on the First Virtual Partition

The WLM configuration wizard will be used throughout this example scenario. This tool is a Java-based wizard that configures one WLM configuration file at a time. When managing multiple partitions, it is necessary to run the wizard in each partition. The wizard allows users to define one or more workloads running in each OS image and to allocate CPU resources to those workloads. The WLM wizard has many screens available that do not apply to this example scenario or are simply navigation choices, such as selecting whether to configure another workload or continue on in the wizard. The screens and choices that aren't relevant to this example scenario are not shown.

The WLM wizard is started on the zoo21 vPar by executing the command `/opt/wlm/bin/wlmcw`. This command starts the graphical user interface. When the wizard begins, the user must specify the maximum number of CPUs that will exist in the partition. This value is used later in the wizard to adjust the maximum capacity for each of the workloads. For this example, the maximum number of CPUs is set to eight, which is the total number of CPUs in the nPartition.

After the user specifies the maximum number of CPUs, the workload identification screen of the wizard is presented, as shown in Figure 15-4. This screen provides the ability to specify the name of the workload group, whether the workload is for an Oracle database server, and whether the group is based on a PSET. If the workload is identified as an Oracle database server, then the subsequent screen of the wizard is customized for Oracle workloads and facilitates the configu-

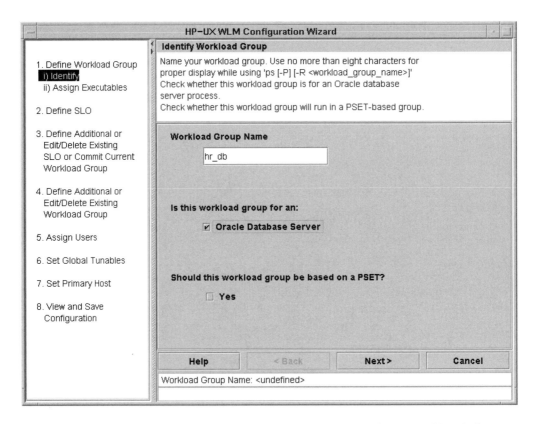

Figure 15-4 Workload Manager Configuration Wizard Specifying Workload Identity

ration of WLM. In this example, the first workload being defined is hr_db. This name is used throughout the resulting configuration file to refer to the hr_db workload. The workload is an Oracle database, so the corresponding checkbox is selected. Finally, the workload will not be based on PSETs because sub-CPU resource sharing is desired for this configuration. Therefore, the corresponding PSET checkbox is not selected.

Since the workload was identified as an Oracle database, the next screen displayed is specific to Oracle database workloads. The screen shown in Figure 15-5 enables users to specify the Oracle database home directory and the ORACLE_SID for the workload. Both of these values are used to identify the workload processes within the system. Since there are two instances of the Oracle database running within the zoo21 vPar, it is necessary to configure the Oracle values not only to distinguish the hr_db workload from other processes on the system but also to distinguish the Oracle instances from one another.

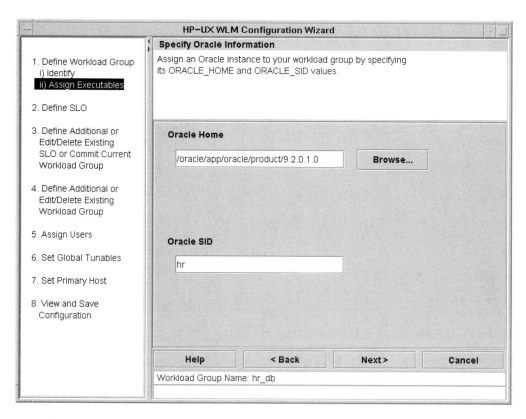

Figure 15-5 Workload Manager Wizard Oracle Information

The next step is to specify the name of the SLO for the hr_db workload and its priority. The name of the SLO is used in the configuration file and is also prominent in the WLM monitoring application. Therefore, a name that can be readily associated with the workload is advisable. The priority values range from 1 to 100, with 1 being the highest priority. In this case, the hr_db_SLO will be given a priority of 10. It will be the highest-priority workload in the configuration, but starting at 10 allows a higher-priority workload to be added at a later time without having to adjust the priorities of the existing workloads.

Since the hr_db workload has the highest priority, resources will continue to be allocated to it until its SLO is satisfied. This configuration can result in a workload with a lower priority getting starved because the hr_db workload has both the highest priority and a maximum entitlement of all 800 CPU shares. Therefore, if the hr_db needs all 800 CPU shares to meet its SLO, it will get them. As should be apparent, the result can be dramatic for lower-priority workloads.

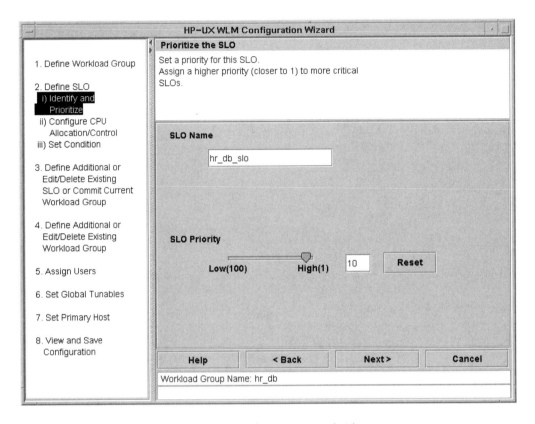

Figure 15-6 Workload Manager Wizard Service Level Objective

In this example scenario, CPU usage is used as the metric for CPU allocation as shown in Figure 15-7. Using this metric, additional CPU resources will be added to the workload when the workload is using more than 75% of its entitlement. Resources will be released from the workload when the workload is using less than 50% of its entitlement. The result of this policy is that WLM will attempt to keep the utilization of workload's CPU entitlement between 50% and 75%.

WLM also supports a fixed CPU allocation policy that provides a static allocation of resources to a workload. This option is useful in situations where regardless of utilization of the workload's CPU entitlement, the allocation of resources should remain the same. The drawback of fixed resource allocation is that the overall system resource utilization will likely be lower because unused resources will not be shared with other workloads.

When metric-based policies are selected, a workload's entitlement will be adjusted based on the performance, usage, or other type of metric associated with the workload or the system. For example, example WLM configuration files are provided with WLM that illustrate how workload entitlements can be adjusted based on the number of users connected to an Oracle database. The various Workload Manager toolkits that are shipped along with WLM provide a set of example configuration files and data collectors that can be used to tightly integrate applications with WLM for metric-based policies. The following steps should be considered when implementing a metric-based policy:

1. The first decision to make is which metric to be used for the goal. If a response-time value is readily available from the application, it is usually a good choice. Another commonly used metric is the length of the request queue. When choosing a metric, it's important to experiment to reach an understanding of how the metric changes based on adjustments to the resources allocated to the application.

2. Next, a mechanism must be developed to provide the metric to WLM. A very simple scriptable interface for WLM allows data to be passed from any script or command. If the metric data is available in a log file, a script can be created to pull it out and send it to WLM. Alternatively, if a command can be executed to extract the metric data, a simple script can be created that runs the command in a loop. The script should output data to WLM at least once every WLM_INTERVAL; WLM will not make resource adjustments to a workload's entitlement if it doesn't have new metric data for the application. WLM sets the environment variable $WLM_INTERVAL when the data collectors are invoked so the value can be used to ensure that data is provided every interval.

3. Finally, the goal must be defined. It is helpful to monitor the metric data under normal conditions to determine the typical value for the metric. For example, if response time is the metric to be used, then experiments should be performed when the application is under normal load to determine an appropriate goal for the response time. If the typical response time is two seconds but this application is consuming too many resources, the goal can be lowered to five seconds. This will allow this application to continue to get a reasonable response time and at the same time have less of an impact on the performance of other workloads on the system.

See the *HP-UX Workload Manager User's Guide* for more information on integrating applications with WLM.

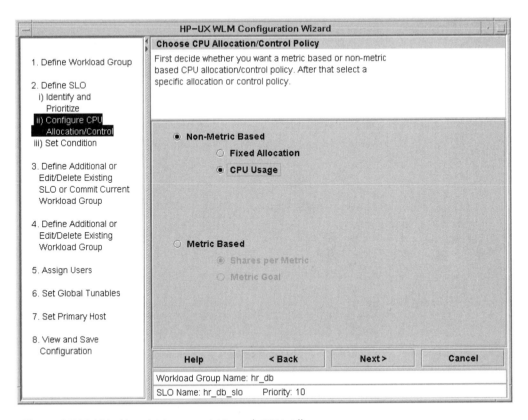

Figure 15-7 Workload Manager Wizard CPU Allocation

The next screen, Figure 15-8, enables users to limit the amount of CPU resources that will be allocated to the hr_db workload. One CPU is represented as 100 shares. This allows partial CPU entitlements to be configured. For example, allocating 250 shares would result in the equivalent of 2.5 physical CPUs. Figure 15-8 shows the range of minimum and maximum CPU entitlements from 100 (1 CPU) to 800 (8 CPUs). The maximum value presented on this screen (800 CPU shares) reflects the maximum number of CPUs specified in the first screen of the WLM configuration process, which asked for the maximum number of CPUs that will exist in the partition.

Tip

> When you are configuring vPars that will be used with WLM, HP recommends that you configure the minimum number of CPUs to be one for every vPar and the maximum to be the total number of CPUs in the server or nPar. The WLM configuration can be used to specify less-extreme values if the settings used in the vPars configuration are not appropriate for the workloads. The benefit of this configuration is that the WLM boundaries can be adjusted dynamically, whereas the minimum and maximum values of vPars require a reboot to modify.

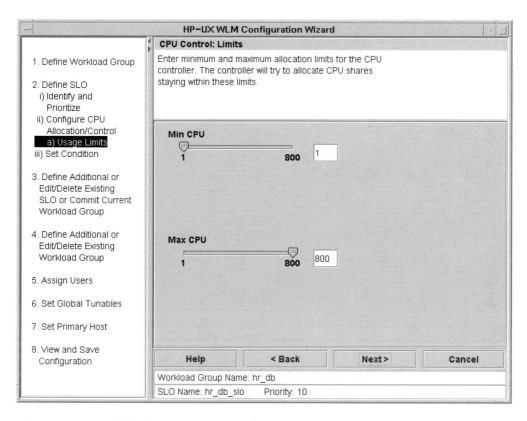

Figure 15-8 Workload Manager Wizard CPU Limits

After the minimum and maximum number of CPU shares have been specified, the next screen (which is not shown) allows you to specify a condition string. The condition string can be used to specify the days of the week in which the policy is applicable. It can also be used to activate a policy only when a given metric is above a certain threshold, such as the number of users logged into the system. In this example scenario, no condition string is specified; this means that the policy applies at all times, under all conditions.

At this point in the wizard, all of the configuration settings for the hr_db workload have been completed. The WLM configuration wizard allows additional workloads for the partition to be specified. In this case, another workload definition is required for the payroll_db. Figure 15-9 shows the first step for configuring the second workload. The configuration of the payroll_db workload is performed on the system where the workload will run, which happens to be the same system where the hr_db is hosted, the zoo21 vPar. This is the same screen shown in Figure 15-4. The vast majority of the configuration steps for the payroll_db are identical to the hr_db. The primary difference is the priority that is assigned to the workload. In this example, the hr_db is the highest-priority workload and the payroll_db is the lowest. Therefore, when the hr_db database instance requires resources, it will get as much as it needs up to the maximum entitlement.

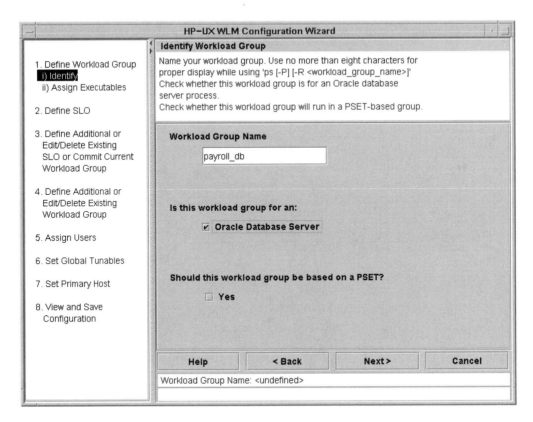

Figure 15-9 Workload Manager Wizard Identify Workload Group

After you have completed all of the configuration steps for the payroll_db workload, the screen shown Figure 15-10 appears. At this point, additional workloads could be configured by selecting the Add Another Workload Group option. In this example, both the payroll_db and the hr_db have been configured, so the appropriate selection is Proceed to Next Step.

Assigning users to the workload groups is the next step in the configuration wizard, which is not shown. When users are assigned to a workload group, processes owned by the specified users are associated with the workload group and are allocated resources according to the specified SLOs. This screen is not shown because both the hr_db and payroll_db workloads are identified by the process specification and Oracle SID, not the users executing the workloads.

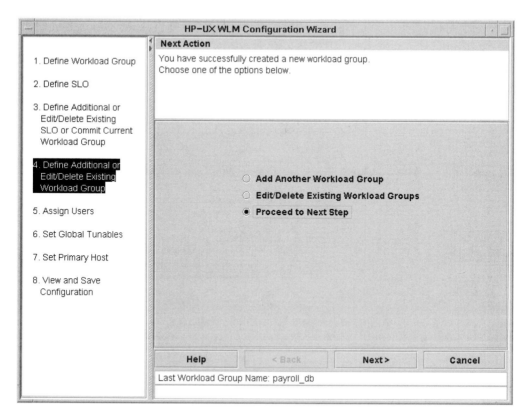

Figure 15-10 Workload Manager Wizard Proceed to Next Step

Global WLM tunables can be configured next. In this example, only the distribute_excess tunable is modified. This tunable directs WLM to allocate unused resources to alternate workloads instead of the default behavior, which is to allocate the unused resources to the OTHERS group. The only workload groups that will receive the excess resources are those with active workloads. Those with condition strings that result in the workload being inactive will not receive resources. The global tunables screen is not shown.

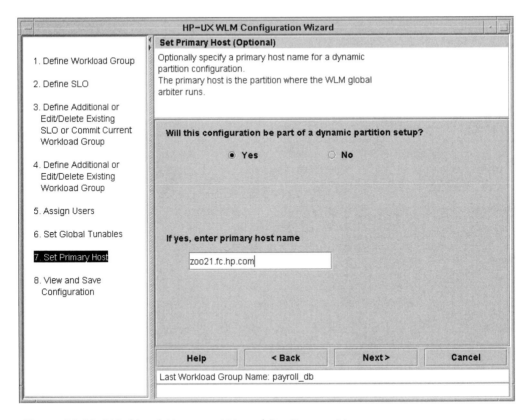

Figure 15-11 Workload Manager Wizard Set Primary Host

Figure 15-11 shows the screen for configuring the primary host for the workload group. The primary host is responsible for running the wlmpard daemon, which serves as the global arbiter. In addition, the configuration of the wlmpard daemon is performed on the system selected as the primary host. This scenario uses zoo21 as the primary host. As a result, zoo21 will run the wlmpard daemon. This daemon is responsible for deciding where and when CPUs should be migrated between the zoo21 and zoo19 vPars.

The final step in the WLM configuration wizard is shown in Figure 15-12. The configuration file that has been built must be saved to disk. Before you save the file, you can click on the View Configuration button to preview the configuration that will be saved. Generally configuration files are saved in the /etc directory.

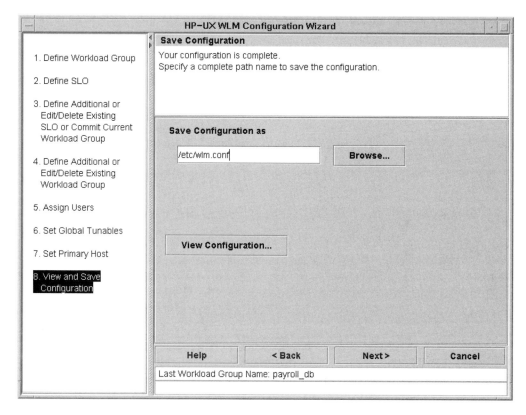

Figure 15-12 Workload Manager Wizard Save Configuration

Viewing the Generated WLM Configuration File

The resulting configuration file for zoo21 is shown in Listing 15-1. This file contains the WLM configuration parameters for both workloads in zoo21. It does not contain any information for the workloads in zoo19, nor does it provide the configuration settings for the global arbiter, wlmpard. Each of these requires a separate configuration file.

Listing 15-1 Workload Manager Configuration File for zoo21

```
# cat /etc/wlm.conf
#
# HP-UX WLM configuration: originally created using wlmcw(1M).
#
# See wlmconf(4) and /opt/wlm/share/doc/WLMug.* for details.
#
# Validate with /opt/wlm/bin/wlmd -c /etc/wlm.conf
```

```
# Activate with /opt/wlm/bin/wlmd -a /etc/wlm.conf
#

#
# Primary host for the dynamic partition setup.
#
primary_host = "zoo21.fc.hp.com";

#
# The PRM structure is used to define workload groups
# and optionally assign applications and users to
# those groups.
#
prm {
    groups =
        payroll_db : 3,
        hr_db : 2;

    apps =
        payroll_db : /oracle/app/oracle/product/9.2.0.1.0/bin/oracle "ora*pay
roll",
        hr_db : /oracle/app/oracle/product/9.2.0.1.0/bin/oracle "ora*hr";
}

#
# SLO (Service-Level Objective) structure.
#
slo payroll_db_slo {
        # Priority of this SLO.
        pri = 20;
        # The workload group this SLO applies to.
        entity = PRM group payroll_db;
        # Request no less than mincpu of available shares.
        mincpu = 1;
        # Grant no more than maxcpu shares for this SLO.
        maxcpu = 800;
        # Allocate available CPU shares to achieve goal.
        goal = usage _CPU;
}

#
# SLO (Service-Level Objective) structure.
#
slo hr_db_slo {
        # Priority of this SLO.
        pri = 10;
        # The workload group this SLO applies to.
        entity = PRM group hr_db;
        # Request no less than mincpu of available shares.
        mincpu = 1;
        # Grant no more than maxcpu shares for this SLO.
        maxcpu = 800;
        # Allocate available CPU shares to achieve goal.
        goal = usage _CPU;
}
```

```
#
# Global tune structure is used to set values to
# global tune variables.
#
tune {
        # Set interpretation of share:
        #    1 => share is 1/100 of one CPU
        #    0 => share is 1/100 of all CPUs
        # Do not set to 0 if using PSET groups.
        absolute_cpu_units = 1;

        # If resources remain, give to user-defined groups
        # (1 = yes; 0 = no)?
        distribute_excess = 1;

        # Set rate (seconds) at which WLM changes resource
        # allocations:
        wlm_interval = 5;
}
```

Creating the Workload Manager Partitions Configuration File

In addition to the WLM workload configuration file, a configuration file is required for the wlm-pard daemon as shown in Listing 15-2. This file can be adapted from the one provided by WLM in the /opt/wlm/examples/wlmconf directory. The systems listed in the partitions list constitute a partition set. In this example, the partitions in the partition set are the two vPars in this configuration, zoo19 and zoo21. The interval parameter in the configuration file directs WLM to consider moving CPUs between vPars every 10 seconds. Setting this value higher results in less-frequent migration of CPUs but can result in unnecessarily long delays in migrating resources when they are needed.

Important

> The vPars listed in the partitions configuration file must reside within the same nPartition or server. Since CPUs cannot be migrated across nPartitions or servers, it isn't possible for WLM to perform resource adjustments in an environment where the virtual partitions don't reside within the same nPartition.

Listing 15-2 Workload Manager Partitions Configuration File for zoo21

```
# cat /etc/wlmpar.conf
#
# Adapted from /opt/wlm/examples/wlmconf/vpar_usage_goal.wlmpar
#
vpar {
    partitions = zoo21 : zoo21.fc.hp.com,
                 zoo19 : zoo19.fc.hp.com;
    interval = 10;
}
```

Starting Workload Manager on the First Virtual Partition

Now that both configuration files are in place on zoo21, you should verify the syntax of the file. The command /opt/wlm/bin/wlmd -c /etc/wlm.conf will verify that the configuration file contains no errors. This step is especially important when the WLM configuration is edited by hand.

The next step is to start WLM daemon on the zoo21 vPar with the command /opt/wlm/bin/wlmd -a /etc/wlm.conf. After running this command, the WLM daemon will be running and adjusting resources allocated to each of the workloads within zoo21. However, you have not yet started the global arbiter, so no resources will be migrated between the two vPars.

In order to start the global arbiter, its configuration file should be checked for errors. The commands to validate and start the wlmpard daemon are very similar to those used for the wlmd daemon, but the global arbiter's command is wlmpard instead of wlmd. To check the configuration file for the global arbiter, execute the command /opt/wlm/bin/wlmpard -c /etc/wlmpar.conf. Assuming there are no errors, you can start the global arbiter with the /opt/wlm/bin/wlmpard -a /etc/wlmpar.conf command.

In addition to starting the two WLM daemons responsible for ensuring SLOs are being met, you can start another daemon that enables you to remotely monitor the workloads and their SLOs using the WLM GUI. This daemon can be started by executing the /opt/wlm/bin/wlmcomd command.

The final configuration task for zoo21 is to configure WLM so that it automatically starts when the system is booted. A configuration file is provided in /etc/rc.config.d/wlm for this purpose. The file should be modified so the wlmd daemon is automatically started by setting the variable WLM_ENABLE to 1. The global arbiter variable WLMPARD_ENABLE should also be set to 1, and the remote monitoring daemon WLMCOMD_ENABLE should be set to 1 if desired. HP also advises that you explicitly configure the location of the wlmd and wlmpard configuration files for the respective daemons. If these two configuration files are not explicitly configured, WLM will use the configuration files that were used the last time each of the daemons was executed.

Configuring Second Virtual Partition

The configuration of the zoo19 vPar is almost identical to the configuration of the zoo21 vPar. The names and priorities of the workloads are different, but everything else is the same. Therefore, simply copying the /etc/wlm.conf configuration file from zoo21 to zoo19 and editing the lines for the workload names is the easiest method.

The file shown in Listing 15-3 is the resulting configuration file for zoo19. Notice that the primary host is zoo21.fc.hp.com. Only one of the vPars serves as the primary host. Also notice that the names of the workload groups and their priorities have been updated to reflect the workloads running within this vPar.

Listing 15-3 Workload Manager Configuration File for zoo19

```
# cat /etc/wlm.conf
#
# HP-UX WLM configuration: originally created using wlmcw(1M).
#
# See wlmconf(4) and /opt/wlm/share/doc/WLMug.* for details.
#
# Validate with /opt/wlm/bin/wlmd -c <filename>.
# Activate with /opt/wlm/bin/wlmd -a <filename>.
#


#
# Primary host for the dynamic partition setup.
#
primary_host = "zoo21.fc.hp.com";

#
# The PRM structure is used to define workload groups and optionally assign
# applications and users to those groups.
#
prm {
    groups =
        sales_db : 2,
        finance_db : 3;

    apps =
        sales_db : /oracle/app/oracle/product/9.2.0.1.0/bin/oracle
"ora*sales",
        finance_db : /oracle/app/oracle/product/9.2.0.1.0/bin/oracle "ora*fi-
nance";
}

#
# SLO (Service-Level Objective) structure.
#
slo sales_db_slo {
        # Priority of this SLO.
        pri = 15;
```

```
        # The workload group this SLO applies to.
        entity = PRM group sales_db;
        # Request no less than mincpu of available shares.
        mincpu = 1;
        # Grant no more than maxcpu shares for this SLO.
        maxcpu = 800;
        # Allocate available CPU shares to achieve goal.
        goal = usage _CPU;
}

#
# SLO (Service-Level Objective) structure.
#
slo finance_db_slo {
        # Priority of this SLO.
        pri = 12;
        # The workload group this SLO applies to.
        entity = PRM group finance_db;
        # Request no less than mincpu of available shares.
        mincpu = 1;
        # Grant no more than maxcpu shares for this SLO.
        maxcpu = 800;
        # Allocate available CPU shares to achieve goal.
        goal = usage _CPU;
}

#
# Global tune structure is used to set values to
# global tune variables.
#
tune {
        # Set interpretation of share:
        #    1 => share is 1/100 of one CPU
        #    0 => share is 1/100 of all CPUs
        # Do not set to 0 if using PSET groups.
        absolute_cpu_units = 1;

        # If resources remain, give to user-defined groups
        # (1 = yes; 0 = no)?
        distribute_excess = 1;

        # Set rate (seconds) at which WLM changes resource
        # allocations:
        wlm_interval = 5;
}
```

Starting Workload Manager on the Second Virtual Partition

The zoo19 vPar does not require a configuration file for the wlmpard because zoo21 is serving as the primary host. The next step is to check the syntax of the configuration file by using the command `/opt/wlm/bin/wlmd  -c  /etc/wlm.conf`. Just as with the zoo21 vPar, the WLM daemon is then started with the command /opt/wlm/bin/wlmd -a /etc/wlm.conf. Assuming that there are no errors in the configuration, the WLM daemon is now running and adjusting resource entitlements for each of the workloads within zoo19. Since the global arbiter is running on zoo21, resources will now be migrated between the two vPars as the workloads demand. As with zoo21, HP recommends that you start the daemon that enables remote monitoring of the workloads and their SLOs using the WLM GUI. This daemon can be started by executing the /opt/wlm/bin/wlmcomd command.

The final configuration task for zoo19 is to configure WLM so it automatically starts when the system is booted. A configuration file is provided in /etc/rc.config.d/wlm. This file should be configured to automatically start wlmd by setting the WLM_ENABLE variable to 1. The global arbiter daemon is not configured for zoo19, as it should run only on zoo21. The remote monitoring daemon can be enabled by setting the WLMCOMD_ENABLE variable to 1. HP advises that you explicitly configure the path to the configuration file for wlmd.

Overview of Monitoring Workloads with Workload Manager

Because Workload Manager doesn't require any user interaction to perform its normal operations, it can be easy to forget that it is running in the background. Several monitoring interfaces make it possible to see what WLM is doing. The first monitoring interface is the wlminfo command. This command provides a number of subcommands that allow all of WLM's actions and metrics to be monitored. The following subcommands are supported by the wlminfo command:

Group: provides a listing of all of the groups defined on the partition where the command is executed

SLO: shows all of the SLOs defined on the partition where the command is executed

Par: provides information about CPU allocations across multiple nPartitions or vPars

Metric: displays information about all the metrics that are being passed into WLM

There is also an interactive mode to the wlminfo command. This is invoked by specifying the -i flag on the command line that brings up the WLM graphical user interface.

The WLM GUI can be invoked in a number of ways. It can be invoked from the command line using either wlminfo -i or wlmgui. Since the GUI is a Java application, it can be executed from any HP-UX, Linux, or Windows system.

Since both zoo21 and zoo19 have been configured to allow remote monitoring through the wlmcomd daemon, the WLM GUI can be used to monitor the workloads. In this scenario, the WLM GUI will be executed on zoo21. The command /opt/wlm/bin/wlmgui will bring up the screen shown in Figure 15-13.

This dialog is used to specify the partition set to be monitored. For this example, zoo21.fc.hp.com is entered into the Hostname field. The default port number will be used, so the Port field is left blank. The Login and Password fields must be specified. Since zoo21 is the primary host, the corresponding checkbox should be selected. Clicking on the Add host button adds zoo21.fc.hp.com as the primary host to the list of partitions. Finally, clicking on the Load

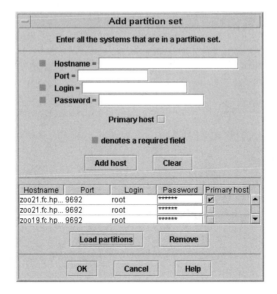

Figure 15-13 Workload Manager Graphical User Interface Adding a Partition Set

partitions button loads the names of all the partitions within the partition set into the list. Remember, the partitions in this partition set were defined in WLM partition configuration file shown in Listing 15-2. Notice that two instances of zoo21 are listed. This is expected because the first entry is the primary host instance and the second is the partition to be monitored. Selecting OK on this screen contacts each partition and displays the initial screen.

Once you are in the WLM GUI, a number of different screens are available as shown in Figure 15-14. The three primary tabs along the top of the screen provide the following functions:

Monitor: enables monitoring of a set of workloads being managed by WLM

Modify: allows the workload configurations to be updated for a set of partitions, including remote partitions. Every option supported by the configuration file can be modified using this interface.

Deploy: provides an interface to activate a configuration that has been modified

The panel on the left of the screen shown in Figure 15-14 enables you to define sets of partitions that are being managed or monitored as a group. Typically these groupings would be the sets of partitions on nodes where WLM is running. However, there is no requirement that all of the systems listed run under the same primary host. Instead, the list of partitions could be any arbitrary set of partitions where WLM is running. It is possible to create a partition set for all the partitions that are running the instances of an Oracle Real Application Clusters (RAC) or WebLogic cluster, for example. Certainly WLM cannot reallocate resources between partitions on different nodes, but graphs can be created that show what resources are being allocated to each of the nodes in the cluster.

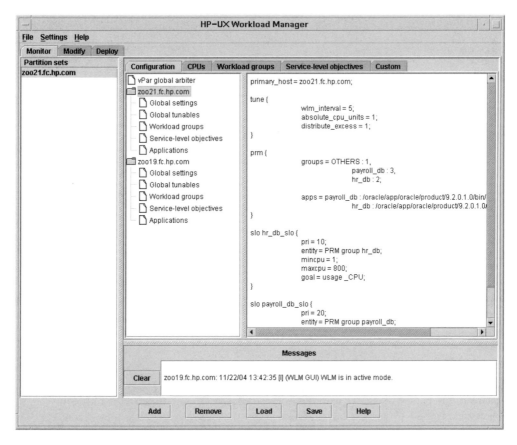

Figure 15-14 Workload Manager Configuration Viewer

The five tabs on the upper-right-hand side of the screen shown in Figure 15-14 provide the following functions:

Configuration: displays the currently active configuration for the selected partition. The configuration shown in this screen is a read-only view. The top-level Modify tab must be used to alter the configuration.

CPUs: in a multipartition configuration, the graphs available on this tab show how the CPUs are allocated to each of the partitions.

Workload Groups: provides graphs showing how the CPU resources are being allocated to each of the workload groups running inside a particular OS instance.

Service Level Objectives: allows a specific SLO that is active in a partition set to be selected and then graphs the metric and goal that is being used to drive CPU entitlements for the workload. In addition, a separate graph is displayed that shows the amount of CPU being applied to the workload.

Custom: provides a flexible interface to create a graph with any combination of data that WLM is collecting.

In addition to the standard tabs and graphs, you can create a dashboard view by selecting the desired graphs and clicking the New Window button, which opens a new window containing only the selected graph. Performing these steps with each desired graph enables you to tile multiple graphs for a dashboard view of the most important metrics relating to the running workloads.

Finally, the panel in the lower-right-hand corner displays all messages written to the WLM message log on all of the managed systems.

The screen shown in Figure 15-15 illustrates two SLO graphs available for the hr_db_slo. The top graph shows the high and low usage thresholds that control when the hr_db_slo will request more CPU resources and when it will release unused resources. In this case, Workload Manager's goal is to keep CPU utilization between 50 and 75%. In this graph it is clear that there was a period of time when the hr_db_slo was at 100%. During this time, all of the available CPUs

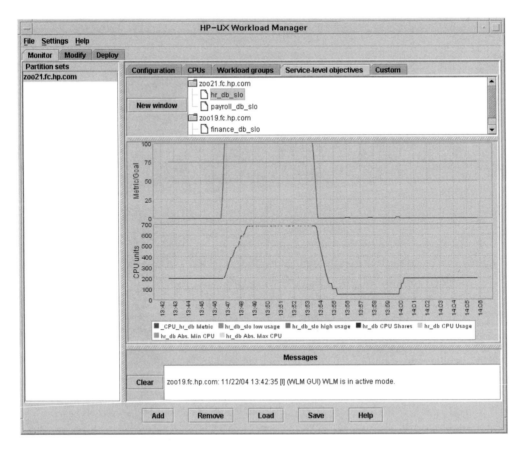

Figure 15-15 Workload Manager HR Group Service Level Objectives Graph

that could be migrated to the zoo21 were assigned to the workload and the workload continued to consume all of the CPU resources.

The lower graph shows the number of shares allocated to the workload, which was 700 during peak utilization; seven CPUs were allocated to the hr_db workload. It is also apparent from the lower graph that the hr_db workload consumed the entirety of the allocated resources during the workload's peak. As soon as the resources were no longer required, the workload's entitlement was adjusted and the resources were made available to the other workloads in the partition set.

The screen shown in Figure 15-16 provides similar graphs to those discussed for the hr_db_slo, but these are for the finance_db_slo. The top graph shows the percent of resources being consumed by the workload. In this example, the workload began to peak at about 13:51 hours. Careful examination of the lower graph shows that it wasn't until 13:54 that additional shares were allocated to the workload. The reason for this apparent delay is because the hr_db_slo was assigned a higher priority and the hr_db workload consumed all of the available

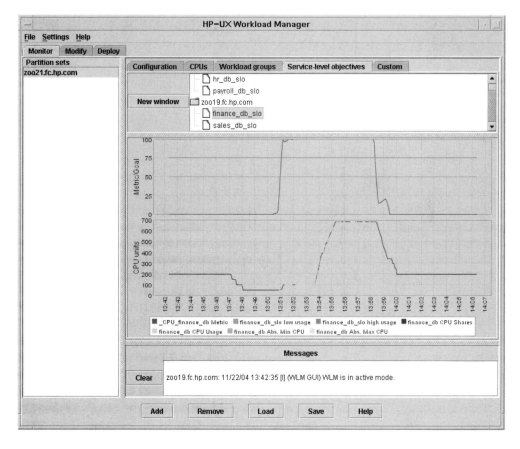

Figure 15-16 Workload Manager Finance Group Service Level Objective Graph

resources. If you look back at Figure 15-15, you will see that the hr_db workload was at 100% utilization between the time of 13:51 and 13:54. As a result, even though the finance_db_slo was requesting additional resources, they were not allocated because the hr_db workload had a higher priority. As soon as the hr_db workload's demand decreased, the resources were allocated to the finance_db workload.

The final graph shown for these workloads is in Figure 15-17. This graph shows the number of CPUs allocated to the selected partition. Each vPar began with four CPUs. When the hr_db workload became busy, three of the CPUs in zoo19 were moved to zoo21. After the hr_db workload lightened, the CPUs were moved to the zoo19 vPar, where the finance_db workload needed them.

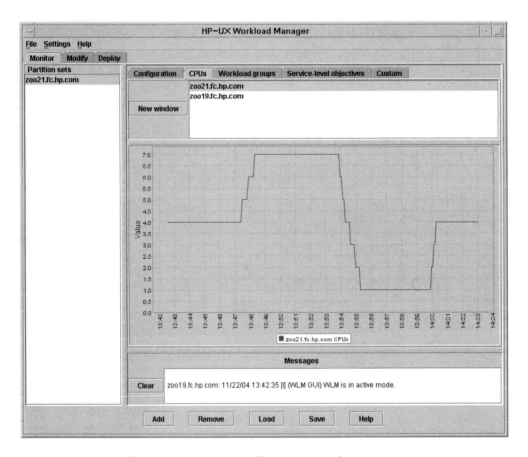

Figure 15-17 Workload Manager CPU Allocation Graph

Modifying the Workload Manager Configuration

The screen shown in Figure 15-18 provides an interface for modifying any attribute supported by WLM. The selected portion of the configuration is the Service-level objectives for the zoo21 vPar and the hr_db_slo. In this screen, the priority, the minimum and maximum CPU, or any other parameter could be modified. The WLM GUI also provides a mechanism to deploy new or modified configurations using the Deploy tab. This allows remote configuration and modification of WLM managed workloads through a graphical user interface.

Workload Manager Virtual Partition Scenario Summary

The scenario described in this section provides an example of deploying WLM to manage multiple workloads running in separate vPars. Each of the workloads is configured with a specific

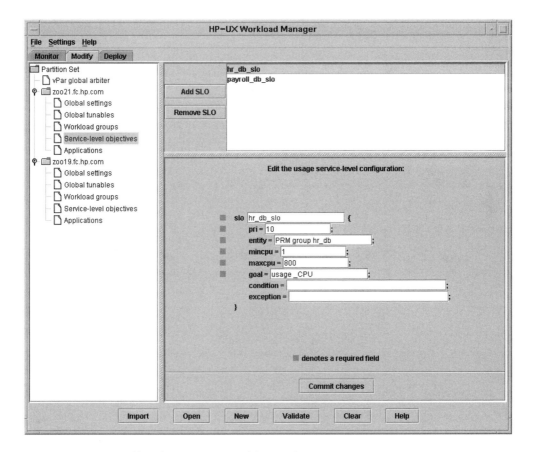

Figure 15-18 Workload Manager Modify Configuration Screen

priority and SLO. These priorities and SLOs are used by the global arbiter running in one of the vPars to determine when CPUs should be migrated from one vPar to another. The end result is a dynamic environment that ensures the highest-priority workloads receive the necessary resources. Additionally, the implementation of WLM yields overall higher hardware utilization because resources that aren't busy can be used by another workload or even be moved to a different vPar.

Workload Manger and Serviceguard Example Scenario

This scenario discusses the use of WLM in a Serviceguard cluster. In this scenario there are two nodes in the cluster, each of which has nPartitions residing in different complexes. The first nPartition's primary role is a testing nPartition and it also serves as the failover node for a Serviceguard package. The second nPartition is a production nPartition that serves as the preferred node for running the Serviceguard package.

Table 15-2 provides an overview of the configuration of the two nPartitions. The Serviceguard cluster hosts a single Serviceguard package, which is a Tomcat application server. The primary node for the Tomcat package is zoo16; rex04 serves as a failover node (also referred to as an adoptive node) only when the zoo16 nPartition is down or otherwise unavailable.

When the Tomcat package is running on the rex04 nPartition, two unlicensed Temporary Instant Capacity CPUs can be activated as needed to ensure that the Tomcat application has the required resources. This allows the unlicensed CPUs to be inactive a majority of the time; they get activated only when the Tomcat package fails over to the rex04 nPartition and the application is busy enough to warrant activating them. The result is a highly available application without the requirement of redundant, idle hardware.

This scenario describes the process of configuring WLM to monitor the Tomcat Serviceguard package on rex04. When the package is active on the node and the application's CPU utilization goes above 75%, WLM will be configured to automatically activate unlicensed Temporary Instant Capacity CPUs. When the workload is migrated back to zoo16 or its utilization goes below 50%, WLM will deactivate the unlicensed CPUs.

Table 15-2 Configuration of nPartitions in Serviceguard Cluster

nPartition	Number of CPUs	Number of Active CPUs	Number of Inactive CPUs	Temporary Capacity	Serviceguard Package Role
zoo16	4	4	0	No	Primary
rex04	4	2	2	Yes	Secondary

The process of configuring the Serviceguard cluster used in this scenario is described in Chapter 16, "Serviceguard."

Overview of WLM and Serviceguard Scenario

This example scenario consists of the following steps. These steps are discussed throughout the example scenario.

1. Configure WLM on the Adoptive Node

   The first step in this scenario is to configure WLM on the adoptive node. WLM is not used on the primary node in this example because a single workload is running in the nPartition.

2. Integrate WLM with Temporary Instant Capacity

   After generating the initial WLM configuration, the Temporary Instant Capacity configuration is augmented with the configuration using a template that WLM provides.

3. *View the WLM Configuration*

   Next, the final configuration file, including Temporary Instant Capacity integration, is described.

4. *Start Workload Manager*

   This step validates the syntax of the WLM configuration file. It also starts the wlmd daemon.

5. *Monitor Workloads with Workload Manager*

   Configuration of WLM is complete at this step and the workloads can be easily monitored with WLM. This step shows the WLM tools available for monitoring workloads that are being managed by WLM including the Temporary Instant Capacity log file.

Configuring Workload Manager

WLM is not configured on zoo16. When the Tomcat workload is running on the primary host, the entire nPartition is dedicated to the Tomcat server, so there is no need to configure WLM on that nPartition. The configuration of WLM described in this section occurs on rex04. The rex04 nPartition has several testing workloads running on it, so it is important to configure WLM to ensure that when the Tomcat package is activated on the testing nPartition it receives the resources necessary to meet its SLO.

Workload Manager will be configured using the graphical configuration wizard. The wizard does not currently support configuration of Temporary Instant Capacity. Therefore, the basics of the workload configuration will be specified using the configuration wizard and the Temporary Instant Capacity configuration parameters will be manually added to the configuration file.

Note

HP recommends that you configure the Serviceguard packages on the node before you configure WLM. This will enable WLM to automatically discover the Serviceguard packages.

The screen shown in Figure 15-19 shows the identification page for the workload group. In this scenario, the name of the workload group is tomcat_pkg. This workload is not an Oracle database server and it will not be based on a PSET, so those options are not selected.

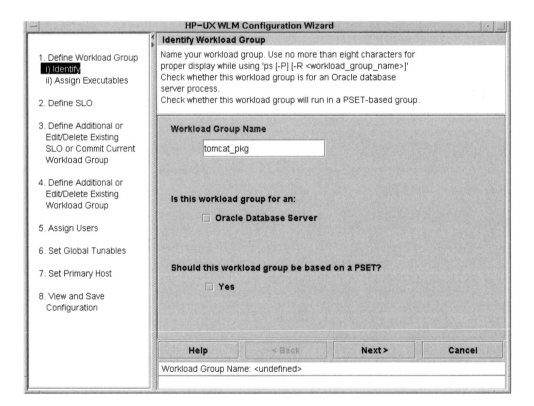

Figure 15-19 Workload Manager Wizard Specify Workload Group Name

The next screen of the configuration wizard allows the executable path to be specified. The path to the Tomcat application server is difficult to specify because the actual process that runs for the duration of the application is a Java process, which means that the parameters to the Java Virtual Machine must be examined to determine which Java process is Tomcat. Instead of configuring WLM to identify Tomcat by its executable location, a specific user (www) will always run the application; therefore the workload will be identified by user instead of executable path. Configuration of the user is shown in a subsequent screen.

After the executable path screen, the CPU allocation screen is displayed. This is the same screen shown during the vPar WLM scenario in Figure 15-17. As with the vPar scenario, the non-metric-based CPU usage policy will be used for the tomcat_pkg workload. When the tomcat_pkg workload is consuming more than 75% of the entitled CPU resources, WLM will allocate additional resources to the workload. When consumption of CPU resources by the tomcat_pkg falls below 50% of its entitlement, WLM will release resources.

The screen shown in Figure 15-20 contains the configuration of the SLO for the tomcat_pkg. The name of the SLO is defined to be tomcat_slo and the priority is 1. The tomcat_pkg workload is the highest-priority workload on the rex04 testing nPar.

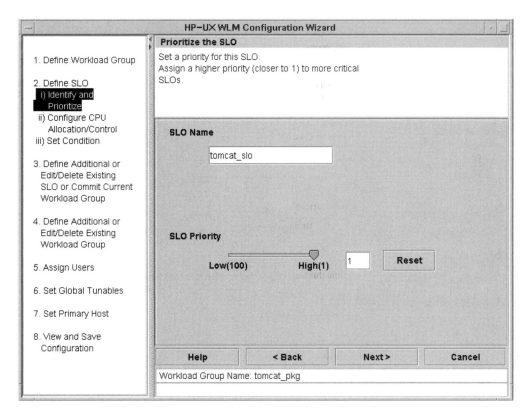

Figure 15-20 Workload Manager Wizard Configure SLO

The next screen, shown in Figure 15-21, illustrates Serviceguard integration with WLM. The name of the Serviceguard package is tomcat_pkg. In this case, the WLM workload group and the Serviceguard package have the same names; however, there is no requirement that the two names be the same. WLM displays the set of packages that are configured to run on this system in the Select a Serviceguard Package list. Since this workload is a Serviceguard package, the package is selected. This causes the wizard to create conditions for the tomcat_slo. The packages will be inactive when the package is not running on this system, thus ensuring that resources are not wasted by reserving space for a workload that is running on another system the vast majority of the time.

Next the WLM wizard displays a screen that enables users to specify the CPU limits. This screen is similar to the one shown in Figure 15-8. The CPU limits for this workload should be set to a minimum of one and a maximum of four. As a result of this setting, the tomcat_pkg is allowed to consume up to four CPUs. When more than two CPUs are active, Temporary Instant Capacity will be utilized. The Temporary Instant Capacity configuration occurs in subsequent

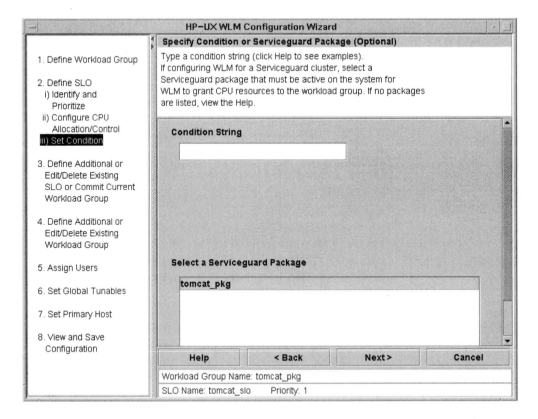

Figure 15-21 Workload Manager Wizard Select Serviceguard Package

steps; at this point, nothing has been configured that would cause Temporary Instant Capacity to be used. If the maximum value of three were specified instead, a maximum of one CPU would be activated with temporary capacity instead of two.

Identifying the workload by executable path is problematic in this case because the workload is a Java application. Therefore, the workload will be identified by the user who owns the process. For this scenario, the user www will own the Tomcat server. The sole purpose of this user is to run the Tomcat application. All processes owned by this user will be assigned to this WLM group. Activities that do not relate to this workload should not be initiated by the www user because they will be considered part of the Tomcat application and will have a high priority on the system.

The screen shown in Figure 15-22 allows the user to select the workload group along with the user or group name. In this case, the name of the user, www, is input.

The final screen shown for configuring the WLM group is presented in Figure 15-23. This screen provides the ability to distribute the excess resources to alternate workload groups instead of allocating the excess resources to the OTHERS group. In addition, this screen provides

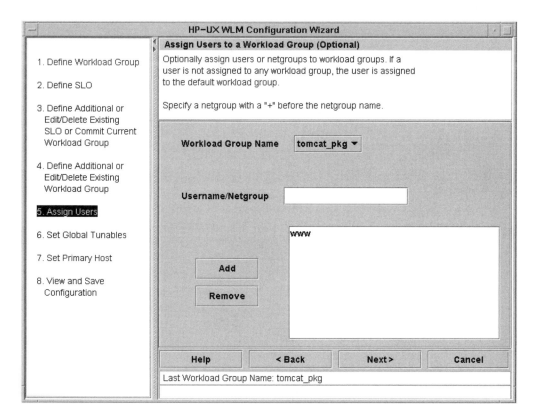

Figure 15-22 Workload Manager Wizard Assign Users

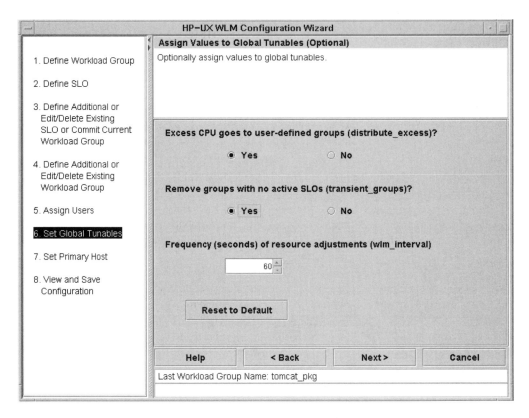

Figure 15-23 Workload Manager Wizard Global Tunables

the ability to configure WLM so only groups with active workloads are allocated resources. When you are configuring a workload that corresponds to a Serviceguard package, the transient_groups option should be set to Yes. The result is a workload that only consumes resources when the corresponding package is running on the local partition. Accordingly, the transient_groups option is set to Yes for this example.

Important

> When configuring workload groups to be associated with Serviceguard packages, selecting Yes for the transient_groups parameter is especially important. If this option is set to No, all workloads will be allocated a minimum of 1% of a CPU. For a single application, this may not be a major concern, but in situations where tens or even hundreds of packages have workload groups defined, it can become a significant waste of resources.

Integrating WLM with Temporary Instant Capacity

The configuration of the tomcat_pkg is complete except for the Temporary Instant Capacity configuration elements. The file is saved by the WLM configuration wizard in the user-specified location of /etc/wlm.conf. The Temporary Instant Capacity configuration components are then added manually. The file `/opt/wlm/toolkits/utility/config/minimalist.wlm` can be used as a guide for augmenting the configuration file generated by the WLM configuration wizard. Listing 15-4 shows the final WLM configuration file for rex04.

Lines 1 through 17 were generated by the configuration wizard except for line 4, which was manually added. These lines define the tomcat PRM group and associate the www user with the tomcat_pkg workload group.

Line 4 and the associated SLO defined from lines 19 to 25 define a second workload group, excess, which is assigned an extremely low priority. This workload group is configured to always request the same amount of resources, 400 shares, or four CPUs. In addition, no processes will run in this workload group. The only purpose of the workload group is to request all of the excess shares on the system. As a result of its low priority and lack of processes, the workload group will receive resources only when the system has unused capacity. When the utility data collector, utilitydc, notices that the excess group is receiving additional resources, it deactivates unlicensed processors. Conversely, when the excess group is receiving no resources, the utilitydc realizes that all of the system's resources are being consumed and activates additional unlicensed CPUs.

The first three settings in the tune structure defined from lines 27 to 33 were defined using the WLM configuration wizard. The coll_argv tune attribute defined on line 31 was manually added as part of the Temporary Instant Capacity configuration to specify the default data collector. The wlm_interval on line 32 was also added for Temporary Instant Capacity integration. This setting is the number of seconds WLM should wait between checking the performance data. In this case, WLM will check the performance data every 10 seconds. As will be described later, this does not necessarily mean that it will activate or deactivate unlicensed CPUs every interval.

The tune structure defined from lines 35 to 38 was generated by the WLM configuration wizard. This setting results in the tomcat_pkg receiving resources only when the associated Serviceguard package is active.

The final tune structure, defined from lines 40 to 48, is used by the excess_slo to activate and deactivate unlicensed processors. Line 43 specifies the name of the excess workload group. Line 44 indicates that the system contains unlicensed processors. Line 45 specifies that there should always be at least two processors active. In most cases, this value should represent the number of licensed processors in the system. If the value is set too high, temporary capacity will be consumed at all times. Setting the value too low may cause too many licensed processors to be inactive and licensed resources will become unusable. Line 46 instructs WLM to wait for 6 intervals before adjusting the number of unlicensed processors. The interval in this configuration is set to 10 seconds. As a result, WLM requires a workload to be above the SLO usage goal for at least 60 seconds (6 intervals multiplied by 10 seconds per interval) before unlicensed CPUs are activated. Similarly, WLM will wait for 60 seconds before deactivating unlicensed CPUs. This number in combination with the wlm_interval setting can be tuned to ensure that unlicensed CPUs are activated for the most appropriate amount of time without activating and deactivating processors too rapidly or too slowly. Finally, line 47 specifies the contact information for the authorizing administrator for activating unlicensed CPUs.

Listing 15-4 Workload Manager Configuration File for rex04

```
 1  prm {
 2      groups =
 3          tomcat_pkg : 2,
 4          excess:60;
 5
 6      users =
 7          www : tomcat_pkg;
 8  }
 9
10  slo tomcat_slo {
11          pri = 1;
12          entity = PRM group tomcat_pkg;
13          mincpu = 1;
14          maxcpu = 400;
15          goal = usage _CPU;
16          condition = metric tomcat_pkg_active;
17  }
18
19  slo excess_slo {
20          pri = 100;
21          entity = PRM group excess;
22          mincpu = 400;
23          maxcpu = 400;
24          goal = metric ticod_metric > -1;
25  }
26
27  tune {
28          absolute_cpu_units = 1;
29          distribute_excess = 1;
30          transient_groups = 1;
31          coll_argv = wlmrcvdc;
32          wlm_interval = 10
33  }
34
35  tune tomcat_pkg_active {
36      coll_argv = wlmrcvdc
37          sg_pkg_active tomcat_pkg;
38  }
39
40  tune ticod_metric {
41      coll_argv =
42          /opt/wlm/toolkits/utility/bin/utilitydc
43              -g excess
44              -i temporary-icod
45              -m 2
```

```
46                  -f 6
47                  -d "Bryan Jacquot:bryanj@rex04.fc.hp.com:555.555.4700";
48 }
```

Starting Workload Manager

The last step to be performed before starting WLM is validation of the configuration. The WLM command /opt/wlm/bin/wlmd -c /etc/wlm.conf should be used to ensure that there are no errors in the configuration file. After the configuration file has been validated, it is activated with the /opt/wlm/bin/wlmd -a /etc/wlm.conf command.

At this point, the WLM configuration is active. As long as the Serviceguard package is running on zoo16, there will be no user-visible changes to the rex04 nPartition. When the tomcat_pkg Serviceguard package does fail over to rex04 as the adoptive node, the WLM SLO for the tomcat_pkg workload will be activated. As the workload demands increase, WLM will activate unlicensed CPUs in rex04 to meet the SLOs. When the workload demands decrease or when the package is migrated back to zoo16, any unlicensed CPUs that have been activated will be deactivated. In order to monitor the tomcat_pkg workload on rex04, the wlmcomd daemon must be started by executing the /opt/wlm/bin/wlmcomd command.

To ensure that WLM starts after rebooting rex04, the /etc/rc.config.d/wlm file should be updated. The WLM_ENABLE variable should be set to 1, and if remote monitoring is desired, the WLMCOMD_ENABLE variable should be set to 1 as well. The WLM_STARTUP_SLOFILE variable should also be explicitly configured to ensure that the proper configuration file is used when WLM starts.

Monitoring Workload Manager

When the Serviceguard cluster package is not running on rex04, the workload group is disabled, as is apparent in the output following wlminfo command.

```
# /opt/wlm/bin/wlminfo slo -s tomcat_slo

Sun Dec  5 15:16:01 2004

SLO Name     Group        Pri    Req Shares  State Concern
tomcat_slo   tomcat_pkg    1      -        0  OFF   Disabled
```

No resources are consumed by this workload because it is disabled. When the zoo16 node is unavailable or has failed, the Tomcat package will be migrated to rex04. Figure 15-24 shows the tomcat_slo graphs available from the wlmgui command. Notice in the upper graph that when the CPU usage of the tomcat_slo is above 75%, the workload is requesting more CPU resources. Because of the minimum of a 60-second delay in activating unlicensed CPUs, the erratic nature of the workload in the upper graph becomes smoother in the CPU allocation graph. None of the

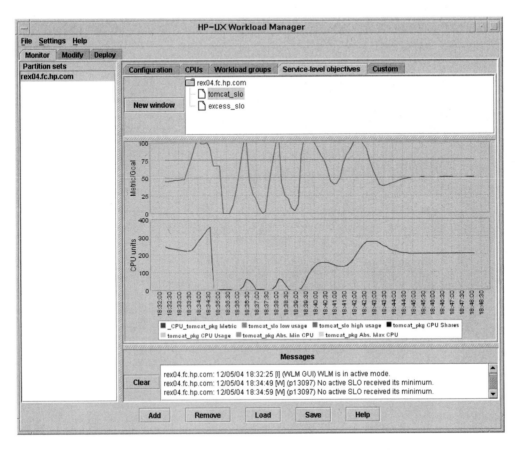

Figure 15-24 Workload Manager Service Level Objectives Graph

utilization spikes between the time of 18:35 and 18:39 resulted in any substantial change in the number of shares assigned to the workload, and consequently no unlicensed CPUs were activated during that period.

The graph shown in Figure 15-25 illustrates the number of CPUs active in the rex04 nPar. In this case, all CPU values above 2 indicate periods when Temporary Instant Capacity is being consumed. From this graph it is readily apparent that CPUs are being activated and deactivated quite regularly. As a result, it may be appropriate to increase the wlm_interval value, increase the number of intervals WLM will wait to make Temporary Instant Capacity changes, or both. The result would be a flatter graph that would show only sustained workload peaks causing Temporary Instant Capacity to be allocated and only continued workload lulls causing deallocation of unlicensed CPUs.

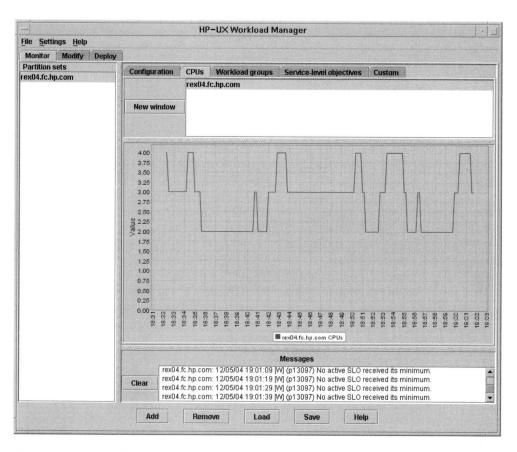

Figure 15-25 Workload Manager CPU Graph

Viewing the Instant Capacity Log

Because WLM automatically activates and deactivates processors, it becomes increasingly important to monitor the usage of temporary capacity. As described in Chapter 11, "Temporary Instant Capacity," the administrative e-mail address should be configured so every WLM activation and deactivation of unlicensed CPUs can be monitored. In addition, a detailed log is maintained by the Instant Capacity infrastructure. Listing 15-5 shows an example Instant Capacity log file when WLM is automatically activating and deactivating CPUs.

Listing 15-5 Instant Capacity Logfile with Workload Manager CPU Activations and Deactivations

```
# cat /var/adm/icod.log

Date:                       12/05/04 18:56:36
Log Type:                   Configuration Change
Total processors:           4
Active processors:          2
Intended Active CPUs:       2
Description:                Surplus resources
Changed by:                 Workload-Manager

Date:                       12/05/04 18:59:41
Log Type:                   Configuration Change
Total processors:           4
Active processors:          3
Intended Active CPUs:       3
Description:                SLOs failing
Changed by:                 Workload-Manager

Date:                       12/05/04 19:00:16
Log Type:                   Temporary capacity debit
CPU minutes debited:        30
Licensed processors:        14
Active processors:          15
nPar    Active
ID      CPUs
0                            4
1       3
2       4*
3       4*
Temporary capacity available:  198 days, 0 hours, 0 minutes

Date:                       12/05/04 19:00:18
Log Type:                   Configuration Change
Total processors:           4
Active processors:          4
Intended Active CPUs:       4
Description:                SLOs failing
Changed by:                 Workload-Manager

Date:                       12/05/04 19:01:22
Log Type:                   Configuration Change
Total processors:           4
Active processors:          3
Intended Active CPUs:       3
Description:                Surplus resources
Changed by:                 Workload-Manager
```

Summary

Workload Manager builds on many of the technologies available in HP's Virtual Server Environment. WLM allows administrators to configure the desired service level objective for a set of workloads, and it takes over from there.

One of the many capabilities of Workload Manager is its ability to dynamically migrate CPUs between vPars as shown in the first example scenario. Running WLM in this model allows multiple operating systems to retain a high level of isolation yet attain an unsurpassed level of resource sharing. Workload Manager can also be used to monitor Serviceguard packages and activate SLOs only when a package is active. This integration allows significant flexibility, especially when Instant Capacity, Temporary Instant Capacity, or Pay per use technologies are integrated into the solution, as shown in the second example scenario. The result is a highly available application that will receive the required resources but does not require resources to be left idle or underutilized. Instead, the idle resources are inactive and are only activated when the workload requires.

This chapter has described just a small subset of the capabilities available through WLM. WLM integrates with almost every technology in HP's Virtual Server Environment. Toolkits are available for a variety of widely used enterprise applications. Each of these technologies and integration points can be implemented as the workloads require. It should also be apparent from the example scenarios covered in this chapter that WLM configurations can start as very simple goal-based SLOs and can be incrementally augmented as additional features and integrations are required.

16

Serviceguard

Chapter Overview

When I was in high school, a NASA engineer visited from Kennedy Space Center to give a presentation. The presentation covered topics ranging from gravity to centripetal force. I don't recall all of the details from the presentation, but one quote has stayed with me. The quote was in regard to the safety consciousness of the NASA engineers. He said, "In fact, you'll notice every engineer at NASA wears both suspenders and a belt. Just to be sure there's always a backup." I have since learned that the "suspenders and a belt" notion has been around for decades and has become a common figure of speech. However, the concept behind this statement is far from a figure of speech. In many environments ranging from space flight to enterprise data centers, a single point of failure can have dire consequences.

The product that provides the "suspenders and a belt" safety feature in HP's Virtual Server Environment is HP Serviceguard. When Serviceguard is configured properly, an application can run within a cluster without a single point of failure. Any hardware or software component can experience a failure, but the result will not affect the availability of the application.

This chapter begins with an overview of commonly used Serviceguard terms. Next an overview of Serviceguard is discussed, including a description of the planning process for a cluster. The chapter ends with an example scenario consisting of the configuration of a Serviceguard cluster and a package to run within the cluster. The result is an application that can withstand hardware failures that would otherwise have drastic affects on the workload. But with the use of Serviceguard, end users don't notice a difference.

The configuration of a Serviceguard cluster can vary widely based on the requirements of the workload and various hardware configurations. This chapter will focus on a single example scenario to highlight the overall process of configuring a cluster and will not attempt to discuss all of the supported variations in the configuration of the cluster. The mechanics of configuring the hardware and the operating system for a cluster operation are not covered in detail. HP's "Managing Serviceguard" document provides extensive details on the configuration of hardware and the operating system to be used in a Serviceguard cluster.

Serviceguard Terminology

The following terms are used throughout the remainder of this chapter and in the Serviceguard documentation.

Cluster: a set of two or more nodes that have enough hardware and software redundancy that a hardware or software failure will not significantly disrupt service

Package: a workload that has been configured to run on a cluster. A package is capable of running on more than one node in the cluster and can be migrated from node to node for maintenance or in the event of a hardware or software failure.

Primary Node: the node where a package is configured to run most of the time. Generally a package runs on its primary node unless the node fails or requires maintenance, in which case the package is moved to an adoptive node.

Adoptive Node: a node where a package is configured to run when the primary node is unavailable

Cluster Heartbeat: a message sent from each node in the cluster to every other node in the cluster using either the network or a serial line. The cluster heartbeat is used to determine when a node has failed or is no longer accessible. In the event that a node becomes unreachable, the remaining nodes in the cluster will reform the cluster without the failed node.

Cluster Lock: required when a cluster is forming and exactly half of the nodes in the cluster are available. The cluster lock prevents two separate instances of the same cluster from creating a situation known as split-brain syndrome. Only the set of nodes that acquires the lock is able to form the cluster. A cluster can be configured to use either a cluster lock disk or a quorum server for locking purposes.

Lock Disk: a specific storage device available to all nodes in the cluster that holds the cluster lock

Quorum Server: a system separate from any node in the cluster; it runs a daemon that is responsible for giving a cluster lock to only one set of nodes in the cluster

Split-Brain Syndrome: the situation where two halves of a cluster each form a distinct instance of the same cluster. This is problematic because generally the package file systems are not capable of being mounted by multiple systems simultaneously. In addition, package IP addresses should only be active on a single node, which would not be the case when a cluster experiences a split-brain syndrome.

Serviceguard Overview

Serviceguard is a set of software components designed to ensure that workloads are highly available. Because Serviceguard is software based, an initial assumption could be that installation and configuration of the Serviceguard software results in a highly available platform for hosting applications. However, that is not the case. In order to achieve a highly available foundation for running workloads, you must carefully plan and implement both the hardware and the software.

Serviceguard Software Components

Figure 16-1 shows the primary Serviceguard components. Immediately below the workload are the four major components in the Serviceguard application, the package manager, cluster manager, network manager, and object manager. Below the Serviceguard components in the diagram are the volume manager and operating system. These components are the same as the standard HP-UX and Linux volume managers and operating systems. The Serviceguard components are discussed in more detail in the following sections.

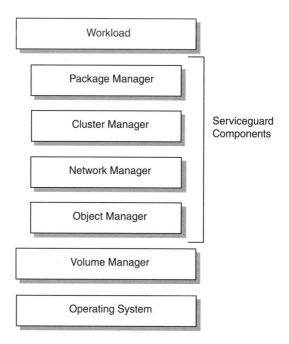

Figure 16-1 Serviceguard Components

Package Manager

The first Serviceguard component is the package manager, which is responsible for deciding where a package should run and executing the control scripts of packages. There are two types of package managers. One of the package managers in each cluster takes on the role of package coordinator, which decides where each package should be running. All package managers, including the package coordinator, perform the following functions:

1. Take responsibility for starting and stopping packages that are supposed to be running on the local node.

2. Monitor the services, resources, and subnets required for normal running of the package.

Workload failures in a cluster can usually be classified in one of two categories. The first is when a node running the workload becomes unreachable on the network and does not respond to heartbeat messages. As discussed in the next section, the cluster manager is responsible for detecting this failure condition and migrating packages accordingly. The second category of workload failures happens when a node is running normally and responding to heartbeat messages, but the application is experiencing a problem. In this situation, the package manager is responsible for detecting the failure. The package manager monitors several aspects of the workload to detect a workload failure. These include:

Services: application processes are monitored as services. The package manager starts these services when the package is started and then monitors whether these processes are running. If a service process stops running, the package manager attempts to restart it based on the package configuration. If that fails, it stops the package and fails it over to another node.

Subnet: the package manager monitors the availability of the subnets required by the package. If there is a failure and a standby network interface is available, the package manager instructs the network manager to switch over to the standby interface. If no standby is available, the package will fail over to another node.

EMS Resources: EMS resource monitors can be created to monitor any attribute relevant to the application's status. The package manager can then be configured to monitor those EMS resources. If a resource exceeds the specified threshold, the package manager fails the package over to another node in the cluster.

Cluster Manager

The next Serviceguard component is the cluster manager, which is responsible for initializing the cluster. It also monitors the health of the cluster and decides when a failure should occur. When a node leaves or joins the cluster, the cluster manager controls the reformation of the cluster.

The cluster manager monitors the health of cluster nodes by sending heartbeat messages to all nodes in the cluster at every heartbeat interval. The interval is configurable. Setting this value lower will cause failovers to happen more quickly but may result in false failovers due to network congestion or intermittent network failures.

Network Manager

The third component of Serviceguard is the network manager that is responsible for ensuring the networking infrastructure for the cluster remains available, even in the event of a network card, network cable, or network switch failure. To accomplish this task, the network manager migrates a package's IP address along with the package to keep the address of the package constant, regardless of where the package is running. In addition, the network manager can enable a standby network adapter should an active network adapter experience a failure.

Object Manager

Finally, the Object Manager is responsible for responding to Serviceguard Manager client requests for information about the cluster. When a user starts Serviceguard Manager and specifies a cluster node to connect to, the object manager on the target node services the requests. If the object manager is not running, the connection fails.

Serviceguard Hardware Planning

The first step for configuring a Serviceguard cluster is planning how the cluster will be implemented. The hardware configuration of the cluster is crucial for achieving a highly available platform for workloads. The following list provides an overview of the planning steps that should be considered when configuring a cluster.

Note

The *Managing Serviceguard* user's guide provides extensive documentation and planning worksheets that assist in the planning process. HP highly recommends that you consult the user's guide when going through the planning process for a Serviceguard cluster.

Hardware planning should consider every aspect of the hardware's configuration while paying special attention to any component that is a single point of failure. The loss of any one component should not affect the workload in a high availability environment. The hardware planning steps are generally broken down into planning for highly available power, storage, and networking.

Power is an aspect of planning that can be easily overlooked but is crucial for you to perform thoroughly. This includes ensuring that no single power circuit outage would cause a loss of enough resources to prevent the cluster from operating. Each individual component does not need to be connected to a separate power circuit, but the key is to ensure that the loss of any one power circuit does not prevent the cluster from operating. As a simple example, each copy of a mirrored data disk should be on a separate power circuit; that way, at least one copy of the mirrored disk will be available if a power circuit fails. For even more power reliability, you can use an uninterruptible power supply (UPS) to protect from short-term power losses. In addition, many devices now have multiple power cords that allow a single device to have redundant power connections. These power cords should be connected to separate power circuits.

Storage devices must be carefully planned. Every storage device must be configured with a redundant mirror, including the root device. In addition, steps must be taken to ensure that the failure of a single storage adapter or cable will not result in the loss of all the copies in a mirrored-disk configuration.

Networking is the final aspect of hardware planning. There should be redundant network devices for each LAN connection, including the heartbeat connection. Each of the LAN cards in a redundancy set should be connected to a separate LAN switch, and those switches should be on distinct power circuits. The desired result is a cluster that will continue to function until a failed component—a power circuit, a network switch, a network cable, or a network adapter-is repaired. The repair should be performed as soon as possible because another failure could result in loss of cluster connectivity.

Serviceguard Software Configuration Planning

After completing the hardware planning, the next step is planning for the software configuration of the cluster. This also includes planning for any packages that will be configured to run on the cluster and planning for the cluster lock. The following list provides more details about each of the primary software planning topics.

Cluster Planning involves deciding how the cluster will be configured, especially with regard to how failovers will occur. A cluster could be configured with eight nodes, for example, seven of them active and one a standby. The standby node serves as a failover for all seven of the other nodes. Alternatively, the cluster may contain as few as two nodes, each node serving as a failover for the other. Another aspect of cluster planning is deciding how the networking interfaces will be configured, including the heartbeat connections. It is important to consider aspects such as whether a separate LAN is required for the heartbeat. If the data LAN is used for the heartbeat and it becomes saturated, then the heartbeat messages may not get transmitted in a timely fashion, which could result in a cluster failure. The cluster lock is another aspect of cluster planning.

Cluster Lock Planning is an important factor to consider as part of planning the entire cluster. Either a lock disk or a quorum server is required for a cluster lock. A lock is acquired only when a cluster fails and exactly half of the cluster nodes are available to reform the cluster. In this situation, the cluster lock will be used to ensure that the other half of the cluster nodes do not also reform a cluster. When there is no lock, split-brain syndrome occurs, a circumstance when two instances of the same cluster are running at the same time.

Storage Software Planning for a cluster involves deciding which volume manager and file systems will be used for the disks containing the data and programs necessary for the packages. The HP Logical Volume Manager (LVM), the VERITAS Volume Manager (VxVM), or the VERITAS Cluster Volume Manager (CVM) may be used as the volume managers in a Serviceguard cluster. The type of file system within each volume must also be considered. To a large degree, the type of file system is dictated by the application.

Package Planning involves deciding where the package should run and which nodes will serve as adoptive nodes in the event of a failure. Another part of package planning is whether the package will be configured to run automatically when the cluster is started and how the adoptive node will be chosen in the event of a failure. The next node in the list of alternate nodes can be used or Serviceguard can be configured to start the package on the node that has the least number of packages running. Finally, the behavior of the package after the primary node is restored must be considered. The package can continue to run on the adoptive node until the package is manually moved back to the primary node or Serviceguard can be configured to automatically move the package back to the primary node when it becomes available.

After completing the planning phases, the configuration and implementation of the cluster can begin. The example scenario described in the next section provides a concrete example of configuration of a Serviceguard cluster using the Serviceguard Manager graphical user interface.

The Serviceguard Manager application used in the example scenario is delivered as a separate product from the core Serviceguard application in the bundle B8325BA. The application is available for Linux, Windows, and HP-UX. In addition to running the application natively on a Serviceguard Linux or HP-UX cluster, a Windows desktop can be used to remotely manage the cluster configuration.

Serviceguard Example Scenario

This scenario describes the process for configuring the Serviceguard cluster that was used in the scenario in Chapter 15, "Workload Manager," where the integration of Serviceguard with Workload Manager was highlighted. Two nPartitions will be configured in a Serviceguard cluster responsible for hosting a Tomcat application server in a Serviceguard package. The zoo16 nPartition is the primary host for the package. The rex04 nPartition serves as the adoptive node for the package when zoo16 is unavailable. When not serving as the adoptive node for the Serviceguard package, rex04 is used for testing purposes. As shown in the Workload Manager scenario, when the Serviceguard package is active on rex04, it is the highest-priority workload and gets most of the resources on the system if it needs them.

Cluster Hardware Configuration

The diagram shown in Figure 16-2 provides a detailed view of the hardware configuration for the two nodes in the cluster. Each of the nPartitions has a mirrored root disk attached to separate SCSI interfaces. If a disk, SCSI cable, or SCSI interface card were to fail, one of the mirrored disks would continue to be available. In addition, the data disks are also mirrored on separate SCSI buses to ensure that at least one of the disks will be available.

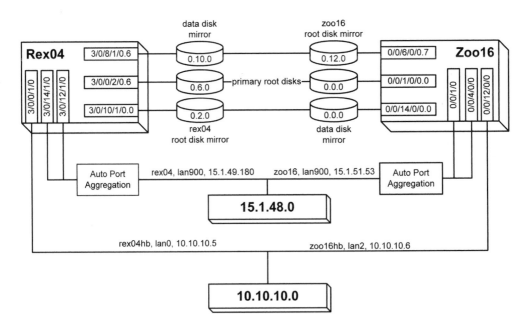

Figure 16-2 Cluster Hardware Configuration

Each of the nPartitions has three network adapters. Two of them are configured in HP-UX with auto-port aggregation; a single IP address is assigned to two of the interface cards. Using this configuration, either of the cards, network cables, or switches could fail and the nPartitions network connectivity would not be lost. A separate network interface is connected to a dedicated heartbeat LAN. This LAN is isolated from the rest of the network to ensure that network saturation on the production LAN doesn't result in delayed transmission of heartbeat messages, which would cause the cluster to fail. The primary LAN interfaces are also used to transmit heartbeat messages to prevent cluster failure if one of the devices on the heartbeat LAN fails.

The final aspect of hardware configuration is power. Each of the nPartition servers must be connected to separate power circuits. In addition, each of the LAN switches and each copy of the mirrored disks should be connected to separate power circuits.

The next step is to configure the operating environment. This consists of setting up the operating system and core applications on each of the nodes in the cluster.

Operating Environment Configuration

The next step in configuring a cluster is to set up the operating environment. Starting with the kernel, all nodes in the cluster should have their kernel tunables set consistently to ensure that the packages will operate as expected in the event of a failure. Next, the shared storage must be mountable by any node in the cluster, but none of the nodes should mount the storage unless the package is active on the node. Shared storage devices should either not be listed in the /etc/fstab file or they should be commented out such that they are not automatically mounted.

The final steps necessary for configuring the operating environment are related to networking. The Serviceguard commands rely heavily on network communication and name resolution. Every node must be able to resolve the hostname for every other node in the cluster. Therefore, the /etc/hosts file on each node in the cluster should contain the hostnames and IP address of every node in the cluster. To ensure reliable name resolution, the /etc/nsswitch.conf file should be modified such that the /etc/hosts file is used as the primary source for resolving hostnames. Domain name system (DNS) or other name-resolution services may be added to the /etc/nsswitch.conf file as alternate name resolution services. Finally, HP highly recommends that you set up all the nodes in the cluster to use the network time protocol (NTP) to ensure that the clocks on all the nodes are synchronized.

Quorum Server Configuration

At this point the hardware and operating environments for the cluster have been configured. Before you configure the cluster and the cluster packages, you must set up the quorum server unless you are using a lock disk. In this scenario, zoo7 will be used as the quorum server. The first step for setting up a quorum server is to install the software package, which is contained in the product bundle B8467BA. After installing the software, you need to add the following entry to the /etc/inittab file (the location of the log file can be altered as needed):

```
qs:345:respawn:/usr/lbin/qs >> /var/adm/qs/qs.log 2>&1
```

After adding the entry to the /etc/inittab file, you'll need to edit the authorization file to allow cluster nodes to use the quorum server. A quorum server can be used by multiple clusters. The file /etc/cmcluster/qs_authfile defines the cluster nodes that are allowed to use the quorum server. This file has a very simple format that consists of one system's hostname per line. Every node in the cluster should be listed in this file. The /etc/cmcluster/qs_authfile file for this scenario contains the following entries:

```
# cat /etc/cmcluster/qs_authfile
zoo16.fc.hp.com
rex04.fc.hp.com
```

Finally, start the quorum server by using the command init q. As specified in the /etc/inittab file, the quorum server will use the file /var/adm/qs/qs.log to log messages. The configuration of the quorum server is now complete, and the process of configuring the cluster and the package can begin.

Cluster Software Configuration

Configuring the software aspect of the cluster is the next step. This example scenario will use the graphical user interface Serviceguard Manager to perform the configuration of the cluster and the package. These steps can also be performed by editing a configuration file instead of using the GUI. If you choose to edit the configuration file directly, you can create a template for the cluster configuration by executing the following command:

```
# cmquerycl -v -C /etc/cmcluster/zoocat.ascii -n zoo16 -n rex04
```

Before starting Serviceguard Manager, you should perform two steps on each of the nodes in the cluster. First, you should include the file /etc/cmcluster.conf in any user's .profile file who will be managing the cluster. This file defines variables that specify the location of files and directories Serviceguard uses. Second, you must create the /etc/cmcluster/cmclnodelist file on every node so Serviceguard Manager will be able to create a cluster using the nodes. For this scenario, the file is identical on both zoo16 and rex04 and contains the following two lines:

```
# cat /etc/cmcluster/cmclnodelist
rex04 root
zoo16 root
```

Now the Serviceguard Manager GUI can be started. It is located in /opt/sgmgr/bin/sgmgr. The first screen shown is a welcome screen that allows a previous file to be opened or a live set of systems to be configured. For this example, the default setting is selected and Serviceguard Manager is connected to live systems.

Following the welcome screen, the screen in Figure 16-3 is displayed. This screen is used to specify the server, username, and password and provides the means to select the option to view all unused nodes. In this case, zoo16 is specified as the server and the option to View All Clusters and Unused SG Nodes is selected. When you click on the Connect button, Serviceguard Manager discovers all of the clusters and unused nodes on the local network.

Tip

> If an unused node does not appear in Serviceguard Manager, it is likely that
> the /etc/cmcluster/cmnodelist file was not properly created or the file does
> not contain an entry for the server and user specified in the Serviceguard
> Manager login screen.

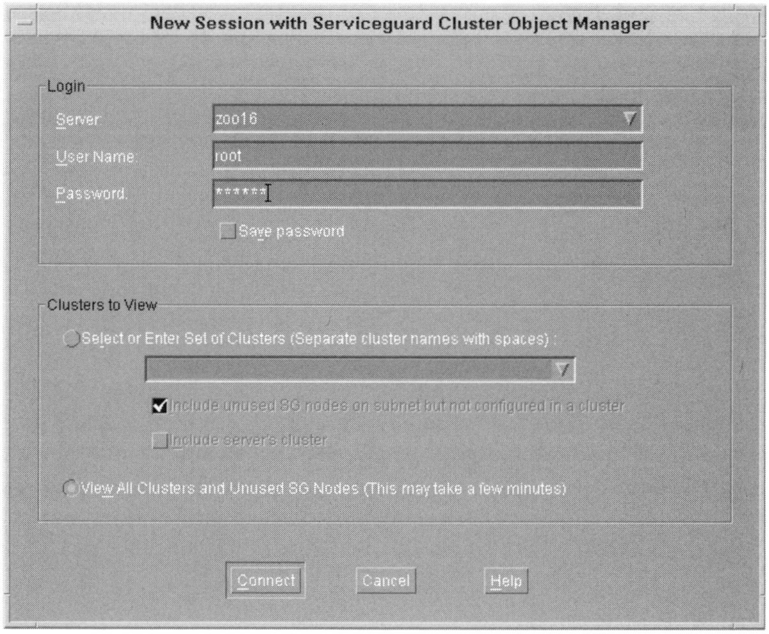

Figure 16-3 Serviceguard Manager New Session Screen

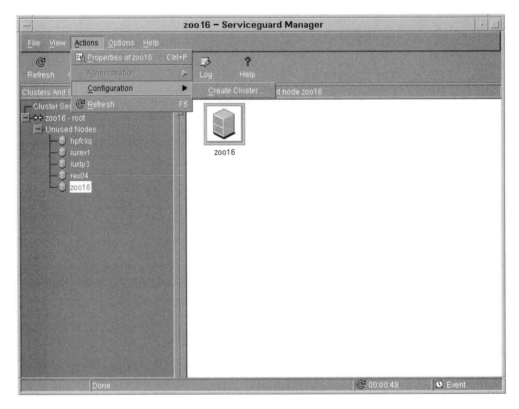

Figure 16-4 Serviceguard Manager Main Screen

The screen shown in Figure 16-4 is the main Serviceguard Manager window. Notice that all of the unused nodes are listed on the left-hand side. In this case, the two of interest are zoo16 and rex04. Zoo16 is selected and then the Create Cluster action is selected from the Actions menu.

Selecting the Create Cluster action produces the dialog shown in Figure 16-5. It provides the ability to configure all the parameters that can be specified in the configuration file. The first step in configuring the cluster is specifying the name of the cluster. The cluster in this scenario is named zoocat, which is specified in the Cluster name field. After the cluster name has been specified, the first tab to be completed is the Nodes tab. Both rex04 and zoo16 are selected from the list on the right-hand side and added to the Cluster node list. After the nodes in the cluster have been selected, the next step is to configure the parameters for the cluster.

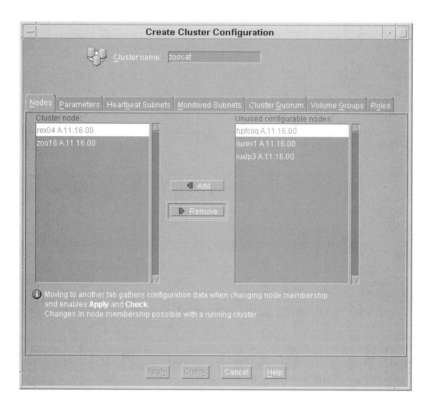

Figure 16-5 Serviceguard Manager Cluster Node Configuration Screen

Figure 16-6 shows the Parameters tab of the cluster configuration screen. The following parameters can be configured on this screen.

Heartbeat Interval: the number of seconds between the transmissions of heartbeat messages. This value should be at least half of the Node Timeout value. The default value of one second is used in this scenario.

Node Timeout: the number of seconds the network manager will take to determine that a node has become unavailable. The higher this value is set, the slower cluster reformations will occur, but a lower value can result in more frequent reformations due to temporary network or system utilization spikes. The node timeout is set to four seconds in this scenario.

Autostart Timeout: the amount of time a node will wait before it stops trying to join a cluster. This value should be set to at least the amount of time it takes for the slowest booting system to boot. The default value of 600, or 10 minutes, is used in this example.

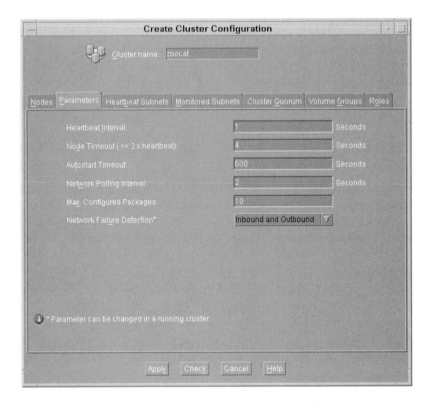

Figure 16-6 Serviceguard Manager Parameter Configuration Screen

Network Polling Interval: the frequency with which network devices being managed by the Serviceguard network manager are checked to ensure that they are able to send and receive data. The default value of 2 seconds is used in this case.

Max Configured Packages: the maximum number of packages that can be configured in the cluster. This value cannot be changed while the cluster is running, so it is important to set this value high enough during the initial configuration. The default value of 10 is used in this scenario.

Network Failure Detection: the algorithm used by the Serviceguard network manager to determine when a network device has failed and should be replaced by a standby interface. The default value of Inbound and Outbound is used for this scenario. This setting tells Serviceguard to count the inbound and outbound network failures separately and to declare a card down only when both values have reached a critical level. The alternate choice tells Serviceguard to combine the inbound and outbound network failures and declare a card down when the total number of failures has reached a critical level.

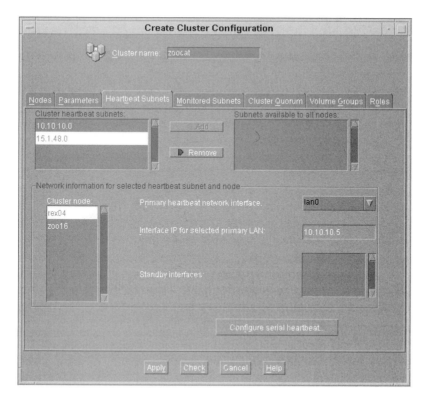

Figure 16-7 Serviceguard Manager Heartbeat Subnet Configuration

The screen shown in Figure 16-7 provides an interface to specify the heartbeat subnets for the cluster. In this example, both the 10.10.10.0 and 15.1.48.0 networks will be used as heartbeat networks. The 10.10.10.0 subnet is dedicated to the cluster heartbeat and the 15.1.48.0 network is used as a secondary carrier.

The lower portion of the screen provides the ability to specify which network interface should be used as the primary heartbeat network. In this scenario, rex04 will use lan0 as the primary network interface because it is connected to the 10.10.10.0 dedicated heartbeat network. For zoo16, lan2 is selected because it is also connected to the 10.10.10.0 network. There are no standby interfaces on either system, so that field is left blank.

The screen shown in Figure 16-8 provides the ability to specify additional subnets that will be monitored by Serviceguard to ensure that they are functioning properly. In this example, both of the subnets used by the cluster nodes are used as heartbeat subnets, so there is no need to configure them again in the Monitored Subnets tab. In fact, only networks that are not configured to be heartbeat subnets appear in this screen.

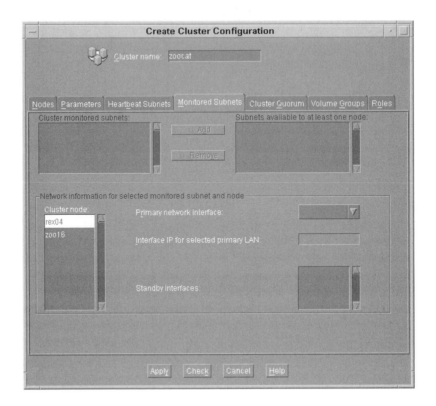

Figure 16-8 Serviceguard Manager Monitored Subnets
Configuration

The next task is configuring the cluster quorum as shown in Figure 16-9. This scenario uses a quorum server that is running on a separate node, zoo7. Here the hostname for the quorum server is specified and the polling interval is configured. This value is how frequently the quorum server will be polled to ensure that it is available. Finally, a timeout extension can be specified that provides a grace period when the quorum server can be unavailable without being marked as down.

The next tab is for configuring Volume Groups. In this example, there are no shared cluster volume groups, so the tab is left blank. The final tab that requires information when you are creating a cluster is the Roles tab. This tab can be used to give non-root users the ability to

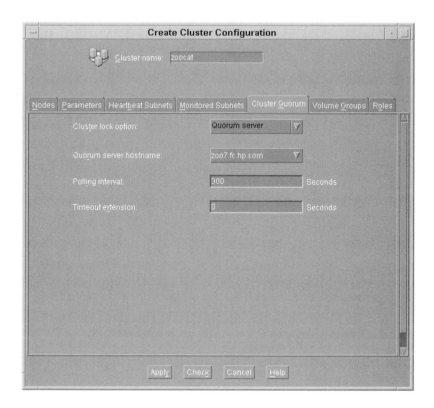

Figure 16-9 Serviceguard Cluster Quorum Configuration

perform administrative duties on the cluster. Figure 16-10 shows that a non-root user, bryanj, has been granted cluster-wide administrative privileges. User roles are added by clicking on the Add button and then specifying the following information:

Role: the three choices are Monitor, Admin all packages, or Admin cluster-wide. The Monitor role provides read-only access for the specified user or set of users. The Admin all packages role enables users to monitor and perform administrative duties on the packages, such as moving, halting, and starting packages. Admin cluster-wide provides full read-write access to the cluster and package configuration and administration tasks.

User: a specific user name or a generic choice of Any authenticated user. The Any authenticated user option is useful for giving all authenticated users on the system monitor privileges, for example.

Host: specifies which host should allow the access. This can be configured to be a specific Serviceguard node, any node in the cluster, or any Serviceguard node.

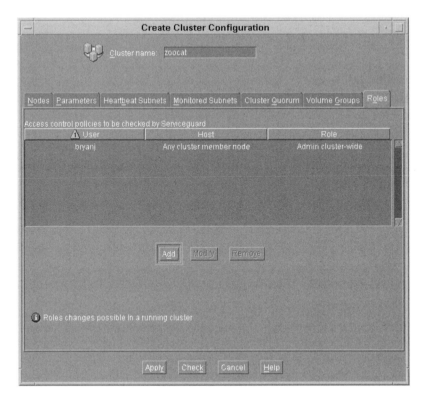

Figure 16-10 Serviceguard Manager Roles Configuration

In this scenario, the user bryanj has cluster-wide administrative privileges from any node in the zoocat cluster. The final step in configuring the cluster is to perform a validation of the cluster's configuration.

The screen shown in Figure 16-11 is the Operation Log detailing the process of checking the configuration for the zoocat cluster. This task can be initiated at any time during the configuration process by clicking on the Check button at the bottom of the screen to verify the inputs that have been specified. In addition, if the cluster is being configured by editing the configuration file directly, then the following command can be used to check the configuration file:

```
# cmcheckconf -v -k -C /etc/cmcluster/zoocat.ascii
```

As the output from the command shows, there are no errors in this configuration, so it can be safely applied to all of the nodes in the cluster.

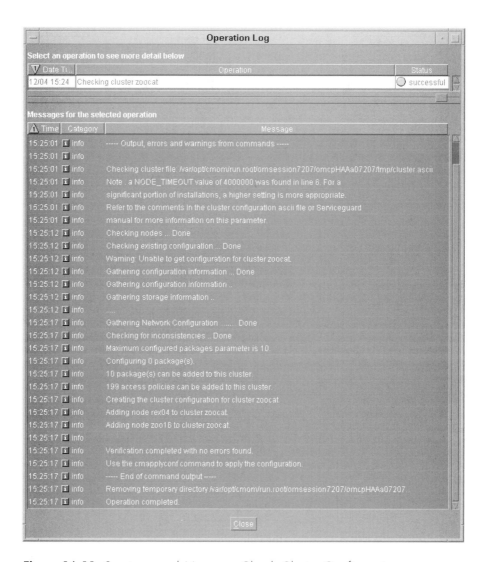

Figure 16-11 Serviceguard Manager Check Cluster Configuration

Figure 16-12 shows the main Serviceguard Manager screen after the Apply button on the cluster configuration dialog has been clicked. When editing the configuration file directly, use the following command to apply the configuration to all nodes in the cluster:

```
# cmapplyconf -f -v -C /etc/cmcluster/zoocat.ascii
```

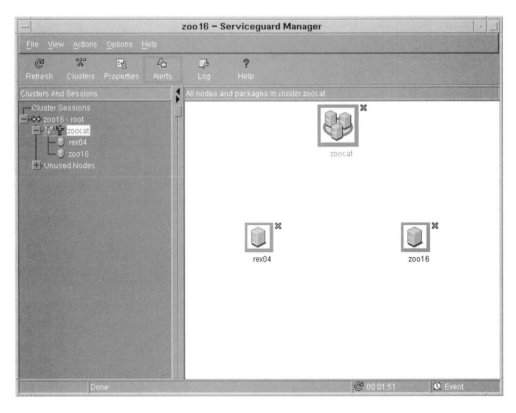

Figure 16-12 Serviceguard Manager Inactive Cluster View

This screen shown in Figure 16-12 illustrates the cluster and the two nodes that are part of the cluster. Currently the cluster and all of the nodes are in the down state because the cluster has not been started.

Before demonstrating the process of configuring a package for the cluster, a quick look at the configuration file generated by Serviceguard Manager is warranted. The file shown in Listing 16-1 shows the textual configuration of the cluster.

Listing 16-1 Serviceguard Cluster Configuration File

```
# cat /etc/cmclcuster/zoocat.ascii
CLUSTER_NAME    zoocat
HEARTBEAT_INTERVAL      1000000
AUTO_START_TIMEOUT        600000000
MAX_CONFIGURED_PACKAGES 10
NETWORK_POLLING_INTERVAL        2000000
NODE_TIMEOUT    4000000
NETWORK_FAILURE_DETECTION       INOUT
NODE_NAME rex04
```

```
NETWORK_INTERFACE lan0
  HEARTBEAT_IP 10.10.10.5
NETWORK_INTERFACE lan900
  HEARTBEAT_IP 15.1.49.180
NODE_NAME zoo16
  NETWORK_INTERFACE lan2
  HEARTBEAT_IP 10.10.10.6
  NETWORK_INTERFACE lan900
  HEARTBEAT_IP 15.1.51.53
QS_HOST zoo7.fc.hp.com
QS_POLLING_INTERVAL     300000000
USER_NAME bryanj
USER_HOST CLUSTER_MEMBER_NODE
USER_ROLE full_admin
```

Package Toolkit Configuration

The next step in configuring the cluster is preparing the application to run as part of a Serviceguard package. In this scenario, the Tomcat server will run within the package. This section applies specifically to the Tomcat application; however, it is shown as an example of the general procedures that must be followed to run an application within a Serviceguard package. Every application will have unique configuration files and startup/shutdown scripts.

The Serviceguard application includes several toolkits that are delivered in the /opt/cmcluster/toolkit directory. The standard toolkits provided with Serviceguard facilitate integration with Oracle, Tomcat, and other applications. To use the Tomcat toolkit, copy all of the files under /opt/cmcluster/toolkit/tomcat to the /etc/cmcluster/pkg/tomcat_pkg directory. Then you can customize the files without polluting the original files.

The Tomcat directory includes a configuration file; several scripts for starting, stopping, and monitoring Tomcat; and a file containing documentation for the toolkit. The first file of interest is the hatomcat.conf file, which is shown in Listing 16-2. This file is used to define the home and base directories for the Tomcat server. Additionally, the Java home directory is specified in this file. The remaining parameters in the file need not be modified unless the environment requires you to do so. Once you have updated the configuration file, execute the /etc/cmcluster/pkg/tomcat_pkg/toolkit.sh script specifying the start and stop parameters to ensure that Tomcat can be started and stopped using the toolkit scripts. You should correct all errors associated with running the command before you continue with the configuration of the package. After the script is functioning properly, it is crucial to copy the script and the configuration files to the exact same location on all of the nodes in the cluster and ensure that they have the appropriate permissions set.

Important

> Before continuing, it is vital that you copy the package toolkit configuration files to all nodes in the cluster. Failure to do so will cause the package to fail during a package migration. Regardless of which package or toolkit you are using, each node must have a copy of all associated scripts and configuration files necessary to run the package.

Listing 16-2 Tomcat HA Toolkit

```
# cat /etc/cmcluster/pkg/tomcat_pkg/hatomcat.conf
#!/usr/bin/sh
#########################################################
# HA Tomcat Toolkit User Configuration Script
# Version: B.02.11
###################################################
# This script contains a list of predefined variables
# that the toolkit user must assign proper values on
# them. With no function and running statement in it,
# this script purely provides the user a simple format
# of configuration data and, eventually, will be
# included by the toolkit main script in order to run
# toolkit functions.
#
# This script includes all user configuration features
# and it is the only toolkit interface to the user.
###################################################

# Define the Catalina Home directory. This is the base
# directory where Tomcat is installed. /opt/hpws/tomcat
# is the default installation location

CATALINA_HOME=/tomcat/opt/hpws/tomcat

# Define the Catalina base directory. This is the
# base directory where Tomcat configuration files
# like server.xml reside. To know more please refer
# Tomcat configuration guide. If this is not defined
# the toolkit will use CATALINA_HOME as the base
# directory. This should be unique for each tomcat
# instance and usually residing on the shared disk

CATALINA_BASE=/tomcat/opt/hpws/tomcat

# The userid used to start the tomcat daemon. It can
# be either www or root.  No other user can start
# tomcat. It is advisable  that tomcat is not started
# as root since it may lead to security vulnerabilities

TOMCAT_USER=www
```

```
# Base directory of Java Development kit. This software
# is a pre-requisite for
#running Tomcat
```

JAVA_HOME=/opt/java1.4

```
# Maintenance  flag is used to bring this toolkit
# into maintenance  mode.  If set to yes then this
# will enable maintenance feature in the toolkit.
# Tomcat Toolkit will look out for a file
# "tomcat.debug" in the tomcat package file directory
# where all the tomcat toolkit files reside.  If the
# file exists monitoring is paused,  tomcat can be
# brought down for maintenance and package would
# not be failed over to the adoptive node even though
# tomcat instance has been brought down for maintenance.
# After the maintenance work, it is the user's
# responsibility to make sure that Tomcat is brought
# up properly.  You should delete the file
# "tomcat.debug" in the package directory.  This
# would enable toolkit to continue monitoring Tomcat
# server  application.
#
# Note if Maintenance flag is set to "no" then the
# above feature would not be available.

MAINTENANCE_FLAG="yes"


# Define the parameters for monitor process.
# You can either use default or alternative values
# for the following three variables. Uncomment and
# update the variable values if you want to alter them.

# This is the tomcat server listening port. This is
# configured in the configuration file
# $CATALINA_BASE/conf/server.xml. The toolkit checks the
# existence of tomcat process by periodically checking
# whether this port is listening. If multiple instances
# of tomcat are configured then this port needs be unique
# for each instance.

MONITOR_PORT=8081

# The interval (in seconds) between checking if Tomcat
# server daemon is up and running. The default setting
# is 5 seconds.

MONITOR_INTERVAL=5

# The number of times to attempt to check the tomcat
# server daemon before giving up and  exiting. The default
# setting is 2 times.

RETRY_TIMES=2
```

After configuring Tomcat to start and stop using the Serviceguard toolkit scripts, update the default Tomcat configuration file, /etc/rc.config.d/hpws_tomcat, to prevent Tomcat from being started when the operating system is booted. Failure to perform this step could result in two instances of Tomcat attempting to use the same network port, which will cause the second instance to fail during startup.

The final step in configuring Tomcat to run in a Serviceguard package is to add an alias for the Serviceguard package's IP address. In this example, the package will be assigned the IP address that resolves to the hostname zoo14.fc.hp.com. Since clients will be connecting to the Tomcat server using the package IP address or hostname rather than the address of zoo16 or rex04, you must configure the server to respond to the requests. To configure Tomcat with the package hostname, the following text is added to the /tomcat/opt/hpws/tomcat/conf/server.xml configuration file.

```
[...]
    <!- Define the default virtual host ->
    <Host name="localhost" debug="0" appBase="webapps"
     unpackWARs="true" autoDeploy="true">

       <Alias>zoo14.fc.hp.com</Alias>
[...]
```

Creating a Serviceguard Package

After configuring the Tomcat application to run within a Serviceguard package, the next step is to configure the package so it uses the newly customized configuration files. Figure 16-13 shows the Serviceguard Manager screen with the Create Package menu item, which is available from the Actions menu. As with the cluster configuration process, instead of using Serviceguard Manager to create the package configuration, the tasks can be performed from the command line and by manually editing the configuration files. To create a configuration template, the following command can be used:

```
# cmmakepkg -p /etc/cmcluster/tomcat_pkg/tomcat_pkg.config
```

After creating the package template, it must be manually edited according to the needs of the package.

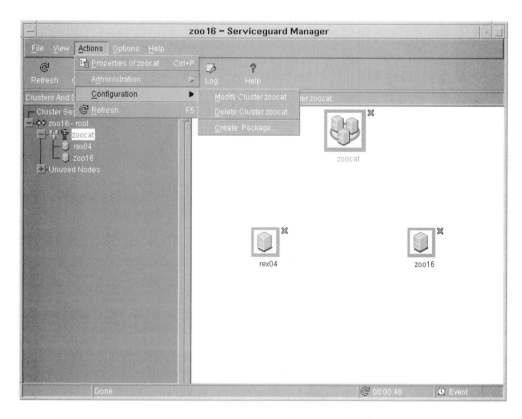

Figure 16-13 Serviceguard Manager with Newly Created Cluster

The screen shown in Figure 16-14 provides the ability to configure the name of the package, which is specified as tomcat_pkg in this scenario. Also shown in this screen is the Nodes tab, which provides the ability to specify which nodes the package will run on and the order in which nodes will be selected. Both zoo16 and rex04 can host the package, and zoo16 is placed at the top of the list so it is the primary node. The adoptive node will be rex04.

The next tab is for configuring the parameters of the package. The following parameters can be specified for each package:

Package auto run allows a package to be started automatically when the cluster starts on the first available node. This option also allows the package to be started automatically on an adoptive node if the primary node experiences a failure. If this option is not selected, the package will require manual intervention to start and migrate when a node fails.

Local LAN failover enables Serviceguard to transfer the package's IP address to a standby network interface. In this example, the checkbox is selected, but it has no effect on the configuration because there are no standby network adapters in either node.

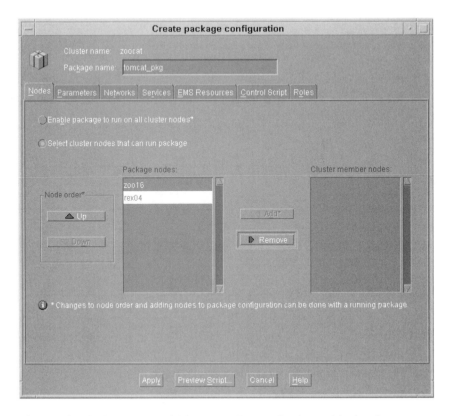

Figure 16-14 Serviceguard Manager Create Package Nodes Screen

Node fail fast tells Serviceguard to issue a transfer of control (TOC) in the system when a failure occurs. This setting causes an abrupt termination on the node that experiences a failure but allows the package to be started on an alternate node more quickly.

Failover policy is used to determine which node will be used when starting a package. The default, using the configured node policy, uses the nodes listed on the Nodes tab in order starting from the top. The alternate choice, min package node, uses the node with the fewest number of packages running to host the package.

Failback policy lets you specify what action Serviceguard should take when the package is not running on the primary node but the primary node is capable of running the package. For example, if the primary node fails and the package is moved to an adoptive node, this setting dictates the action Serviceguard should take when the primary node is restored. By default, the package must be migrated back to the primary node manually. However, it can be set to automatic, in which case Serviceguard would migrate the package back to the primary node as soon as it becomes available.

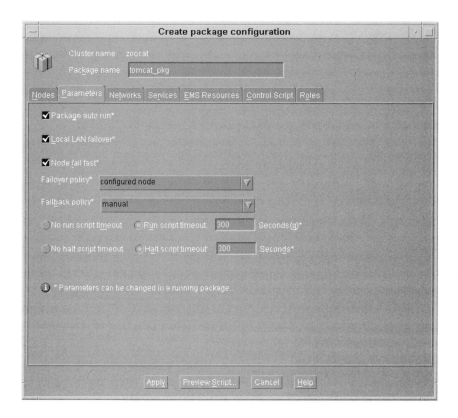

Figure 16-15 Serviceguard Manager Package Parameters Screen

Run script timeout provides a mechanism to limit the amount of time a script should be allowed to run before it is regarded as failed.

Halt script timeout is similar to the Run script timeout except that it applies to the time allowed for the halt script to run before it is regarded as failed.

The next step is to configure the networks to be used by the package. The screen in Figure 16-16 shows the available networks in the zoocat cluster. The 15.1.48.0 network has been selected because it will be the only network used for the package. (Remember that the 10.10.10.0 network is dedicated as the heartbeat network.)

The bottom portion of the screen is used to configure the IP address to be associated with the package. In this case, zoo14.fc.hp.com, or 15.1.51.51, is assigned to the package. This IP address is input in the Specify IP address on the subnet field and then added to the list of Configured IP Addresses by clicking on the Add button.

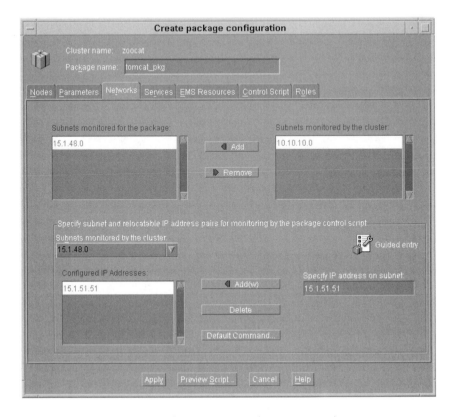

Figure 16-16 Serviceguard Manager Package Networks Screen

The next step in configuring the package is to specify the services to be associated with the package. The screen in Figure 16-17 shows the list of services associated with the package. Selecting a service from the list and then clicking on the modify button allows a service to be edited. Clicking on the Add button results in the dialog shown in Figure 16-35, which allows a new service to be created for the package.

The dialog shown in Figure 16-18 provides the settings for configuring a package service. The following options are available in this dialog:

Service fail fast determines whether Serviceguard should treat the failure of the service as the failure of the node. Since this option is selected for the Tomcat package, Serviceguard will reboot the node if the service fails and will perform a transfer of control (TOC) on the node if the reboot does not correct the issue.

Service halt timeout is used when a service is being halted. The amount of time specified in this field is the number of seconds Serviceguard will wait after the service has been sent the SIGTERM signal before sending the SIGKILL signal.

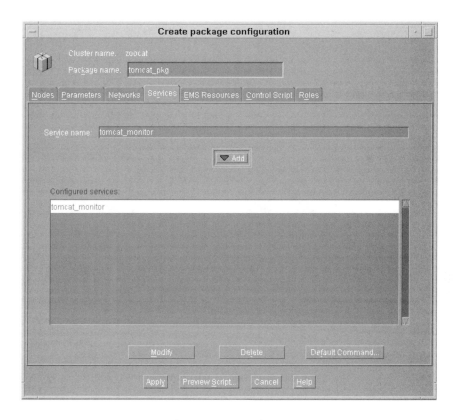

Figure 16-17 Serviceguard Manager Package Services Screen

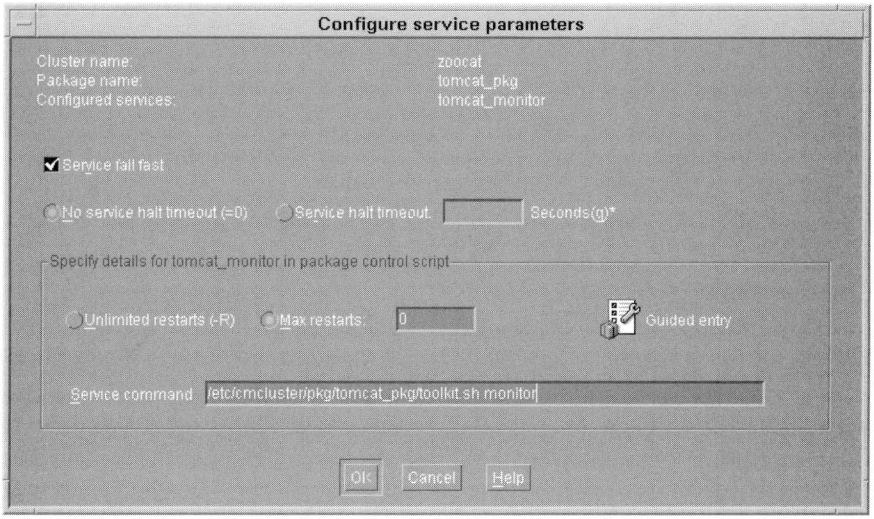

Figure 16-18 Serviceguard Manager Service Parameters Screen

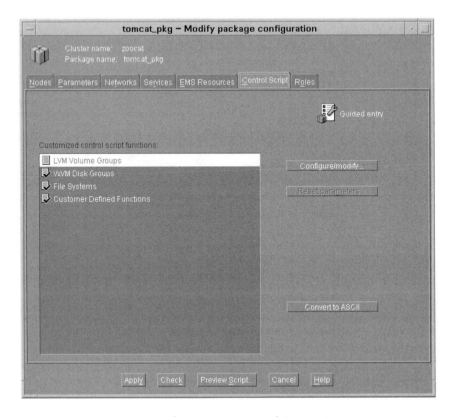

Figure 16-19 Serviceguard Manager Control Scripts Screen

Number of restarts is the number of times Serviceguard should attempt to start the service when starting the package.

Service command is the command-line interface that starts the service. This scenario uses the command that is part of the Tomcat toolkit with the `monitor` option. This service will periodically check to ensure that the Tomcat server process is running and that the application is listening on the network port.

The next tab specifies EMS Resources to be monitored by Serviceguard. In this example scenario, there are no EMS resources specified as a package dependency, so the screen is left blank.

The next tab is the Control Script tab, which is used to customize the control script for the package. The control script can be customized to specify the LVM volume groups, VxVM disk groups, and file systems. In addition, customer-defined functions can be implemented, which are generally used to start and stop the package. There are no LVM groups associated with the Tomcat package in this scenario so there are no customizations necessary for that portion of the script. Each of the other three possible customization choices are selected; the next step is to click on the Configure/modify button for each customization.

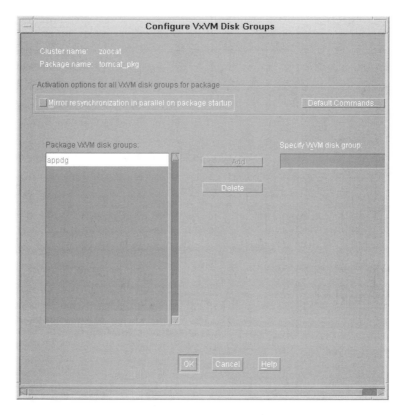

Figure 16-20 Serviceguard Manager Disk Group Screen

The screen shown in Figure 16-20 shows the settings for the VxVM disk groups. In this example, the name of the package VxVM disk group is appdg. This value is input into the Specify VxVM disk group field and then the Add button is clicked on to add it as a package VxVM disk group. The Mirror resynchronization in parallel on package startup option specifies that Serviceguard should not wait for a problem with a disk mirror to be corrected before starting the package. In most cases the default value, unchecked, should be used for this setting.

The next customization of the control script is shown in Figure 16-21. This dialog allows you to specify which file systems are associated with the package. Options are also available that let you tune file system checking and mount operations that are performed when migrating the package.

The table in the lower half of the dialog lists the file systems that will be mounted when the package is activated. Clicking on the Add button allows additional file systems to be appended to the list. Values for each of the columns shown in the table can be specified when associating a new file system with the package.

The final customization of the control script for customer defined functions is shown in Figure 16-22. In this example, the script that was provided as part of the Tomcat toolkit is specified

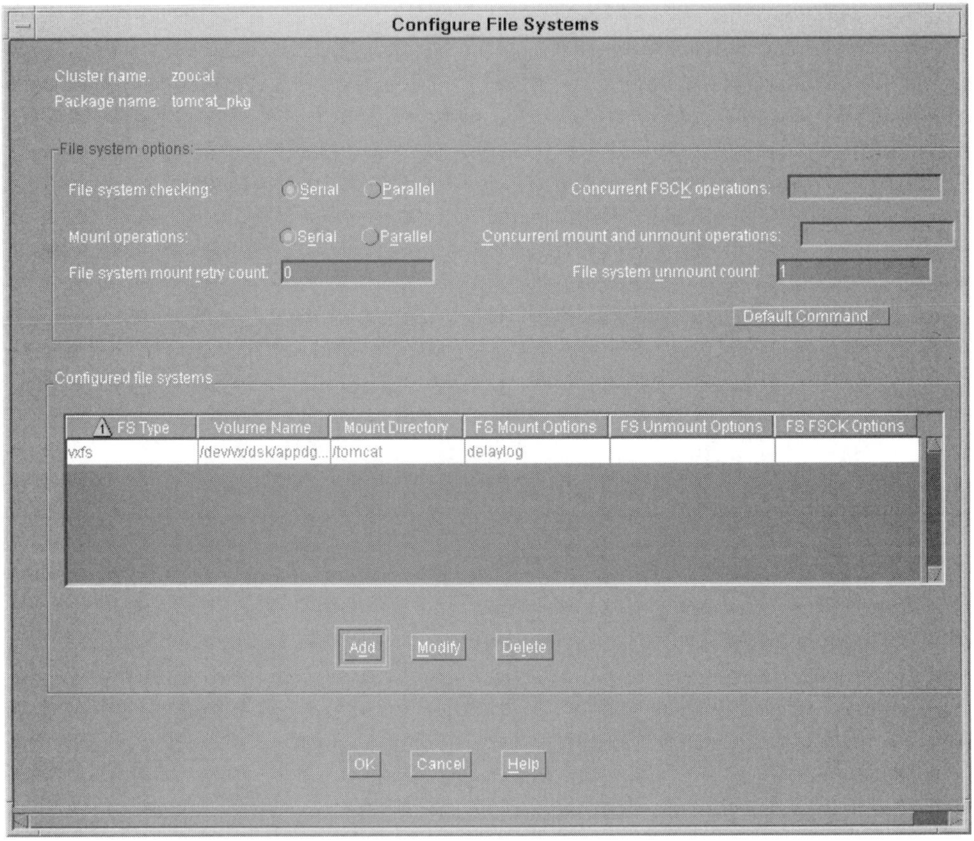

Figure 16-21 Serviceguard Manager File System Screen

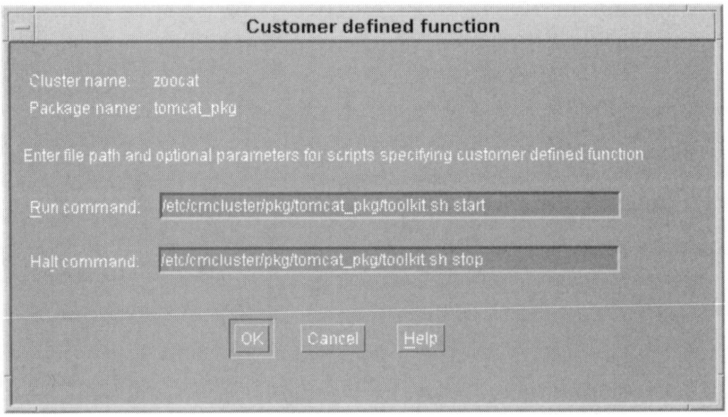

Figure 16-22 Serviceguard Manager Run and Halt Package Commands

to start and stop Tomcat. These are the same commands that have already been verified to properly start and stop the Tomcat server.

The final option provided as part of configuring the package is the Roles tab. This screen is used to define package specific roles in addition to those that may have already been configured at the cluster level. The roles configured in this section apply only to the package, whereas those shown previously can apply to the entire cluster. For this scenario, no package specific roles will be defined.

At this point, you can click on the Preview Script button to look at the script before you apply it to the nodes in the cluster. In addition, the Check button tells Serviceguard to perform verifications on the generated configuration file. If you are manually editing the configuration file, you can checked it by executing the following command:

```
# cmcheckconf -v -P /etc/cmcluster/tomcat_pkg/tomcat_pkg.config
```

The next step is to apply the configuration to all of the nodes in the cluster. Clicking on the Apply button will deploy the package configuration and script to all the nodes in the cluster. From the command line, you can use the following command to apply the configuration:

```
# cmapplyconf -v -f -P /etc/cmcluster/tomcat_pkg/tomcat_pkg.config
```

The package configuration has now been distributed to each of the nodes in the cluster. The content of the package configuration file is shown in Listing 16-3. Upon careful inspection of this file a common question is, "Where are all of the settings that were specified in Serviceguard Manager for starting and stopping Tomcat?" The answer to this question is shown in Listing 16-4, which is the package control script that is also created as part of the Serviceguard Manager package configuration process.

Listing 16-3 Serviceguard Package Configuration File

```
# cat /etc/cmcluster/tomcat_pkg:
PACKAGE_NAME tomcat_pkg
PACKAGE_TYPE FAILOVER
FAILOVER_POLICY CONFIGURED_NODE
FAILBACK_POLICY MANUAL
NODE_NAME zoo16
NODE_NAME rex04
AUTO_RUN YES
LOCAL_LAN_FAILOVER_ALLOWED YES
NODE_FAIL_FAST_ENABLED YES
RUN_SCRIPT /etc/cmcluster/tomcat_pkg/tomcat_pkg.sdf.sh
RUN_SCRIPT_TIMEOUT 300
HALT_SCRIPT /etc/cmcluster/tomcat_pkg/tomcat_pkg.sdf.sh
HALT_SCRIPT_TIMEOUT 300
SERVICE_NAME tomcat_monitor
SERVICE_FAIL_FAST_ENABLED NO
SERVICE_HALT_TIMEOUT 0
SUBNET 15.1.48.0
```

The file shown in Listing 16-4 is the control script that will be executed when starting and stopping the package. This file contains not only the variables but also the commands that are used. A template for the control script can be created using the following command line and manually editing the file instead of using Serviceguard Manager:

```
# cmmakepkg -s /etc/cmcluster/tomcat_pkg/tomcat_pkg.sdf.sh
```

Listing 16-4 Serviceguard Package Control Script

```
# cat /etc/cmcluster/tomcat_pkg/tomcat_pkg.sdf.sh
[...]

. ${SGCONFFILE:=/etc/cmcluster.conf}

# Set PATH to reference the appropriate directories.
PATH=$SGSBIN:/usr/bin:/usr/sbin:/etc:/bin

# CVM DISK GROUP ACTIVATION:
CVM_ACTIVATION_CMD="vxdg -g \$DiskGroup set activation=exclusivewrite"

# VxVM DISK GROUPS
VXVM_DG[0]=appdg

# FILESYSTEMS
FS_FSCK_OPT[0]=""
LV[0]="/dev/vx/dsk/appdg/tomcatvol"
FS[0]="/tomcat"
FS_TYPE[0]="vxfs"
FS_MOUNT_OPT[0]="";
FS_UMOUNT_OPT[0]="";
FS_FSCK_OPT[0]=""

# VOLUME RECOVERY
VXVOL="vxvol -g \$DiskGroup startall"        # Default

# FILESYSTEM UNMOUNT COUNT
FS_UMOUNT_COUNT=1

# FILESYSTEM MOUNT RETRY COUNT.
FS_MOUNT_RETRY_COUNT=0

CONCURRENT_VGCHANGE_OPERATIONS=1
CONCURRENT_FSCK_OPERATIONS=1
CONCURRENT_MOUNT_AND_UMOUNT_OPERATIONS=1
```

```
IP[0]=15.1.51.51
SUBNET[0]=15.1.48.0

# SERVICE NAMES AND COMMANDS.
SERVICE_NAME[0]=tomcat_monitor
SERVICE_CMD[0]="/etc/cmcluster/pkg/tomcat_pkg/toolkit.sh monitor"
SERVICE_RESTART[0]=""

function customer_defined_run_cmds
{
  /etc/cmcluster/pkg/tomcat_pkg/toolkit.sh start
  test_return 51
}

function customer_defined_halt_cmds
{
  /etc/cmcluster/pkg/tomcat_pkg/toolkit.sh stop
  test_return 52
}
[...]
```

Activating the Cluster

The cluster and the Tomcat package have both been created and applied to all of the nodes in the cluster. However, the cluster is still not active and the package is not running. The screen shown in Figure 16-23 shows the cluster, each of the nodes in the cluster, and the package. To start the cluster, the Run cluster zoocat item is selected from the Actions menu. This command starts the cluster and the package since the auto run option was specified for the Tomcat package. As an alternative to using Serviceguard Manager, the following command can be used to start the cluster:

```
# cmruncl -v
```

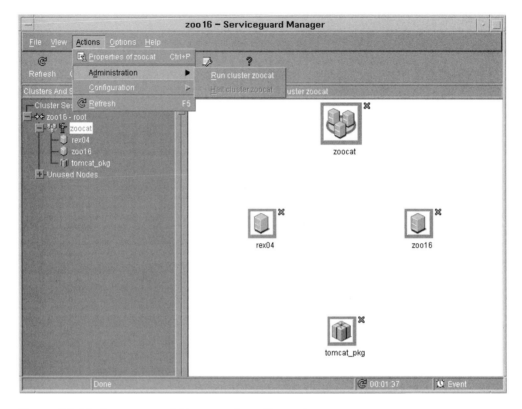

Figure 16-23 Serviceguard Manager Run Cluster Action

The screen shown in Figure 16-24 depicts the cluster and the package as both being active. As is evident from the tree hierarchy, the tomcat_pkg is running on the primary node, zoo16.

Alternatively, the command line can be used to view the status of the cluster and the package, as shown in Listing 16-5.

Listing 16-5 Serviceguard Cluster Status from Command Line

```
# cmviewcl

CLUSTER          STATUS
zoocat           up

   NODE          STATUS         STATE
   rex04         up             running
   zoo16         up             running

      PACKAGE      STATUS       STATE       AUTO_RUN      NODE
      tomcat_pkg   up           running     enabled       zoo1
```

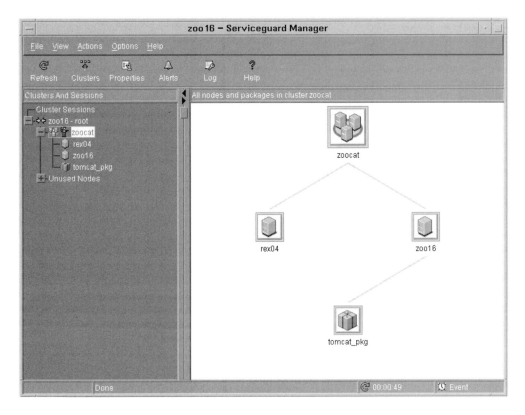

Figure 16-24 Serviceguard Manager with Cluster and Package Active

At this point, the cluster and package are both running. In order to ensure that the package will operate as expected in a failure situation, HP highly recommends that you go through a series of tests to ensure that the cluster and the package behave as expected.

Testing the Cluster

Testing of the cluster is a very important step to ensure that the package behaves as expected. A simple configuration error could cause the package to fail to start on an adoptive node when the primary node fails. The screen shown in Figure 16-25 is a simple web page accessed through the Tomcat server. Notice that the URL (which is internal to HP) in the browser window contains zoo14, which is the package's hostname. Also notice that the content of the page shows the server that is running the Tomcat application. In this case, the server is running on zoo16.

In Serviceguard Manager, you can use the Move package to node item on the Action menu to test whether the package can be migrated to rex04. If the command is successful, the package

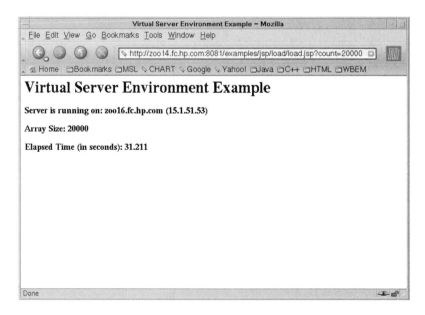

Figure 16-25 Example Page When Tomcat Package Is Running on Primary Node

will be quickly migrated to rex04. From the command line, the package can be moved by executing the following three commands:

```
# cmhaltpkg -v tomcat_pkg
# cmrunpkg -v -n rex04 tomcat_pkg
# cmmodpkg -e tomcat_pkg
```

The screen shown in Figure 16-26 demonstrates the extreme power Serviceguard provides. Notice that the URL in the browser is identical, but the web page now shows that the Tomcat server is running on rex04 instead of zoo16. In the situation where zoo16 has failed, users will see little, if any affect because the package will be quickly started on rex04.

After you have completed the cursory test that ensures that the package can be moved from one node to another, you should perform several additional tests. These tests are based on simulating hardware failures. Testing of each network card should be performed by individually unplugging the network cable to each of the network cards. The cluster should continue to function, even when a cable has been removed from one network card. Storage should be tested to ensure that each of the disks can be removed and the package can continue to function. Finally, power circuits should be tested to ensure that a failure of a single circuit will not affect more of the cluster than expected.

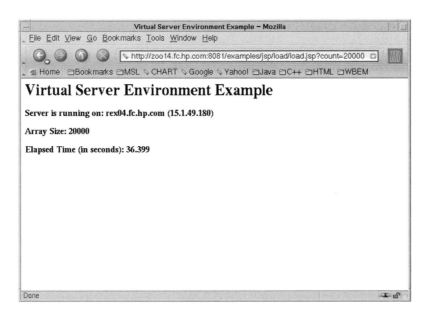

Figure 16-26 Example Page When Tomcat Package Is Running on Adoptive Node

Summary

Since my initial encounter with the NASA engineer who told the story about engineers wearing both a belt and suspenders, I've learned that the phrase is commonly used when referring to systems designed with a high degree of fault tolerance and redundancy. HP Serviceguard provides the belt and suspenders for workloads. Serviceguard clusters can be configured to host numerous packages and regardless of whether a node experiences a failure, the package can continue operations on an adoptive node. The result is highly available workloads with hardware and software fault tolerance.

Serviceguard can be configured in large or small clusters. As was shown in this chapter, a cluster can be configured in an environment as simple as a primary node and an adoptive node. The example scenario showed how to configure the cluster and the Serviceguard package using both Serviceguard Manager and the command line. Several toolkits are provided to ease the integration of Serviceguard with several enterprise applications.

Serviceguard has an extremely powerful set of capabilities. The key to success when implementing a Serviceguard cluster is proper planning. If the appropriate steps are taken to plan the cluster, implementation is greatly facilitated. In addition, proper hardware planning and configuration is crucial to the availability of workloads.

Within HP's Virtual Server Environment, Serviceguard provides the tools to ensure that your workloads are wearing both a belt and suspenders.

17

Virtualization Manager

Chapter Overview

Every year approximately 8 million commercial airline flights transport more than 500 million passengers across the United States.[1] The aircraft form a web of traffic across the skies, congregating at various hubs throughout the country. At every intersection in the web of airline traffic are the air traffic controllers, who see to it the airline passengers and cargo are safely sent on their way and received without incident. Air traffic controllers rely on several tools to keep the airplanes safely traveling the skies. Among the most central is the Final Approach Spacing Tool (FAST).[2] This software tool brings together several components that are critical for maintaining safe and reliable air travel. For example, the FAST software integrates the radar and weather systems. Additionally, the FAST tool has integrated components that analyze the route and trajectory of each aircraft. The FAST tool brings numerous technologies that have existed individually for long periods of time together under a single interface. Using this tool, air traffic controllers are able to more efficiently and safely use the available airspace and ground support resources while ensuring that aircraft and passengers arrive safely at their destinations.

HP's Virtualization Manager is similar in many ways to the FAST tool. Virtualization Manager is a set of graphical user interfaces and technologies that bring the technologies in HP's Virtual Server Environment together into a single console. Administrators using Virtualization Manager have all the information they need to deploy workloads, monitor applications, and maintain the health of the datacenter. Like the air traffic controllers who rely on FAST to safely direct aircraft, administrators who depend on Virtualization Manager are better equipped to efficiently utilize hardware resources while ensuring that workloads meet their service-level objectives.

---

[1] USA Department of Transportation press release, "October Airline Traffic: Ten-Month Domestic Traffic," available at http://www.bts.gov/press_releases/2005/bts004_05/html/bts004_05.html.

[2] Center-TRACON Automation System under Dr. Dallas Denery, "Final Approach Spacing Tool," available at http://www.ctas.arc.nasa.gov/project_description/fast.html.

Virtualization Manager is integrated into the HP Systems Insight Manager (SIM) product that has been available for several years. Because of Virtualization Manager tight integration with HP SIM, this chapter discusses several features of HP SIM in concert with the discussion of Virtualization Manager.

This chapter begins by discussing the most commonly used terminology relating to HP SIM and the VSE management suite. Next, the chapter provides an architectural overview of the VSE management suite. It concludes with a detailed tour of HP SIM and the VSE management suite.

It should be noted this chapter was written using pre-release versions of the VSE management suite and HP Systems Insight Manager. Some of the screens shown in this chapter will vary slightly from the final products.

Virtualization Manager Terminology

HP Systems Insight Manager (HP SIM): a centralized management tool that provides consistent multisystem management capabilities. Virtualization Manager is tightly integrated with HP SIM; as a result, all of the features available from HP SIM are also readily available when using the VSE management suite.

Central Management Server (CMS): the central server in the management domain that is running the HP SIM and Virtualization Manager software packages. Most of the operations performed by Virtualization Manager are initiated from the CMS.

Management Domain: the set of managed systems that have been placed under the control of HP SIM and Virtualization Manager. Virtualization Manager's management domain is a subset of HP SIM, as Virtualization Manager provides management capabilities for only HP 9000 and HP Integrity servers.

Managed System: a system under the control of HP SIM. Managed systems have trust relationships with the CMS that enable administrators to configure and monitor the managed systems from the CMS.

System List: a set of managed systems that are grouped together for administration purposes. Custom system lists can be created to facilitate system management. Custom system lists may be formed by specifying the set of attributes in a query, such as "all HP-UX servers," or by selecting a specific list of servers, such as "server A, server B, etc."

Workload: a collection of processes within an OS image running on a managed system whose performance is managed as a single unit. Examples include the processes that belong to an application or all processes owned by a specific user.

System Page: a summary page provided by HP SIM that provides information and links for a system in the management domain.

User-Based Security: a feature in HP SIM that enables administrators to delegate management duties by providing granular control over which users can perform which tasks on which systems. Virtualization Manager takes advantage of user-based security so that each administrator can be granted permission to perform management tasks on the systems for which they are responsible.

Virtualization Manager Overview

Virtualization Manager is a web-based system administration tool that is tightly integrated with HP SIM. All of the VSE technologies discussed in this book will be supported by Virtualization Manager. The purpose of Virtualization Manager is to provide a consolidated monitoring and administration point for all VSE technologies. Graphical views of system configurations are one of the primary features of the tools. These views depict the relationships between VSE technologies such as the nPartitions that contain virtual machines and the virtual partitions that are being managed by Global Workload Manager (gWLM). The views also depict the systems that contain gWLM PSETS and FSS groups in shared resource domains. In the past, each of these technologies had a technology-specific user interface. However, Virtualization Manager unites these technologies under a single administration console for seamless monitoring and management of VSE technologies.

The HP VSE management software consists of three primary components. The first component, Virtualization Manager, provides visualization and configuration capabilities for all of the VSE technologies. The visualization aspect of this component provides graphical displays of Virtualization Manager's management domain. The configuration aspect of this component provides direct access to each of the VSE management tools. For example, the management tool for Integrity Virtual Machines is seamlessly integrated with Virtualization Manager.

The second primary component of the VSE Management Software is Global Workload Manager, which is discussed in detail in Chapter 19. This component allows policies to be associated with workloads that in turn provide resource controls to ensure that workloads receive the necessary resources while maximizing hardware utilization.

The third and final component of the VSE Management Software is the Capacity Advisor. Capacity Advisor is described in detail in Chapter 18. This component enables capacity planners to analyze historical workload utilization data for the purposes of planning for workload migrations or new workload introductions. Taken in whole, the three components of the VSE management suite provide the capabilities necessary to effectively and efficiently manage a Virtual Server Environment.

Within Virtualization Manager four primary views are available. The first is the System view, which graphically displays the hierarchical layout of the systems in the VSE management domain. The second is the Workload view, which displays a list of workloads in the management domain. This view contains only workloads. Systems that are not directly running workloads, such as VM hosts, are not shown in the Workload view. As another example, if an nPartition complex contains four nPartitions that are each running workloads, then the System view would display the complex and the four nPartitions. On the other hand, the Workload view would display only the four nPartitions because the complex is not running a workload directly. The third view in Virtualization Manager is the Shared Resource Domain view, which displays the systems and workloads being managed by gWLM. The final Virtualization Manager view is the view. This view displays the capacity-planning scenarios that have been created for analysis and planning purposes.

Overview of Architecture of the Management Software

Figure 17-1 shows the management domains relevant to the Management Software. The outermost box indicates the set of systems in HP SIM's management domain. This domain includes a variety of system types such as HP NonStop servers, HP 9000 servers, HP Integrity servers, IA-32 servers, IA-32 workstations, printers, and network switches. HP SIM also supports a variety of operating systems, such as HP-UX, Linux, Windows, OpenVMS, and HP NonStop.

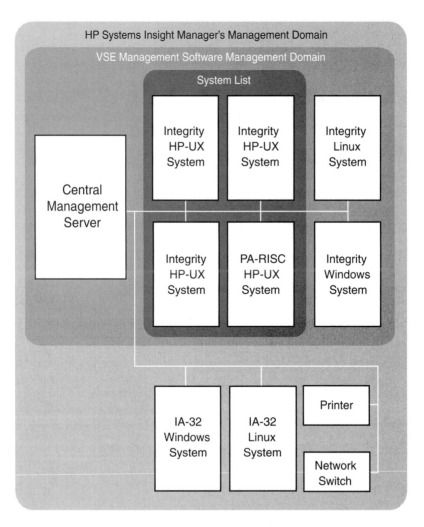

Figure 17-1 HP Systems Insight Manager and VSE Management Domains

The VSE Management Software's management domain is a subset of HP SIM's management domain. HP 9000 and HP Integrity servers are the focus of the VSE Management Software, and thus the management domain for the VSE Management Software is restricted to those hardware platforms. As the diagram indicates, the CMS itself can be part of the management domain. The VSE Management Software supports the HP-UX and Linux operating systems initially, and it will support Windows operating systems in a future revision.

Within the VSE Management Software's domain, the innermost box shown in the diagram depicts a specific set of systems that have been grouped together in a customized system list for management purposes. A system list can be created as a collection of specifically chosen systems or system lists can be defined as a query such that all systems that meet a certain criteria are contained in the list. In Figure 17-1, the four HP-UX servers in the system list could be part of a collection where each system was specifically added to the list. Or the system list could have been defined as a query for all systems running the HP-UX operating system. The difference between the two methods of creating system lists is that HP SIM automatically updates the system lists defined as queries when a new system is added to the management domain, but system lists defined as a collection of systems must be manually updated by the administrator. In the case where four HP-UX servers are specifically added to the collection, a new HP Integrity server running HP-UX that is added to the management domain will not be automatically included in the system list. However, if the system list is defined as a query based on the operating system, adding a new HP Integrity server running HP-UX would result in HP SIM automatically expanding the list to include the new server.

The diagram shown in Figure 17-2 illustrates the communication mechanisms between the HP SIM CMS and the managed systems. Every managed system in the management domain requires that a specific set of software be present and running. The required software varies based on the VSE technologies in use. Generally speaking, a utilization Web-Based Enterprise Management (WBEM) provider tracks resource utilization for processors, memory, disks, and network interfaces. In addition, most VSE technologies have a specific WBEM provider that the VSE Management Software uses to collect status and configuration information from the managed systems. Examples of these technology-specific WBEM providers include nPartition, virtual partition, and virtual machine WBEM providers. In other cases, VSE technologies rely on a proprietary agent on the managed system that provides the capabilities necessary for the technology. gWLM and Serviceguard both rely on such proprietary agents.

In addition to the VSE Management Software GUI, a set of VSE Management Software daemons runs on the CMS. These daemons are responsible for keeping the data on the CMS up to date. Every managed system is also required to have a secure shell SSH server available to allow the remote execution of commands. The VSE Management Software relies on an SSH client on the CMS to execute the VSE Commands on the managed systems when configuration changes are performed.

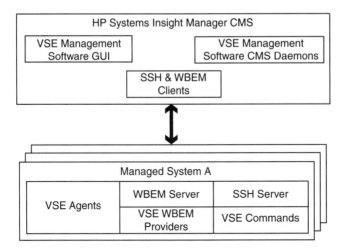

Figure 17-2 Architecture of HP Systems Insight
Manager and VSE Managed Systems

Virtualization Manager Tour

This section provides a high-level tour of Virtualization Manager. Since Virtualization Manager is tightly integrated with HP SIM, the first portion of the tour will cover several fundamental features of HP SIM. Knowledge of these HP SIM features will help you implement and effectively use Virtualization Manager. The discussion below describes configuring the automated system discovery mechanism, creating custom system lists, and defining user-based security authorizations. Following the HP SIM tour, a tour of Virtualization Manager is provided.

HP Systems Insight Manager Tour

The VSE management suite's integration with HP Systems Insight Manager allows many features in HP SIM to be used from within Virtualization Manager. The screen shown in Figure 17-3 is the HP SIM home page. From this page, many properties, actions, and tasks are available. The upper-left-hand pane is the system status area; it contains counters for events received from the management domain. This status pane shows the events that haven't been cleared and provides direct access to the interface where the events can be viewed and addressed. Below the System Status pane is the System Lists. The hierarchy contained in the System Lists pane is one of the primary system navigation mechanisms in HP SIM and Virtualization Manager. Like file explorers, the hierarchy can be expanded until the appropriate collection of systems is found. HP SIM is shipped with a standard hierarchy of system lists, and the lists can be customized based on the requirements of the system administrators. In addition, private lists can be created that

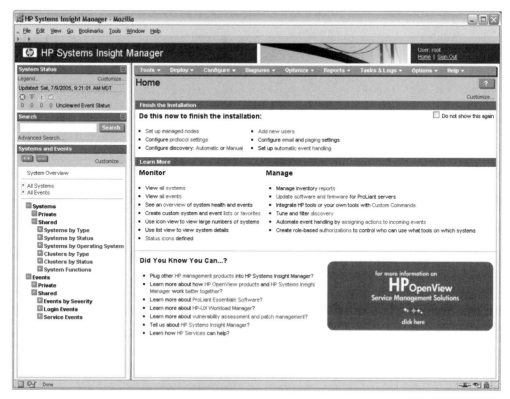

Figure 17-3 HP Systems Insight Manager

are specific to a particular user. This allows each administrator to have a customized management environment.

Immediately below the banner that extends across the top of the screen is the action menu. A vast array of tasks can be invoked from this menu. Tasks such as installing software, generating inventory reports, and launching Virtualization Manager are all available from this menu.

Directly below the action menu is the area of the screen known as the workspace. This area is used by the various tools and components of HP SIM to display the content of the application. This area of the screen is where most administrative duties are performed from within HP SIM. When Virtualization Manager is launched, it occupies all of the HP SIM workspace.

After installing and starting HP SIM, the next step to be performed is configuring the automated system discovery mechanism. The screen shown in Figure 17-4 provides an interface for this purpose. SIM uses the settings defined on the Automatic Discovery page to regularly scan the specified network addresses for systems to be included in the management domain. When new systems are found, they are automatically added to the HP SIM management domain. Furthermore, the inventory information stored in the HP SIM database is updated for existing systems during the automated discovery process. The automatic discovery screen has many options that let

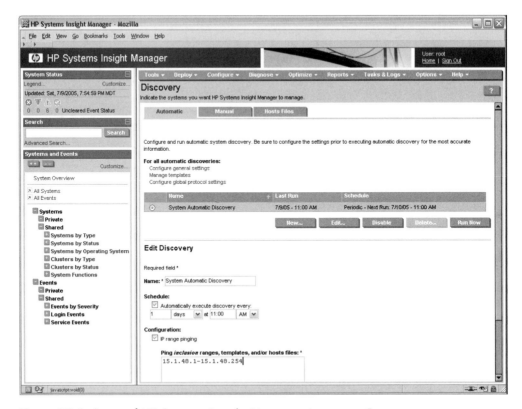

Figure 17-4 Setup of HP Systems Insight Manager Automatic Discovery

users tailor the discovery process according to the requirements of an environment. For example, the protocols used to discover systems and gather system information can be tuned according to each environment's requirements. In general, Simple Network Management Protocol (SNMP) and WBEM are the two services used to gather system information.

When the discovery process is complete, the HP SIM database will contain information for each of the systems found. The contents of the database are then reflected in the System Lists folders. Opening a folder in the System Lists pane displays the discovered systems that match the criteria for the selected folder, as shown in Figure 17-5.

Selecting the All Systems list from the left-hand pane changes the workspace and shows a detailed table view of all the systems in the HP SIM management domain. The screen shown in Figure 17-5 illustrates a table view of all systems found by the HP SIM discovery. This System view shows the status, name, type, address, and additional information for each system in the selected system list. From this list, users may select a system and invoke an action by choosing a tool from the actions menu.

The default system lists provided by HP SIM are adequate for many environments. Among the default set of lists are queries for All Servers, All Clients, All VSE Resources, and All Printers. In addition, system lists that group systems by operating system type, by status, and by function

Figure 17-5 HP Systems Insight Manager System List

are available by default. While these default lists make the first use of the application easy, customization of the system lists allows administrators to group systems more logically based on business function. For example, a system list can be created that contains each of the systems in a three-tiered application. This type of grouping allows an administrator to manage the set of systems responsible for a specific application as a cohesive group without the clutter of unrelated systems.

Figure 17-6 shows the Customize Lists interface in HP SIM that is used to create new system folders. Using this screen, specific systems may be included in a custom list. Alternatively, a query can be defined such that systems that match a given criteria are contained in a folder. For example, the screen shown in Figure 17-6 illustrates the creation of a list that selects all systems running the HP-UX B.11.23 operating system.

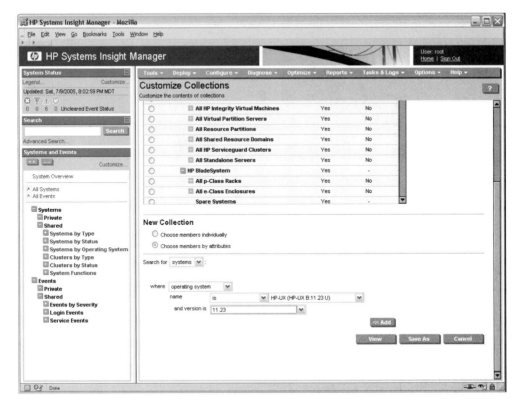

Figure 17-6 HP Systems Insight Manager Customizable System Lists

The system list shown in Figure 17-5 displays all of the systems in the All Servers folder. When the name of one of the systems in the list is selected, the System Page for the selected system is displayed. An example System Page is shown in Figure 17-7. The page shown in this example is for the rex04 nPartition that has been used in several examples throughout this book. This page shows detailed information for the system and provides links to more information. The events that have been received from the system are also available from the system page.

The final HP SIM feature to be covered in the HP SIM tour is user-based security. HP SIM provides a way for specific users, tools, and systems to be grouped together into an authorization. When configured, each authorization allows the specified user to execute the specified tools on the specified systems. The specified user has the ability to perform these management actions without being authenticated with super-user credentials. Instead, the user authenticates to HP SIM with his/her own login credentials and performs actions they would otherwise not be able to do because of insufficient privilege.

To fully appreciate the power behind this feature, consider the case where system administrators are not allowed login to systems as root. Instead users are forced to login with their unique user names to allow tracking of the changes made to the system. In this type of environment,

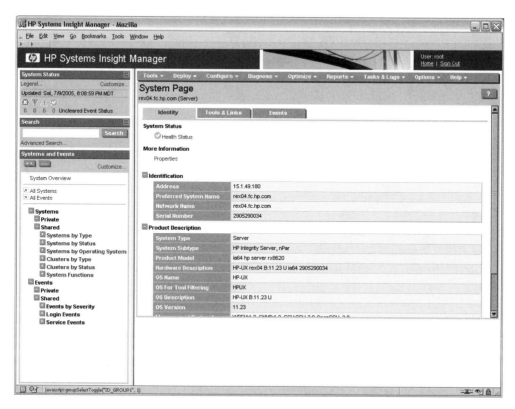

Figure 17-7 HP Systems Insight Manager System Page

simply disallowing the use of the root account would render most system administrators ineffective because many system administration tasks require root privileges. However, the user-based security facility in HP SIM provides non-super-users with the ability to execute a specific set of privileged tools on a specific set of systems. Once user-based security is configured, HP SIM determines whether the user is authorized to perform a selected action on the target system; and if the user is authorized, HP SIM then performs the action with elevated privileges on behalf of the user.

The screen shown in Figure 17-8 is the Users and Authorizations page that is used to configure user-based security. This configuration interface consists of four steps. The first step configures the set of users who will have permission to use HP SIM. The second step configures toolboxes, which are a collection of tools that a user or set of users has permission to execute. Next, system groups can be created that specify the set of systems where the selected user is allowed to perform the actions contained in a toolbox. Finally, the authorizations step combines the user, the

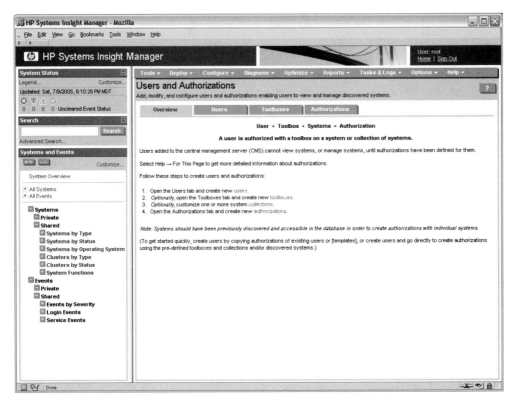

Figure 17-8 HP Systems Insight Manager User Based Security

toolbox, and the system group into an authorization that allows the selected user to run the selected tools on the selected systems.

Virtualization Manager Tour

All of the topics discussed in relation to HP SIM apply directly to Virtualization Manager. Using these facilities in HP SIM greatly increases the security and effectiveness of HP SIM, Virtualization Manager, and the other applications integrated with HP SIM.

Figure 17-9 shows Virtualization Manager System view. This view provides a graphical layout of the systems and VSE technologies being used in the VSE management domain. The System view graphically represents the systems in the management domain by layering boxes within boxes. The outermost boxes in the System view are the physical servers in the management domain. These boxes can be either nPartition or stand-alone servers. Within the outermost boxes, smaller boxes indicate technologies contained within the server. For example, the Production Superdome shown in Figure 17-9 contains multiple nPartitions. Additionally, the Web nParti-

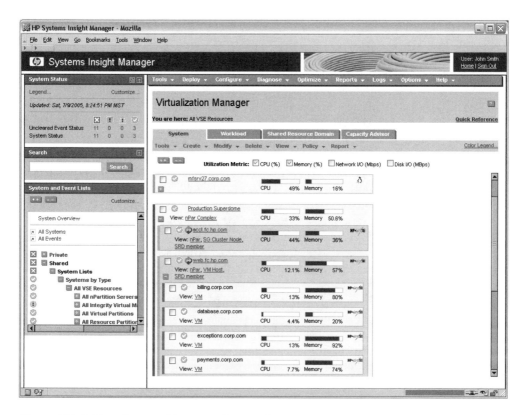

Figure 17-9 Virtualization Manager System View

tions is further divided with Integrity Virtual Machines. Each virtual machine is drawn within the containing nPartition. The same approach is applied for virtual partitions, Secure Resource Partitions, and VSE management workloads. This approach makes it simple to determine which systems are affected by a system configuration change, and the systems that may suffer side effects from the changes are readily visible. As an example, consider the case where a new cell must be added to an nPartition. If the nPartition contains Integrity Virtual Machines, the nPartition cannot be rebooted without coordinating the downtime with the owners of all the virtual machines. The graphical relationship between the VSE technologies involved in this example has not been available in the past, which made management of the various VSE technologies more difficult. Virtualization Manager's ability to unify the management of VSE technologies simplifies this process.

In addition to the partitioning technologies being displayed in the System view, systems that are members of Serviceguard clusters and gWLM shared resource domains are noted as such. This enables quick access to the details and management capabilities for clusters and shared resource domains by simply clicking on the appropriate link. Eventually every technology in HP's Virtual Server Environment will be represented in Virtualization Manager

System view; thus allowing centralized management and visualization for all of the VSE technologies.

Beyond the configuration and status of the systems in Virtualization Manager System view, the resource utilization is also displayed for all the workloads in the VSE management domain. Furthermore, the resource utilization data is aggregated up the hierarchy, which means that utilization data is displayed for an entire Superdome that consists of the aggregation of the utilization for the nPartitions contained in the Superdome. Another example of the data aggregation is that an nPartition containing multiple virtual partitions will have utilization data shown for each Virtual Partition in addition to the aggregated value for the nPartition. This model provides detailed utilization metrics from the lowest-level workload up to the highest-level server. The result is a view of the overall resource utilization for each of the servers in the VSE management domain.

The Virtualization Manager System view also provides seamless integration with a majority of the VSE configuration tools. Management tools for nPartitions, virtual machines, gWLM PSETS and FSS groups, and Serviceguard clusters can be invoked from the Virtualization Manager System view by selecting actions from the action menu. The actions for the Virtualization Manager are available in the menu immediately below the System, Workload, Shared Resource Domain, and Capacity Advisor tabs. This menu contains actions that are specific to VSE technologies, whereas the HP SIM menu at the top of the screen contains actions that apply to the entire HP SIM management domain.

The resource utilization meters shown in the Virtualization Manager System view can also be clicked, resulting in a display of historical utilization graphs for the selected system or workload. An example Capacity Advisor historical utilization graph is shown in Figure 17-10. This screen allows the type of metric to be changed in addition to allowing the interval to be selected. The historical utilization graphs provide additional context to the real-time utilization values shown in the System view. In many cases the historical views provide the necessary context to understand whether the real-time utilization value is either too high or too low by comparing the current value against the system's historical utilization patterns.

The second top-level view of the Virtualization Manager is the Workload view. This view provides a flat list of workloads in the VSE management domain. This view shows the status of the

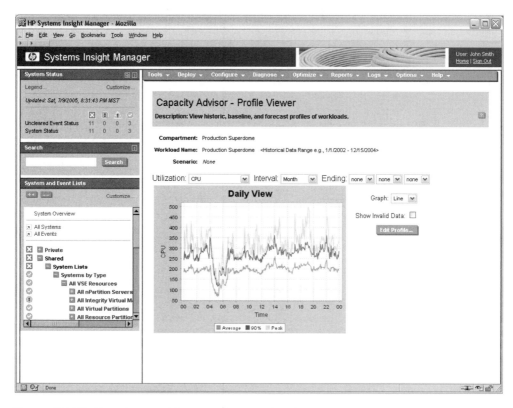

Figure 17-10 Virtualization Manager Historical Utilization Report

system where the workload is running, whether the workload is being managed by gWLM, workload utilization metrics, and several other informational pieces of data. An important difference between the Workload and System views is that the Workload view only shows systems that are directly running workloads. In other words, the Workload view is filtered to remove nodes that aren't directly running applications. Consider an nPartition that contains two virtual partitions. The two virtual partitions are shown on the Workload tab, but the nPartition is not. This view is tailored for monitoring the workloads in an environment without attempting to depict the relationships between the systems and workloads.

In addition to monitoring workloads, the Workload view also allows actions to be performed. By selecting a workload, the Virtualization Manager action menu can be used to perform tasks such as changing the gWLM workload policy associated with the workload or changing the definition of the workload to include additional processes.

Figure 17-11 Virtualization Manager Workload View

By default, Virtualization Manager Workload view shows workloads at the operating system, PSET, or FSS group level. This means that all of the processes running in each operating system are treated as a single workload unless gWLM PSETs or FSS groups are in place, in which case the utilization data is available at finer levels of granularity. In situations where resource utilization tracking is desired at finer levels of granularity without the use of PSETS or FSS groups, Virtualization Manager allows a workload definition to be created and deployed for any set of executables or users on a system. This workload definition provides the ability to monitor the real-time resource utilization as well as the collection of historical data.

Figure 17-12 shows the screen that allows Virtualization Manager workloads to be defined. Using this screen, the workload is assigned a name and description along with the users and executables that constitute the workload. After creating the workload definition, Virtualization Manager System and Workload views display the workload and its resource utilization. It is important to understand that these workload definitions provide only real-time and historical

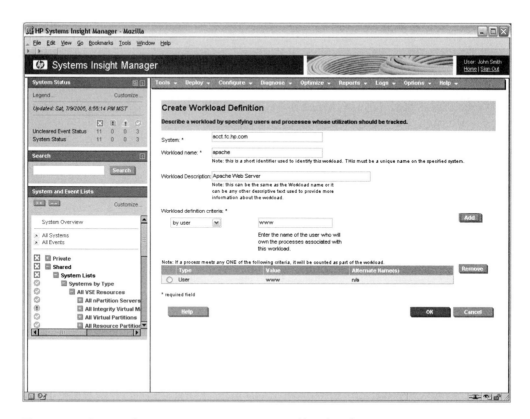

Figure 17-12 Virtualization Manager Create Workload Definition

monitoring capabilities. No resource control is provided with Virtualization Manager workload definitions. However, after you monitor the workloads for a period of time to understand the workloads' utilization patterns, you can associate a gWLM policy with the workload that will enforce utilization limits or allocate resources to ensure that all workloads receive the necessary resources.

Figure 17-13 shows the third top-level view of the Virtualization Manager, which is the gWLM Shared Resource Domain view. This view shows all of the gWLM shared resource domains that have been defined on the CMS. The view provides the ability to select a shared resource domain to get more details on the contained workloads and the status of their policies. From this screen, actions can be selected to create a new shared resource domain, modify an existing shared resource

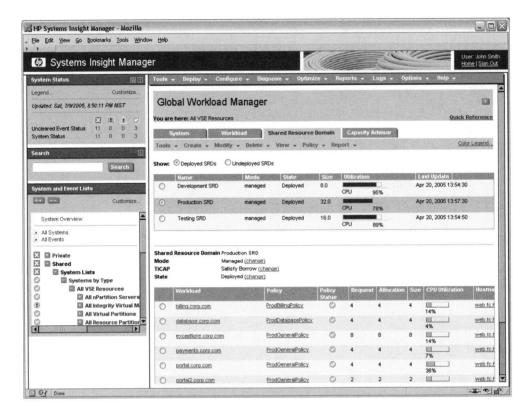

Figure 17-13 Global Workload Manager Shared Resource Domain View

domain, or even modify the policies associated with the workloads contained in a shared re-source domain. The gWLM portion of the VSE Management Software is described in detail in Chapter 19, "Global Workload Manager."

The final top-level view of Virtualization Manager is shown in Figure 17-14. The Capacity Advisor tab shows all of the capacity advisor scenarios which have been defined. Using this view, what-if simulations can be performed to assist in answering questions such as, "Where should I place my new workload?" or "What would the effects be of moving this workload?" The Capacity Advisor portion of the VSE Management Software is discussed in detail in Chapter 18, "Capacity Advisor."

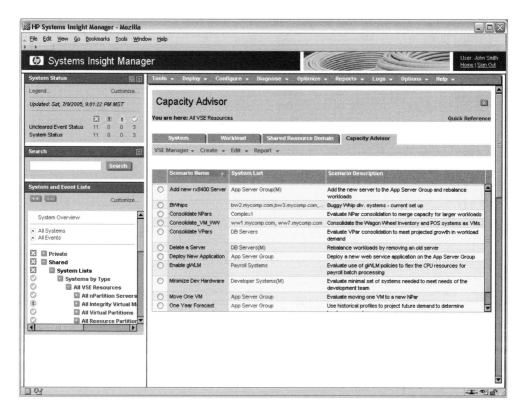

Figure 17-14 Capacity Advisor View

Summary

Air traffic controllers depend on the Final Approach Spacing Tool to ensure that the airways are safely and efficiently used. FAST brings together many systems in one tool to provide air traffic controllers with the capabilities they need to more effectively use the airport and airspace. In fact, initial tests showed that FAST has increased arrival rates and departure rates, while ensuring passenger and aircraft safety.[3]

HP's Virtualization Manager provides an analogous integrated set of tools for system administrators. VSE configuration and visualization, workload and policy management, and scenario analysis tools are all available from this single console. Virtualization Manager enables

---

[3]T. J. Davis, D. R. Isaacson, J. E. Robinson III, W. den Braven, K. K. Lee, and B. Sanford, "OPERATIONAL TEST RESULTS OF THE PASSIVE FINAL APPROACH SPACING TOOL," available at http://ntl.bts.gov/lib/000/300/399/davis_06_97.pdf

existing resources to be utilized more effectively while ensuring that workloads are allocated adequate hardware to meet their service-level objectives.

In addition to Virtualization Manager's visualization and configuration capabilities, gWLM and Capacity Advisor are both seamlessly integrated. Furthermore, Virtualization Manager is integrated with HP Systems Insight Manager, which provides features such as user-based security, event management, and automated system discovery. This suite provides a comprehensive set of management tools with unique features made available only through the integration of the individual components in HP's Virtual Server Environment.

Virtualization Manager provides the single console that allows administrators to manage their Virtual Server Environment more efficiently. Just as FAST unites a set of tools that allow air traffic controllers to be more effective, Virtualization Manager gives administrators the information and capabilities to transform their data centers into Virtual Server Environments.

18

Capacity Advisor

Chapter Overview

Each of the technologies in HP's Virtual Server Environment provides environments with unique characteristics for hosting workloads. nPartitions, virtual partitions, virtual machines, and Secure Resource Partitions provide varying degrees of workload isolation, ranging from complete hardware isolation using nPartitions to resource isolation within an operating system using Secure Resource Partitions. In addition, each technology provides varying levels of granularity and flexibility with regard to resource allocation. The Utility Pricing strategies of HP's Virtual Server Environment, which include Instant Capacity and Temporary Instant Capacity, provide a means to purchase systems without initially activating all of the hardware, and pay per use provides an option to pay for only the resources that are actually consumed. Finally, using tools in the VSE Management Software allows workloads to be managed in a highly available and policy-based environment. As a result of the combined technologies in HP's Virtual Server Environment, many different choices and options are available for workload deployment in enterprise data centers.

While each of the VSE technologies fills a vital role in the overall solution, several questions can be difficult to answer without specialized tools. Questions such as, "If I consolidate these workloads, will the resulting system be able to handle the combined load?" and "How do I know how big to make my virtual machines?" are often asked but difficult to answer. Another question that can be perplexing is, "I'm deploying a new workload; where is the best place to put it?" In order to help capacity planners answer these types of questions and more, HP's Virtual Server Environment offers the Capacity Advisor product. Capacity Advisor automates the steps that are traditionally performed manually by capacity planners, thereby freeing the capacity planners to focus on planning for future workload introductions, migrations, and consolidations.

This chapter begins with an overview of Capacity Advisor. It describes a common Capacity Advisor use model and introduces the most commonly used terms relating to Capacity Advisor. It illustrates one of the many reasons for capacity planning by describing a planning scenario that was performed to determine whether two production workloads in HP's internal IT department could be consolidated. The chapter concludes with an example scenario that walks through a workload consolidation. In the consolidation example, three workloads running in separate nPartitions are evaluated to determine whether a single nPartition with fewer total resources is able to host the workloads. The goal of the scenario is to reduce the hardware necessary for the workloads while increasing resource utilization.

It should be noted this chapter was written using prototypes of the Capacity Advisor. The screens shown in this chapter will vary slightly from the final product.

Capacity Advisor Overview

Capacity Advisor is a component of the VSE Management Software as described in Chapter 17, "VSE Virtualization Manager." The Capacity Advisor tool collects workload utilization data for every workload in the enterprise data center. This data is collected on a daily basis from each system and is stored on the HP Systems Insight Manager CMS. The collected workload utilization data is referred to as a workload's historic profile.

A workload's historic profile is its resource consumption history. This information consists of historic metrics for CPU, memory, disk I/O, and network I/O utilization. Reports and graphs are available for each metric in the workload's historic profile. In addition to generating reports and graphs, a historic profile can be edited using the Historic Profile Editor.

The historic profile editor can be used to mark data points as invalid in a workload's historic profile. Atypical events occur in computing environments that skew the actual resource requirements for a workload. For example, an intermittent hardware failure can cause an application to require unnecessary retries and thus record unusually high utilization metrics. For these events, the historic profile editor in Capacity Advisor can be used to invalidate the unusually high data points. The unwanted data points can be invalidated according to a given date range or it can discard values above a certain threshold.

After ensuring that the historic profile accurately reflects the nature of the workload, the next step is editing the workload's forecast. A forecast is an extrapolation of the baseline data into the future. Forecasting allows growth trends to be input in order to adjust for expected increases in resource requirements. In situations where the resource requirements for a workload are expected to change, the forecast editor allows the forecast for a workload to be modified. For example, if a workload is expected to grow 10% over the next 12 months, the forecast editor can be used to scale the workload accordingly.

As part of editing the workload's forecast, the workload's baseline can also be tailored. A baseline is a workload's resource utilization blueprint based on its historic profile. One way to create a baseline is to select a specific day in the workload's history as the representative sample to be used for planning purposes. Workloads that have daily repeating usage patterns such as backup systems are candidates for this type of baseline. Another way is to create a baseline from an arbitrary period of historic data. Workloads that are cyclical on a weekly basis are best modeled with this type of baseline. Several more options exist for creating baselines. It is important to remember that baselines should be created using the appropriate dataset for the workload. Only baselines that accurately reflect the business's use model of the workload are useful for capacity-planning purposes.

Editing of the baseline is performed using the Capacity Advisor baseline editor. Unless you made modifications, Capacity Advisor derives the baseline directly from historic information. In some cases the baseline does not require modification. However, most of the time workloads are event driven or cyclical in nature and adjusting the baseline results in a much more accurate and reliable model for capacity-planning purposes. For example, a payroll workload that runs on a biweekly basis requires editing of the baseline in order to accurately plan for the workload and its requirements in the future. Consider a situation where a payroll workload is being consolidated with a workload that runs at the end of each month. Using the baseline editor for each of these workloads to specify the exact nature of the workload makes it readily apparent that consolidating these workloads might not be feasible because some days payroll is processed on the same day as the month-end processing. This simple example illustrates why it is important to create an accurate baseline. If the baseline for the payroll workload does not accurately reflect the workload, the capacity-planning scenario evaluating this consolidation might overlook the problematic times where the peaks for the two workloads are aligned.

The final aspect of editing a workload's forecast is accounting for expected events in the workload's future. Events such as obsolescing a workload or doubling a workload's user base due to a merger can be specified as part of the forecasting process. These events further ensure that the capacity-planning activities performed on a workload are reliable and properly account for known events in a workload's future.

Once the workloads' historic profiles and forecasts have been customized, the next step is creating a Capacity Advisor scenario. This process allows many workloads to be evaluated as a group. A scenario is a set of systems and workloads combined together for capacity-planning purposes. Using the workload forecasts, what-if scenarios can be evaluated to determine if workload migrations, consolidations, or introductions will be successful. Hypothetical systems and workloads can also be defined within a scenario to provide what-if planning facilities. The hypothetical systems can be used to assist in answering questions such as "Will these workloads perform acceptably on the system I'm purchasing?" Additionally, scenarios can be used to evaluate the effects of moving a workload from one system to another. Essentially, capacity-planning scenarios provide a test-bed for performing analysis using both real and hypothetical systems and workloads. These scenarios are reliable because they are based on historic workload utilization data. The historic data is then used to create a forecast and baseline for the workload. The Capacity Advisor product allows capacity planners to effectively and accurately plan for changes in the datacenter.

A Reason for Capacity Planning

Before diving in to the Capacity Advisor example scenario, one of the many reasons for capacity planning is illustrated using an experiment that was performed using data from production workloads in HP's internal IT department. In this experiment, the data for two production workloads was collected. The data was then used to determine whether consolidating the two workloads would result in reduced hardware requirements. Of course, reducing the number of required CPUs results in a reduction in both hardware costs and software licensing costs.

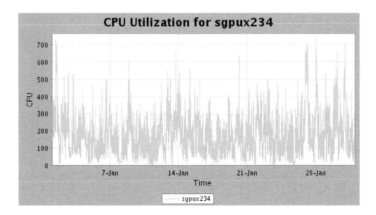

Figure 18-1 First Workload's Resource Utilization for the Month of January

The graph shown in Figure 18-1 depicts the resource utilization for the first workload to be examined in HP's internal IT department. The graph shows the CPU utilization for the month of January. The scale of the y-axis is based on CPU shares, with 100 shares equaling one physical CPU. This workload consumed roughly seven CPUs at its highest peaks.

The graph shown in Figure 18-2 is the CPU utilization for a second workload HP's internal IT department examined. As with the previous graph, the y-axis of the graph is based on CPU shares. This workload consumed almost eight CPUs at its highest peak. When the two graphs are examined together, it appears the utilization patterns of the workloads are closely aligned and experience peaks at roughly the same time. However, as shown in the next graph, that is not necessarily the case.

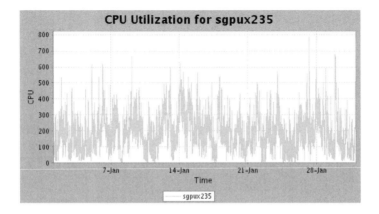

Figure 18-2 Second Workload's Resource Utilization for the Month of January

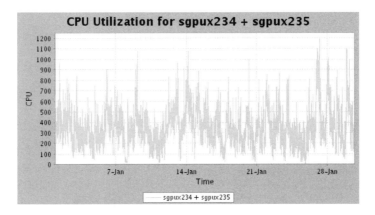

Figure 18-3 Combined Utilization for Both Workloads

After seeing these two graphs, the question arises, "How much hardware, if any, can I save by consolidating these workloads?" The initial answer from looking only at the previous two graphs could be "None." The first workload requires seven CPUs and the second requires eight CPUs, so the consolidated system must have 15 CPUs. However, Figure 18-3 shows the aggregation of the two consolidated workloads. From this graph it is clear that while the peaks appear to line up very closely, they are offset enough to provide an opportunity for hardware savings. In this case, the sum of the two workloads is less than 12 CPUs. This is a 20% savings in hardware without a reduction in the quality of service or response time.

From this simple experiment based on production workloads in HP's internal IT department, it is obvious that careful capacity planning can truly result in higher system utilization and reduced hardware requirements; both will result in cost savings. The following section walks through an example Capacity Advisor scenario that describes how the product can be used to effectively and reliably plan for workload consolidations.

Capacity Advisor Example Scenario

This scenario involves three production workloads that are each running in separate nPartitions, as shown in Figure 18-4. The goal of the scenario is to determine whether one of the nPartitions can be eliminated and the resources of the other two nPartitions can be combined into a single nPartition that will host all three workloads. This environment reduces the number of operating systems that require maintenance and licensing by two-thirds and reduces the hardware required by one-third. However, these savings must be weighed against the potential costs associated with poorly performing workloads if the workloads peak at similar times or otherwise have resource contention during their normal operation.

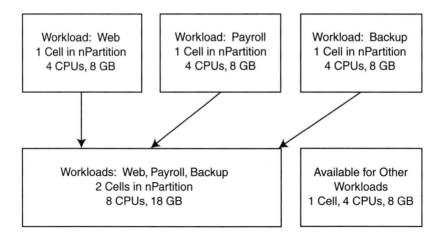

Figure 18-4 Example Scenario Workload Consolidation

Table 18-1 lists the workloads to be consolidated in this example scenario. The workloads in this example have been chosen for illustration purposes. In a real-world situation, it would be unlikely for the payroll, web, and backup workloads to be candidates for consolidation on the same system because of their unrelated business purposes. Nevertheless, these workloads have characteristics that are important to understand from a capacity-planning perspective and result in an insightful example.

As shown in Table 18-1, all of the workloads are hosted on separate nPartitions that contain four CPUs and 8 GB of memory. The web workload is the primary web portal for the workgroup. This workload has cyclical usage patterns that are similar each day of the week and from one week to the next. The second workload, payroll, runs on a biweekly basis. Finally, the backup workload runs every night and has a predictable daily usage pattern. The table also represents the expected growth in each of the workloads over the next year. This information will be used to adjust the forecast for each workload.

Table 18-1 Workloads for Consolidation

Workload Name	Usage Pattern	CPUs	Memory	Expected Growth
Web	Daily and Weekly	4	8 GB	10% annually
Payroll	Biweekly	4	8 GB	none
Backup	Nightly	4	8 GB	5% annually

Editing the Web Workload Historic Profile

The screen shown in Figure 18-5 is the Workload area of the VSE management suite. This view shows all of the workloads and several of their respective properties. From this view, the capacity advisor action for modifying the workload profile is available. The web workload is selected and the edit workload profile action is taken from the VSE management suite menu.

Figure 18-6 shows the historic profile in the workload profile viewer. This view graphically represents the historic resource usage pattern for the web workload that is being evaluated for consolidation. This screen allows each of the four metrics (CPU, memory, disk I/O bandwidth, and network I/O bandwidth) to be viewed individually. Options are also available that adjust the time period and data resolution.

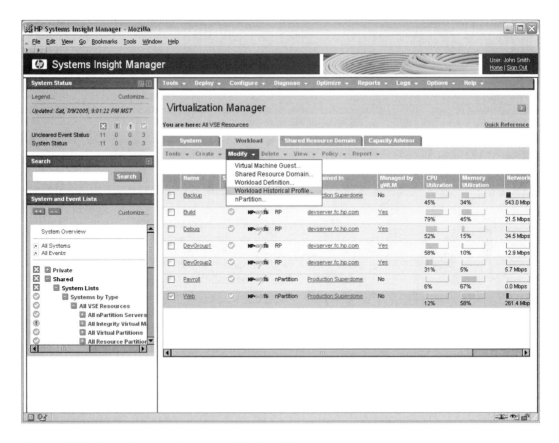

Figure 18-5 Virtualization Manager Workload View

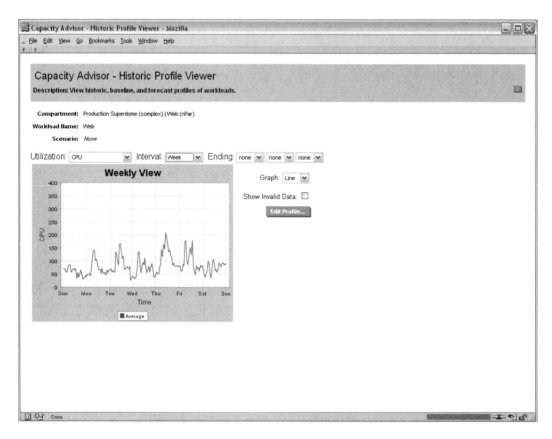

Figure 18-6 Capacity Advisor Historic Profile Viewer

The screen shown in Figure 18-7 provides a mechanism to modify a workload's historic profile. This can be performed in one of two ways. First, all data points over a given threshold can be marked as invalid. This operation flattens the peaks of a workload that are unusually high. The second way to modify a workload's historic profile is to mark data as invalid during specific date ranges. Using this mechanism, time periods that experience unusually high or low resource consumption can be marked as invalid to prevent the data from falsely affecting capacity-planning scenarios.

In this example, there is no need to mark data as invalid. However, the screen illustrates how data points between April 17th and April 25th would be marked as invalid for the workload if the user clicked the OK button.

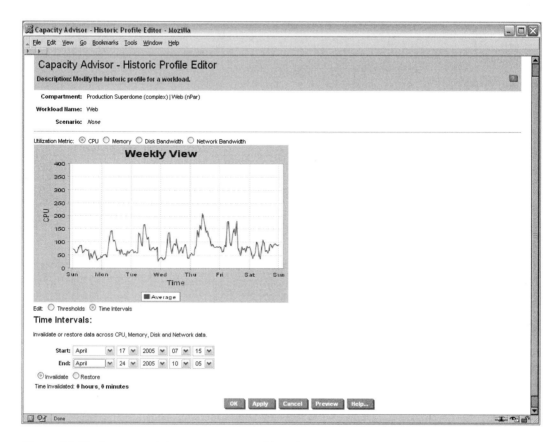

Figure 18-7 Capacity Advisor Historic Profile Editor

The next step is to edit the forecast. By default, the forecast is generated directly from the historic profile. The screen shown in Figure 18-8 is the default forecast for the workload. Notice that this view is based on historic data but will not take data points that have been marked invalid into account. In many cases, the forecasts require customizations such as incorporating expected growth rates and usage patterns. The Capacity Planning forecast editor allows these types of customizations and more to be performed in order to accurately reflect the nature of workloads.

Figure 18-9 shows the forecast editor in Capacity Advisor. The expected growth rate for CPU, memory, network I/O, and disk I/O can all be specified using this interface. After specifying the expected growth rates for the workload, what-if scenarios will properly account for the expected growth rate for the workload; this will produce more-accurate planning. This example illustrates the use of linear growth rate, but compounding growth, also referred to as exponential growth, can be modeled with the forecast editor.

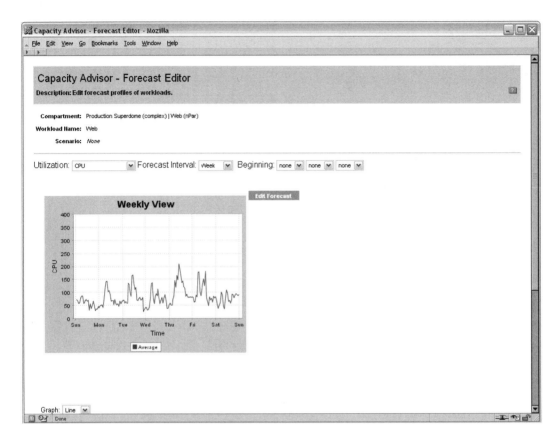

Figure 18-8 Capacity Advisor Forecast Viewer

In addition to specifying growth rates, Capacity Advisor allows specific events to be added to the forecast. Any event affecting the workload that occurs in the future can be added to the forecast. Examples of such events are mergers or reorganizations that change the scope or nature of the workload.

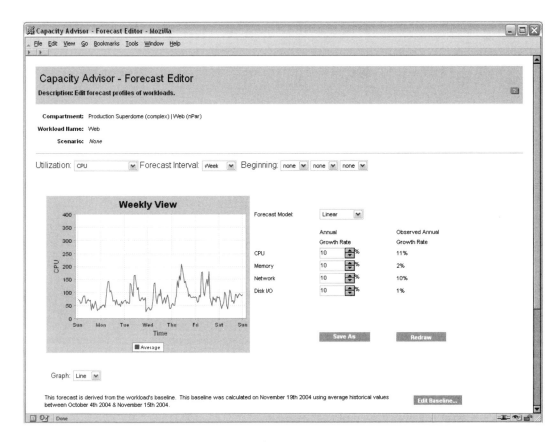

Figure 18-9 Capacity Advisor Forecast Editor

The workload's baseline can now be tailored using the Capacity Advisor Baseline Editor. The screen shown in Figure 18-10 is the default baseline for the web workload. This baseline is derived directly from the historic profile for the workload. If the historic profile accurately represents the workload's profile, then the default baseline may not need to be altered. However, in many cases, the nature of the workload is best represented by customizing the baseline according to the business function of the workload. For example, the web workload has a fairly regular usage pattern throughout each day and each week. The same days of the week generally experience the same average workload, and throughout each day the usage pattern is quite regular. As a result, this baseline will be tailored based on the workload's known usage patterns.

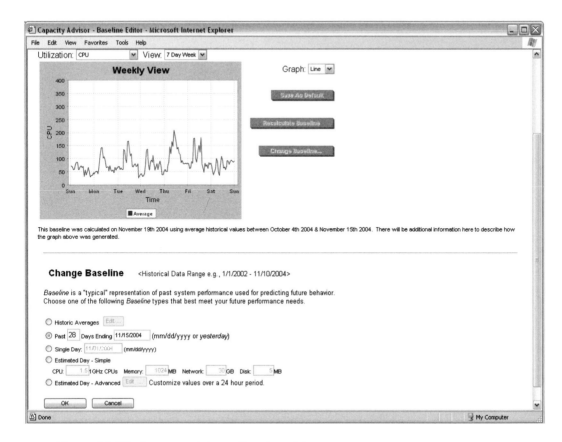

Figure 18-10 Capacity Advisor Baseline Editor

The interface shown in Figure 18-11 allows the baseline for the workload to be customized. In this case, the option to use the past four weeks is selected. This option modifies the baseline so it reflects the past four weeks of historic utilization data. Workloads that have regular usage patterns over a weekly basis can be modeled accurately using this type of baseline.

At this point, the web workload profile has been fully customized. The historic profile has been verified to ensure that all of the data points are valid, the forecast has been adjusted for expected future growth, and the baseline has been tailored to reflect the usage patterns of the workload. The web workload profile is now ready to be incorporated in capacity-planning scenarios. Before diving into the what-if scenarios, we will need to customize the other two workloads.

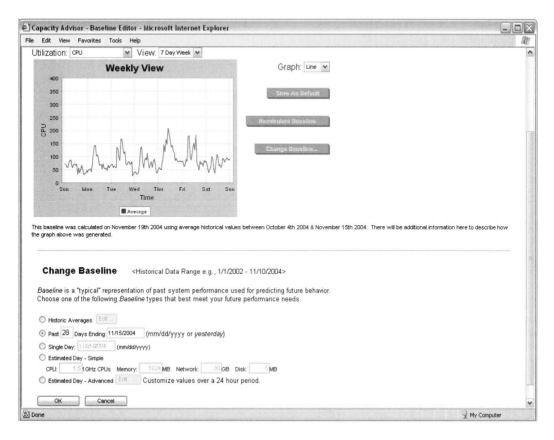

Figure 18-11 Capacity Advisor Baseline Editor for Web Workload

Editing the Payroll Workload Profile

The next workload profile to be edited is the payroll workload. As with the web workload, the screen shown in Figure 18-5 is the launching point for the workload profile customization. Similar to the web workload, the historic profile for the payroll workload will not be modified to remove outlying data points. Since the resource requirements for the payroll workload are expected to be flat over time, the forecast will not be adjusted.

The first customization for this workload is the editing of the baseline. As shown in Table 18-1, the Payroll workload runs on a biweekly basis. Customizing the baseline for this workload makes the forecasting and what-if scenarios much more reliable and realistic. In order to customize the baseline for this workload, a specific two-week period will be used for forecasting. As shown in Figure 18-12, a two-week period ending on the most recent payday has been specified for this workload's baseline.

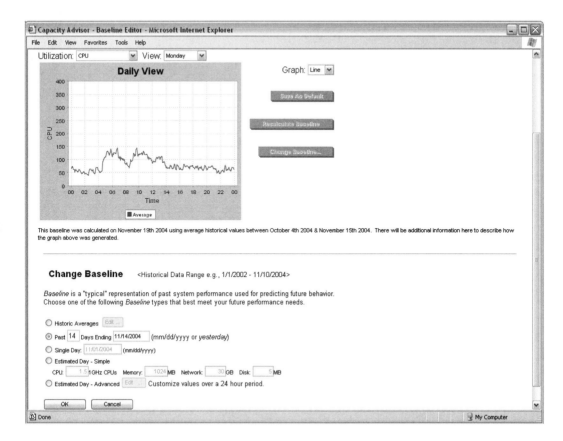

Figure 18-12 Capacity Advisor Baseline Editor for Payroll Workload

The customization of the payroll workload is complete at this point. The historic profile did not require manipulation and the forecast was not altered as there is no expected growth in the workload over the next year. Finally, the baseline has been customized to incorporate the resource usage pattern of the workload. The next step in this scenario is to edit the workload profile for the backup workload.

Editing the Backup Workload Profile

The final workload to be customized in this scenario is the backup workload. As is typical for backup workloads, it runs on a nightly basis. The workload profile is edited by selecting it in the screen shown in Figure 18-5. The first step in editing the workload is correcting any issues in the historic profile. This workload's historic profile is accurate and does not need alteration. The next step is modifying the forecast. The forecast for the backup workload is adjusted for the expected increase in the number of systems in the environment that will require backup services. Therefore, as shown in Table 18-1, the expected growth rate of 5% is reflected in the fore-cast editor for the workload.

The workload's baseline will be tailored according to the workload's resource usage patterns. Every day of the year is the same for this workload. As a result, the workload's baseline will be based on a single day. The screen shown in Figure 18-13 illustrates a change in the baseline to reflect a single day of the workload's historic profile.

All three of the workloads' profiles have been edited to accurately reflect their utilization patterns. Their baselines have been tailored according to the business function each workload serves and their forecasts have been customized according to the expected growth in resource requirements. The next step in this example is to create a Capacity Advisor scenario to perform what-if experiments with the workloads.

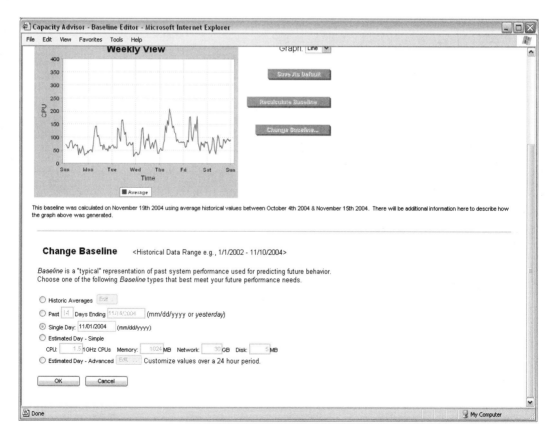

Figure 18-13 Capacity Advisor Single-Day Baseline Editor

Creating a Capacity Advisor Scenario

In order to perform what-if experiments with Capacity Advisor, a scenario must be created. The scenario defines the set of systems that will be used in the experiments. Hypothetical workloads and systems can also be added to scenarios to assist in the planning process. For this example, the Capacity Advisor scenario will contain the web, payroll, and backup workloads and the respective nPartitions where each of the workloads is currently hosted.

The screen shown in Figure 18-14 shows the first step of the Create New Scenario wizard in Capacity Advisor. This step involves selecting the appropriate systems to be included in the scenario.

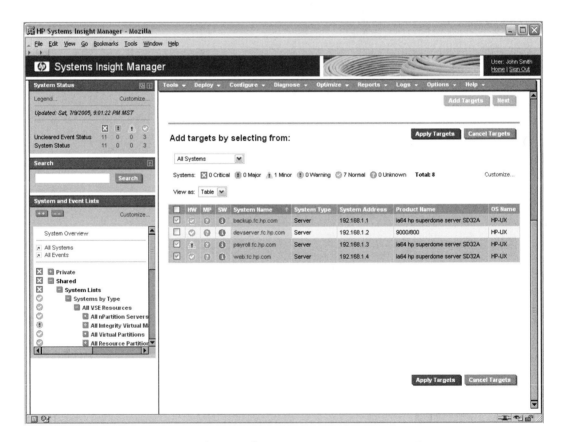

Figure 18-14 Capacity Advisor Select Systems in Create New Scenario

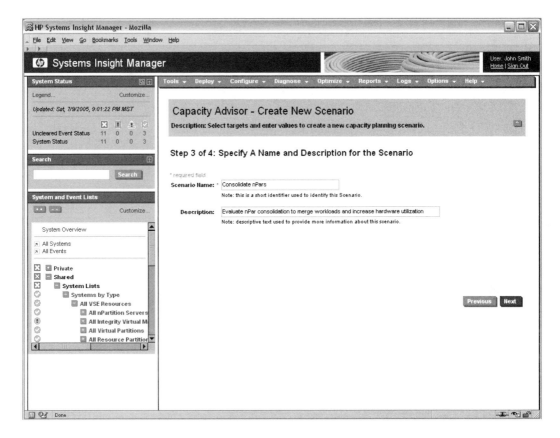

Figure 18-15 Specify Scenario Name and Description in Create Scenario Wizard

After selecting the systems, the name and description of the scenario must be specified as shown in Figure 18-15. This text is used as an identifier for the scenario and is displayed on the Scenario view of Capacity Advisor.

Creating a Hypothetical System and Performing a Capacity-Planning Experiment

Since the goal of this scenario is to determine whether a single nPartition with eight CPUs and 16 GB of memory will adequately meet the resource requirements for these three workloads, a hypothetical system will be added to this scenario. The screen shown in Figure 18-16 shows the tool for defining a new hypothetical system. As an alternative to creating a new system, the system capacity for one of the existing nPartitions could have been hypothetically increased. After creating the hypothetical system, what-if experiments can be performed that simulate the consolidation of the three workloads to the hypothetical system.

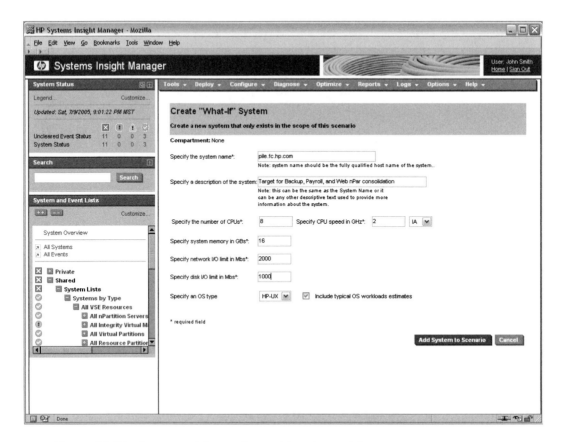

Figure 18-16 Capacity Advisor Create Hypothetical System

Before performing experiments using this scenario, the simulation interval should be set to reflect the time period to be used for performing the capacity-planning analysis. In this situation, the interval has been set two years in the future. Using a time interval in the future allows the workloads' forecast to be taken into account. This ensures that the workloads will have adequate resources at a future point. Failure to set the simulation interval appropriately could produce the result that although a workload consolidation appears to fit on the target system, a year or two in the future the system doesn't have the capacity to meet the expected growth in the workloads' resource requirements.

The next step in this scenario is performing a what-if experiment using the newly defined hypothetical system and the three workloads that have been edited to accurately reflect their historic and future resource requirements.

The screen shown in Figure 18-17 is the What-If Move Workload screen. This interface allows the selected workloads to be moved to the hypothetical system. This interface does not actually move the workloads. Instead, it serves as a test-bed for performing capacity-planning scenarios.

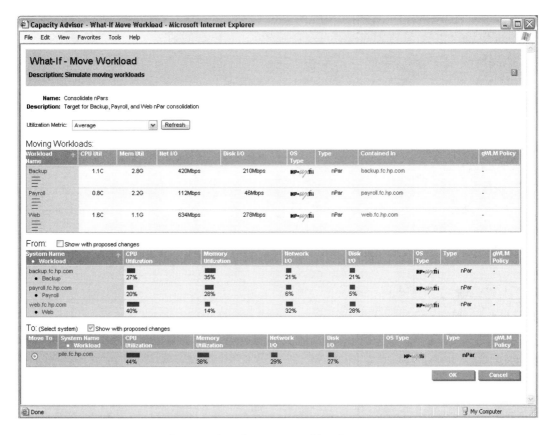

Figure 18-17 Capacity Advisor What-If Move Workload

In this case, the three workloads are selected to be moved to the hypothetical system. The upper portion of the screen shows each of the workloads and their resource profiles. The middle of the screen shows the current nPartition servers where the workloads are currently running. Finally, the bottom of the screen shows the hypothetical system as the target for the workloads. When this What-If Move Workload screen is approved, the follow-on screens for this capacity-planning scenario will show the workloads as if they have been moved. From these screens, reports can be generated to evaluate whether the hypothetical system and the workloads will receive their required resources.

Since the hypothetical system in the scenario now contains the three workloads being evaluated for consolidation, the system is selected as the target for reports. Figure 18-18 shows the interface for creating a system report. This interface provides a wide variety of options for customizing the report. In this example, the options to generate overall system and workload summaries are selected along with the utilization profiles and sustained load reports for the hypothetical system and the workloads.

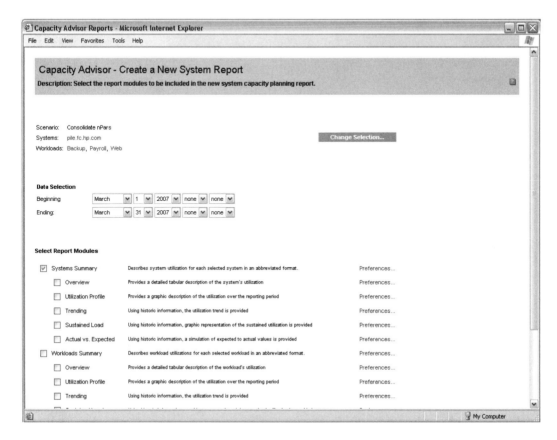

Figure 18-18 Capacity Advisor Scenario Report Generator

As with the simulation interval for the what-if scenarios, the date range for generating system reports should generally be set to a point in the future. In this case, the time interval for the report has been set to the entire month of March two years in the future. This takes the forecast for the workloads into account. The generated report will then indicate the resource utilization at the specified time period in the future.

The screen shown in Figure 18-19 illustrates one of the many graphs that are generated in the resulting Capacity Advisor report. This graph shows what the sustained CPU utilization will be for the hypothetical system during March of 2007. The maximum sustained utilization (at least 15 minutes in duration) is 92% for this hypothetical system. This means that the highest workload peak that will be sustained for at least 15 minutes will consume at least 92% of the hypothetical system's resource. An important distinction to understand from the sustained load graph is that the graph doesn't show utilization spikes that are shorter than 15 minutes in duration. In many environments, such short spikes aren't a concern from a capacity-planning perspective; the sustained peaks are generally most significant. In addition to verifying that the CPU load can be

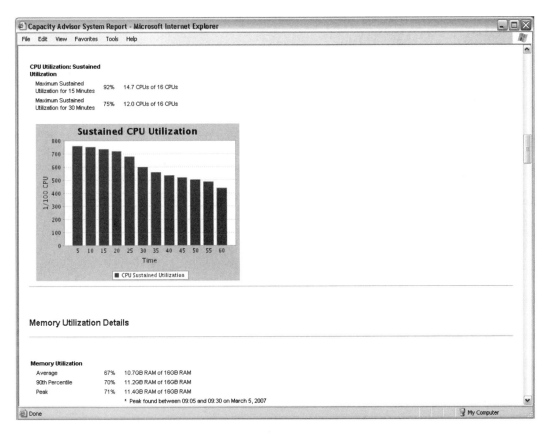

Figure 18-19 Capacity Advisor Workload Consolidation Report

handled by the target system, you should also examine other system resources to ensure that memory and I/O resources will be able to handle the consolidated load.

The graphs and data provided in the Capacity Planning reporting facilities are extensive. These reports provide a wealth of information that is based on historic data and workload-specific baselines. The reports can also be built from hypothetical systems and workloads. As a result of this combination of historic data and fine tuning, the models generated by the Capacity Advisor are highly accurate and reliable.

From the experiment performed in this example scenario it is clear that the three workloads can be safely combined to a single hardware nPartition. This will release one-third of the computing resources for other workloads and will result in higher utilization of the hardware in the consolidated environment. In addition, fewer operating system images will be required to host the workloads; this translates into lower system administration costs to keep the operating systems up to date and running properly.

Summary

The Capacity Advisor component of the VSE management suite provides the data, tools, and reports necessary to make informed decisions regarding workload placement, migration, and consolidation. Using this product, capacity planners are able to analyze each workload's utilization profile. With data in hand, they can create baselines as the foundation for performing what-if scenarios. The baseline can be finely tuned to accurately represent the nature of the workloads, which creates more accurate representations of the workload's resource requirements. Specific workloads may require that you build elaborate recurrences into the baseline, such as peaks on a biweekly basis, in order to reflect the nature of workloads. After adjusting the baseline, you can build a forecast to extrapolate the workload's resource requirements into the future. This forecast can be adjusted based on expected changes in the workload's resource requirements.

After going through the baseline and forecast modification steps, you can create capacity-planning scenarios as a test bed for evaluating workload consolidations, migrations, or placements. These scenarios allow what-if experiments to be performed on both real and hypothetical workloads and systems. These experiments provide an accurate preview of the expected resource utilization because they are based on actual workload utilization metrics.

Capacity Advisor is a crucial component of HP's Virtual Server Environment. It allows capacity planners to more fully utilize the existing resources in the datacenter and provide assistance when placing new workloads or performing workload consolidation. These steps are traditionally difficult to perform and require extensive manual data collection and manipulation. Using Capacity Advisor takes the manual steps out of the process and allows capacity planners to focus on planning the datacenter.

19

Global Workload Manager

Chapter Overview

The Mission Control Center at Johnson Space Center in Houston, Texas, serves as the central directing point for all space shuttle missions. Within the Mission Control Center is the Space Shuttle Flight Control Room. This room constitutes the base operations for the flight-control team, which consists of a wide variety of experts responsible for specific areas of the space shuttle's mission. As the leader of the flight control team, the flight director is responsible for the overall mission. The flight dynamics officer plans for the maneuvers of the craft and monitors the trajectory. The surgeon monitors the health of the crew and coordinates medical operations for the crew.[1]

HP's Global Workload Manager (gWLM) serves an analogous role for managing workloads in enterprise datacenters. Like the flight director in the Space Shuttle Flight Control Room, gWLM serves as the central directing point that monitors and manages workloads and their use patterns and allocates resources. In addition, it makes adjustments in workload resources just as the flight dynamics officer coordinates maneuvers and monitors trajectory of the space shuttle. Real-time reporting facilities in gWLM allow the health of workloads to monitored and reacted to immediately, just as the surgeon monitors the health of the crew.

Global Workload Manager is the second-generation workload management product in HP's Virtual Server Environment. Its predecessor is covered in Chapter 15, "Workload Manager." One of the most important differences between gWLM and WLM is the management model it uses. gWLM offers a centralized management strategy that allows a single console to be used to manage all of the workloads in the datacenter. Also, the configuration options have been greatly simplified and include default settings to ease the introduction of gWLM into new environments. Finally, gWLM offers a new advisory mode that provides a preview of the actions gWLM would take to allocate resources without actually making changes to the system.

---

[1]National Aeronautics and Space Administration, responsible official John Ira Petty, "Mission Control Center," available at http://spaceflight.nasa.gov/shuttle/reference/mcc/index.html

This chapter begins by discussing the vocabulary used throughout this chapter and the gWLM documentation. Then it presents an overview of gWLM that describes its primary use models and architecture. The chapter ends with an example scenario demonstrating gWLM's capabilities. The first part of the example scenario demonstrates gWLM's abilities to migrate CPUs between two vPars based on the policies associated with each vPar. The second part of the example describes the process of using gWLM on the Linux operating system. Global Workload Manager is also supported on OpenVMS, but the example scenario does not illustrate the use of gWLM on OpenVMS.

Global Workload Manager Terminology

The following terms are used throughout this chapter and the gWLM documentation.

Workload: a set of processes that can be identified by an executable, by the owning user name, or by the owning group name. Workloads are the level of granularity with which gWLM monitors the processes within the compartment and makes resource adjustments to ensure that the policy for the workload is being met. From a gWLM perspective, workloads reside within a single compartment. The supported compartment types are virtual partitions (vPars), processor sets (PSETs), and fair-share scheduler (FSS) groups.

Compartment: a vPar, an nPartition, a PSET, or a FSS group that is capable of being managed by gWLM. gWLM is capable of dynamically adjusting the resources assigned to a compartment in order to meet the policy associated with the workload that is running within the compartment. There is a one-to-one mapping between workloads and compartments.

Shared Resource Domain (SRD): the set of compartments over which gWLM is capable of managing resources to ensure that workload policies are met. If workloads are running within vPars, then the SRD is the set of vPars within the nPar or stand-alone server. If the workloads are running within PSETs or FSS groups, then the SRD is the set of PSETs or FSS groups running within the operating system.

Policy: contains the settings used by gWLM to allocate resources to the compartments that contain workloads. Policies can be defined to allocate a fixed amount of resources to a workload, or they can be defined to allocate a variable amount of resources that allows sharing between workloads.

Advisory Mode: allows administrators to see the requests gWLM would make on behalf of workloads in order to meet their policies. While running in advisory mode, gWLM makes no changes to the resources allocated to each compartment. Instead, this mode allows policy and workload definitions to be fine-tuned without affecting the system. After the settings are finalized, gWLM can be switched to managed mode.

Managed Mode: a mode gWLM uses to monitor workload utilization data and make adjustments to the resource allocations of the compartments. The mode for gWLM is specified for each SRD. Therefore, an entire SRD is either in managed or advisory mode.

Central Management Server (CMS): the station where the gWLM CMS daemon runs and where the user interface is hosted. The gWLM CMS daemon communicates with gWLM agent daemons that are running on every managed node under the control of gWLM. The gWLM managed node agent is responsible for monitoring workload utilization and reporting the information back to the gWLM CMS daemon.

Global Workload Manager Overview

Global Workload Manager is the second-generation workload management application in HP's Virtual Server Environment. gWLM's architecture provides a centralized management model for defining workloads and their associated policies. This makes possible resource sharing by utilizing several of the dynamic system capabilities in HP's Virtual Server Environment such as virtual partitions, processor sets, and fair-share schedule groups. The association of policies with workloads increases system utilization by increasing the level of resource-sharing between workloads. Policies can be used instead to isolate resources to specific workloads.

Figure 19-1 shows an example configuration for gWLM. This example illustrates gWLM's flexibility and power in its management of workloads. The Central Management Server (CMS) hosts the HP Systems Insight Manager application, the gWLM CMS daemon, and the gWLM web-based graphical user interface (GUI). The gWLM GUI is tightly integrated with HP Systems Insight Manager and communicates with the gWLM CMS daemon. The gWLM CMS daemon communicates with the gWLM agents running on each operating system under the control of gWLM.

In the CMS depicted in the diagram, four Shared Resource Domains are being managed. The first Shared Resource Domain is SRD 1. This SRD is in managed mode, which means that gWLM is monitoring workload resource utilization and is actively making changes to resource allocation for each compartment. SRD 1 contains three vPars that are all running HP-UX. Notice that the gWLM CMS daemon communicates with a gWLM managed node agent running on each of the vPars.

Important

> Shared Resource Domains containing vPars must reside within the same nPar or stand-alone server. This is because gWLM must have the ability to migrate resources between the compartments within the Shared Resource Domain.

The second SRD shown is SRD 2, which consists of four FSS groups running within a single operating system. Since all of the compartments are contained within a single operating system, only one gWLM agent is required on the system. The gWLM CMS daemon communicates with the gWLM agent to send configuration changes and collect historical utilization data. The gWLM agent is responsible for adjusting the size of each compartment based on the policies and resource utilization metrics of its workloads. This SRD is also in managed mode.

The third SRD, SRD 3, is in advisory mode, which means that gWLM will not make changes to the PSET compartments on this system. Instead, gWLM will provide graphs and reports that

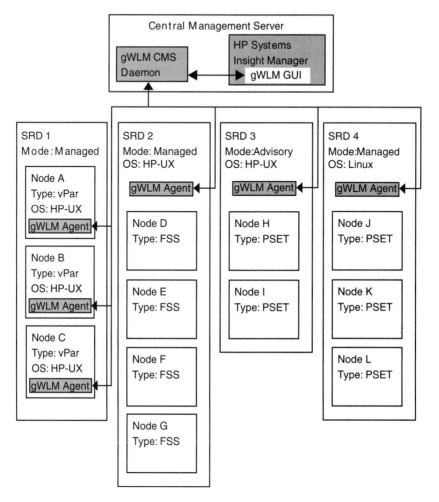

Figure 19-1 Global Workload Manager Example Configurations

show the resource utilization and the associated resource adjustments it would make if it were in managed mode. SRD 3 contains two processor sets that can be adjusted in size based on resource utilization if the SRD was changed from advisory to managed mode.

Finally, SRD 4 shows gWLM's ability to manage workloads running on the Linux operating system. When using Linux, processor sets are the only type of compartment supported. SRD 4 is in managed mode. The same CMS can manage a heterogeneous environment containing HP-UX, Linux, and OpenVMS operating systems (OpenVMS is not shown in the diagram but functions similarly to Linux and HP-UX). SRDs must contain homogenous types of compartments and operating systems, but at the CMS level, gWLM can manage a variety of compartment types and operating systems.

Architecture of the Global Workload Manager Central Management Server

The diagram shown in Figure 19-2 provides a more detailed view of the gWLM CMS architecture, which is quite simple. The two main functions are the graphical user interface and a daemon that handles background tasks that need to be running even when no users are actively using the user interface.

The gWLM screens in the GUI rely on data in the gWLM database on the CMS. The gWLM GUI also interacts with the agents on the managed systems for status display, real-time graphing, and deploying configuration data.

The gWLM daemon running on the CMS ensures that the agents always have a mechanism to upload historical data into the CMS database. It is also responsible for forwarding events to the HP SIM event management system.

Architecture of Global Workload Manager's Managed Node

The diagram show in Figure 19-3 illustrates the architecture of gWLM's managed node. Each node being managed by gWLM must have a gWLM agent running. The major functions performed by the gWLM agent include:

Discovery: The agent discovers the partition configuration of the system. This information is passed to the CMS and is displayed to the administrator when he or she is configuring workloads and policies for a system.

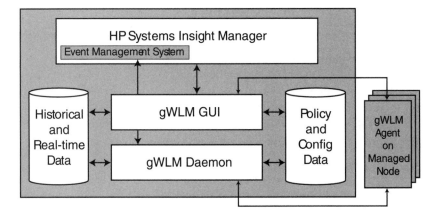

Figure 19-2 Architecture of the gWLM Central Management Server

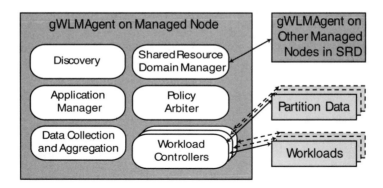

Figure 19-3 Architecture of the gWLM Agent

Application Manager: When the local system has multiple workloads that are being controlled by PSET or FSS compartments, it is necessary to specify which processes on the system should run in each of the compartments. The application manager is responsible for ensuring that these processes are assigned to the correct compartment.

Data Collection and Aggregation: The data that gWLM collects in order to manage workloads is stored locally. It is then aggregated and passed to the CMS for storage in the database.

Shared Resource Domain Manager: The SRD manager is responsible for communicating with other gWLM Agents when the shared resource domain includes multiple partitions running separate operating systems. One agent will be automatically elected the master and will be responsible for resource arbitration for the entire SRD. Once the master is elected, all the other nodes pass their resource requirements to the master for arbitration.

Policy Arbiter: The policy arbiter is responsible for taking inputs from all the workloads in the shared resource domain and deciding how resources will be allocated. In an SRD with multiple OS images, this is performed by the master agent.

Workload Controllers: The workload controllers are responsible for collecting information specific to each of the local workloads and deciding if the workload needs more or less resources to satisfy the policy associated with the workload. This information is then passed to the arbiter, which makes resource allocation adjustments as necessary.

In an SRD with multiple partitions running separate OS images, one of the agents is elected the master and this agent is the only one that does arbitration. To prevent the master from becoming a single point of failure for the entire SRD, the agents are designed to reconnect to one another if they lose communication with the master. If the master node experiences a failure or the agent is not reachable by the other nodes, the other agents in the SRD will renegotiate and elect a new master. This occurs only if the master is the only agent that fails. If multiple partitions fail at the same time, gWLM assumes there has been cata-strophic failure and stops attempting to reallocate resources until the SRD has at least n-1 agents running.

Global Workload Manager Polices

Global Workload Manager supports several different types of policies for controlling resource allocation to workload compartments. gWLM is shipped with a set of default policies that are commonly used. If the default policies are not appropriate for a given workload, new policies can be created or the default policies can be modified. The following four types of policies are available in gWLM:

Fixed policies guarantee that a workload compartment has a fixed amount of re-source allocation. These policies are satisfied before any other type of policy is con-sidered. Using fixed policies allows workloads to receive a constant share of the system's resources; however, fixed policies may result in lower system utilization be-cause resources that are not in use are not allowed to be shared.

Utilization policies are based on specified target utilization values. When the CPU utilization goes above the target utilization value, such as 85%, gWLM will allocate more resources to bring the utilization below the 85% target. Similarly, when the workload's resource utilization drops below the lower utilization target value, such as 60%, gWLM will remove CPU resources from the workload compartment. Using these two example target values, gWLM will attempt to keep the resource utilization of the compartment between 60% and 85%.

Own-Borrow-Lend policies allow a specific amount of CPU resources to be owned by each workload compartment. In addition, these policies specify a minimum number of CPU resources. The difference between the owned CPU resources and the mini-mum is the amount that can be lent to other workloads when they are not being uti-lized by the owning workload. Finally, the maximum value specified defines the maximum amount of CPU resources that should be allocated to the compartment. The difference between the maximum and the owned CPU resources is the amount of CPU resources the workload is allowed to borrow. Own-borrow-lend policies are also referred to as OwnBorrow policies in the gWLM software.

Custom policies allow workload specific metrics to be configured. gWLM uses the de-fined metric to adjust resource allocation based on how the current metric compares to the target value.

Global Workload Manager Example Scenario

This example scenario has two parts. The first part demonstrates the integration of gWLM and virtual partitions on HP-UX. In this example, there are two vPars configured to share CPU resources based on an own-borrow-lend policy. The second part of the scenario demonstrates the use of gWLM in a Linux environment using processor affinity which is standard in the 2.6 version of the Linux kernel. gWLM uses the processor affinity capabilities in the Linux kernel in a way that resembles the functionality of PSETs on HP-UX. At the end of the scenario, the two parts are brought together in an illustration of gWLMs; monitoring capabilities for all workloads being managed from the CMS.

It should be noted that Global Workload Manager version 1.0 was used in this example scenario. While it is not illustrated in this scenario, version 2.0 of Global Workload Manager adds support for Instant Capacity, Temporary Instant Capacity, and Pay per use. It will integrate with Integrity Virtual Machines and Serviceguard. Finally, version 2.0 of Global Workload Manager will be integrated with Virtualization Manager as described in Chapter 17, "Virtualization Manager."

Global Workload Manager and Virtual Partition Scenario

The first example scenario discussed illustrates the use of gWLM in a virtual partition environment. There are two vPars, zoo19 and zoo21, configured within the same nPartition named zoo9. Each of the vPars is running two instances of the Oracle database. This is the same configuration used in Chapter 15, "Workload Manager." Table 19-1 illustrates the configuration for each of the vPars with respect to the gWLM configuration.

An important distinction when comparing gWLM version 1.0 to Workload Manager is that gWLM does not allow workload compartments in a single SRD to be hierarchical. For example, an SRD may contain multiple vPars or an SRD may contain a single vPar that then contains processor sets or FSS groups. However, an SRD cannot contain multiple vPars that are also hosting processor sets or FSS groups. When gWLM is managing an SRD comprised of multiple vPars, all of the processes within the vPar are considered the workload. Therefore, gWLM treats the sales_db and finance_db workloads that are running in the zoo19 vPar as a single workload. If either of them are busy, gWLM will allocate more resources to the zoo19 vPar if zoo21 is not fully utilizing those it owns. This also means that the sales_db and finance_db are on equal ground with respect to workload priority and resource allocation. In the example scenario shown in Chapter 15, "Workload Manager," the finance_db was given a higher priority; thus, if it was busy, the sales_db workload would get its resources only after finance_db had met its service-level objectives. The benefit of the gWLM model is a major simplification in the configuration and management of the workloads because workloads within each vPar need not be individually specified and monitored.

Table 19-1 Virtual Partition Configurations

Virtual Partition	Workload Name	CPUs Owned	Minimum Number of CPUs	Maximum Number of CPUs	Shared Resource Domain
zoo19	zoo19.vpar.dbs	4	1	7	zoo9.vpars.dbs
zoo21	zoo21.vpar.dbs	4	1	7	

Configuring Managed Nodes

The first step in configuring gWLM is to set up and boot the vPars according to the requirements of each of the workloads. This includes memory allocation, network connectivity, and storage configuration. HP highly recommends that you configure each vPar's minimum number of CPUs to be 1 and the maximum number of CPUs to be the total number of CPUs in the nPartition or stand-alone system. Configuring the minimum and maximum values as described enables gWLM polices to be created that specify the desired minimum and maximum number of CPUs. The benefit of relying on gWLM policies instead of the vPar configuration to define the minimum and maximum number of CPUs is that gWLM policies can be changed without rebooting the operating system. Chapter 5, "Virtual Partitions," explains the process of configuring vPars similar to those used in this example scenario.

Before configuring gWLM, the workloads must also be configured and running, at least to the point where the workload can be identified by gWLM. In this case, the Oracle databases are up and running before the configuration process for gWLM is started.

After configuring each of the vPars and their workloads, the next step is to install the gWLM agent software on each of the vPars. This software is contained in the bundle T2743AA and will be shipped as part of the HP-UX 11i Operating Environments starting in 2005. For Linux, the software is available in a Red Hat Package Manager (RPM) package named gWLM-Agent-A.xx.yy. The exact version number has been removed because the version number will change with each release of the gWLM agent.

HP recommends that you configure the gWLM agent to start automatically at boot time on all of the managed nodes. This will ensure that the gWLM agent will be restarted in the event of a system failure or scheduled reboot. The gWLM agent can be configured to start automatically by editing the configuration file located at `/etc/rc.config.d/gwlmCtl` for HP-UX and `/etc/sysconfig/gwlmCtl` for Linux. The variable `GWLM_AGENT_START` to should be set to 1.

The next step involves the optional configuration of the properties file for the gWLM agent. This file is located in `/etc/opt/gwlm/conf/gwlmagent.properties`. For most installations the default properties file is adequate; however, you can configure properties such as the logging level and timeout using this file.

Finally, the gWLM agent should be started using the following command:

```
# /opt/gwlm/bin/gwlmagent
```

Configuring Global Workload Manager's CMS

The configuration of the gWLM managed nodes is complete and now the gWLM CMS software must be configured. This example scenario does not describe the process of installing and configuring the HP Systems Insight Manager product. That product must be installed and properly configured before continuing through the scenario.

After installing and configuring HP Systems Insight Manager, the first step is to install and configure the gWLM CMS software that is contained in the bundle T2412AA. At the first release of gWLM, HP-UX is the only supported operating system for the CMS. HP recommends users allocate 4GB of space in the /var directory for every 100 workloads. This space will allow approximately two years' worth of data to be stored for capacity-planning and performance management purposes. This space recommendation applies only to the CMS, not the managed nodes.

The next step is to initialize the gWLM CMS by running the following command:

```
# /opt/gwlm/bin/gwlminitconfig -initconfig
```

Next, the gWLM CMS daemon should be configured to start automatically when the CMS server is restarted or experiences a system failure. This is done by changing the GWLM_CMS_START variable to 1 in the /etc/rc.config.d/gwlmCtl file.

The next step involves configuring the properties file for the gWLM CMS daemon and gWLM user interface. For most installations the default properties file is adequate and does not require editing. The file is located in /etc/opt/gwlm/conf/gwlmcms.properties and contains variables such as the logging level, caching sizes, and settings for the graphs displayed in the GUI.

After you have modified the gWLM configuration files, you'll need to take steps to ensure that the communications between each of the gWLM agents and the CMS are secure. The gwlmsslconfig(1M) manual page describes this procedure in detail. It involves creating certificates on each of the managed nodes and copying the public key to every node in the Shared Resource Domain, including the CMS. This step is not required, but HP recommends it.

Finally, the gWLM CMS daemon should be started by executing the following command:

```
# /opt/gwlm/bin/gwlmcmsd
```

Creating the Global Workload Manager Policy

At this point, gWLM agents are running on both of the vPars and HP Systems Insight Manager and the gWLM CMS daemon are both configured and running. The next step is to create a new policy for the zoo19 and zoo21 vPars using the gWLM GUI. In this example scenario, the CMS is rex04. Directing a web browser to the standard HP SIM URL opens the HP Systems Insight Manager main screen. In this example, rex04.fc.hp.com is the hostname of the CMS, so that value is specified in the URL

```
https://<CMS hostname>:50000
```

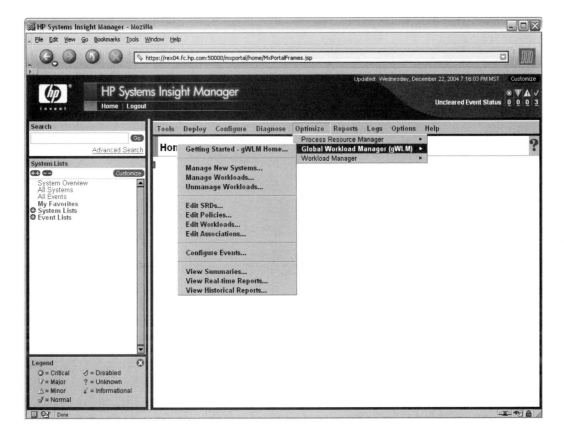

Figure 19-4 gWLM Action Menu

The screen in Figure 19-4 shows HP Systems Insight Manager with the list of gWLM actions. This menu is reached by selecting the Optimize menu and then Global Workload Manager (gWLM). From this menu, most of the actions available within gWLM are readily accessible. To create a new policy, select Edit Policies.

Figure 19-5 shows the list of gWLM policies currently defined on the CMS. From this page, a new policy can be created or an existing policy can be modified or removed. The other tabs shown in this view are the list of SRDs on the Shared Resource Domains tab, the list of workloads on the Workloads tab, and the associations between workloads and policies on the Associations tab.

Many standard polices are shipped with gWLM. In many cases, a new policy does not need to be created because the pre-defined policies are adequate. However, in this scenario, the maximum number of CPUs for each of the vPars will be seven because each vPar must have one

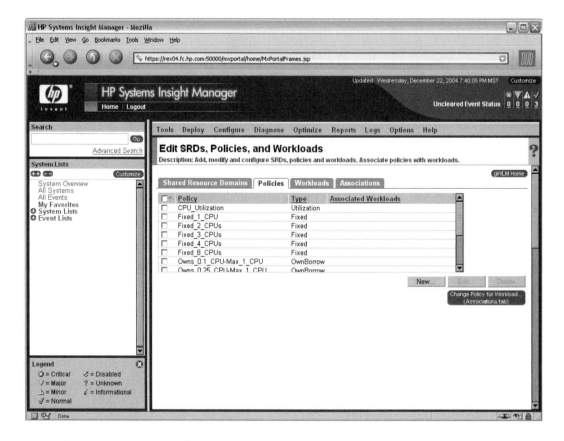

Figure 19-5 gWLM Policy List

CPU. So neither vPar can have all eight of the CPUs in the zoo9 nPar. As a result, the standard policy of owning four with a maximum of eight is close to what is needed, but it is not correct. You must create a new policy by clicking on the New button.

The screen in Figure 19-6 is the interface that allows a new policy to be defined. For this scenario, a new own-borrow-lend policy will be defined. Specify the name of the policy first, then select the type OwnBorrow. Finally, specify the minimum, owned, and maximum number of CPUs according to the values listed in Table 19-1. When you click on the OK button, the policy is created and is displayed in the list of existing policies. The newly created policy will be used in the next step, which goes through the Manage New Systems wizard.

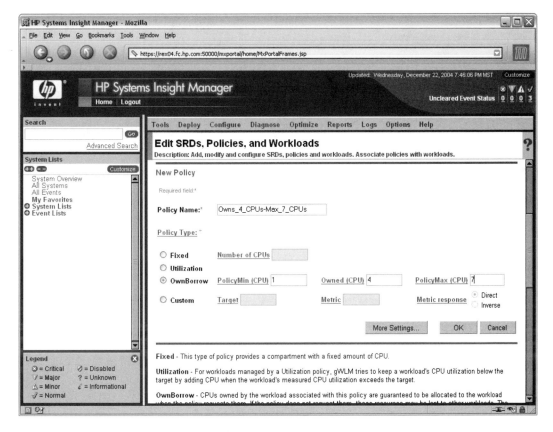

Figure 19-6 gWLM Create New Policy Screen

Manage New Systems with Global Workload Manager

The two vPars must now be configured to operate under the control of gWLM in a Shared Resource Domain with the newly created policy associated with each of them. This is performed by selecting the Manage New Systems action from the main Global Workload Manager (gWLM) menu in HP Systems Insight Manager. The screen in Figure 19-7 is the first step of the Manage New Systems wizard. The first task is defining the systems to be part of the Shared Resource Domain. In this example, zoo19 and zoo21 are specified in the System list field. Clicking on the Next button causes gWLM to contact each of the gWLM agents on the systems to determine what type of compartment is being managed.

Important

> The gWLM agent must be running on every node specified in the list of systems for the nodes to be discovered.

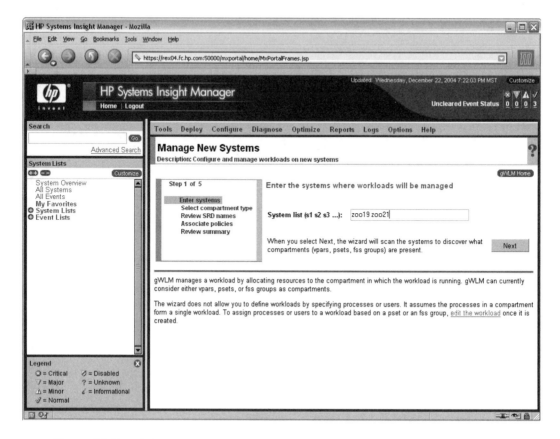

Figure 19-7 gWLM Manage New Systems Screen

After you have specified the set of systems to be part of the shared resource domain, gWLM queries the gWLM agents on each of the systems. The resulting compartment layout is shown in Figure 19-8. gWLM discovered that both vPars are within the same nPartition, zoo9, and within the same complex named zoo. gWLM has also selected the default compartment type according the information discovered. For this scenario, the compartment type is vPar, in which case, gWLM will create a single SRDs. If the compartment type were changed to PSET or FSS group, then gWLM would create a separate SRDs. This is because gWLM version 1.0 does not support hierarchical compartments. When the vPars are members of the SRD, as they are in this example, gWLM does not support additional compartments within the vPars.

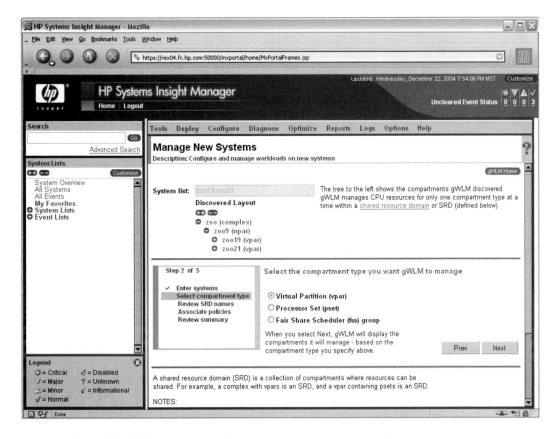

Figure 19-8 gWLM Manage New Systems Compartment Type Screen

The next step of the Manage New Systems wizard, shown in Figure 19-9, is to specify the name of the Shared Resource Domain and to decide whether it should operate in advisory or managed mode. For this example, the name is specified as `zoo9.vpar.dbs`. Initially the shared resource domain will be placed in advisory mode so that no configuration changes will be made by gWLM. The graphs and reports will display the actions gWLM would take if it were in managed mode, but it will not make changes to the vPars while it is in advisory mode.

Next a policy must be associated with each of the vPars. Remember that all of the processes in each of the vPars are considered to be a single workload, so the policy is associated with the

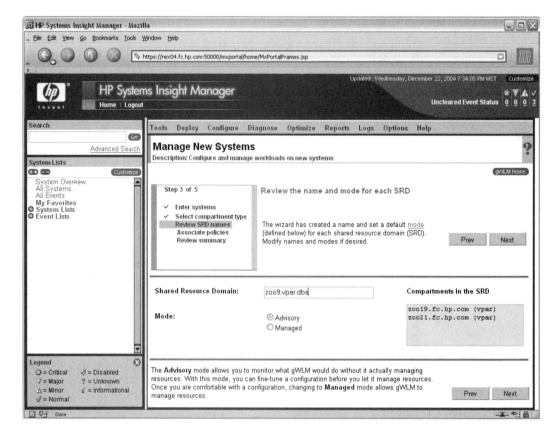

Figure 19-9 gWLM Manage New Systems SRD Name and Mode

entire vPar, not for individual Oracle database instance. The screen in Figure 19-10 provides an interface to define the name of the workloads and associate a policy with them. The name of the workload should be globally unique within the CMS to allow individual workloads to be recognized and managed. The hostname or any other identifier can be used for the name of the workload. In this example, the name of the vPar is specified along with the word "vpar" to make it clear that the workload is a vPar, followed by the type of workload running within the vPar, which is "dbs" in the example.

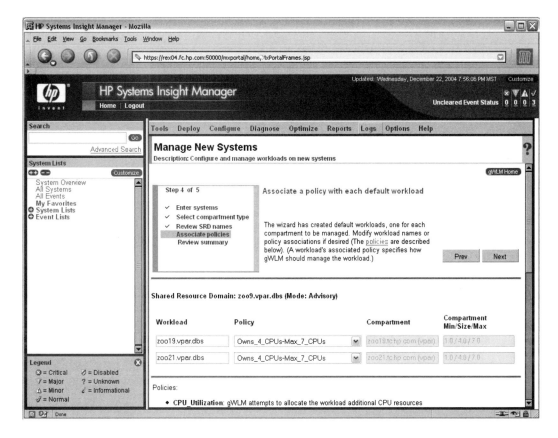

Figure 19-10 gWLM Manage New Systems Policy Association Screen

After specifying the names of the workloads, the next step is to choose the policy to be associated with the workloads. This is the step where the policy defined earlier in this example is selected. From the list of policies, the Owns_4_CPUs-Max_7_CPUs policy is chosen for each of the vPars.

The final step in the Manage New Systems wizard is the summary screen shown in Figure 19-11. This screen provides the details of the workloads and their associated policies. When the Finish button is clicked on, gWLM will deploy the policies to each of the vPars and begin to monitor the systems. Since the shared resource domain is in advisory mode, no changes will be made to the CPU allocation between vPars based on their utilization. Instead, the gWLM reports and graphs will show the resource allocation changes it would make if it were in managed mode.

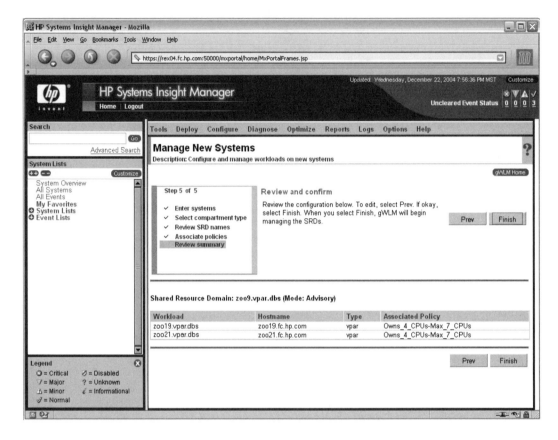

Figure 19-11 gWLM Manage New Systems Summary Screen

Monitoring Workloads in Virtual Partitions

One of the most valuable tools provided in the gWLM GUI is the graphing of workload utilization and allocation. The value comes from being able to see the current workload utilization in conjunction with the resource allocation changes that gWLM would make in managed mode. Figure 19-12 shows the real-time report for the zoo19 vPar, which is available by selecting View Real-time Reports from the gWLM action menu.

During the time period from 12:06 to 12:10 shown in Figure 19-12, the workload CPU utilization was very low. During that same period, as the graph shows, the allocation of resources would be decreased. It is important to realize that the gWLM graphs showing resource allocation while in advisory mode depict only the first step gWLM would take. In this example, the graph shows that a single CPU would be removed from zoo19, but in reality, after removing one CPU, gWLM would likely continue removing CPUs until the minimum value was reached because the CPU utilization is less than one CPU in zoo19 during the aforementioned time period.

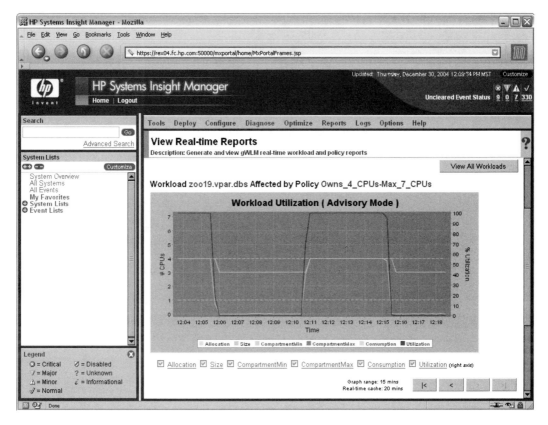

Figure 19-12 Workload Utilization in Advisory Mode for zoo19

In addition to the utilization and allocation traces, the graph also displays the minimum and maximum compartment sizes, which are constant in this scenario.

Figure 19-13 shows the workload utilization graph for zoo21. This graph shows that the workload in the zoo21 vPar is constantly at peak utilization. A careful comparison of the graph shown in Figure 19-12 and Figure 19-13 reveals gWLM's power. During the same time period of 12:06 to 12:10, CPU utilization in zoo21 was extremely high. If gWLM had been in managed mode, it would have added CPUs to the zoo21 vPar because the zoo19 vPar wasn't using them. Again, the height of the CPU allocation trace isn't the important factor. Instead, the movement of the trace indicates when gWLM would make a resource allocation change.

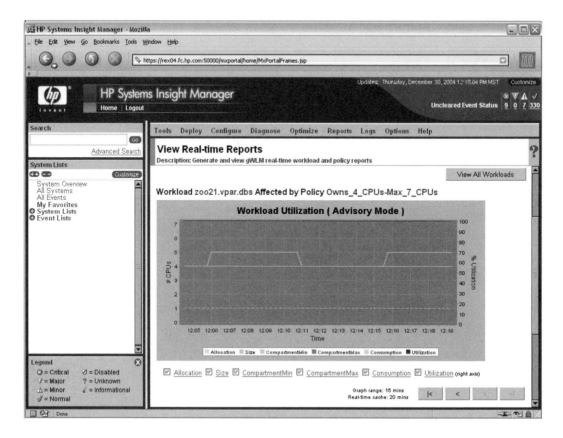

Figure 19-13 Workload Utilization in Advisory Mode for zoo21

Converting the Shared Resource Domain to Managed Mode

At this point, gWLM has been running for an adequate amount of time for the user to feel comfortable with its capabilities. Therefore, the SRD is being converted from advisory to managed mode. This is performed by selecting the Edit SRDs item from the Global Workload Manager action menu. This action opens a screen similar to that shown in Figure 19-5, except that the Shared Resource Domains tab is selected. From this screen, select the zoo9.vpar.dbs SRD and click on the Edit button. The resulting Edit Shared Resource Domain screen is shown in Figure 19-14. This window provides mechanisms for changing the name, toggling the mode, and switching the state of the SRD. In this instance, only the mode is changed from advisory to managed. When you click on the OK button, the change takes affect immediately and gWLM begins actively managing the resources in the two vPars.

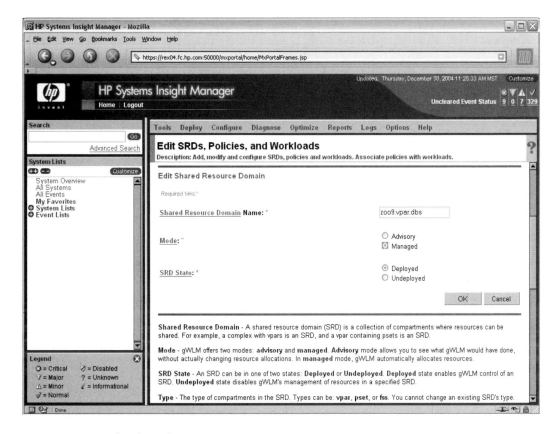

Figure 19-14 Edit Shared Resource Domain

Monitoring Workloads in Managed Mode

Once you have changed the mode of the SRD to managed, the real-time reports will provide a clear view of the actions gWLM is taking while it ensures that each workload is receiving its required resources and that the overall resource utilization is as high as possible. The graph in Figure 19-15 shows that the actions taken match closely with the hypothetical resource changes that were shown when the SRD was in advisory mode. From the time period of 12:36 to 12:40, the resource utilization of the zoo19 vPar was low, and its size was reduced to a single CPU. During the period from 12:40 to 12:44, additional CPUs were added to zoo19 until it reached the maximum compartment size of seven CPUs. Viewing the workload utilization for zoo21 will complete the picture regarding the overall resource utilization for the entire zoo9 nPartition.

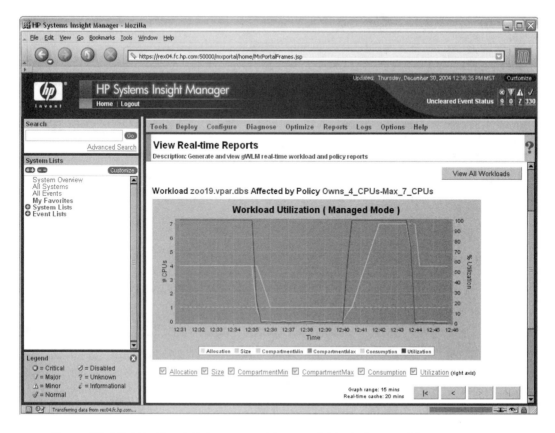

Figure 19-15 Workload Utilization in Managed Mode for zoo19

The graph in Figure 19-16 shows the workload utilization for zoo21. Using the time values to correlate the resource allocation between the two graphs, from 12:36 to 12:40 the zoo21 vPar was consuming close to 100% of its resources. Since zoo19 was idle during the same period, zoo21 was allocated its compartment maximum of seven CPUs. At 12:40, the workload in zoo21 began to lighten, and as a result, CPUs were migrated to zoo19.

Reporting with Global Workload Manager

At this point, the workloads in each of the vPars are running under the control of gWLM. However, because of gWLM's automation capabilities, a common question gWLM customers ask is, "How have my workloads been running and what has gWLM been doing with the resources available?" The gWLM product provides a workload reporting tool. Three types of workload reports are available from the `gwlmreport` command:

A *Resource Audit* report shows detailed information for the specified workloads, including the shared resource domain and compartment, policy, and utilization information.

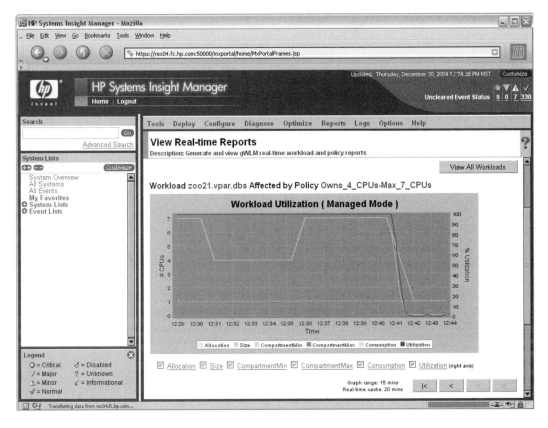

Figure 19-16 Workload Utilization in Managed Mode for zoo21

A *Top Borrowers* report provides utilization information for each of the specified workloads and provides a clear picture of which workloads are consuming the bulk of the resources.

A *Data Extraction* report provides an interface to extract data from gWLM's workload database in a machine-readable format for use in alternate data analysis tools.

A resource audit report for the zoo19.vpar.dbs workload is shown in Listing 19-1. Two of the most important sections in the report are the Samples and Utilization sections. The Samples section provides a summary of the overall gWLM state during the samples represented in the report. Of particular interest are the Borrow and Want2Borrow metrics. If the Borrow metric is regularly high, one or more workloads are frequently borrowing resources. This is not necessarily indicative of a problem, but continued patterns may indicate that the policies should be reconfigured to more accurately reflect each workload's requirements. Second, if Want2Borrow is high on a regular basis, one or more workloads is requesting more resources than it has been allocated. Again, this does not necessarily represent a problem, but it could indicate that the policies are not properly configured for the requirements of the workloads. Finally, the Utilization section at the end of the report shows the peak, average, and minimum resource utilization. In addition, the trade balance field shows that zoo19 had a negative trade balance. This means that zoo19 was lending resources more often than it was borrowing from zoo21. A Top Borrowers report is shown in Listing 19-2.

Listing 19-1 Global Workload Manager Resource Audit Report

```
# /opt/gwlm/bin/gwlmreport resourceaudit \
> -workload=zoo19.vpar.dbs
Generating report for workload(s) [zoo19.vpar.dbs].
Please be patient, this may take several minutes.
#---------- Resource Audit for zoo19.vpar.dbs----
#- Report information:
    ReportDate=2004/12/31 10:39:25 MST
    Workload=zoo19.vpar.dbs

    TotalSamples=    1076
    AvgSampleDuration=0.9979117565055762 (min)
    ReportDateRange= [2004/12/30 - 2004/12/31]
    PossibleSamples= 1346.812622697556

#-- Workload context information (from most recent sample):
#- Shared Resource Domain info:
    SRDName=         zoo9.vpar.dbs
    SRDMode=         Managed
#- Policy info:
    PolicyName=      Owns_4_CPUs-Max_7_CPUs
    PolicyType=      OwnBorrow
    PolicySettings=  [min=1.0/own=4.0/max=7.0]
#- Compartment info:
    CompartmentName=   zoo19
    CompartmentType=   vpar
    CompartmentHost=   zoo19.fc.hp.com

#- Samples info:       (%)      (count)
    Total=           100.0%     1076
    OwnedOnly=       041.0%     441
    Borrowing=       005.6%     60
    Lending=         053.4%     575
    Able2Lend=       058.7%     632
    Want2Borrow=     038.1%     410
    CompClipped=     000.0%     0
    PolClipped=      001.2%     13
    PriClipped=      047.4%     510

#- Utilization: info
    AvgUtil=         049.19
    MaxUtil=         100.00    (Date occurred=2004/12/30
                               20:03:00 MST)
    TradeBalance=    -001.19   (negative=Lending,
                               0=Own,
                               positive=Borrowing)
    AvgUtilWhileLending=       021.01
    MaxUtilWhileLending=       100.00    (Date occurred=
                                          2004/12/30
                                          20:03:00 MST)
```

Listing 19-2 Global Workload Manager Top Borrowers Report

```
# /opt/gwlm/bin/gwlmreport topborrowers \
> -workload=zoo19.vpar.dbs \
> -workload=zoo21.vpar.dbs \
> -duration=1day \
> -startdate=2004/12/30
Generating report for workload(s) [zoo19.vpar.dbs,
                                   zoo21.vpar.dbs].
Please be patient, this may take several minutes.
#---------- Top Borrowers Report ------
#- Report information:
    ReportDate=2004/12/31 toc=1104514326563

Workload          Number   Lend/Own/Borrow Avg      TradeBalance
                  Samples     %/%/%        Util
zoo21.vpar.dbs    564      5.0/41.5/53.5   088.27   001.20
zoo19.vpar.dbs    564      53.5/41.5/5.0   049.01   -001.20
```

The first portion of this example scenario is now complete. Both vPars are running under the control of gWLM and the workloads are being actively monitored. The detailed reporting capabilities provide a mechanism to generate monthly, weekly, or even daily reports. The next portion of the example scenario configures a Linux nPartition to use processor sets that will provide resource isolation between the workloads running within the nPartition.

Global Workload Manager and Linux Processor Sets Scenario

This example illustrates the use of gWLM to provide resource isolation, whereas the previous part of the example scenario focused on maximizing resource sharing. Table 19-2 shows the configuration of the three processor sets within the zoo20 nPartition.

Table 19-2 Linux Processor Set Configurations

Processor Set	Workloads	CPUs Owned	Shared Resource Domain
zoo20.pset0.default	All other processes	1	zoo20.psets.tomcat_samba
zoo20.pset1.samba	App: /usr/sbin/smbd App: /usr/sbin/nmbd	1	
Zoo20.pset2.tomcat	User: www	2	

The first processor set will be allocated a single CPU and will run all processes that are not associated with one of the other two workloads. The second processor set will be dedicated to running a Samba server and is also assigned a single CPU. This workload is specified by using the full path to the application's executables. The final processor set is for the Tomcat application server. The processor set is assigned two CPUs and is identified by the name of the user who owns the Tomcat process. The name of the SRD for these three processor sets will be zoo20.psets.tomcat_samba.

Manage New System with Global Workload Manager

The first step in creating the processor sets for the zoo20 nPartition is to go through the Manage New Systems wizard. The first step of the wizard, which is not shown, provides an interface to specify the systems to be managed. In this case, the only system in the SRD is zoo20. The next step, shown in Figure 19-17, displays the layout of the discovered system. Notice that there is

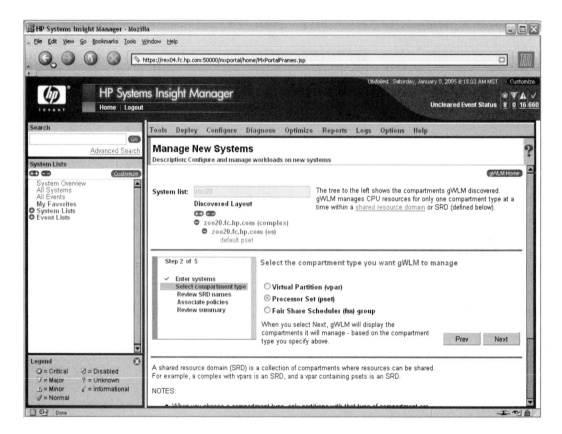

Figure 19-17 Manage New Systems Wizard Processor Set Compartment Type

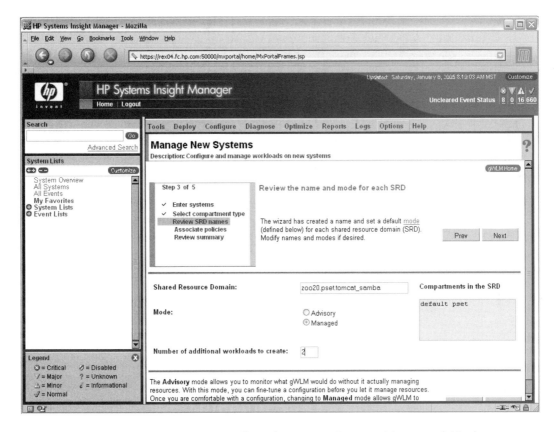

Figure 19-18 Manage New Systems Shared Resource Domain Name and Mode

only the default PSET under the zoo20 nPartition at this time. Since the compartment type will be PSET in this part of the scenario, that option is selected.

Clicking on the Next button takes you to the screen in Figure 19-18. This screen provides the interface to specify the name of the SRD and the mode. The mode is set to Managed from the beginning for this part of the scenario. Since the PSETs will be fixed in size, gWLM won't be making any changes to the compartments even in managed mode. Finally, the number of workloads in addition to the default PSET is specified. In this case, two workloads will be added.

The next screen is shown in Figure 19-19. This screen allows you to specify the names of the workloads and select a policy to be associated with each of the workloads. Allocate a single CPU to the default PSET by selecting the Fixed_1_CPU policy. Similarly, assign a single CPU to the Samba workload. Allocate the final two CPUs in the nPartition to the Tomcat workload by selecting the Fixed_2_CPUs policy. Both of the policies used in this part of the scenario are standard policies provided by gWLM.

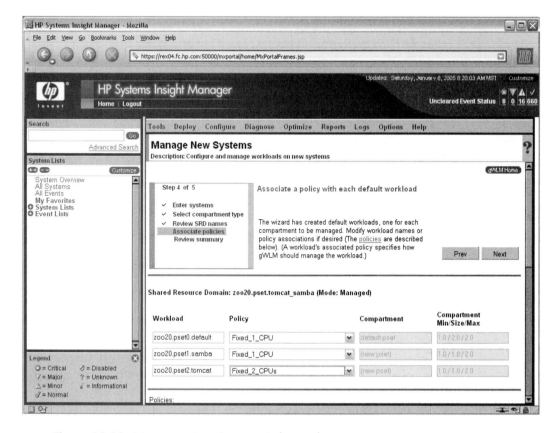

Figure 19-19 Manage New Systems Policy Selection

After the names for the workloads have been specified and the policies have been selected, the SRD summary is displayed. Selecting Finish on summary screen causes the SRD and the associated processor sets to be created. The next step in the scenario is to edit the two new workloads for Tomcat and Samba so that the processes are placed within the correct PSET.

Edit Workloads

After creating the SRD for zoo20, you'll need to modify workload definitions for the Tomcat and Samba applications. Use the Edit Workloads option in the gWLM action menu to display the list of workloads. From this screen, select the Samba workload and click on the Edit button; this will take you to the screen shown in Figure 19-20. Click on the New button below the Applications tab to add a new application entry for the workload. The first Application Pathname

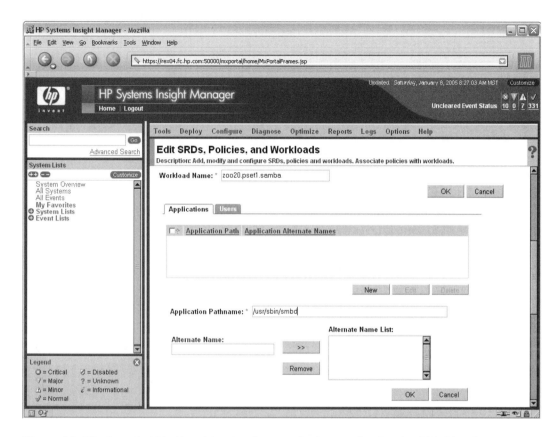

Figure 19-20 Specify Workload by Application Pathname for Samba Workload

to be specified is /usr/sbin/smbd for this example. When the application path has been specified, click on the OK button below the Alternate Name List. Repeat this process for the
/usr/sbin/nmbd executable, which is also associated with the Samba application. The final result is the list of application paths that contains the set of executables that constitute the workload. After entering both of the executables, clicking on the OK button below the Workload
Name field updates the workload.

Now the Tomcat workload must be modified. Select this workload from the list of workloads
by clicking on the Edit button. This workload will be identified by username instead of executable path. Tomcat is a Java-based application, and it is somewhat difficult to distinguish Java
processes from one another, so it is often more effective to identify the workload by the name of
the user who owns the process. For this example, the user www is specified in the screen shown
in Figure 19-21 and it will be the username of the user who owns the processes associated with
the Tomcat application. Clicking on OK on this screen updates the Tomcat workload definition.

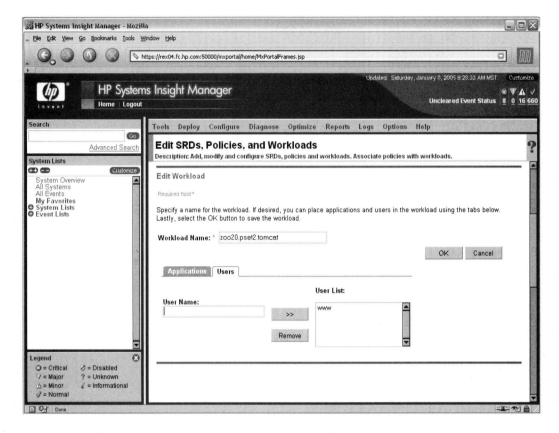

Figure 19-21 Specify Workload by User Name for Tomcat Workload

Monitoring Processor Set Workloads

At this point, the three processor sets are configured and gWLM is monitoring their resource usage. The graph shown in Figure 19-22 illustrates the default processor set and its resource consumption. This graph provides a prime example of a situation where using gWLM can be beneficial when applications are stacked on the same system. In this case, a process or set of processes running in the default PSET is consuming the entirety of its resource allocation. If gWLM and the associated processor sets were not in place, the processes consuming the CPU resources could overtake the Tomcat and Samba processes resulting in unsatisfied end-users. However, with gWLM in place, the processes are restrained to a single processor and cannot affect the CPU resources allocated to the other two workloads.

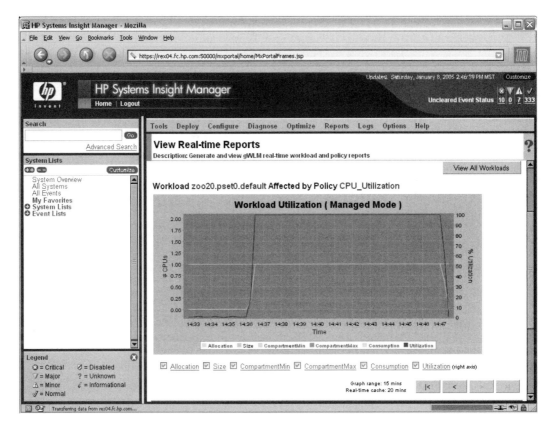

Figure 19-22 Workload Utilization for the Default Workload

The graph shown in Figure 19-23 further illustrates the default processor set possibly overtaking the other workloads and gWLM's actions to isolate the workloads. Notice that during the same time period between 14:36 to 14:47 when the default PSET workload was at peak utilization, the Tomcat workload had excess capacity. If Tomcat needed the CPU resources, they were immediately available. The obvious drawback to the fixed resource allocation approach is that the unused resources are not shared and can be underutilized.

As of now, the workloads in the zoo20 nPartition are isolated from one another in terms of CPU resources. Each workload receives a fixed allocation of CPU resources and those resources are guaranteed to be available regardless of whether they are being used. The task of administering the workloads under the control of gWLM is very lightweight at this point.

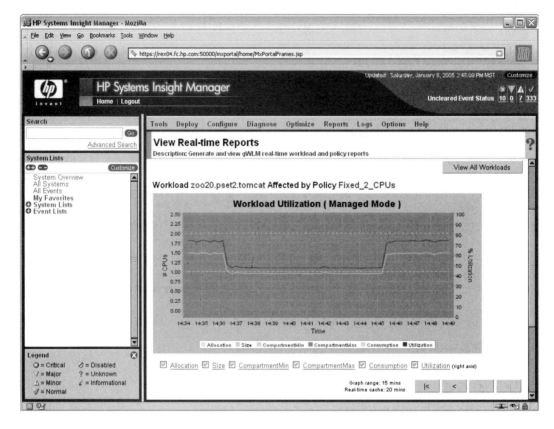

Figure 19-23 Workload Utilization for Tomcat Workload

Viewing the Workload Summary

With both of the shared resource domains in this example scenario up and running, monitoring and occasional minor configuration adjustments based on workload utilization changes are the only interactions you will need to have with gWLM. The screen shown in Figure 19-24 provides a high-level summary of the SRDs defined on the CMS for the two parts of this example scenario. This summary shows the overall CPU resource utilization and status for all of the SRDs on the CMS in a single view.

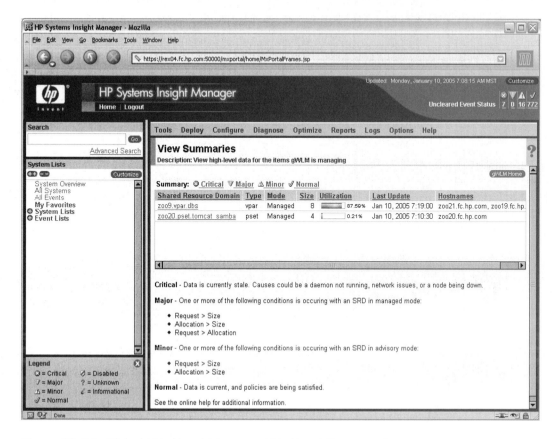

Figure 19-24 Global Workload Manager Workload Summary Screen

In addition to the graphical summary screen shown in Figure 19-24, gWLM also provides a command-line interface to monitor the SRDs or workloads. The output shown in Listing 19-3 is the monitoring command-line interface, which continually refreshes. As with the graphical view, the list of SRDs is displayed along with their respective size and CPU resource utilization.

Listing 19-3 Global Workload Manager Monitor Command

```
# /opt/gwlm/bin/wlm monitor

Thu Jan 8 15:25:15 2005
Number of deployed Shared Resource Domains: 2

Shared Resource Domain    Allocation      Size  Utilization

zoo9.vpar.dbs             8.00 CPU    8.00 CPU       87.7 %
zoo20.psets.tomcat_samba  4.00 CPU    4.00 CPU        0.8 %

Totals                   12.00 CPU   12.00 CPU       58.7 %

Thu Jan 8 15:25:30 2005
Number of deployed Shared Resource Domains: 2

Shared Resource Domain    Allocation      Size Utilization

zoo9.vpar.dbs             8.00 CPU    8.00 CPU       87.6 %
zoo20.psets.tomcat_samba  4.00 CPU    4.00 CPU        0.4 %

Totals                   12.00 CPU   12.00 CPU       58.5 %
```

Summary

Just as the Space Shuttle Flight Control Room is the base for the flight-control team that manages and monitors all operations of the space shuttle, gWLM is the base for monitoring and managing the workloads in an enterprise datacenter. gWLM provides powerful capabilities for defining how resources should be allocated to workloads and the policy that dictates how those resource allocations are modified, if at all, based on resource utilization.

gWLM can be used to migrate CPUs between virtual partitions based on the resource utilization within each vPar. In addition, gWLM is capable of managing both fair-share scheduler groups and processor sets within an operating system instance. Linux support is provided through the use of a feature of the 2.6 version of the Linux kernel known as CPU affinity, which has similar characteristics to HP-UX PSETs. Finally, gWLM is also supported on OpenVMS.

Within HP's Virtual Server Environment, gWLM serves as the flight-control room for managing workloads and their resource allocation.

References

nPartition Servers

HP System Partitions Guide: Administration for nPartitions

    http://docs.hp.com

HP Superdome Web Page

    http://www.hp.com/go/superdome

Virtual Partitions

Installing and Managing HP-UX Virtual Partitions

    http://docs.hp.com

Virtual Partitions Product Web Page

    http://www.hp.com/products1/unix/operating/manageability/partitions/
virtual_partitions.html

Ignite-UX & vPars Cookbook

    http://itrc.hp.com

HP Virtual Partitions

    Published by Prentice Hall PTR ISBN # 0-13-065419-1

HP-UX 11i System Administration Handbook and Toolkit

    Published by Prentice Hall PTR ISBN # 0-13-101883-3

Integrity Virtual Machines

Not available at the time of printing.

Secure Resource Partitions

HP Process Resource Manager User's Guide
> http://docs.hp.com

Process Resource Manager Product Web Page
> http://www.hp.com/go/prm

Using HP PRM with Oracle Databases
> http://www.hp.com/products1/unix/operating/prm/info.html

Instant Capacity

Instant Capacity (iCAP) User's Guide
> http://docs.hp.com

Instant Capacity Product Web Page
> http://www.hp.com/go/icod

Temporary Instant Capacity

Instant Capacity (iCAP) User's Guide
> http://docs.hp.com

Instant Capacity Product Web Page
> http://www.hp.com/go/icod

Installing and Administering Internet Services
> http://docs.hp.com

Pay Per Use

Pay per use User's Guide
    http://docs.hp.com

Workload Manager

Workload Manager User's Guide
    http://docs.hp.com
Workload Manager Product Web Page
    http://www.hp.com/go/wlm

Serviceguard

Managing Serviceguard User's Guide
    http://docs.hp.com
Serviceguard Product Web Page
    http://www.hp.com/go/serviceguard
HP-UX 11i System Administration Handbook and Toolkit
    Published by Prentice Hall PTR ISBN # 0-13-101883-3
HP Auto Port Aggregation Support Guide
    http://docs.hp.com

Virtualization Manager

Not available at the time of printing.

Capacity Advisor

Not available at the time of printing.

Global Workload Manager

Global Workload Manager User's Guide
    http://docs.hp.com
Global Workload Manager's Product Web Page
    http://www.hp.com/go/gwlm
Getting Started with gWLM
    http://docs.hp.com
gWLM: Reference and Additional Topics
    http://docs.hp.com
HP gWLM Version A.01.00 Release and Installation Notes
    http://docs.hp.com

Product Versions

This appendix provides the product and firmware versions (where appropriate) used in the example scenarios throughout this book. This information is intended to make it clear exactly which version of each product is shown so you can quickly understand why differences may be seen between this book and the products running in your environment.

Chapter 4 nPartition Servers

HP-UX Partition Manager Product Version
    B.11.23.02.00.03.03
HP-UX Partition Commands Product Version
    B.11.23.05
HP-UX nPartition WBEM Provider Version
    B.11.23.01.03.00.06
Manageability Firmware Revision
    A.5.021
System Firmware Version
    1.015

Chapter 5 Virtual Partitions

HP-UX Virtual Partitions Revision
    A.03.01.03

Manageability Firmware version

7.24

System Firmware version

35.3

Chapter 6 Integrity Virtual Machines

Pre-release versions of Integrity Virtual Machines and the Integrity Virtual Machines management GUI were used in the examples shown in this book.

Chapter 7 Secure Resource Partitions

Process Resource Manager

C.02.03.03

Process Resource Manager Sw-Lib

C.02.03.03

Process Resource Manager Sw-Krn

C.01.02

Chapter 10 Instant Capacity

HP-UX Instant Capacity Software Product Version

B.06.01 and B.06.03

HP-UX Partition Manager Product Version

B.11.23.02.00.03.03

HP-UX Partition Commands Product Version

B.11.23.05

HP-UX nPartition WBEM Provider Version

B.11.23.01.03.00.06

Manageability Firmware Revision

A.5.021

System Firmware Version

1.015

Chapter 11 Temporary Instant Capacity

HP-UX Temporary Instant Capacity Software Product Version
> B.06.01 and B.06.03

Manageability Firmware Revision
> A.5.021

System Firmware Version
> 1.015

Chapter 12 Pay Per Use

HP-UX Pay Per Use Software Product Version
> B.07.00

Manageability Firmware Revision
> A.5.021

System Firmware Version
> 1.015

Chapter 15 Workload Manager

Workload Manager
> A.02.03.03

Workload Manager Utilities
> A.02.03.03

Workload Manager Toolkits
> A.01.07.03

Process Resource Manager
> C.02.03.03

Process Resource Manager Sw-Lib
> C.02.03.03

Process Resource Manager Sw-Krn
> C.01.02

Chapter 16 Serviceguard

Serviceguard
    A.11.16.00
Serviceguard Manager
    A.04.00
Serviceguard Tomcat Script Templates
    B.02.11
HP Auto Port Aggregation
    B.11.23.05

Chapter 17 Virtualization Manager

Pre-release versions of Virtualization Manager and HP Systems Insight Manager are used in this book.

Chapter 18 Capacity Advisor

A pre-release version used in this book.

Chapter 19 Global Workload Manager

Global Workload Manager CMS
    A.01.00
Global Workload Manager HP-UX Agent
    A.01.00
Global Workload Manager Linux Agent for SLES 9 Linux
    A.01.00

C

Product Command-Line Interfaces

Chapter 4 nPartition Servers

partition(5) — Overview information concerning the nPartition command line interfaces.

parmgr(1M) – Partition Manager graphical user interface for managing nPartition servers

    HP-UX path: /opt/parmgr/bin/parmgr

    Windows path: Start-> Programs -> HP Insight Management Agents -> HP System Management Home Page

    Linux path: /opt/hp/hpsmh/sbin/smhstart

cplxmodify(1M) — Modify an attribute of an nPartition server complex.

    HP-UX path: /usr/sbin/cplxmodify

    Windows path: C:\Program Files (x86)\Hewlett-Packard\nParCommands\cplxmodify.exe

    Linux path: /usr/sbin/cplxmodify

parcreate(1M) — Create a new nPartition.

    HP-UX path: /usr/sbin/parcreate

    Windows path: C:\Program Files (x86)\Hewlett-Packard\nParCommands\parcreate.exe

    Linux path: /usr/sbin/parcreate

parmodify(1M) — Modify an existing nPartition.

    HP-UX path: /usr/sbin/parmodify

    Windows path: C:\Program Files (x86)\Hewlett-Packard\nParCommands\parmodify.exe

    Linux path: /usr/sbin/parmodify

parstatus(1) — Display the status and configuration for nPartition servers.

    HP-UX path: /usr/sbin/parstatus

    Windows path: C:\Program Files (x86)\Hewlett-Packard\nParCommands\parstatus.exe

    Linux path: /usr/sbin/parstatus

parremove(1M) — Remove an existing nPartition.

    HP-UX path: /usr/sbin/parremove

    Windows path: C:\Program Files (x86)\Hewlett-Packard\nParCommands\parremove.exe

    Linux path: /usr/sbin/parremove

parunlock(1M) — Unlock the data structures stored in the management processor of nPartition servers.

    HP-UX path: /usr/sbin/parunlock

    Windows path: C:\Program Files (x86)\Hewlett-Packard\nParCommands\parunlock.exe

    Linux path: /usr/sbin/parunlock

fruled(1) — Turn on, turn off, and flash attention indicators in nPartition servers.

    HP-UX path: /usr/sbin/fruled

    Windows path: C:\Program Files (x86)\Hewlett-Packard\nParCommands\fruled.exe

    Linux path: /usr/sbin/fruled

frupower(1M) — Display the status and control power to hardware components in nPartition servers..

    HP-UX path: /usr/sbin/frupower

    Windows path: C:\Program Files (x86)\Hewlett-Packard\nParCommands\frupower.exe

    Linux path: /usr/sbin/frupower

Chapter 5 HP Virtual Partitions

vpartition(5) - Overview information concerning the Virtual Partition command line interfaces.

vparresources(5) — Overview of Virtual Partition resources and their requirements.

vparboot(1M) — Boot a Virtual Partition.

    HP-UX path: /usr/sbin/vparboot

vparcreate(1M) — Create a new Virtual Partition.

    HP-UX path: /usr/sbin/vparcreate

vpardump(1M) — Manage Virtual Partition monitor dump files.

    HP-UX path: /usr/sbin/vpardump

vparextract(1M) — Extract memory images from a running Virtual Partition.

    HP-UX path: /usr/sbin/vparextract

vparmodify(1M) — Modify an existing Virtual Partition.

    HP-UX path: /usr/sbin/vparmodify

vparreloc(1M) — Manage the vmunix file.

    HP-UX path: /usr/sbin/vparreloc

vparremove(1M) — Remove a Virtual Partition.

    HP-UX path: /usr/sbin/vparremove

vparreset(1M) — Perform either a hard or soft reset of a Virtual Partition.

    HP-UX path: /usr/sbin/vparreset

vparstatus(1M) — Display the status and configuration for Virtual Partitions.

    HP-UX path: /usr/sbin/vparstatus

vparutil(1M) — Manage SCSI parameters on SCSI controllers from a Virtual Partition.

    HP-UX path: /usr/sbin/vparstatus

Chapter 6 Integrity Virtual Machines

This section was written using a pre-release version of Integrity Virtual Machines. Therefore, some of the commands referenced may vary from the final product.

hpvmboot — Boot an Integrity Virtual Machine.

    HP-UX path: /opt/hpvm/bin/hpvmboot

hpvmclone — Clone an Integrity Virtual Machine

    HP-UX path: /opt/hpvm/bin/hpvmclone

hpvmcreate — Create a new Integrity Virtual Machine.

    HP-UX path: /opt/hpvm/bin/hpvmcreate

hpvmmodify — Modify the attributes of a virtual machine.

    HP-UX path: /opt/hpvm/bin/hpvmmodify

hpvmreload — Reload the Integrity Virtual Machine's configuration information.

    HP-UX path: /opt/hpvm/bin/hpvmreload

hpvmremove — Remove an existing Integrity Virtual Machine.

    HP-UX path: /opt/hpvm/bin/hpvmremove

hpvmreset — Reset an Integrity Virtual Machine.

    HP-UX path: /opt/hpvm/bin/hpvmreset

hpvmstatus — Display the status and configuration for one or more Integrity Virtual Machines.

> HP-UX path: /opt/hpvm/bin/hpvmstatus

hpvmvswitch — Control an Integrity Virtual Machine.

> HP-UX path: /opt/hpvm/bin/hpvmvswitch

Chapter 7 Secure Resource Partitions

prm(1) — overview of Process Resource Manager

xprm(1) - Launch the PRM graphical user interface (GUI).

> HP-UX path: /usr/bin/xprm -> /opt/prm/bin/xprm

prmanalyze(1) - Analyze accounting files for data on resource usage and contention to help plan PRM configurations.

> HP-UX path: /usr/bin/prmanalyze -> /opt/prm/bin/prmanalyze

prmavail(1) - Display resource availability to help plan PRM configurations.

> HP-UX path: /usr/bin/prmavail -> /opt/prm/bin/prmavail

prmconfig(1) - Configure, enable, disable, and reset PRM. Also, validate PRM configuration files and control PRM's message logging.

> HP-UX path: /usr/bin/prmconfig -> /opt/prm/bin/prmconfig

prmlist(1) - Display the current PRM group, memory, user, application, and disk configuration information.

> HP-UX path: /usr/bin/prmlist -> /opt/prm/bin/prmlist

prmloadconf(1) - Create a PRM configuration file or update an existing configuration file.

> HP-UX path: /usr/bin/prmloadconf -> /opt/prm/bin/prmloadconf

prmmonitor(1)- Monitor current PRM configuration and resource usage by PRM groups.

> HP-UX path: /usr/bin/prmmonitor -> /opt/prm/bin/prmmonitor

prmmove(1) - Move processes or groups of processes to another PRM group.

> HP-UX path: /usr/bin/prmmove -> /opt/prm/bin/prmmove

prmrecover(1) - Reactivate processes left suppressed after an unexpected termination of the PRM memory daemon.

> HP-UX path: /usr/bin/prmrecover -> /opt/prm/bin/prmrecover

prmrun(1) - Run an application in its assigned group or in a specified group.

> HP-UX path: /usr/bin/prmrun -> /opt/prm/bin/prmrun

prmagt(1) - The HP PRM SNMP read-only agent. This gets started at boot time, and should always remain running. It can be used to gather statistics from any machine running PRM.

> HP-UX path: /usr/bin/prmagt -> /opt/prm/bin/prmagt/prmagt

Chapter 10 Instant Capacity

icod(5) — Overview of Instant Capacity software.

icod_modify(1M) — Configure Instant Capacity including activation and deactivation of processors, applying code words, and setting contact information.

> HP-UX path: /usr/sbin/icod_modify

icod_notify(1M) — Configure and test the email notification system of Instant Capacity.

> HP-UX path: /usr/sbin/icod_notify

icod_stat(1M) — Display the status and system information for a system containing Instant Capacity.

> HP-UX path: /usr/sbin/icod_stat

icodd(1M) — The Instant Capacity daemon.

> HP-UX path: /usr/lbin/icodd

Chapter 11 Temporary Instant Capacity

See Instant Capacity commands.

Chapter 12 Pay Per Use

ppu(5) — Overview of Pay per use software.

ppuconfig(1M) — Configure the Pay per use daemon

> HP-UX path: /usr/sbin/ppuconfig
>
> Windows path: C:\Program Files (x86)\Hewlett-Packard\ppu\ppuconfig.exe

ppud(1M) — The Pay per use daemon

> HP-UX path: /usr/lbin/ppud

ppuservice — The Pay per use service for Microsoft Windows.

> Windows path: C:\Program Files (x86)\Hewlett-Packard\ppu\ppuservice.exe

Chapter 15 Workload Manager

wlm(5) - Workload manager overview

wlmd(1M) - Starts WLM and activates a configuration.

    HP-UX path: /opt/wlm/bin/wlmd

wlminfo(1M) - Provides various WLM data.

    HP-UX path: /opt/wlm/bin/wlminfo

wlmcw(1M) - This graphical configuration wizard greatly simplifies the process of creating a WLM configuration.

    HP-UX path: /opt/wlm/bin/wlmcw

wlmgui(1M) - This graphical interface allows you to create, modify, and deploy WLM configurations both locally and remotely. In addition, it provides monitoring capabilities.

    HP-UX path: /opt/wlm/bin/wlmgui

wlmpard(1M) - Starts the WLM global arbiter for cross-partition management.

    HP-UX path: /opt/wlm/bin/wlmpard

wlmsend(1M) - Sends metric values to a named rendezvous point for wlmrcvdc to forward to WLM.

    HP-UX path: /opt/wlm/bin/wlmsend

wlmrcvdc(1M) - Receives metric values from a named rendezvous point and forwards them to the WLM daemon.

    HP-UX path: /opt/wlm/lbin/wlmrcvdc

wlmckcfg(1M) - Validates WLM configuration files for Servicecontrol Manager integration.

    HP-UX path: /opt/wlm/bin/wlmckcfg

wlmemsmon(1M) - The WLM EMS monitor provides information on how well WLM and the managed workload groups are performing.

    HP-UX path: /opt/wlm/lbin/wlmemsmon

wlmcomd(1M) - Services requests from the WLM graphical user interface.

    HP-UX path: /opt/wlm/bin/wlmcomd

wlmprmconf(1M) - Converts a PRM configuration file into a WLM configuration file.

    HP-UX path: /opt/wlm/bin/wlmprmconf

Chapter 16 Serviceguard

cmapplyconf(1M) - Verify and apply Serviceguard cluster configuration and package configuration files

HP-UX path:	/usr/sbin/cmapplyconf
Red Hat Linux path:	/usr/local/cmcluster/bin/cmapplyconf
SuSE Linux path:	/opt/cmcluster/bin/cmapplyconf

cmcheckconf(1M) - Check high availability cluster configuration and/or package configuration files

HP-UX path:	/usr/sbin/cmcheckconf
Red Hat Linux path:	/usr/local/cmcluster/bin/cmcheckconf
SuSE Linux path:	/opt/cmcluster/bin/cmcheckconf

cmdeleteconf(1M) - Delete either the cluster or the package configuration

HP-UX path:	/usr/sbin/cmdeleteconf
Red Hat Linux path:	/usr/local/cmcluster/bin/cmdeleteconf
SuSE Linux path:	/opt/cmcluster/bin/cmdeleteconf

cmgetconf(1M) - Get cluster or package configuration information

HP-UX path:	/usr/sbin/cmgetconf
Red Hat Linux path:	/usr/local/cmcluster/bin/cmgetconf
SuSE Linux path:	/opt/cmcluster/bin/cmgetconf

cmhaltcl(1) - Halt a high availability cluster.

HP-UX path:	/usr/sbin/cmhaltcl
Red Hat Linux path:	/usr/local/cmcluster/bin/cmhaltcl
SuSE Linux path:	/opt/cmcluster/bin/cmhaltcl

cmhaltnode(1) — Halt a node in a high availability cluster.

HP-UX path:	/usr/sbin/cmhaltnode
Red Hat Linux path:	/usr/local/cmcluster/bin/cmhaltnode
SuSE Linux path:	/opt/cmcluster/bin/cmhaltnode

cmhaltpkg(1) — Halt a high availability cluster.

HP-UX path:	/usr/sbin/cmhaltpkg
Red Hat Linux path:	/usr/local/cmcluster/bin/cmhaltpkg
SuSE Linux path:	/opt/cmcluster/bin/cmhaltpkg

cmhaltserv(1M) - Halt a service from the high availability package halt script

HP-UX path:	/usr/sbin/cmhaltserv
Red Hat Linux path:	/usr/local/cmcluster/bin/cmhaltserv
SuSE Linux path:	/opt/cmcluster/bin/cmhaltserv

cmmakepkg(1) — Create a high availability package template file

HP-UX path: /usr/sbin/cmmakepkg

Red Hat Linux path: /usr/local/cmcluster/bin/cmmakepkg

SuSE Linux path: /opt/cmcluster/bin/cmmakepkg

cmmodpkg(1M) - Enable or disable switching attributes for a high availability package.

HP-UX path: /usr/sbin/cmmodpkg

Red Hat Linux path: /usr/local/cmcluster/bin/cmmodpkg

SuSE Linux path: /opt/cmcluster/bin/cmmodpkg

cmquerycl(1) — Query a cluster or node configuration information

HP-UX path: /usr/sbin/cmquerycl

Red Hat Linux path: /usr/local/cmcluster/bin/cmquerycl

SuSE Linux path: /opt/cmcluster/bin/cmquerycl

cmruncl(1) — Run a high availability cluster.

HP-UX path: /usr/sbin/cmruncl

Red Hat Linux path: /usr/local/cmcluster/bin/cmruncl

SuSE Linux path: /opt/cmcluster/bin/cmruncl

cmrunnode(1) — Run a node in a high availability cluster.

HP-UX path: /usr/sbin/cmrunnode

Red Hat Linux path: /usr/local/cmcluster/bin/cmrunnode

SuSE Linux path: /opt/cmcluster/bin/cmrunnode

cmrunpkg(1) — Run a high availability package

HP-UX path: /usr/sbin/cmrunpkg

Red Hat Linux path: /usr/local/cmcluster/bin/cmrunpkg

SuSE Linux path: /opt/cmcluster/bin/cmrunpkg

cmviewcl(1M) - View information about a high availability cluster.

HP-UX path: /usr/sbin/cmviewcl

Red Hat Linux path: /usr/local/cmcluster/bin/cmviewcl

SuSE Linux path: /opt/cmcluster/bin/cmviewcl

cmviewconf(1M) - View Serviceguard cluster configuration information

HP-UX path: /usr/sbin/cmviewconf

Red Hat Linux path: /usr/local/cmcluster/bin/cmviewconf

SuSE Linux path: /opt/cmcluster/bin/cmviewconf

Chapter 17 VSE Management Suite

Command-line interfaces for Virtualization Manager suite were not available at the time of writing this book.

Chapter 18 Capacity Advisor

This section was written using a pre-release version of capacity advisor. Therefore, some of the commands referenced may vary slightly from the final product.

capcollect(1M) - Collect utilization data from systems for capacity planning.

> HP-UX path: /usr/sbin/capcollect
>
> Linux path: /usr/sbin/capcollect

capprofile(1M) - Extract, display, invalidate and remove utilization profile data for workloads.

> HP-UX path: /usr/sbin/capprofile
>
> Linux path: /usr/sbin/capcollect

capreport(1M) - Generate text or HTML reports of historical or projected future capacity based on the existing configuration or on a scenario.

> HP-UX path: /usr/sbin/capreport
>
> Linux path: /usr/sbin/capcollect

Chapter 19 Global Workload Manager

Note: the manual sections for the references below are located in section 1M on HP-UX and section 8 for Linux except where otherwise noted.

General Global Workload Manager Commands

The following commands can be executed on both the HP Systems Insight Manager CMS and each of the gWLM managed systems.

gwlm — Global Workload Manager overview

gwlmsslconfig — Configure a system to secure communications for gWLM.

> HP-UX path: /opt/gwlm/bin/gwlmsslconfig
>
> Linux path: /opt/gwlm/bin/gwlmsslconfig

gwlmexportkey — Export a key from the local system.

    HP-UX path: /opt/gwlm/bin/gwlmexportkey

    Linux path: /opt/gwlm/bin/gwlmexportkey

gwlmimportkey — Import a key from a remote system to the local keystore

    HP-UX path: /opt/gwlm/bin/gwlmimportkey

    Linux path: /opt/gwlm/bin/gwlmimportkey

Global Workload Manager HP Systems Insight Manager CMS Commands

The following commands are executed only on the HP Systems insight manager CMS.

gwlminitconfig — Perform the initial system configuration of the system as a CMS for gWLM.

    HP-UX path: /opt/gwlm/bin/gwlminitconfig

    Linux path: /opt/gwlm/bin/gwlminitconfig

gwlmcmsd — Global Workload Manager daemon that runs on the HP Systems Insight Manager CMS.

    HP-UX path: /opt/gwlm/bin/gwlmcmsd

    Linux path: /opt/gwlm/bin/gwlmcmsd

gwlmreport — Display workload utilization summary reports.

    HP-UX path: /opt/gwlm/bin/gwlmreport

    Linux path: /opt/gwlm/bin/gwlmreport

gwlmxml — Overview of the file structure that can be used as input to the gwlm command line interface.

    HP-UX manual section — 4

    Linux manual section — 5

Global Workload Manager Managed System Commands

The following commands are executed only on the gWLM managed systems.

gwlmagent — Global Workload Manager agent daemon that runs on gWLM managed systems.

HP-UX path: /opt/gwlm/bin/gwlmagent

Linux path: /opt/gwlm/bin/gwlmagent

gwlmplace — Place a process in a gWLM workload.

HP-UX path: /opt/gwlm/bin/gwlmplace

Linux path: /opt/gwlm/bin/gwlmplace

gwlmsend — Send metric data to gWLM for use with a custom policy.

HP-UX path: /opt/gwlm/bin/gwlmsend

Linux path: /opt/gwlm/bin/gwlmsend

Index

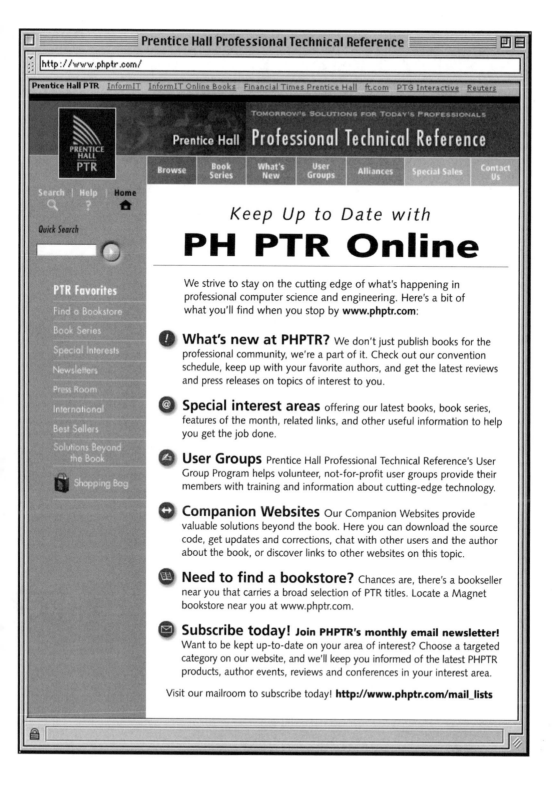

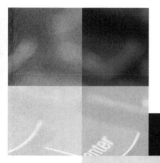